P. F. M. FONTAINE

THE LIGHT AND THE DARK

A CULTURAL HISTORY OF DUALISM

VOLUME IX

J.C. GIEBEN, PUBLISHER
AMSTERDAM

THE LIGHT AND THE DARK

P.F.M. FONTAINE

THE LIGHT AND THE DARK

A CULTURAL HISTORY OF DUALISM

VOLUME IX

GNOSTIC DUALISM IN ASIA MINOR
DURING THE FIRST CENTURIES A.D.
II

J.C. GIEBEN, PUBLISHER
AMSTERDAM 1994

To my friend since my grammar-school days,
Joop Kramer, fellow-historian,
able diplomat,
and his wife Aagje Moussault,
my friend since our first days in
the University of Amsterdam,
art-historian, enthusiastic tour conductor

No part of this book may be translated or reproduced in any form, by print, photoprint, microfilm, or any other means, without written permission from the publisher.

© by P.F.M. Fontaine / ISBN 90 5063 346 3 / Printed in The Netherlands

"For all things are called
light and darkness"

Parmenides

CONTENTS

Preface — xv

I LEFTOVERS FROM THE JAR — 1

1. The Treatise on Resurrection — 1
2. The Gospel of Philip — 4
   a. Nominalism — 4
   b. Pleromic emanations — 5
   c. The rulers of the world — 5
   d. Man — 6
   e. The Fall — 7
   f. Christ the Saviour — 9
   g. Two races of men — 10
   h. Unity restored — 11
3. The Hypostasis of the Archons — 14
   a. On the tract itself — 14
   b. The two worlds — 15
   c. Matter — 16
   d. Sabaoth — 17
   e. Mankind — 18
   f. Eve — 19
   g. The role of the serpent — 19
   h. Cain and Abel — 20
   j. Seth and Norea — 21
4. On the Origin of the world — 22
   a. The first work — 22
   b. The Shadow — 23
   c. Cosmogony — 23
   d. Yaldabaoth the Demiurge — 24
   e. The conversion of the Demiurge — 25
   f. The Demiurge's counter-offensive — 26
   g. Beauties from above — 26
   h. Paradise — 27
   j. Creation — 28
   k. The origination of mankind — 29

		l. The Father intervenes	31
		m. The Apocalypse	32
		n. Conclusion	32
5.	On the soul		32
		a. The Fall of the soul	32
		b. The healing of the soul	33
		c. The celestial wedding of the soul	34
6.	The First Apocalypse of James		34
7.	The Second Apocalypse of James		35
8.	Authoritative Teaching		36
9.	The Concept of our Great Power		38
10.	The Apocalypse of Peter		40
11.	The Trimorphic Protennoia		42
Notes to Chapter I			44

II THE MARCIONITE CHURCH — 53

1.	What we know of Marcion's life		53
		a. Uncertainties and some facts	53
		b. Banished from Sinope	54
		c. Marcion in Rome	55
		d. His breach with the Church	56
		e. Marcion's dualistic tendencies	57
2.	Cerdo, the forerunner		59
		a. What we know of his life	59
		b. His doctrine	59
3.	Marcion and the scriptural tradition		60
		a. The New Testament distorted by Judaizers	60
		b. Marcion and the Gospel of Luke	61
		c. Marcion and the Pauline Letters	62
		d. A New Testament that was free of Judaism	63
4.	The 'Antitheses'		63
5.	The separation of Law and Gospel		63
6.	Marcion's ditheism		64
7.	The Nature of the Demiurge		66
8.	Matter as a third principle		67
9.	The creation of the world and mankind		68
10.	The Law and the prophets		69
11.	Marcion and the Jews		70
12.	Marcion's rejection of history		71
13.	Mankind a sorry lot		71
14.	The unknowable god		72

15.	Redemption	73
16.	The role of Christ	74
	a. Marcion's docetism	74
	b. Christ an emanation from the supreme god	74
	c. Did Marcion's Jesus preach a new god?	75
	d. The act of redemption	76
	e. A dramatic scene	76
	f. Who will be saved	77
	g. A Marcionite act of faith	78
17.	The day of reckoning	79
18.	Marcion's Gnostic dualism	79
	a. Marcion's dualism	79
	b. Marcion and the Gnosis	82
19.	The Marcionite way of life	83
20.	The Marcionite Church	84
21.	The interior history of the Marcionite Church	85
	a. Apelles	85
	b. A religious dispute	86
	c. Creation	88
	d. The Bible	88
	e. Christ	89
	f. The role of Knowledge	90
	g. The saving of the souls	90
	h. Apelles' dualism	91
22.	Marcionism seen as a threat to the Catholic Church	91
	a. Orthodoxy at war	91
	b. A longer life in the cast	93
	c. What made Marcionism so attractive	94
23.	The relationship of the Catholic and Marcionite Churches	94
Notes to Chapter II		97

III	MANDA, THAT IS KNOWLEDGE	108
1.	Mandaeans forever!	108
2.	The Mandaeans discovered	109
3.	The origin of Mandaeism	109
	a. The Jordan region	109
	b. A connection with John the Baptist?	110
	c. Mandaeans and Christ	111
	d. Mandaeans and Christianity	112
	e. Mandaeans and Jewry	112
4.	The myth of Mandaean origin	113

5.	The mental roots of the sect	114
6.	The religious literature of the Mandaeans	115
7.	Two worlds	116
8.	Mandaean theogony	117
	a. The first principles	117
	b. The manas and uthras	118
	c. Manda dHayye	119
	d. War in the underworld	120
9.	The descent of the Redeemer into the underworld	121
	a. How the underworld is organized	121
	b. Hibil prepared for his task	121
	c. The descent to Krun	122
	d. The return of Hibil	123
	e. What this means	124
	f. The Ruha version	125
	g. What this myth means	127
10.	Mandaean cosmogony	128
	a. Ptahil the Demiurge	128
	b. Ptahil's failure	129
	c. Ruha's failed attempt	129
	d. Ptahil tries again	130
	e. The planets interfere	131
11.	The creation of man	132
	a. Ptahil the Demiurge	132
	b. Adam created	132
	c. Mankind's double origin	132
	d. Man's dislike of the body and the world	134
	e. The Mandaeans and the female sex	135
	f. Adakas and Adam	136
	g. The Adamites	137
12.	The monistic version	138
	a. The two worlds are brothers	138
	b. A pleromic Demiurge	138
	c. About Adam and 'his tribe'	139
13.	The Mandaean apocalypse	140
14.	The rehabilitation of the Demiurge	141
15.	Mandaean hierarchy, ritual, and sacraments	142
Notes to Chapter III		142

IV	MANI'S WORLD-RELIGION	151
1.	The standard-bearer of dualism	151

2.		The rediscovery of Manichaeism	152
3.		Modern scholarship on Manichaeism	153
4.		The present stance of scholarship	155
5.		Mani's life	155
	a.	Place and date of Mani's birth and his parents	155
	b.	Arsacid and Sasanian religious policy	156
	c.	Patek's religion	157
	d.	The sect of the Mughtasila	158
	e.	Was there a relationship between the Mughtasila and the Elkasiates?	159
	f.	Young Mani as a Mughtasila	162
	g.	On the road to 'apartheid'	162
	h.	The dissident	163
	j.	Mani's mission	164
	k.	The date of Mani's first public appearance	165
	l.	What did Mani look like?	165
	m.	Mani's missionary activities	166
	n.	Mani's encounter with King Shapur I	167
	o.	Further missionary travels	168
	p.	Mani's end	169
6.		Mani's literary output	170
7.		The main characteristics of the Church of Justice	171
8.		Mani's dualistic starting-point	172
	a.	The two principles	172
	b.	Two 'gods' or one?	174
9.		The origin of Mani's dualism	175
	a.	Did it stem from Iran?	175
	b.	Could something in Mani's early years have been the cause of his dualism?	176
10.		The two worlds and their sovereigns	178
	a.	Two contingent worlds	178
	b.	Two sovereigns	179
11.		An offensive against the upper world	180
	a.	Particles of the Light captured by Darkness	180
	b.	An inconsequence pointed out	180
12.		Celestial counter-measures	181
	a.	The suffering god	181
	b.	The Mother of Life	182
	c.	Primordial Man enjoins the battle with Darkness	183
	d.	The meaning of this move	184
13.		Contrarieties in the lower sphere	184
14.		A twofold rescue operation	185

	a.	Primal Man recovered	185
	b.	The search for Primal Man's armour	186
15.	The cosmic structure		187
16.	A new offensive from above		188
17.	A sweeping design		190
18.	The creation of Adam		191
	a.	Adam as a microcosmos	191
	b.	The function of human sexuality	192
	c.	The dark side of Eve	192
19.	The appearance of Jesus		193
	a.	Jesus a mythical figure	193
	b.	Jesus the spender of Knowledge	194
	c.	A warning against women	195
20.	Mankind spoils the liberation process		195
	a.	Eve as the tool of the demons	195
	b.	Cain and Abel	196
	c.	Eve seduces Adam	196
	d.	Adam saved by Shatil	197
	e.	What all this means	197
21.	The suffering Jesus		198
22.	The prophets and the Church		199
23.	The three seals		199
	a.	The seal on the mouth	200
	b.	The seal on the hand	201
	c.	The seal on the womb	202
24.	The faithful Manichee a strict dualist		202
25.	At the hour of death		203
	a.	The death of a Manichee	203
	b.	The death of a non-Manichee	204
26.	Manichaean apocalypse		205
27.	The Church of Justice		206
	a.	The Electi	206
	b.	The Auditores	207
	c.	The relationship of Electi and Auditores	208
	d.	The hierarchy of the Church of Justice	209
	e.	Manichaean sacraments	209
	f.	Early missionary activities	210
	g.	Roman reactions	210
	h.	Further expansion in the west	211
	j.	Successes in the eastern world	211
28.	Conclusion: Manichaean dualism		212
Notes to Chapter IV			213

| V | LOOKING BACK AT THE GNOSIS | 228 |

Part I Scholars and their opinions   228

1. How to introduce the Gnosis   228
2. The drawbacks of specialization   229
3. Christianity the origin of the Gnosis?   230
   a. The hallmark of the Gnosis according to Simone Pétrement   230
   b. The New Testament as the basis of the Gnosis   230
   c. All Gnostic systems interrelated   231
   d. Pétrement's workmanship   233
   e. How the report on Simon the Magician is handled   234
   f. Simone Pétrement's theory of Apollos   235
   g. The 'gnosticizing' of Paul and John   238
   h. 'Knowledge'   241
   j. Conclusion   242

Part II Was there a Christian Gnosis?   243

1. A 'Christian' Gnosis   243
2. How to approach this question   243
3. Confusion of terms   245
4. Did the Gnostics see themselves as Christians?   245
5. Were Gnostics members of the Church?   246
6. The name of Christian   248
7. Points of resemblance   249
8. Gnostics and the Bible   250
9. Gnostic language   251
10. History and its absence   252
11. Jesus Christ   253
12. The notion of God   254
13. Heaven and Pleroma   255
14. Ideas of gender   256
15. Creation   257
16. The Fall   258
17. The Demiurge   260
18. Revelation   261
19. Redemption   261
20. The conclusion   262

Part III The place of the Gnosis in Antiquity   263

1.	'Unbehagen in der Kultur'	263
2.	Syncretism and autonomy	263
3.	The Gnosis, the contemporary world, and history	264
4.	Gnostic dualism	265
5.	Why the opposite view?	267
6.	The anticosmic attitude	268
7.	The 'all-or-nothing' syndrome	270
8.	The alien god	271
9.	The Gnostic and the Christian Redeemer	272
10.	The concept of election	273
11.	The Gnosis as theosophy	275
12.	Comprehensibility and incomprehensibility	277
13.	Behind the times?	278
Notes to Chapter V		278
Bibliography		283
General index		297

PREFACE

"Fundamentally life is a very simple affair." With these lapidary words the parish priest began his sermon during the wedding ceremony for a couple of my friends. And he was quite right ; life is a simple thing. That is to say, for those who are happy. For them life is simple, just because they are happy. Or they are happy, because they know that life is simple. But it is not so for dualists : for them life is not simple but twofold. By this I do not mean that, as we all know, everything in this life has its reverse, that nothing is absolutely perfect, and that no one is absolutely happy or completely miserable. No, by this 'twofold' I mean that for dualists life, existence, the cosmos, perhaps even Being itself, fall into two separate categories.

1. Dualism : what it is and what it is not

In all previous volumes of this series I have followed this definition of dualism : two utterly opposed conceptions, systems, principles, groups of people, or even worlds, without any intermediate terms between them. They cannot be reduced to each other; in some cases the one is not even dependent on the other. The opposites are considered to be of a different quality - so much so that one of them is always seen as distinctly inferior and hence must be neglected or destroyed.

In dualism there are quite a number of subdivisions possible. The most important of these is that between radical (or absolute) and relative dualism. In radical dualism the two principles, systems, or worlds are absolutely coeval; they are both from eternity, and there is no interdependence whatsoever between them. This is the case, for instance, in Manichaeism. In relative dualism, which occurs in many Gnostic systems, one system or group of people is dependent on another. However strongly opposed they may be, they can, nevertheless, not do without each other.

With regard to the subject of dualism, misunderstandings abound. Our western way of thinking, based on Greek metaphysics and having developed by way of medieval scholasticism and seventeenth-century rationalism, and after that going through the school of the Enlightenment, makes us argue in terms of logical systems. A reviewer of my work reproached me at one point because I had failed to establish the thesis that dualism is a key-concept for historians of culture [1]. But it was never my intention to adopt such a thesis. Dualism has to say something about concepts, or perhaps rather it does something with concepts, but it is not a concept itself. It is about discontinuity and discrepancies, about antagonisms and disharmony. In short, it is about what does not 'fit', about what does not go together. It is, fundamentally, anti-holistic.

Dualism is not an intellectual system, neither is it an ideology, a philosophy, or a religion; instead, it is a mental phenomenon. It cannot be set over against non-dualistic systems, for then we would be comparing things of a different order. The term 'dualistic system' is, although I use it myself, basically a contradiction in adiecto. There have, indeed, been a number of attempts to create such a system. Recapitulating what I wrote in the Preface of Volume V (pp. XX/XXI) and amplifying this in the light of the subsequent volumes, I am able to present the following 'dualistic systems' : the Pythagorean fraternity (Vol. I, Ch. 1.15), the Orphic religion (Vol. I, Ch. IV.10), the philosophies of Empedocles, Heraclitus, and in particular, Parmenides (Vol. I. Ch. II.6, 8, and 9), those elements in Plato's teaching that show a strong tendency towards dualism (Vol. III, Ch. III.20-22), Zoroastrianism (Vol. IV, Ch. IV.8 and 9), and still more Iranian Zervanism (Vol. V, Ch. II.22), in India Yoga in particular (Vol. V, Ch. V.22), Chinese Daoism (Vol. V, Ch. III.25), and, finally, the numerous Gnostic systems as described in Volumes VII, VIII, and the present one. This is rather a meagre harvest for the long periods and the many civilizations I have studied. Furthermore, the impact of these systems was not great. Pythagoreans and

Orphics, Yogis and Daoists, as well as almost all Gnostic communities never became mass movements. Although Valentinianism and Manichaeism enjoyed a reasonable success, only Zervanism came close to becoming a national religion.

Add to this that nearly all dualistic systems not only remained restricted in membership and extent but also confined in time. Most of them - I am thinking here especially of Gnostic systems - were only short-lived. Manichaeism lived on for more than a millennium, but finally foundered in the backgardens of China. Mandaeism exists until the present day but is tucked away in the marshlands of Lower Iraq. Of the philosophies only Platonism remained influential throughout the ages, probably more because of its non-dualistic elements than of the dualistic ones. It is my conviction that it is precisely their dualism, that is their predilection for disconnectedness, that made the impact of these systems so feeble and their span of life so short. In the end it was always the 'holistics' that won the day.

2. Dualism and monism

I believe it is invariably the 'holistics' who contend that monism is the exact opposite of dualism. This is a constantly recurring theme of western thought. Those who relish this idea - and they are not few - do not realize that this opposition is dualistic in itself, for in their eyes it is a case of either-or. Monism can generate dualism. It is simply not feasible to bring all metaphysical, cosmic, and human phenomena under one heading; there will always remain an intractable remnant. This remnant will 'rebel' against the monistic monopoly which will lead to a dualistic situation. In fact, monism and dualism belong in the same category, that of forcing all kinds of reality into one single straightjacket [2].

3. Dualism as an anthropological phenomenon

I shall not again discuss the fairly general misunderstanding that all dualisms are of Iranian provenance, or at least have an Iranian background. Time and again I have argued that dualism is an independent phenomenon, and that Iranian dualism is only one dualism among many [3]. Very often it is treated as though it were only a religious phenomenon, the proper subject for historians of religion; not rarely the field of philosophy is also included.

My own thesis, however, is that dualism is an anthropological phenomenon, something that is common to all humanity, occurring everywhere and in all periods of history. And if I am right in positing that it is something anthropological, something generally human, then we should look for it in all fields of human life, not one excluded. This is why I gave my work the subtitle of 'A cultural history of dualism'; this expresses my intention to place the occurrences of dualism in a far wider context than that of religion or philosophy.

4. The origin of dualism

a. The role of personal circumstances

If Iranian dualism is not the fountainhead of all dualism, the question arises where we should look for its origin. If dualism is basically human, it must express a human proclivity. In most people this rarely if ever comes to the surface or not at all. But in others it becomes a definite attitude that colours their whole conception of life, their way of thinking, their behaviour, and their relation with fellow-beings. In our treatment of the Gnosis we encountered instance after instance of this. Is this relishing of the sharpest possible oppositions something pathological? Not necessarily. In a book I wrote on Hitler [4], the greatest and fiercest dualist of modern times, I argued that he was not a pathological case; I am convinced that an international panel of famous psychiatrists would have declared him fully responsible for his actions.

I am quite sure that personal circumstances can kindle this propensity to dualism that, perhaps, is slumbering in every human being; usually such circumstances will occur in early youth or adolescence. In Antiquity we are poorly endowed with detailed biographies; only very rarely do we get a glimpse of personal developments. It is only in the cases of Plato (Vol. III, Ch. III.22), the apostle John (Vol. VII, Ch. IV.5b), and the prophet Mani (the present volume, Ch. IV.8) that I feel able to describe how and why a possibly innate tendency to dualism grew stronger in the course of their lives.

b. The role of more general circumstances

However influential personal circumstances may be, I doubt whether they offer a sufficient explanation. Perhaps dualists also feed on less personal and more general experiences. I am not thinking here of abstract philosophical reasonings or the impact of certain religious ideologies. It could rather be that the acceptance of a peculiar creed, a Gnostic one for instance, is the outcome, first of circumstances in the personal sphere, and, secondly, of a confrontation with 'existential' issues, I mean such as concern humanity in general.

Ioan Couliano, the victim of a vile political murder, once wrote that "the 'dualism of the west' has a social history", adding that he himself would not write this history. "It is up to others to write it" [5]. I don't know whether I am qualified to compose this 'social history of dualism', but I feel that this is more or less what I am attempting to do in this series. The problem that is occupying me is whether there is something in the world, something really present, that might give rise to dualism, something that does not wholly fit, such as loose ends, gaps in fundamental explanations, unsolved contradictions. Let us take a sharp look at this.

5. What is a paradox?

Philosophy and mathematics know of paradoxes. Now, what is a 'paradox'? "A paradox, in the original sense of the word", says the author of an article in a encyclopaedia of philosophy, "is a statement that goes against generally accepted opinions" [6]. I assume that it is for this reason that another philosophical encyclopedia carries no entry on 'paradox' but rather offhandedly relegates it to the article on 'the absurd' [7]. R.M. Sainsbury defines the concept of paradox as "an apparently unacceptable conclusion derived by apparently acceptable reasoning from apparently acceptable premises" [8]. Logicians and mathematicians are no great lovers of paradoxes; they spoil their game. What they are out for is consistency and identity. They can admit a paradox only as something incidental or accidental, hoping that sounder reasoning may eliminate it [9]. Whitehead and Russell even developed a theory by means of which the occurrence of paradoxes can be avoided. According to them, "an analysis of the paradoxes to be avoided shows that they all result from a certain kind of vicious circle" [10].

It is an undeniable fact indeed that many paradoxes are only apparently so, among them most paradoxes that stem from the ancients who were very fond of them, especially the Sophists. One might think here of the famous paradox of Achilles and the tortoise [11]. The swift-footed hero gives the tortoise an ample start, but he proves unable to overtake the slow animal because he is constantly halving the distance
still separating him from it. Since the tortoise keeps crawling on, however slowly, Achilles, by halving the difference, will never succeed in coming abreast with it : there will always remain a distance to be halved. One of the reasons for invalidating this paradox is that, as Whitehead/Russell would say, "it has no consonance with common sense". For the argument is based on the assumption that on onlooker would be able to observe the finally infinitesimal distance between the runner and the tortoise, which, of course, is practically impossible [12].

6. The later history of the paradox

Medieval scholastics did not show any affinity with the idea of paradox. What had seemed paradox in the eyes of pagan philosophers became soundly orthodox. The so often misquoted paradox 'credo quia absurdum' is not to be found in any Christian author of late Antiquity or the Middle Ages [13]. With the advent of the Renaissance the paradox began to slowly regain prestige. It became so popular then that a modern scholar spoke of 'paradoxia epidemica' [14]. Many authors of that period loved to go against the grain, but whether they really developed impeccable paradoxes is another question.

The great Enlightenment prophet, Rousseau, declared that he had rather be "a man of paradoxes than a man of prejudices" [15] which inspired Proust to say that "the paradoxes of today are the prejudices of tomorrow, because the thickest ... of present-day prejudices once had a moment of newness" [16]. Just like this French novelist, Goethe was no lover of paradoxes; he equalled 'the appetite for paradoxes' with 'the spirit of contradiction' [17]. But Schopenhauer declared truth as such to be paradox [18], an idea that would have filled medieval scholastics with horror, while Yorck von Wartenburg even went so far as to state that "paradoxicality is a hallmark of truth" [19].

Although logicians and mathematicians always hope to have the best of paradoxes, poets and dramatists think differently. Whereas Mackie wanted to understand paradoxes "without becoming ensnared in them" [20], the romantic author Novalis obviously loved to be 'ensnared'. Although he put it interrogatively, he found that "the highest principle would comprise the highest paradox in its task"; this would be "a proposition that ... ever again would become incomprehensible, how often believed to have been understood" [21]. The dramatist Dürrenmatt pointed to the occurrence of chance. "People who act according to plan want to attain a certain end. Chance hits them most horribly, when they attain just the opposite of this end ... (This) is not senseless, it is paradox." And he cited the story of Edipus as a case in point [22].

XXII

Moving back along this road, we meet Kierkegaard who stated in his journal what the real, the ontological significance is of the paradox. "The paradox is not a concession but a category, an ontological definition expressing the relation between an existing, acknowledging mind and eternal truth" [23].

6. The fundamental question

In her book 'Purity and Danger' Mary Douglas writes as follows [24]. "Purity is the enemy of change, of ambiguity and compromise ... The yearning for rigidity is in us all. It is part of our human condition to long for hard lines and clear concepts. When we have them, we have either to face the fact that some realities elude them, or else blind ourselves to the inadequacy of the concept. The final paradox of the search for purity is the attempt to force experience into logical categories of non-contradiction. But experience is not amenable, and those who make the attempt find themselves led into contradiction." In this connection, one thinks of the Gnostic dualists with their rigid distinction of the lower and upper worlds and their division of mankind into two totally different and opposed sets. They do this for the sake of purity indeed, the purity of the elect.

Yet another quotation, this time from a very famous work, 'Varieties of religious experience' by William James [25] who mentioned the interesting notion "of there being elements of the universe which make no rational whole in conjunction with the other elements, and which, from the point of view of any system which those elements make up, can be only considered so much irrelevance and accident, so much 'dirt' as it were, as 'matter out of place'". It is, of course, typical of such a highly sophisticated intellectual as James to refer to those elements which do not fit into 'any system' as 'dirt'.

The paradox, therefore, throws up the fundamental question whether we, as human beings, however intelligent we may be, are able to grasp, to comprehend Being as a whole. Or, in other words, whether there is not a gap between Being and our comprehension of it. Behind this question lurks another one. If there is nothing wrong with our intellect, is Being at fault then? Or is our comprehension defective and is Being unified and uniform?

7. Some paradoxes

Haskell B. Curry prints a list of paradoxes, which he terms 'logical antinomies', and which appear in scientific literature [26].

a. The paradox of the barber

A well-known and popular paradox is that of the barber (probably due to Russell). The council of a certain town in Spain, the name of which is sometimes given as Sevilla, orders the barber (there is obviously only one barber there) to shave all the men in town who do not shave themselves, and only those. But what about Figaro himself? If he shaves himself, he does not shave all the men who do not shave themselves; if he does not shave himself, he likewise does not shave all the men who do not shave themselves. But the barber can easily dodge the problem by growing a beard. The council's order did not lay down that he should remain beardless. This turns this paradox into a pseudo-paradox.

b. The liar paradox

A harder nut to crack is the 'liar paradox', the best-known one there is. The most simple form of it is the statement 'I am lying'. If the speaker really is lying, it is a lie that he is lying, which means that he is speaking the truth. But if he is speaking the truth, then indeed ..., and so on. The more sophisticated form is that of Epimenides the Cretan who said : "All Cretans are liars". We are obviously trapped in a vicious circle here in the same way [27]. Whoever its author was, when it became known, it caused an enormous uproar; some people felt that it meant the end of rational thinking, Philites of Cos, for instance, who for this reason committed suicide. But the statement 'I am lying' does not involve the speaker who, confronted, for instance, with an astute police officer, may finally admit that he has been lying, in which case he is believed. So it is with Epimenides who certainly does not apply his statement to himself. For else he would openly advertise that he is an inveterate liar. And who would do this [28]?

c. Grelling's paradox

We really get into the epicentre of the logical earthquake with 'Grelling's paradox', published in 1908 by Kurt Grelling. It is the 'paradox of heterologicality'. Some words are applicable to themselves and only to themselves. Such a word is 'short', another 'polysyllabic', yet another 'vague'. These are called 'autological'. Words that are not applicable to themselves are called 'heterological', for instance 'monosyllabic' or 'green' or 'useless'. A good example is 'symbol' which is not a symbol itself but a concept. The great problem here is that, if 'heterological' is 'heterological', it is by the same token 'autological'; but if it is 'autological', it is also 'heterological'. And now there is no way out [29].

d. Russell's paradox

An equally watertight paradox is that of Russell [30]. When he communicated it in June 1903 by letter to Gottlob Frege, who is considered to be the founder of mathematical logic, his correspondent sent his answer almost by return of post. Frege proved deeply shocked; in his opinion the discovery of this paradox had shaken the foundations of the system of logic on which he, Frege, intended to build arithmetic [31].

We consider a tree as an object. All possible trees taken together form a new object which we call a 'class'; a class, therefore, is an object consisting of individual objects. As an individual I am an object too, a Dutchman. As a Dutchman I am a member of the class comprising all Dutchmen; since Dutchmen are Europeans, their class forms part of a class comprising all Europeans. But this class also comprises Englishmen,

Portuguese, Fins, Greeks, and so on. The class 'Europeans', in consequence, is a class of classes. Even a class of all classes would be conceivable, something like 'mankind', or Plato's Idea of the Good, the source of all other ideas.

Now Russell distinguished proper and improper classes. Proper classes are those which are not members of themselves. The class of numbers, for instance, is a 'clean' case, since this class is not a number itself. Improper classes are those which are members of themselves, like the class of all ideas which is an idea itself. All proper classes taken together form the class of proper classes. This class I call R, the 'Russell class'. However, R, the general class, is a proper class itself, and, in consequence a member of itself. This signifies, by the same token, that it is not a proper class but an improper one.

But, my sharpwitted reader will say, you start from the premise that R is proper class itself. Let us assume that it is an improper class. OK! If R is an improper class, it is not a member of the class of proper classes; in logical consequence, it then is a proper class. However, suppose that R is a member of itself; hence it is a proper class; hence it is not a member of itself. On the other hand, suppose that R is not a member of itself; hence it is a proper class, hence it is a member of itself. Now we see why Frege became so upset.

8. Is there a solution?

Those who occupy themselves with problems like these can be divided into optimists and pessimists. The optimists, as I have already mentioned, trust that hard work and acute thinking will succeed in eliminating all paradoxes. Perhaps Russell himself was one of these; he thought that his paradox could be solved. But others are not so hopeful. As John van Heijenoort writes, "no rule could be formulated that would by itself eliminate all paradoxes, and only the paradoxes ... The known paradoxes had to be eliminated by a radical and thorough reconstruction of logic and set theory that involved much more than the plucking out of paradoxes" [32]. In other words, to get rid of paradoxes, a totally new system of logic would have to be developed that would be paradox-free.

And Curry concludes that "the problem of explaining the paradoxes remains an important open problem. Although there is a vast literature devoted to them and a great variety of explanations has been offered, yet there is at present no one explanation which is universally accepted. It seems that a complete reform of logic is called for" [33]. But would what has always been known as 'logic' since Aristotle, still be 'logic'? Would it not rather be a 'metalogic'? And have we any guarantee that this totally new system too would not contain a paradox?

9. Gödel's theorem

In 1930 a twenty-four year old Austrian mathematician, Kurt Gödel (1906-1978), presented to the Wiener Akademie der Wissenschaften a proposition that soon became known as 'Gödel's theorem' [34]. Gödel's essay cannot have been agreeable reading for logicians and mathematicians. It disturbed the relative peace that prevailed in the different compartments of logic. Slowly but certainly the confusion caused by the possibility of there being unsolvable paradoxes had been overcome. In 1879 Gottlob Frege had proposed a system of formal logics that seemed to promise perfect consistency. As John van Heijenoort expresses it : "It seemed to embody the Aristotelian ideal of a perfect deduction from first principles" [35].

a. The Hilbertian ideal

As late as 1922 the German mathematician David Hilbert acknowledged that mathematics would be a poor affair indeed if it did not possess solidity. In former days mathematicians had, according to him, trusted too much to intuitive evidence; this had led the discipline into difficulties. This is what my teacher of maths in grammar-school did, way back in 1933, when, in the very first lesson, he told us that we would start from some premises which he called 'axioms'; axioms, he added, were propositions which could not be proved but did not need proof, since they were evident enough. Of course, none of us asked him what was the guarantee of this evidence. Intuition probably. But is our intuition infallible?

Hilbert admitted that we cannot do without intuitive evidence. But at the same time he proposed that a logical system must be possible that would comprise the concrete, extra-logical, intuitive, or 'lived' (mathematical) objects. There was a field, he thought, in which we would encounter pure truth, a field higher than 'ordinary' mathematics that had proved not to be entirely free of paradoxes. This would be the field of 'meta-mathematics', written in a system of symbols showing that mathematics did not contain contradictions. Mathematical thought seemed on the verge of overcoming all inconsistencies [36].

b. A theorem with a catastrophic effect

And then there appeared out of the blue a young upstart of a mathematician who categorically declared that there is no such thing as complete coherence, that there nowhere exists a wholeness that is without dents and fissures. Gödel's theorem is known as the 'incompleteness theorem'. The (fundamental, intrinsic) incompleteness (of logico-mathematical) systems consists in the fact that in the last resort they are undecidable. "On the basis of reasonable assumptions, one can show that the formula so constructed is neither provable nor disprovable". Curry stated that this assertion had 'a catastrophic effect on mathematical logic' [37].

The theorem in 'Reinkultur' is not accessible to these who have no training in formal logic (being a mathematician is not sufficient). It is rendered in signs, symbols, and numbers, one of which, the 'Gödel number', was his own addition; consisting of two lemmata and some forty-six introductory definitions, it occupies twenty-five pages in print. The non-mathematician need not be ashamed of his or her incomprehension; at the time of its publication hardly anybody understood it [38].

Rendering the theorem in ordinary language makes it somewhat less precise, but this is the only alternative. What we may reasonably expect of formal logic is that its propositions do not contain contradictions, or that it is able to state unequivocally and irrefutably what is true and what is not true. Now Gödel did not start from the truth concept; he was not looking for criteria to dissolve the antinomy trueuntrue. His problem was that of deducibility : can the desired result be inferred from the data we possess?

Gödel asserted that an arithmetical proposition is undecidable (unentscheidbar) if, within its own system, it is impossible to prove whether or not it is true. Every arithmetical system, even an elementary one, may contain contradictions (referring to relations between numbers, for instance the impossiblity to disprove that 2x3=5). Every formal system that is large enough to allow operations like adding up and multiplying is subject to such restrictions! Gödel's theorem did not, of course, wreck the whole system of mathematical logic. But it frustrated its pretensions. It showed to what extent this kind of logic is effective; it followed from the theorem that the reach of this logic is not unlimited. No system of logics is capable of solving its own problems in their entirety. Monod said that such systems cannot describe their own structure integrally; Jean Martel wrote that no system 'boucle sur lui-même', does not have the power to make itself perfectly closely-reasoned [39]. Thomas Kuhn went somewhat further by stating that "no paradigm that provided a basis for scientific research ever completely resolves all its problems" [40].

If an arithmetical system contains a contradiction, it is inconsistent. But from Gödel's theorem it follows that, even if a contradiction is deduced, this does not prove that the system is consistent. To make a system consistent one has to appeal to the one higher system that is larger and possesses ampler means of argumentation. But the inexorable consequence of Gödel's theorem is that this system too is subject to the same restrictions : it is incapable of making itself consistent. Once again it will be necessary to appeal to a still larger system, only to hit again on the same problem. Finally, one could appeal to the largest system of all, for instance the universe, - if this can be described arithmetically , - only to discover the same restriction.

d. An example

Let me give an example. Our chronology can be presented in purely arithmetical terms. At this moment of writing it is 23.11.1993 at 12.16.30 hrs; everybody understands that it is the end of November about noon. Chronology is indeed a highly detailed and exact arithmetical system but not without its contradictions and anomalies. For instance, not everywhere in the world it is 12.16 hrs at this moment, although my intuition tells me that it is everywhere 'now', nor is it everywhere the same day, although my intuition says that it is everywhere 'to-day'.

We know precisely what a year is; it is the period our globe needs to rotate around the sun; at this moment it stands at exactly the same spot on the ecliptica where it was on November 23, 1992. But what about the 29th of February? In the year before the leapyear there was no February 29! Where then was the earth exactly one year ago? On the spot of February 28 or on that of March 1? This would entail that February 28 and 29 are the same day, just as February 29 and March 1. And this again would mean that February 28 and March 1 are the same day. Or February 29 does not exist! Never! This is an anomaly that remains undecidable within our chronological system (in practice we are able to live with it because we are forced to). For the Gödelian theorem it follows that it will not do to refer to a higher system, for instance the solar system, and from there to the Milky Way, and from there to the universe as the supreme court. For even this court cannot provide a solution.

e. Conclusion

All attempts to lift Gödel's theorem out of the saddle have misfired. We are forced to admit that Hilbert's ideal of an absolute mathematics, of an absolute logic, has receded beyond the horizon. There will always remain contradictions, inconsistencies, and anomalies.

XXX

10. The law of entropy

In his famous and much discussed essay 'The Two Cultures' C.B. Snow reproached the scholars of the humanities for not knowing how the second main law of thermodynamics reads. The first main law, yes, is that of the conservation of energy, but the second ...? Although I belong to the humanities myself, I have had occasion to note that many physicians who, by reason of their discipline, are acquainted with these laws, do not realize that they are at variance with each other. The first law, that of the conservation of energy, says that the total amount of energy in the universe remains equal. To put it as simply as possible : what is lost here is added there.

The second law of thermodynamics is called 'the law of entropy', also known as 'the principle of Carnot', because it was first formulated by the French physician Sadi Carnot in 1824 [41]. Nobody paid any attention to his essay. The principle was reformulated in 1865 by R. Clausius [42] and is, therefore, also known as 'the principle of Clausius' (or of Carnot-Clausius).

Whereas the law of the conservation of energy implies that energy is always useful, always produces something, for instance movement or rotation, the law of entropy says that there is also a degradation, a loss of energy. Clausius stated in as many words that his principle conflicts with that of the conservation of energy. It is also incompatible with the prevailing tendency in science to consider all processes as reversible; they are all seen as non-historical, that is, time plays no role in them; there is no change, everything remains virtually the same. But the law of entropy implies that processes are be irreversible, that they are 'historical', that there is a change, because first there is more and later there is less. Scientists do not love this idea!

Let me explain this more amply. Suppose they give me a box and sixteen billiard-balls, eight red, eight white; if I lay them in the box, they will cover its bottom entirely. They tell me to do this, but before I begin, they blindfold me. This leaves me with in all 12.870 possibilities of placing;

the chance that I make an orderly pattern, say, regularly one white, one red, is very small indeed. But let them give me a hundred balls, again half white, half red. I now have 10 to the 29th possibilities, and my chance of a regular pattern has become infinitesimally small. In other words, there is an overwhelming possibility that I will make a chaos of it [43].

Left us shift our argument to the world of atoms. Since there exist innumerable atoms, the chance that they will form an orderly pattern of themselves is infinitely small. The most probable thing is that there will be a situation of 'chaos', and the least probable that they will form configurations of a regular type. Viewed from a statistical point of view, our conclusion must be that atoms in a closed system will show a tendency to move from a situation of improbability (orderliness) to one of probability (chaos); the atoms will tend to divide themselves evenly over the available space. This happens when you throw bath-salts into your bath. In a few moments the pellets will disappear; they lose their coherence (order) entirely.

Now it is true that an amount of energy is set free through the disruption of the coherence - the energy that was invested in keeping together the 'improbable' construction; insofar the law of the conservation of energy comes into its own. The freed energy is converted into heat; the speed of the atoms increases enormously. But this results in a loss of energy since heat, as a source of energy, is almost useless. A good example is a nuclear explosion; the enormous amount of energy needed to keep the pattern of the fissionable material intact is set loose at the moment of the explosion and is converted into an inconceivable amount of heat. This heat is absolutely useless, if we don't consider the annihilation of people and cities as 'useful'. This is pure one-way traffic : the heat cannot be converted into binding energy.

The yardstick with which we measure the irreversible process of the loss of energy is called 'entropy'; the more energy is converted into heat, the greater the entropy. In consequence, scientists have to face the fact that an entirely coherent description of the field of nature is impossible; there is a flaw, a fundamental contradiction.

XXXII

11. Quantum mechanics

a. A short history of 'atomism'

'Atom' is a Greek word meaning 'indivisible'. The first atomic theory was propounded in the fifth century B.C. by Democritus and Leucippus, and on this the foundations of atomism were laid. Its basic idea was that matter consists of the smallest possible indivisible particles. It will be clear that this classical atomic theory is wholly at variance with modern atomism which is based on the premise that atoms are divisible and that, in consequence, there exist particles smaller than atoms. Nevertheless, the Greek mind had made an important leap : it left the realm of the visible behind and moved into the world of the invisible and unobservable [44].

Not much was heard of atomism again until the seventeenth century. Democritus's theory had the attention of several Renaissance scholars but what Descartes brought forward was considered authoritative. He developed a corpuscular theory according to which matter consisted of small material particles with specific physical properties and subject to mechanical laws. Later in the century Robert Boyle added that those particles not only had physical but also chemical properties. On the basis of this theory Lavoisier composed the first list of chemical elements.

b. Modern atomic theory

The real founder of modern atomic theory was Robert Dalton who, in the first years of the nineteenth century, stated that atoms were particles with the properties of chemical elements. However, he still clung to the age-old idea of Democritus that (chemical) atoms were inchangeable. This means that, although they are unobservable, they remain imaginable since they are fixed things bound together in a compound that finally is a visible object, however small.

In the course of that century it became increasingly clear that atoms are not the smallest particles; they are structures of particles themselves. This led to the construction of the famous atomic model of Bohr (or of Rutherford-Bohr) in 1913 that shows the atom as a structure consisting of a nucleus around which electrons wheeled in fixed orbits; in other words, it was a kind of solar system. Many of us will remember this model from their lessons in physics or chemistry in grammar-school. The teachers were glad to use it since it made so perfectly plain what an atom looked like - somewhat plainer than it really is, as Bohr himself understood very well! Anyhow, the mysterious atom seemed to have regained some measure of visibility.

c. The shift to quantum mechanics

It was, however, this same Bohr who, together with others, was instrumental in utterly destroying every idea, not only of making an atom 'visible', but still more of even the possibility of imagining it or conceiving it. In several steps, from the work of Niels Bohr through the investigations of Max Planck, Louis de Broglie, and E. Schrödinger to that of Werner Heisenberg, in the course of the twenties a totally new form of physics was developed that has become known as 'quantum mechanics'.

Quantum mechanics abandoned the idea that the particles of an atom can be 'localized', that is, can be located at an exactly definable place and that, if they move (which they constantly do), the velocity can be determined with which they go from one place to another. Quantum mechanics says that this is impossible; we have now to do with what Heisenberg called 'uncertainty relations'. That electrons would describe regular orbits is only the product of a (false) hypothesis which makes Bohr's atomic model ripe for the dustbin. Neither location nor speed of the particles can be determined at the same moment; there no longer are coordinates but only 'relations' which only can be expressed in mathematical terms.

If the idea that the internal structure of an atom has now lost every form of conceivability makes the reader feel somewhat uncomfortable, he or she finds him- or herself in very good company. An excellent scholar like Popper always remained highly sceptical. And the great Einstein himself could never bring himself to accept what quantum mechanics told him; it proved impossible for him to believe that physical reality in its inner core should be something indeterminate, that there is no such thing as 'the exact state of the microparticle'. According to Pais, "his attitude regarding quantum mechanics was one of scepticism" [45]. In December 1926 he wrote to Born that "quantum mechanics is very impressive. But an inner voice tells me that it is not the real thing. The theory produces a good deal but hardly brings us closer to the secret of the Old One (= God - F.). I am at all events convinced that he emphatically does not throw dice" [46].

d. Philosophical consequences

The philosophical consequences of this new theory are immense indeed! The realm of reality seems to have become dualistically divided between a world we can observe, describe, imagine, conceive of, and comprehend, and another deeper lying world that is beyond every form of comprehension and imagination. And this second world seems to be the basic one on which all other reality rests. I for one would call this a 'derealization' of reality. The mental effects of this all are probably not very healthy. Of course, hardly anybody knows what quantum mechanics is. But lessons in school and popular expositions have fostered the vague but unpleasant impression that the core of reality is a seething and dangerous volcano. People couple this with the fear they have of nuclear fission, in particular of atomic bombs and nuclear warheads but also of nuclear plants. All this has a destabilizing effect and makes people feel uncertain and threatened in their own world [47].

There are, indeed, those for whom this new mathematical concept is definitely the last word in our understanding of physical nature. However, this was also alleged for the two central views of nature that preceded it. The first was that of the world seen as an organism; its great prophet was Aristotle who put this idea under the high protection of the Prime Mover. The second model was that of the world understood as a mechanism, with Newton as its prophet. To Voltaire, God was 'the eternal machinist' [48]. Both these models have one great advantage : they are imaginable. The word 'organism' reminds us of the human body and suggests to us the ancient relationship of macrocosmos and microcosmos. The word 'mechanism' is far more bloodless and lifeless, but still, we are able to visualize it as a machinery.

Now, after the introduction of quantum mechanics, the world is presented in terms of relations of numbers. With this the last vestige of 'picturesqueness' has disappeared from physics. Of course, not a few physicists honestly believe that with this development the last and most definite word in physics has been spoken. Some of them now speak of God as a mathematician. But there is a poor chance that the newest model will prove the ultimate since neither of the two previous ones could hold its own. For this and other reasons the famous historian of science, Stanley L. Jaki, thinks that "the replacement of theories in science will go on as before" [49].

12. An all-comprising theory?

Is nature playing cat and mice with us? Or hide-and-seek? Or to put it into more scientific terms, does there exist something like a 'final theory of nature', an ultimate theory containing the first principles, the 'archai', which the pre-Socratic philosophers so eagerly looked for (but each of them suggesting another 'archê') [50]? From these first principles, no longer expressed in philosophical terms but modo mathematico, the laws governing the physical universe might be deduced so that we would finally possess a coherent and non-contradictory pattern of all that is going on in organic and anorganic matter. If this were possible, then we would be able to pinpoint every action, every movement, every phenomenon in nature into its natural and logical place in the all-comprising system.

There are phycisists, and not the least ones, who believe that such a theory is possible. Heisenberg is one of them. In 1958 he announced that he had developed a mathematical model in which all physical phenomena are included, but since then very little has been heard of this. More recently the Nobel Prize winner Steven Weinberg, a highly erudite and widely read man, published a book called 'Dreams of a Final Theory' (1992); he calls his book "a great intellectual adventure, the search for the final laws of nature" [51]. He is more modest than Heisenberg, since he does not contend that he has developed such a theory but only that he is 'dreaming' of it. But to him it is a dream that one day will become true.

Weinberg's conviction is partly based on his hopes for an experiment in the physical field, an experiment that has still to be undertaken and that will cost enormous amounts of money (to be provided by the Americal tax-payer). If this experiment succeeds, it will be proved that there exists a particle which at the same time can be described as at once the most fundamental although still purely hypothetical particle. It is hoped and believed that this particle "will supply the remaining key unlocking the secrets of the Final Theory of mathematical physics" [52].

This mysterious particle is thought to be 'the giver of mass to other particles' (i.e. to those we know already); as Penrose in his review of Weinberg's book expressed it : "Its complete role is not just as God in heaven, but as a God who also deigns to live among his mortal subjects" [53]. It is, so to speak, the missing link. Quantum mechanics is to play a large part in this endeavour. "Quantum mechanics may survive not merely as an approximation to a deeper truth ... but as a precisely valid feature of the final theory" [54]. But in the very last words of his book Weinberg proves non-committal on the possibility of this theory. "Whether or not the final laws of nature are discovered in our lifetime, it is a great thing for us to carry on the tradition of holding up nature to examination, of asking again and again why it is the way it is" [55].

If Weinberg himself is non-committal, other excellent phycisists remain downright sceptical. About these 'grandiose ideas' Penrose stated that "we are, at best, a very long way from any kind of ultimate understanding of the nature of our universe" [56]. And Jaki is of the opinion that "at present the prospect of this, - (i.e.) of modern physics to find one day its final mathematical form and synthesis - are extremely meagre" [57]. As a

XXXVII

layman I must confess that I could easily do without a Final Theory if it would cost those billions of dollars which would be the price of the intended experiment (it would involve the boring of a tunnel with a length of 83 km) [58].

13. Is something wrong with the universe?

Should we categorically state, after having pondered deeply on all that was written above, that the universe is not a coherent whole? Are we forced to renounce all holistic dreams? Do we have no other choice than to wander aimless and forlorn among the ruins of what we supposed to be a cosmos - ruins which, viewed as they stand, are still impressive and picturesque, but can no longer be seen as part of the complex in which they had seemed to be integrated? Or was there never such a complex? Answering these anguished questions is no easy task. There are two possibilities. The first is that the universe really is a coherent whole but that our fractured brains are not, and perhaps never will be, able to perceive it as such. The second is that the universe is not without flaws indeed, and that, for this reason, we see it as devoid of ultimate logicality.

In order to decide between these two possibilities, we cannot do without philosophy. Making use of Gödelian terms once again, we must say that science as it is, as a discipline, has not sufficient means at its disposal for making valid decisions on fundamental points. The Polish-English philosopher Leszek Kolakowski starts from the non-positivist but now generally accepted premise that the person of the observer cannot be eliminated from the description of physical events. I for one would add that the more 'fundamental' these phenomena are, the more 'present' the observer is. Kolakowski then puts us between Kant and Plato.

To Kant the intellect was all and matter was nothing, that is, utterly formless; matter only acquires form (becomes perceptible, intelligible, describable, computable) because the (sovereign) intellect imposes a priori forms on it, forms that exist in his mind, and only there, but not in matter. But to Plato it looked quite differently. In his view reality possesses

XXXVIII

forms of its own, and the human mind is able to discover these because "the reality is mind-like, and the very act of recognition, as Plato would have it, presupposes an affinity, or even a loving kinship, between my mind and the mind of the world" [59].

In my opinion, Kant makes man into God, or perhaps rather, into the Creator - the Creator not of matter (which is presupposed) but of the cosmos as an orderly and intelligible complex. His position is curiously dualistic since this order exists in the mind only and not in reality. In his view reality has no ontological status at all. The Platonic position, however, accords autonomy to reality which possesses its own forms independently of the human intellect; metaphorically speaking, reality has a mind of its own. And the human mind and that of the world correspond.

Now the great question is, what makes them correspond? If there is kinship between them, something or someone must have fathered them both. The answer is given by the scholastic concept of the 'analogia entis', the 'analogy of being', which concept is due to Thomas of Aquinas. It presupposes a God who is the creator of the universe and all that it contains. Since I believe in such a God, it is impossible for me to reason as though I didn't. The analogy concept says that there is analogy (but not identity!) between the mind of God and the human mind. It does not argue as though reality itself had a mind.

God, as the Creator, has imposed order on the universe, an order that is autonomous indeed. Since man is his creature too, God has also imposed his order on the mind. And since this is 'mind', and not matter, it represents and resembles the divine mind. It is because of this analogy that man is capable of discovering the order that there is in nature; it is at the basis of every science and every discipline, even of theology.

But once again, although there is analogy, there is no identity. If the human mind really were identical with that of God, man would be God. Then, and only then, he would be capable of seeing the universe as a perfect harmony without flaws, contradictions, and anomalies. Assuming that God created the world and imposed order on it, we must also assume that he did this well and did not leave loose ends dangling. That we cannot perceive this perfect harmony - the 'harmony of the spheres' - is not the fault of the universe, still less of God, but of our own imperfection. Perhaps Adam and Eve in Paradise were better conditioned to see the ultimate harmony of all that is. But since we do not live in Paradise, we have to be content with what Popper called 'piecemeal engineering', realizing that grandiose vistas are not within our reach. We can do no more than penetrate slowly into the mysteries of nature, knowing all the time that every revealed secret will hide another secret, that every resolved problem will pose another problem, and that every levelled anomaly will confront us with a new anomaly.

13. A-symmetrical man

a. The non-symmetry of the body

If we assume that harmony supposes or is expressed by symmetry, then there is no complete harmony in the human constitution, neither internal nor external. First of all, we have the remarkable fact that mankind is dual, because its consists of males and females. It is a mistake to maintain that this is necessary because otherwise there would be no procreation. Among the great numer of reproduction systems which exist in nature there are also a-sexual ones. There is no reason to go deeply into the raison d'être of human gender here; what is important in our context is that it is dual, a-symmetrical. Male and female are complementary but also different and opposite. In volume after volume, at the appropriate places, I have expounded how this duality may lead, and often really does so, to dualistic contrasts, more often than not to the detriment of women.

But the human person is not symmetrical internally either; the two halves of the human body are not identical [60]. For instance, the perpendicular running through the body does not divide the heart into equal halves; it stands obliquely on the water-level line, at an angle that, if I am correctly informed, is exactly the same as that formed by the axis of the earth with the ecliptica. How curious!

b. Right against left

But if we may consider this as a intriguing but harmless curiosity, the difference between our right and left hands is by no means harmless [61]. Robert Hertz, an anthropologist, gave his essay the title of 'The Pre-Eminence of the Right hand, followed by the subtitle : 'A Study in Religious Polarity'. Three things should strike us : the right hand occupies a privileged position; there is a polarity between both hands; this polarity has a religious character [62]. In Hertz's view this has dualistic connotations. "To the right hand go honors, flattering designations, prerogatives ... The left-hand, on the contrary, is despised and reduced to the role of a humble auxiliary ... The right hand is the symbol and model of all aristocracies, the left hand of all plebeians" [63].

Does this difference have an anatomical cause? It is often thought that the preponderance of the right hand is linked to the left cerebral hemisphere which is supposed the better developed of the two halves of the brain. Modern cerebral neurology is by no means sure that one half would be better equipped than the other; they have different tasks indeed, but do not operate independently from each other [64]. Much, often rather silly, speculation has been based on the idea of 'the two brains' [65]. Hertz had already suggested that, if the privileged position of the right hand is due to the better equipped part of the brain, it is equally conceivable that the left cerebral hemisphere is more developed, because the right has to do the bulk of the work.

At this moment I sit writing with my right hand, while my left hand is completely idle. But if the left hand is properly trained, it can become the compeer of its colleague on the right. Ravel wrote a piano concerto for the left hand for an artist who had lost his right hand in the Great War; this piano concerto is far more than a curiosity, it asks for accomplished playing. The fact that the left hand is a pariah must have other reasons than sheer anatomical ones.

When I was a little boy, I sometimes dared to reach my left hand to a visitor. My mother then sternly reproached me and said : "Give your good hand!", clearly implying that something is wrong with the left hand. In this way, and in many others, it is inculcated into very young children that all honours have to go to the right hand. In primary school we learn to write with the right hand, although it is perfectly possible to write with the left hand, and even with both alternately. Add to this that many instruments and implements are designed for right-handers [66].

The English speak of a 'left-handed compliment' by which they mean a misplaced one, or rather a compliment of doubtful sincerity. In many European languages a clumsy person is described as 'left' : 'links' in Dutch, 'gauche' in French, 'linkisch' in German, while the English do not use 'left' in this sense, but have 'sinister', the Latin for 'left' which is of evil omen. In English as in other languages it can be said of a person that he is born 'with two left hands'. Hertz concludes that "right-handedness ... is an ideal to which everybody must conform and which society forces us to respect by positive sanctions" [67], while the conclusion of Coren is that "it is true that society pressures individuals to become right-handed" [68].

c. A religious origin of the difference in hands?

Hertz thinks that the origin of this a-symmetry must be found in the religious sphere, in the difference between the sacred and the profane [69]. In our secularized world this origin is forgotten, but we are reminded of it when, during a wedding ceremony, the officiating priest says to the couple : "Give each other the right hand". In a great many cultures there is a dualistic difference between the sacred and the profane, dividing the whole universe into two spheres. Hertz writes that "social polarity is still a reflection and a consequence of religious polarity" [70].

All that is strong, powerful, healthy is located in the sacred sphere, whereas everything that is weak, powerless, impure has its place in the profane sphere. A very early expression of this in European thought is the Pythagorean list of opposites in which the good items are on the right side and the wrong ones on the left [71]. "How", asks Hertz, "could man's body, the microcosm, escape the law of polarity that governs everything?" [72]. So the left hand is doomed to be the loser. Man is a 'homo duplex', a double being, who "possesses a right and a left that are profoundly differentiated" [73].

14. The scourge of war

a. Our violent history

May we expect harmony and coherence in the human world, among mankind in general, among the nations, among states? Putting the question is answering it, and the answer is an emphatic no! In spite of all that took place in this century, we doggedly keep believing that we are living in an age of progress; for this reason many people arrogate to themselves the right to look down on former generations, especially those of the Middle Ages, when people were stupid, narrow-minded, bigotted, superstitious, and not to forget, given to cruelty. But our enlightened era saw the two largest wars of all history, fought all over the globe, with countless victims, more than fell in all the wars of history together. And didn't we see more than five millions Jews transported to the extermination camps, together with a great number of Gypsies? When communism was abolished and the Soviet-Union was carved up into fifteen successor-states, the world hoped for one short moment that we were in for a period of universal peace. We all know what has happened since then; there is no need to describe it.

Our time seems to be the apogee of an extremely long and violent history. There have always been wars, tribal wars, civil wars, guerillas, interstate wars; there is hardly a year in history without war on. War is simply endemic; I am tempted to say that is an 'organic' part of the existence of mankind, if only it were not so thoroughly inorganic. For there is a curious and painful difference between our general longing for peace, our profound desire to be spared the horrors of war, and the constant recurrence of this form of violence on a big scale.

The human dilemma is expressed in a proverb of those pastmasters in the art of violence, the Romans : "Si vis pacem, para bellum", if you want peace, prepare for war. As though peace would only be possible if a nation remains armed to the teeth! This would make peace into no more than an interval between periods of war - which, so much must be admitted - sums up the history of the world fairly well. "History is little more than a register of crimes, sorrows, and misfortunes", sighed Gibbon [74].

b. Why there is war

Do we not all love order? But somehow a vicious law of entropy seems at work in humanity, a strong tendency to turn order into chaos, as though chaos were by far the easier and more self-evident thing. The experienced and worldly-wise Comte de Ségur who in 1812 accompanied Napoleon's Grande Armée to Moscow and back, and saw what happened when a great army lost its coherence, concluded that "order is an effort against nature" [75]. This made the great novelist Robert Musil say that "somehow order changes into a need of homicide" [76].

Why is there war? Let us listen to Doris Lessing. "Everything desintegrated. Anyone who has been in or near war ... knows that time ... when everything falls apart, when all forms of order dissolve ... During this time old scores of all kinds are settled. It is when unpopular officers are killed 'by accident'. It is when a man who has an antipathy for another will kill him, or beat him up. A man who wants a woman will rape her, if she is around, or rape another when she is not; and those who want to be make sure that they are where the raping is ... In short it is a time of anarchy, of looting, of arson and destruction for destruction's sake. There are those who believe that this time out of the ordinary is the reason for war, its hidden justification, its purpose and law, another pattern behind the one we see" [77]. It seems as though humanity is in permanent need of this time off. With this anomaly we have to live. Louis Menand calls this 'the incommensurability of the world' which according to him is the basis of dualism [78].

15. Death as an anomaly

War is not the direst anomaly with which humanity has to cope. There is another, much more painful, hurting far more deeply, because it eats into the very core of our existence. It is death. Ask as many people as you want : "what is the opposite of life?", and they will invariably answer : death. But the opposite of life is non-life, non-being, in the sense of never having existed. Death is anomaly, a non-concept; the idea of life is incompatible with that of death. Those who do not believe in an afterlife - a tiny minority in humanity since its beginnings - do not think that, at the moment of death, they will be confronted with something real, for instance, by the concept or the image of death, but, on the contrary, that they will fade into nothingness. And those who believe in an afterlife think that death will have no power over them.

Death does not form part of the order of creation; it is not 'natural', it should not be there. It is, therefore, not fundamentally important when or how a person dies; what is existentially basic is that we die. "Death was never of God's fashioning; not for his pleasure does life cease to be; what meant his creation but that all created things should have being? No breed has he created on earth but for its thriving; none carries in itself the seeds of its own destruction ... God, to be sure, formed man for an immortal destiny, the created image of his own endless being. But the devil's image brought death into the world" [79]. This is, of course, the biblical view to which not all of us will adhere. But all the same, it expresses very neatly the duality, the dualism which we all experience, that of life and death.

16. Conclusions

I have described a world full of rifts and fissures, of anomalies, contradictions, and oppositions. We are fundamentally incapable of coping with this world, with our existence, with ourselves, incapable as we are of managing the affairs of this world as they should be managed by homo sapiens. We have neither the brains nor the practical abilities for it. We have to be content with muddling on. "As long as we live we live surrounded by dangers", said Saint Teresa of Avila; we may also add : as long as we live we are surrounded by anomalies. By far the greater part of humanity succeeds in getting along reasonably well in an imperfect world; they accept the good and the bad, the sour and the sweet, the light and the dark as being simply a part of their existence. But some people, everywhere, in all times, in every culture, are viscerally unable to do this. These are the dualists.

In the prefaces of previous volumes and here and there in the chapters I have indicated which are the personal, psychological, historical and anthropological conditions under which dualistic attitudes and ideologies may develop. Now we see that there is something in the existential order (or disorder) of the world that may pain certain people so much that they take their refuge in dualism. As the term itself says, it divides the world into two. What one does not like one can put on one side, and what one likes on the other, and then draw the line between them. Thus dualism seems the way to solve some disagreeable problems, even ontological ones.

I must not send this volume into the world without thanking some persons who have helped me. First of all, I must express my gratitude to Dr. F.R. Ankersmit, professor of the theory of history, and Dr. T.A.F. Kuipers, professor of the philosophy of science, both of Groningen State University (NL). At my request they read the Preface with a critical eye, supplied me with a number of remarks, and by doing so, saved me from some errors and mistakes. Then there is, as always, Dr. J.R. Dove, who was naturalized as a Dutchman some time ago; he corrected the English of this volume in his usual precise and courteous way. My daughter Dr. Th.A.M. Smidt van Gelder found the time - heaven knows where - to act as a 'general reader' throughout this whole volume. Both she and Dr. Dove provided me with some sensible hints and remarks. My dear wife Anneke found the time and the courage for correcting the one but last version of the text on typing errors. Finally, my publisher. Mr. J.C. Gieben saw the book through the press in his usual friendly and efficient manner.

XLVI

The responsibility for the whole text rests entirely with me, for the scholarly contents, for the English text, for the typography, and for the lay-out. This volume, like all others, can be read without consulting others, but all the same, the volumes VII, VIII, and IX, containing the argument on the Gnosis and related systems, belong together. To begin with Volume X I shall shift the argument to dualistic phenomena in Roman history.

NOTES TO THE PREFACE

1. See Vol. V, XIII/XIV.
2. See Vol. VI, XXV/XXVI.
3. See my basic statement in Vol. IV, Ch. IV.5.
4. P.F.M. Fontaine, De onbekende Hitler (Hitler the unknown). Baarn (NL), 1992.
5. Couliano, Gnoses dual. 21.
6. John van Heijenoort s.v. 'Logical paradoxes', Enc.Phil., 5, 45.
7. Kathrin Sandkühler s.v. 'Absurde (Das)', Eur.Enz.Phil.u.Wiss., 1, 43-45.
8. Sainsbury, Paradoxes 1.
9. P. Probst s.v. 'Paradox', Hist.Wört.b.Phil. 7, 89.
10. Whitehead/Russell, Princ.math. I, 37.
11. Attributed by Aristotle to Zeno of Elea, Physics 239b and 263a-b.
12. This pseudo-paradox bears a curious resemblance to something that is familiar to many Dutchmen. On a tin of Droste's cocoa we see a picture of a nurse carrying a tray with a cup of cocoa on it and, next to the cup, a tin of Droste's cocoa. On this tin we see a picture of a nurse with ..., and so on ad infinitum. Ad infinitum? In theory, yes. But as children we amused ourselves with following as far as possible the ever smaller nurses with trays on which ..., until even with a large magnifying glass we lost track. To say nothing of the painter who, at a certain moment, was no longer able to paint the picture, so infinitely small it had become.
13. It is usually but falsely attributed to Tertullian who, however, never wrote this but something else, namely that the death of God's son on the cross was "prorsus credibile quia ineptum", De carne Christi 5.4.
14. R.L. Corie, Paradoxia epidemica. The Renaissance tradition of Paradox. Hamden (Conn.), 1976.
15. Rousseau, Émile 323.
16. Proust, Plaisirs 110.
17. Goethe. Dichtung II.8, 350.

18. Schopenhauer, Preisschrift 812.
19. Letter to Dilthey, 13.I.1883, Briefwechsel 249.
20. Mackie, Truth 239.
21. Novalis, Schriften II, 523/524.
22. Dürrenmatt, Physiker. Anhang 92.
23. Kierkegaard, Tagebücher 2, 80, VIII, A 11.
24. Douglas, Purity 162.
25. James, Varieties 129.
26. Curry, Foundations 3-8. Another list is printed by Sainsbury, Paradoxes 145-151. Nice, non-scientific paradoxes are the slogan of Popeye the Sailorman : "I am what I am, and more than I am", and the advertisement of Hassan : "The dates of Hassan are bigger than they are" (recorded by the Dutch author Multatuli = Eduard Douwes Dekker (1820-1887)). A fascinating example of a pseudo-paradox is this one : "Abraham Lincoln was born in a log cabin that he had built with his own hands" (from an essay by an American student).
27. Epimenides the Cretan, who really existed, was probably not the father of this statement; in DL 2.108 we find mentioned a certain Eubulides of Milete, a philosopher who was fond of dialectical arguments and who wrote a (lost) essay called 'The Liar'.
28. The reader will find all the information he or she may want in a book by Rüstow, 'Der Lügner' (see Bibliography).
29. Except that in 1925 the English mathematician F.P. Ramsey said that this is a 'semantical' or 'epistemological' paradox, and, therefore, may become a subject for discussion. He found that the real, 'logical' paradoxes are written in mathematical symbols. Curry, Foundations 7, finds the distinction 'a little vague'; it "tends to be obliterated in modern logic". As a non-mathematician I feel that Ramsey's distinction comes from an idiosyncracy that is not rare among mathematicians, to acknowledge nothing that cannot be written in mathematical symbols.
30. The formulation of this paradox dates from June 1901. In 1903 he dealt with it in his 'Principles of mathematics', Ch. 10, and in 1910 in his 'Principia mathematica' I, 77-83.
31. Van Heijenoort, A Source Book, 124/125 Russell's letter to Frege dd. 3.VI.1902, and 127/128 Frege's response to Russell's letter dd. 22.VI.1902.
32. John van Heijenoort s.v. 'Logical paradoxes', Enc.Phil. 5, 49.
33. Curry, Foundations 7/8.
34. First publication in the Monatshefte für Mathematik und Physik 38, 173-198, Leipzig, 1931. Translation into English in Gödel, Propositions (see Bibliography). The interested reader can easily find an English translation of Gödel's articles in Van Heijenoort, From Frege, 582-617.
35. John van Heijenoort s.v. 'Gödel's theorem'. Enc.Phil. 3, 356.

XLVIII

36. David Hilbert published his far-reaching ideas in several stages : in 1917 he gave a lecture at Zürich on 'axiomatisches Denken' (published in Mathematische Annale, Vol. 78 (1918). Then came 'Neubegründung der Mathematik. Erste Mitteilung', Abhandlungen an dem mathematischen Seminar der hamburgischen Universität, Vol. I (1922), and 'Über das Unendliche', Mathematische Annale, Vol. 95 (1926). For this subject one should also consult Ladrière, Limitations (seen Bibliography).

37. Curry, Foundations 123/124.

38. Nagel & Newman, Gödel's proof, 7.

39. Martel, Dieu cet inconnu 113.

40. Kuhn, Structure 79.

41. S. Carnot, Réflexions sur la puissance du feu (1824).

42. R. Clausius, Über verschiedene Formen die Anwendung bequeme Formen der Hauptgleichungen der mechanischen Wärmetheorie. Annale der physischen Chemie 125 (1865).

43. I borrow this example from J.D. Fast, Materie en leven. De samenhang der natuurwetenschappen (Matter and Life. The coherence of the sciences). Publication of 'Natuur en techniek', 1973 2, 1972 1, p. 99.

44. See Vol. VI, Ch. III.3.

45. Pais, Subtle 440.

46. Quoted by Pais, Subtle 486.

47. A telling example of this fear is that in the summer of 1945 which was cool and very wet, farmers in the Dutch province of North-Brabant told me that this was the effect of the two nuclear bombs on Japan. They obviously feared that the cosmos itself was shaken by these bombs.

48. Voltaire, Traité de métaphysique (1734), Ch. VIII, Oeuvres complètes, seconde partie 1549.

49. Jaki, Relevance 137.

50. See Vol. I, Ch. II.

51. Weinberg, Dreams IX.

52. James Penrose in NY Review of Books, Oct. 21, 1993.

53. See previous note.

54. Weinberg, Dreams 89.

55. Weinberg, Dreams 275.

56. James Penrose in his review of Weinberg's book in NY Review of Books, Oct. 21, 1993.

57. Jaki, Relevance 137.

58. It is described in Weinberg, Dreams, Ch. XII. After the completion of this Preface I read that this project, called the 'Superconducting Super Collider' (SSC), will not be executed; on October 21, 1993 the American House of Representatives voted to cancel funding for it.

59. Kolakowski, Met. Horror 71.
60. Coren, Left-Hander Syndrome 27 : The "apparent symmetry of the human form is actually an illusion". For this reason he calls man 'a lopsided animal'.
61. I am basing what is going to follow mainly on an essay by Robert Hertz, Pre-Eminence (see Bibliography). The original essay was in French and is dated 1909 ('La prééminence de la main droite : étude sur la polarité religieuse', Revue philosophique 68 (1909). Hertz was a highly promising French sociologist whose career was cut short by his death in action on April 13, 1915.
62. There is little, or even nothing at all, about this religious polarity in two recent books on left-handedness, those of Coren, The Left-Hander Syndrome. The Causes and Consequences of Left-Handedness. New York (1992), and of Rik Smits, De linkshandige picador (The Left-Handed Picador). Over links- en rechtshandigheid : feiten en verzinsels. Amsterdam (NL), 1993.
63. Hertz, Pré-Ém. 3. A telling example of this is provided by Smits, Picador 22. During World war II Roosevelt and Churchill paid a diplomatic visit to King Saud of Arabia. Churchill promised him an armour-clad car. This pleased the king greatly. But when the car came, he was not only disappointed but even felt insulted. For this British car had the wheel at the right side. This meant that the king would have to sit, especially during hunting parties, to the left of his driver; in Saudian etiquette this was simply inconceivable. The King never used the car.
64. See Coren, Syndrome, Ch. 6.
65. Coren speaks of 'psycho-neuro-astrology' (title of his Ch. 7).
66. Smits, Picador 201, gives the example of those pens on a chain which we find at office-windows; they are placed at the right side which make them almost unusable for the left-hander.
67. Hertz, Pré-Ém. 5.
68. Coren, Syndrome 70.
69. Hertz, Pre-Em. 7.
70. Hertz, Pre-Em. 8.
71. Vol. I, Ch. I.11.
72. Hertz, Pre-Em. 8.
73. Hertz, Pre-Em. 21.
74. I mislaid the source of this quotation.
75. Ségur, Campagne : "L'ordre est un effort contre la nature".
76. Musil, Mann ohne Eig. I, 465.
77. Lessing, Out of the Fountain 21.
78. Louis Menand, NY Review of Books, 25.VI.1992.
79. Wisd. 1:13-14 and 2:23-24.

CHAPTER I

LEFTOVERS FROM THE JAR

In this chapter a number of short treatises from the Nag Hammadi Library will be analysed which could not find a place in the foregoing volume, because they are not easily, or even not at all assignable to one of the Gnostic systems. All the same, they are too intriguing, and above all, too thoroughly dualistic, to be left indifferently on the side. They are short, in fact too short to contain a fully developed doctrine. Should the reader want to be orientated in general about this doctrine, I must refer him or her to the preface of Volume VIII. However, the second of the texts to be treated here, the Gospel of Philip, presents in a nutshell the most important Gnostic tenets. I believe that a course on the Gnosis could conveniently begin with an analysis of this document with its didactic character.

1. The Treatise on Resurrection

The document in question is to be found in the Codex Jung which is Codex I of the Nag Hammadi Library, and is called 'The Treatise on Resurrection', a short but important treatise [1]. It is in the form of a letter addressed by an unnamed author to a certain Rheginos [2]. This letter dates from the late second century [3]; it is a matter of debate whether it is Valentinian in content. Some think so, even suggesting that Valentinus himself wrote it, but others deny this. Malcolm Peel believes that its author was a late second century Gnostic who, without being a Valentinian, was certainly influenced by this doctrine [4].

The starting-point of the treatise [5] is the enormous and dualistic difference between the All, the Pleroma, the upper, celestial world, that is, and this world, the cosmos. "Strong is the system of the Pleroma; small is that which broke loose (and) became (the) world." The cosmos in this vision is an erratic block without any ontological relation to the Pleroma. The All simply exists but the world came into being [6]. Those who live in this world "exist in corruption" [7]; the end of all is death. "Those who are living shall die ... Everything is prone to change. The world is an illusion [8].

In this world of illusion there is only one thing that is real and true : the Resurrection. "The resurrection does not have the aforesaid character (of illusion); for it is the truth which stands firm" [9]. The tract is directed against those who doubt the Resurrection. "Many are lacking faith in it, but there are a few who find it" [10]. But whose Resurrection is meant in fact? That of Jesus Christ? Perhaps. "He raised himself", says the text [11]. But one gets the strong impression that the author is not referring at all to the event that is related in the New Testament. There is no mention either of the empty tomb or of the apparitions, nor, indeed, are there any references to specific details. Instead, we are told that "Christ transformed (himself) into an imperishable aeon ... having swallowed the visible by the invisible" [12]. This explains why there could be no apparitions : "He put aside the world which is perishing" [13]. The risen one is not Jesus of Nazareth but the Gnostic Christ who breaks entirely with the world, just as the true Gnostic should do.

In accordance with this it is stated that Christ had no terrestrial origin. Mary is not mentioned nor in fact are there any allusions to details of his life on earth. "He was originally from above, a seed of the Truth, before this structure (of the cosmos) had come into being" [14]. The author seems to proclaim a Christian dogma by stating that Christ was the Son of God and the Son of Man, "possessing the humanity and the divinity". But obviously the two natures of Christ do not fit harmoniously together, since he immediately follows the previous statement with the comment that Christ "on the one hand might vanquish death through his being Son of God, and that on the other through the Son of Man the restoration to the Pleroma might occur" [15].

We should not expect an elaborate Gnostic theology in this short treatise, but all the same all the main Gnostic characteristics are present : the dualism between the Pleroma and the cosmos, the dualistic division of mankind into two races, the dualistic nature of the human person, split as he is into 'flesh' (body), subjected to death and decay, and 'Nous' (thought), the part that will survive [16], the rejection of the world, and the role of Knowledge. This last term is used only rarely; the author speaks of 'the Truth', and further on of 'the Solution'. This Solution appears to be incorporated in Christ the Saviour, who, as the Word of Truth, is "the emanation of Truth and Spirit" [17].

The Pleroma is sketchily described as the structure "where many dominions and divinities came into existence" [18]. The hallmark of existence here below is death and corruption, as I wrote already. "Nothing redeems us from this world" [19]. For the ignorant the outlook is gloomy. The text speaks of "the foolishness of those who are without Knowledge" [20]. But then there are those who "have known the Son of Man ... (Great) are those who believe ... Therefore, we (the Gnostics) are elected to salvation and redemption since we are predestined from the beginning ... We shall enter into the wisdom of those who have known the truth" [21].

"What then is the Resurrection? It is always the disclosure of those who have risen" [22]. However, the body will have no part in it. "The visible (physical) members which are dead shall not be saved" [23]. It is a "spiritual resurrection which swallows up the psychic and the fleshly" [24]. In the best Gnostic tradition it is only the Spirit that counts; the soul and the body are good for nothing. It is obvious that the elect should consider the Resurrection as an event that, for them, did occur already. In the New Testament the second Letter to Timothy mentions a certain Hymenaeus and Philetus who contend "that our Resurrection has already taken place; they have shot wide of the truth" [25]. The present text exhort its addressees to "flee from the divisions and the fetters, and already you have the resurrection ... Why not consider yourself as risen?" [26].

The final result of the redemption is that the chosen become one with the Pleroma. "We are drawn to heaven, like beams by the sun, not restrained by anything" [27]. "The All which we are - we are saved. We have received salvation from end to end" [28]. "Imperishability (descends) upon the perishable; the light flows down upon the darkness, swallowing it up; and the Pleroma fills up the deficiency. These are the symbols and the images of the resurrection" [29].

2. The Gospel of Philip

The Gospel of Philip [30] derives its name from Philip the apostle (its real author must have been a non-apostolic Jew who was converted to Christianity), but is not to be found in the New Testament. It "was probably written in Syria in the second half of the third century (A.D.)" and is "generally Valentinian in character", according to Isenberg. This same scholar says that it "is a collection of statements or excerpts concerning sacraments and ethics". As such, it "makes an important contribution to our rather limited knowledge of Gnostic sacramental theology and practice" [31]. However, this section will focus on something else.

a. Nominalism

Already in the exordium the world and 'the other aeon' (the Pleroma) are opposed, the one being compared to the winter and the other to the summer. "Let us sow in the winter so that we reap in the summer." Reaping 'in winter' will only mean 'plucking out', without any harvest. In other words, no kind of fulfilment is possible down here. The author even goes so far as to say that it is not fitting to pray 'in winter' [32].

Not only is there no fulfilment in this world, there is also no clear intellectual perception possible. "Names given to worldy things are very deceptive, for they divert our thoughts from what is correct to what is incorrect." This is unadulterated nominalism. It is astonishing to hear what the author considers 'worldly'. "Thus one who hears the word 'God' does not perceive what is correct, but what is incorrect. So also with 'the Father' and 'the Son' and 'the Holy Spirit' and 'life' and 'light' and 'resurrection' and 'the Church' and all the rest" [33]. I guess this constitutes a barely veiled attack on orthodox Christianity which freely uses all these key-words of faith. "They (the Christians) perceive what is incorrect, (unless) they have come to know what is correct" [34]. It is only the Gnostics who 'know' the correct meaning of these terms.

b. Pleromic emanations

There is a fully developed emanation theory in this Gospel. As usual, in the Pleroma or above it, is the Father. The Father has a Son to whom he has given his own name, Father, which means that the Son has the identity of the Father. This is a secret : "Those who have this name (the Gnostics) know it, but they do not speak it. But those who do not have it do not know it" [35].

c. The rulers of this world

Then there are 'powers', obviously the rulers of this world. "The world came about through a mistake." This is a fundamental Gnostic tenet. "For he who created it wanted to create it imperishable and immortal. He fell short of his desire. For the world never was imperishable, nor, for that matter, was he who made the world" [36]. We are confronted here with a Demiurge, although this term is not used. The Demiurge bungles his work because he is ignorant.

This Demiurge and the rulers of this world are wicked because "they (contend against) man, not wishing him to be (saved)". It is to them that animal sacrifices are brought, "for if man is (saved, there will not) be any sacrifices ..., and animals will not be offered to the powers" [37]. This contains a criticism of the Jewish religion with its animal sacrifices. One is not far off the mark if one perceives in these 'powers' the figure of the Jewish God to whom such sacrifices are brought.

"The powers wanted to deceive man, since they saw that he had a kinship with those who are truly good (= in all probability the Father and the Son - F.). They took the names of those who are good and gave them to those who are not good, so that through the names they might deceive him and bind him to those who are not good (= the powers)" [38]. The meaning of this is that 'the powers', mainly the Jewish God, try to shift the natural allegiance of humanity to themselves rather than to the Father by usurping the names of the Father and the Son in order to lead people astray. "For they (the powers) wanted to take the free man and make him a slave to them forever" [39]. This is a barely concealed attack on Christian orthodoxy which is here accused of misusing the eternal names for its own ends.

d. Man

This is the first element of an anthropology of which only the barest outline is given. Man is created good but has become enslaved by Ignorance. It is impossible for him "to see anything of the things that actually exist (= the things from above) - F.) ... This is not the way with man in the world : he sees the sun without being a sun; and he sees the heaven and the earth and all other things, but he is not these things" [40]. This curious passage is highly revealing. The hallmark of the nether world is distinctiveness and multiplicity. There are millions of distinct individuals, each of them separate and unique.

But in the Pleroma all entities fuse into each other. "(In that place = the Pleroma) you do see yourself - and what you see you shall become."

For the Gnostic this already becomes true here below. "You (sing.) saw something of that place (the Pleroma) and you became those things. You saw the Spirit, you became Spirit. You saw Christ, you became Christ. You saw (the Father), you shall become Father" [41].

Adam had a double origin, one from the Spirit and one from the earth; both are called 'virgins', I suppose in order to stress that he was brought about in an a-sexual manner [42]. "The soul of Adam came into being by means of a breath, which is a synonym for (Spirit)." The author is following more or less the report of Gen. 2 but his conclusion is different. "His soul was replaced by a (spirit)." This must mean that Adam in this way was transformed from a psychic (earthly) being into a pneumatic (Gnostic) one.

This becomes clear from the following comment. "When he was united (to the Spirit), (he spoke) words incomprehensible to the powers"; these words refer to Gnostic Knowledge is meant. It is suggested that the Spirit (Pneuma) did not become a fully integrated part of Adam, since the Spirit is called 'his mother' [43]. This Pneuma must be conceived as a lodestar or a good genius.

e. The Fall

Speaking of this Adam, we must think of him as an androgynous person, for at first Eve was 'in him'. But then she became separated from him "which is the cause of death" [44]. Death, therefore, is not the consequence of the transgression of God's command in Paradise. "If the woman had not separated from the man, she would not die with the man. His separation became the beginning of death" [45]. In all probability this separation is "the Fall which occurred in the beginning" [46]. But it is nowhere explicitly stated why it happened or whose fault it was.

The reader who is acquainted with Vol. VIII of this series will have met the idea of androgynity or bisexuality several times. Gnostics found the fact that there existed males and females deplorable. They would never, unlike the French Assembly, have thunderously applauded that representative who, after having heard a minister categorically stating that between men and women only 'a small difference' existed, in a stentorian voice exclaimed : 'Vive la petite différence!'. Let me quote Mahé : "God is sufficient in himself, but the human being is profoundly deficient. Man and woman need one another to assure their survival. In consequence, the division of the sexes is one of the aspects of this division". This feeling of deficiency gave rise to the myth of original bisexuality [47]. Perhaps we might also say that, in the view of the Gnostics, sexual differentiation is the true paradigma of multiplicity, whereas androgynity is a pleromic phenomenon.

As soon as man and woman were separated, all went wrong. In Paradise Adam ate from the wrong tree. For the Gnostic writer, there were, as in Genesis, two special trees in the Garden, the tree of knowledge and the tree of life. The first one "bears animals, the second bears men. Adam (ate) from the tree which bore animals and he brought forth animals. For this reason the children of Adam worship (animals)" [48]. It will be clear what is meant. The knowledge is not Knowledge, of course, but earthly wisdom which is only misleading, especially with respect to religion. "(That) is why (sins) increased." Adam forgot all about his pneuma and became an 'animal', that is to say, a purely biological being.

Had he, instead, eaten from the tree of life, the one which bears men, "(then) the gods would worship man. (For in the beginning) God created man. (But now men) create God. That is the way it is in the world - men make gods and worship their creation. It would be fitting for the gods to worship men" [49]. The author could not have expressed his thought with more precision. By 'man' pneumatic man is meant, the man who realizes that his true abode is in the Pleroma. It was God's intention that man should feel in this way. As it is, however, humanity has constructed very imperfect religions after its own image. Had it been otherwise, it would have seen the 'powers' (the gods) at its feet.

f. Christ the Saviour

The human race is incapable of remedying this unhappy situation unaided. Christ the Saviour must come to its help. He was 'born from a virgin' [50]; Mary is mentioned as 'his mother' [51]. But, according to this author, she did not conceive by the Holy Spirit. The orthodox Christians "do not know what they are saying. When did a woman conceive by a woman?" [52]. It should be noted that in Gnostic texts, the Spirit is female. But who may be the father of Jesus then? Ménard, the subject of whose doctoral thesis was this Gospel of Philip, admits that it is an obscure point [53].

Perhaps the solution is to be found further on in the text where it is said that "the Father of everything united with the virgin who came down" [54]. Most probably the virgin in question is not Mary but Sophia, the divine wisdom; they unite 'in the great bridal chamber' which is the Pleroma. It is there that "his (Christ's) body came into being on that very day. It left the bridal chamber as one who came into being from the bridegroom and the bride" [55]. This means that Christ, body and soul, had a pleromic origin. This would reduce the role of Mary to no more than an image, perhaps, of what really happened. This is sustained by another sentence. "When we were Hebrews we were orphans and had only our mother, but when we became Christians we had both father and mother (= the Father, or Logos, and the celestial Sophia)" [56]. The reference is not to orthodox Christians but to Gnostics who, in their understanding of Christianity, had another parentage than Jesus (and the orthodox), namely a pleromic one.

"Christ came to ransom some, to save others, to redeem others" [57]. Before he came, "there was no bread in the world ... Man used to feed like the animals, but when Christ came, the perfect man, he brought bread from heaven in order that man might be nourished with the food of man" [58]. There are two levels of human existence. The one is purely biological and does not really differ from the animal way of life; the other is the divine one and is made possible by the Gnostic revelation.

g. Two races of men

This brings us to the well-known Gnostic notion that there are two clearly (and dualistically) distinct races of men. "The heavenly man (Christ) has many more sons than the earthly man. If the sons of Adam are many, although they die, how much more the sons of the perfect man, they who do not die but are always begotten ... All who are begotten in the world are begotten in a natural way, and the others (the Gnostics) in a spiritual way" [59]. Although in this document Jesus and Christ are identified, their names are destined to be used differently. While 'Christ' is the name that is 'revealed', that is, generally known to the world, 'Jesus' is the name to be used by the initiated only [60].

The non-Gnostic is in a bad shape spiritually. The Powers (of the lower world) take him and "make him a slave forever" [61]. He is subject to unclean spirits among whom there are males as well as females. Their obvious aim is to keep men and women apart and to see to it that they do not marry. "The males are they which unite with the souls which inhabit a female form (= the women), but the females are they which are mingled with those in a male form (= the men) ... And none shall be able to escape them ... When the wanton women see a man sitting alone, they leap down on him and play with him and defile him. So also the lecherous men, when they see a beautiful woman sitting alone, they leap down on her and play with her and defile her" [62]. Human beings are the slaves of evil : "if we are ignorant of it (evil), it takes root in us and produces its fruit in our heart. It masters us. We are its slaves ... Ignorance is the mother of (all evil)" [63].

How different is the outlook for the elect! Their prototypes are the three Mary's : Mary the mother of Jesus, Mary Salome (called her 'sister'), and Mary Magdalena; they were the "three who always walked with him" [64]. Of these three not the Virgin Mary but Mary Magdalena seems to have been the most privileged. "(Christ) loved her more than (all) the disciples (and used to) kiss her (often) on her (mouth)" [65]. We must relate this to another notion. "It is by a kiss that the perfect conceive and give birth ... We receive conception from the grace which is in each other" [66].

The kiss is the image or the seal of the spiritual marriage through which pneumatics engender new beings for the Pleroma. The author calls this 'the undefiled marriage, the true mystery' and opposes it to 'the marriage of defilement' with its sexual intercourse, although he admits that there is 'a hidden quality' to it [67]. Jesus, by kissing Mary Magdalena, 'marries' her in a spiritual way and thus declared her to be a pneumatic, fit for the Pleroma, and the prototype of the elect. As Ménard says, "the Gnosis affranchizes one from the cycle of generations and births" [68]. By taking offence at Jesus' kissing of Mary Magdalena [69], the apostles showed that they were still only psychic men, unable to understand this. Those who have been made free through Knowledge - for "who has Knowledge of the truth is a free man" [70] - will "possess everything, the resurrection, the light, the cross, the Holy Spirit" [71]. But they are not numerous [72].

h. Unity restored

The reader who has followed me up to this point will be convinced that we are dealing with a Gnostic-dualistic text. The two great Gnostic dualisms are there : that of the Pleroma and the cosmos, and that of the two races of men. Furthermore, there is dualism of soul and body, of Knowledge and Ignorance, of life and death, of the light and the dark. But as is usual in Gnostic ideology, dualism, division, distinction, multiplicity, opposition, contrast, is neither the original nor the final state of the world. In the end all contrasts will fuse into each other. "Light and darkness, life and death, right and left, are brothers of one another. They are inseparable ... For this reason each one will dissolve into its original nature" [73]. The attitude expressed here is holistic.

What Christ the Saviour came to achieve is to restore unity in the world. The two great means at his disposal are the Eucharist and marriage [74]. In the Eucharist the believer unites him- or herself with Christ whose body is the Logos and whose blood is the Holy Spirit [75]; this entails that he or she already becomes one with the Pleroma, the eternal aeon, the All. The second sacramental means is marriage by which "the fundamental dualism of man and woman is abolished" [76]. It is a remarkable thing that this Gnostic author is not opposed to marriage, not even to its carnal side.

In fact, marriage occupies a central place in this Gospel and is perhaps its most salient feature. In the Old Testament Israel's relation to God is often presented as an analogy to marriage on earth. In the Gospels Jesus is more than once referred to as 'the bridegroom'. Paul in his letters speaks of marriage as a 'great mystery' and said that the relationship of Jesus to the Church was similar to that of a married couple [77]. As Grant states, "it was among Valentinian Gnostics, however, that most was made of marriage as a mystery ... Valentinian ideas seem to be closely related, at least verbally, to New Testament expressions" [78]. I feel that we should keep this phrase 'at least verbally' firmly in mind with respect to this Gospel too, since this is not far from Valentinian doctrine.

Let us begin with a text that I already quoted. "When Eve was still in Adam, death did not exist. When she was separated from Adam, death came into being." As explained above, this denotes that originally there was only one sex, the androgynous one; the existence of two sexes is considered a deficiency, a gross imperfection, so serious that it is the cause of death. But the author follows this more hopefully : "If he (Adam) becomes again complete and attains his former self, death will be no more" [79]. In other words, the state of androgynity is the true identity; its restoration is the eschatological end of the process of redemption.

This is what Christ came for. He "came to repair the separation which was from the beginning and again unite the two, and to give life to those who died as a result of the separation and unite them" [80]. This 'from the beginning' refers to the origin of mankind; whereas twofold sex is the hallmark of humanity in this world, it is androgynity in the Pleroma. This opposition is dualistic in nature, because twofold sex is 'death' and androgynity is 'life'.

The problem with Eve is that she was never properly married to Adam. "Eve separated from Adam because she was never united with him in the bridal chamber" [81]. I take this to mean that Eve became the consort of Adam in a 'biological' way, i.e. by being taken form his side, but that no sacramental, pleromic marriage took place. Whereas Gen. 2 points out that Adam and Eve, as a couple, are the prototype of all married couples, this Gospel stresses the separation and leaves out the rest. Further on, without mentioning his name, the text speaks of Cain. "He became a murderer, just like his father." Who was his father? Adam? Of course not! "He was the child of the serpent." It is not explained here who this serpent was, but in all probability it was Jaldabaoth, the wicked God who is known from Valentinian sources. He seduced Eve, for Cain "was begotten in adultery" [82].

Gnostic sacramental marriage is the image of the celestial union in the Pleroma. Every sort brings forth its own sort, and a god begets a god. Gnostics, therefore, are "the seed of the Son of man ..., the sons of the (heavenly) bridal chamber [83] ... (and) sons of the bridegroom (= the Father) [84]. There is a problem here. "It is impossible for us to tell whether these Gnostics were discussing human or spiritual marriage, or whether in their minds there was a significant difference between the two" [85].

However this may be, marriage in the world is just as much a mystery as the celestial union. "Marriage in the world is a true mystery for those who have taken a wife." We heard already that the author spoke of 'defiled' and 'undefiled' marriages. What is the difference? A 'defiled' marriage is 'fleshly', an 'undefiled' one 'pure'; the first one obeys 'desire', the second 'the will'; the first belongs to 'darkness and night', the second to 'the day and the light' [86]. This means that Gnostic marriage forms part of the Pleroma (= 'light'), the others of the nether world (= 'darkness'). In short, when Gnostic couples unite, it is from love; non-Gnostics do it out of lust. But there must be no mistake : in both cases sexual intercourse is meant. "Great is the mystery of marriage. For (without) it the world (would not have existed). Now the existence of (the world depends on man) and the existence (of man on marriage)" [87].

Gnostics would not be Gnostics if they did not take their distance from 'the others' in matters of marriage too. "A bridal chamber is not for the animals, nor is it for the slaves, nor for the defiled women; but it is for the free men and the virgins" [88]. As Grant writes : "The way of initiation was ... not for everyone". But for the true believers it was "a highly significant picture of salvation as equivalent to marriage and of marriage as an archetype of salvation" [89]. Marriage was seen as a means to overcome the fundamental dualism in the cosmos; for the Gnostic the eschaton had already become a reality. "If anyone become a son of the bridal chamber, he will receive the light ... And none shall be able to torment a person like this even when he dwells in the world ... The world has become the aeon, for the aeon is fullness (Pleroma) for him" [90].

3. The Hypostasis of the Archons

a. On the tract itself

The Hypostasis of the Archons [91] is of an uncertain date, but, according to Bullard, "some evidence points to the third century (A.D.)" [92]. The Archons are the rulers of the cosmos, of the nether world, that is; what this document sets out to prove is that these authorities are a reality (hypostasis) [93]. We must not think of them as mythological or literary figures.

The genre is that of a revelation made by the Great Angel Eleleth to an anonymous questioner; this angel is called 'sagacity' and 'understanding' and the one "who stands in the presence of the Great Invisible Spirit (= the Father)" [94]; so what he dispenses is vintage Knowledge. "Its theological perspective is a vigorous Gnosticism of undetermined sectarian affiliation" [95]. Bullard, whom I am quoting here, then unblushingly states that "the Hypostasis of the Archons shows clearly Christian features and **thus** (my emphasis) can be considered a Christian work" [96]. Scholars who make such glib statements show deplorably little understanding of the orthodox Christian faith.

We should not expect a fully elaborate Gnostic doctrine in this text of some seven printed pages. The primal godhead is here called 'the Father of the Entirety' [97] and 'the Father of Truth' [98]. This Entirety comprises, or should comprise, both worlds, the (higher) invisible world and the (lower) visible one. At first sight this might be taken to mean that they are not seen as dualistically apart, "for by starting from the invisible world the visible world was invented" [99]. However, further on Eleleth explains that "a veil exists between the World Above and the realms that are below; a Shadow came into being beneath the veil" [100].

b. The two worlds

This unequivocally signifies that the two worlds are qualitatively different; whereas the upper world is that of light, the nether one is under a Shadow'. Furthermore, certain things happen in the 'realms below' that do not have their origin in the 'World Above'. In the latter world yet another entity exists that is called 'Incorruptibility' or 'Imperishability'; it is obviously female [101]. Is she an emanation from the Father? Nothing is said about her origin; the tractate is far more interested in the modelling of cosmos and man than in the Pleroma. But it is also said that ' a voice' went out from Incorruptibility [102]. As Bullard notes, "the voice from Imperishability is evidently the voice of Sophia (Wisdom)" [103], also called 'Pistis' (Faith) [104].

Sophia "wanted to create something ...; and her product was a celestial thing (or 'the image of heaven')" [105]. These 'images' could be the constellations [106]. The 'veil' that was mentioned earlier obviously is the work of Sophia; it is the firmament of the fixed stars that, as so often in Gnostic texts, hermetically seals off the cosmos from the Pleroma.

"This is the reason why Incorruptibility looked down into the region (of the Waters) : so that, by the Father's will, she might bring the Entirety into union with the Light" [107]. The cosmos must not be left entirely to itself; the presence of Light in it warrants its essential connection with the upper world. "Sophia stretched forth her finger and introduced Light into matter; and she pursued it down to the region of Chaos. And she returned up (to) her light" [108]. Sophia does not take up her abode in the cosmos; she goes back to the Pleroma after having "placed the vital light-element into the material" [109].

However, there was a nasty incident. When the image of Incorruptibility appeared in the Waters, "the Authorities of darkness (= the Archons) became enamoured of her. But they could not lay hold of that Image, because of their weakness." The Archons cannot prevent the presence of Light in the cosmos, but dangers to it are lurking everywhere. In the most authentically Gnostic-dualistic manner it is explained in what 'the weakness' of the Rulers consisted. "Beings (the Archons, that is) that merely possess a soul ('psuchê') cannot lay hold of those that possess a Spirit ('pneuma'); for they (the Archons) were from Below, while it (Incorruptibility) was from Above" [110].

c. Matter

We heard already of 'Matter'. How did this originate? The Shadow became Matter. Because the firmament (the veil or curtain) shields off the cosmos from the luminous world above, it must needs cast a shadow. This shadow projects itself further downward, which must mean that the constituent parts of the cosmos came into being. That is how Matter and material things came about.

In the Matter which Shadow created, 'a plastic form' was moulded; this became "an arrogant beast resembling a lion", androgynous by nature [111]. This unpleasant being is none other than Jaldabaoth, the Supreme Ruler of the cosmos who is also called Saklas and Samael [112]. "In this astrological setting", writes Bullard [113], "the first-born archon (Jaldabaoth) must be the outermost of planetary spheres, Saturn" [114]. That he is identical with Jahve, the Jewish God, is proved by his arrogant assertion : "It is I who am God, and there is no other apart from me" [115]. This demonstrates not only his arrogance but also his ignorance since he does not know what is above him. After all, he is no more than the king of Matter. Because he is sinning in this way against the Entirety, a voice reached him "from above the realm of absolute power (= the Pleroma), saying : 'You are mistaken, Samael' - which is 'god of the blind'" [116]. The voice is, of course, that of the Father.

Nothing daunted, the first Archon "made himself a vast realm ... And he contemplated offspring from himself". Because of his androgynity, he did not need a consort to do this [117]. "And he created seven offspring, androgynous just like their parent" [118]. This offspring, it goes without saying, are the planetary spheres, but this would, with Jaldabaoth-Samael, make eight planets which would be impossible. Perhaps we have to do with a clerical error or an oversight.

d. Sabaoth

When Samael tells his offspring that he is the god of Entirety, Sophia takes action. "You are wrong, Sakla", she cries ('sakla' is Aramaic for 'fool'); "she breathed into his face, and her breath became a fiery angel for her, - and that angel bound Jaldabaoth and cast him into the Tartarus (the underworld or Hell) below the Abyss" [119]. The battle between the rulers of the upper and nether worlds is on! We also hear that Sophia has a daughter, called 'Zoê' (Life); this means that she is able to oppose the essential life-force to Jaldabaoth.

One of Jaldabaoth-Saklas-Samael's offspring is Sabaoth [120]. Hearing and seeing what Sophia and Zoê had done, "he repented and condemned his father and his mother Matter". This does not imply that his father Jaldabaoth is suddenly no longer androgynous, for he is identical with Matter. He is, self-evidently, a thoroughly hylic being. That Sabaoth is capable of repentance shows that he, in contrast, has a psychic nature. Pneumatics have no need to repent, but psychics can choose either way.

Sabaoth is now installed as the ruler of the seventh heaven in the place of Jaldabaoth. "And he is called God of the Forces, Sabaoth, since he is up above the Forces of Chaos" [121]. His principal task seems to be to keep these forces of chaos in check. Quoting Zandee, Bullard writes that "Jaldabaoth and Sabaoth represent the two choices available to the psychics" [122].

Down there in the Tartarus, Jaldabaoth, seeing his upstart offspring 'in this great splendour' (for he has created "infinitely many angels to act as ministers" [123]), became jealous and, never to be outdone, produced another androgynous being, Envy, who brought forth Death. In its turn Death engendered numerous offspring which took charge of "the heavens of Chaos ... so that the sum of Chaos might be attained (= that the chaos might become complete)" [124].

e. Mankind

But what about mankind? Man is not created by the Father of all but by the Archons, the rulers of the cosmos. They created a being, androgynous like themselves, out of the dust of the soil and "after the Image of God that had appeared (to them) in the Waters" [125]. This means that man has a double origin, from below as well from above. But the rulers proved incapable of infusing life into the figure they had made; it was no more than something hylic. Man "remained upon the ground many days", lifeless, that is. To the Gnostics, matter does not contain life. But "the Spirit came down from the Adamantine Land (=the Pleroma); it descended and came to dwell within him, and man became a living soul", called Adam [126]. In this way Adam became a living being.

It is then related that an injunction is given to Adam to give names to the animals, that he is placed in the Garden, that he is forbidden to eat from the tree of the knowledge of good and evil, and it is further related how the woman was taken from his side. But all the time it is the Archons who are acting, not God. A conspicuous deviation from Gen. 2 is that 'the Spirit-Endowed Woman' said : "Arise, Adam!" (he is obviously still sleeping). "And when he saw her, he said : 'It is you who have given me life; you will be called 'Mother of the Living'" [127].

f. Eve

Now the Archons, miscreants as they are, began to lust after Eve (her name has not yet been mentioned). They pursued her in order to rape her, but she escaped by changing herself into a tree, leaving only an image, a 'shadowy reflection' of herself, with Adam. The stupid Archons threw themselves on this while the real Eve was hiding in the tree that, to all intents and purposes, is the tree of knowledge [128]. This curious passage makes it clear that there are, so to speak, two Eves. The one is the spiritual, the pneumatic Eve who is far above all ideas of sexuality and dwells in the home of Knowledge, the other the carnal, hylic Eve who is a fair object for sexual lust. If we remember that the First Woman is the 'Mother of the Living', the double Eve is not only the prototype of woman, Madonna and Aphrodite at the same time, but also of all human beings, male and female, who are both spiritual and carnal. By the same token it is evident that these parts do not really fit together.

g. The role of the serpent

We are in for some more surprises. The 'Female Spiritual Principle' changed herself into the snake who is going to act as 'Instructor', that is, as teacher of Knowledge; in fact, it is probable that this 'Female Principle', means Sophia, "who is using the serpent to instruct the earthly pair in gnosis" [129]. In Gen. 3 the serpent is out to harm mankind; here it is just the reverse. The ill-intentioned Archons, ignorant as they are themselves, have forbidden Adam to eat from the tree of Knowledge. The serpent exhorts the pair to take its fruit but, having fulfilled this task, "the Principle (Sophia) was taken away from the Snake and left it behind merely a thing of the earth (= just a common animal, no more - F.)" [130].

"And the carnal woman (Eve) ate from the tree; and she gave to her husband as well as herself; and these beings that possessed only a soul (=who were only psychics) ate. And their imperfection became apparent in their lack of Acquaintance (= Knowledge); and they recognized that they were naked of the Spiritual Element" [131]. The departure of the Snake may look like treason, but it was no treason. "It was rather", says Bullard, "that the eating of the tree of knowledge made them aware of their true situation". This is that they were "denuded ... of the spiritual" [132].

From this point the text follows the biblical account in which God takes the first human beings to task and curses the serpent, with the difference that in the Hypostasis it is not the Father of all who is speaking but the chief Ruler. And it is not God but the humans who curse the snake. Finally, the Archons "expelled him (Adam) from the Garden along with his wife ... Moreover, they threw Mankind into great distraction and into a life of toil, so that their Mankind might be occupied by worldly affairs, and might not have the opportunity of being devoted to the Holy Spirit" [133]. We see here the dualistic opposition between the Rulers of the cosmos to the powers of the Pleroma.

h. Cain and Abel

Afterwards Eve bore Cain who became a farmer; then Adam "knew his wife (and) she bore Abel" who became a herdsman [134]. Does this signify that Cain had another father than Abel? There is nothing that leads to this conclusion. However, Bullard is quite right in stating that the phrasing is "somewhat surprising". For there is also a widespread Gnostic idea that Eve bore sons by the archons or by their chief; sometimes Cain and Abel are mentioned as these sons. According to this scholar, "this (text) alone (in the Hypostasis) seems to have no distinctively Gnostic interpretation given it" [135]. In relating the fratricide and its consequences, the Hypostasis again renders the Genesis account, with this proviso that it calls Cain 'fleshly' [136] = hylic, less than psychic. This "assigns Cain to the lowest category of humanity in the Gnostic anthropology" [137]. There is no antinomian glorification in this document.

j. Seth and Norea

At this point the text deviates from the biblical account. It says that first Seth was born to Adam and Eve, but then Norea, who is not mentioned in Genesis. Eve "said : 'He (Adam) has begotten on (me a) virgin as an assistance (for) many generations of mankind'. She is the virgin whom the Forces (the Archons) did not defile" [138]. In this way Eve wreaks vengeance on the Archons who have lusted after her.

The presence of Norea (= Thought) on earth seems to have had a beneficial effect on mankind which began to improve. In consequence, the Archons became jealous and decided on the Flood; however, the Demiurge (the chief Ruler) is intent upon saving Noah and his family from the coming catastrophe and commands him to construct the Ark. We now are straying ever farther from the biblical text. Norea obviously has no wish for Noah to be saved and sets the Ark on fire. But Noah who does not want to have Norea in the Ark, patiently begins to build a second one [139].

Evidently there is a war on between the Demiurge (and Noah) on the one side and Norea on the other. Norea must be considered a pneumatic being, the incarnation of Gnosis. "I am not your descendant; it is from the World Above that I come" [140]. How this is possible since her parents are just plain earthly persons is not explained.

When Norea cried for help, Eleleth, the Great Angel, descended to teach her about 'the Root'. He instructs her in celestial wisdom [141]. When Eleleth has spoken, Norea asks him whether she too is of the stuff of the Archons, that is, whether she too is hylic. But no! "You, together with your offspring (the Gnostics), are from the Primeval Father from Above ... All who have become acquainted with this Way exist deathless in the midst of dying Mankind" [142]. This is the usual dualistic distinction between those who 'live' (the Gnostics) and those who are 'dead' (the others). In the end the Archons will be destroyed, but the chosen "will ascend into the limitless Light ... and will become truly acquainted with the Truth and their Root" [143].

4. On the Origin of the World

The treatise 'On the Origin of the World' [144], that bears a certain resemblance to the 'Hypostasis', was nameless in Antiquity; the title it has now is modern. It cannot be assigned to any known Gnostic system. Bethge and Wintermut think that it "was composed in Alexandria at the end of the third century C.E. or the beginning of the fourth" [145].

a. The first work

In the opening words the author takes issue with the common idea that it all began with Chaos, and that there existed nothing before it. For, he argues, everybody agrees that Chaos is darkness. But if this is so, its obscurity must result from something that casts a shadow over it. This shadow must have been "derived from a work existing from the beginning" [146]. This means that Chaos is an epiphenomenon.

The author calls this first work 'the Boundless One', and from it 'the immortals' came. "Sophia flowed out of Pistis (Faith)". She is a 'likeness' which means that she is an emanation from the Boundless One who is also called "the light which first existed". A light, however, cannot cast a shadow; for this we must descend somewhat further down through the Pleroma (for it is of this that we are speaking).

b. The Shadow

At Sophia's wish, there "appeared a heavenly likeness (emanation) ... which is in the middle between the immortals and those who came after them (mankind) ... It is a veil which separates men and those belonging to the (sphere) above" [147]. Here too this veil is the firmament of the fixed stars; once again the safety-curtain is let down between the upper and the nether worlds. On the inner side, that of the Pleroma, there is no shadow but an 'immeasurable light'; "its outside (= the side of the cosmos) is a shadow. It was called 'darkness' ... The (shadow) is posterior to the first work (which) appeared" [148]. Herewith the dualistic opposition between the Light and the Dark is given. This is identical with that between order and chaos (also called 'abyss') [149].

The appearance of the Shadow is equivalent to the Fall, although this term is not used. Out of the Shadow, "(every) race of gods was brought forth". Inside the darkness itself "a power appeared (as) ruler over the darkness". But suddenly the Shadow, which is obviously personified, realized that "there was one stronger than it", namely the Boundless One. "It became jealous, and when it became self-impregnated, it immediately bore envy." Since that day envy is omnipresent. But it "was found to be a miscarriage without any spirit in it" [150].

c. Cosmogony

This does not forebode any good for the future of the world and of mankind. The world has as yet not come into existence. The cosmogony is related in contemptuously negative terms. "The bitter wrath (or envy) which came into being from the Shadow was cast into a region of Chaos." Thus a negative element is cast into the role of generative principle. "(A) watery substance ... flowed forth (from the Shadow), appearing in Chaos". This was the origination of matter. "Just as the useless afterbirth of one who bears a child, likewise the matter which came into being was cast aside."

This does not mean that it was discarded but that it began to lead a life of its own. "Matter was in Chaos, (existing) in a part of it" [151]. Matter has no ontological status, in contrast to the beings in the Pleroma, but is something confused and undefinable.

Pistis Sophia felt greatly upset when she saw which turn things were taking, and she attempted to create some order in the chaotic mass below. She wanted to stamp 'the pattern of likeness' on it, to fashion it somewhat after the model obtaining in the Pleroma. Of course, this could never succeed, the Pleroma and the nether world being too much different. But anyhow, "a ruler over the matter and all its powers ... appeared out of the waters, lionlike in appearance, androgynous, and having a great authority within himself, but not knowing whence he came into being". He "is ignorant of the power of Pistis". Pistis Sophia gave him the name of 'Yaldabaoth'. Gods and angels and men came into being through him; he, therefore, is the Demiurge. Assuming that she had done enough, Pistis Sophia returned to the Pleroma [152].

d. Yaldabaoth the Demiurge

Yaldabaoth is identical with the Jewish God; actual creation is related in biblical terms, like the Spirit moving to and fro over the waters, the separation of heaven and earth, and that of wet and dry. But soon enough Gnostic mythology takes over. Yaldabaoth created an androgynous being (also incongruously dubbed 'son'), Yao, and a second, Eloai, and a third, Astaphaios. There appeared seven such androgynous beings in all, each one with a masculine and a feminine name. The feminine name of Yaldabaoth him/herself is 'Pronoia Sambathas' which is explained as signifying the Hebdomad. This means that Yaldabaoth controls the seven planetary spheres. Each of the seven 'sons' rules one of these spheres, "seven times more exquisite (than any earthly glory)", full of "armies of divine, lordly, angelic, and archangelic powers, myriads without number, in order to serve" [153].

All this made the Demiurge unbearably arrogant. "I do not need anything, he said. I am God and no other exists besides me", using the biblical words of Jahve [154]. But "when Pistis saw the impiety of the chief ruler, she was angry ... She said, 'You err, Samael', i.e. the blind god ... (The Father of all) will trample upon you like potter's clay ... And you will go down with those who are yours to your mother, the abyss. For in the consummation of your works all of the deficiency which appeared in the truth will be dissolved. And it will cease, and it will be like that which did not come into being" [155]. This world is no more than 'a deficiency of the truth', that is, it has no proper ontological status.

e. The conversion of Sabaoth

One of Yaldabaoth's 'sons', Sabaoth [156], whose feminine name is 'divinity', was converted by the words of Pistis Sophia. "(He) glorified her because she informed them of the deathless man and his light (= of the true destiny of man) ... Then Pistis Sophia stretched forth the finger, and she poured upon him a light from her light for a condemnation of his father". And "he condemned his father on account of the word of Pistis ... He hated his father, the darkness, and his mother, the abyss; he hated his sister (who is) the thought of the Demiurge" [157]. Sabaoth has become the archetype of the Gnostic : he has received the light from above, he utterly rejects the cosmic powers, he is capable of distinguishing real wisdom from the sham-wisdom of this earth. And he thrives on dualistic distinctions.

Because "Sabaoth received the light, he received a great authority against all the powers of Chaos. Since that day he has been called 'the lord of the powers'". From then on the cosmos had two opposed rulers, the Demiurge and Sabaoth. This made the authorities of Chaos very jealous, and a great war ensued. To assist Sabaoth, Sophia sent a group of archangels, and "she established a kingdom for him above everyone". She even gave him her daughter, Zoê (Life); it is not explained how an androgynous being can have a wife.

The task of Zoê was to impart ever more knowledge to Sabaoth. He is identified with the apparition Isaiah had in the famous 'throne-vision' [158]. The four-faced chariot is there, but this would not be a Gnostic document if a curious twist had not been given to a biblical text. For "from this chariot the seventy-two gods receive a pattern ... so that they may rule over the seventy-two languages of the world" [159].

Then "Sabaoth created an angelic church - thousands and myriads, without number, (belong to her)." This church is the prototype of the Gnostic community. It has 'a first-born' who is called 'Israel' as well as 'Jesus Christ', and who is the Saviour (a sample of Gnostic inclusive thinking). He too is instructed about the pleromic order by Sophia "in order that the kingdom might continue for him until the consummation of the heavens of Chaos and their powers" [160].

f. The Demiurge's counter-offensive

Must we believe that the Demiurge looked passively on all the time? Of course not! He snatched Sabaoth away from his exalted place and put Death in his stead. Death too was androgynous and begot seven sons with male names like Jealousy, Wrath, Weeping, and feminine names like Grief, Lust, Quarrelsomeness. Having intercourse among one another, they produced forty-nine androgynous demons. Not to be outdone, Zoê in her turn created seven androgynous powers, all good ones, with masculine names such as the Blessed, Joy, the Beloved, and with feminine names like Peace, Gladness, Rejoicing. "And many good and guileless spirits are derived from these" [161]. This leads to the conclusion that good and evil spirits are fighting one another for the possession of the world.

g. Beauties from above

By now the Demiurge began to feel uneasy. He had discovered that there was indeed somebody above him, and this disturbed him. Recklessly he challenged the highest divinity. "If someone exists before me, let him appear so that we may see his light." And a great light appeared which made the Demiurge ashamed, and not only him but all the powers of the heavens [162].

The light that come from above took the shape of an angel; it was called 'Light-Adam'. Pronoia, the female side of Yaldabaoth, the Demiurge, fell in love with him only to be rejected. For he was light, she was darkness. Then a new being appeared, also androgynous, Eros; if I understand the opaque text well, his origin was the (menstrual?) blood of Sophia. Beautiful as he/she was, all the powers became enamoured of him, but "he burned them".

Now follows a highly remarkable passage, revealing in spite of all its obscurity. "Eros was scattered in all the creatures of Chaos and he was not diminished." This means that the erotic drive is eternal and omnipresent. Coming from above but now dwelling below, Eros "appeared out of the mid-point between light and darkness, (and) in the midst of angels and men the intercourse of Eros was consummated." It is not stated with whom this intercourse took place. The author, however, is not interested in what once happened but rather in the dire consequences. "So ... the first sensual pleasure sprouted on the earth." The text then proceeds with a short poem. "(The man followed) the earth/The woman followed the man/And marriage followed the woman/And reproduction followed marriage/And death followed reproduction" [163]. So this is the sad conclusion : sensual pleasure in the end leads to death; all that lives must die. Like almost all other Gnostic essays, this one too takes a low view of sex.

h. Paradise

Justice (that was not mentioned earlier) created Paradise. In the Garden there are not two but three important trees. The first is the Tree of immortal life which will "give life to the immortal saints who will come out of the molded bodies of poverty (= the redeemed Gnostics)". The second is the

Tree of knowledge, and the third the olive tree from the fruits of which the oil will be pressed that will anoint the "kings and the chief priests of justice, who will appear in the last days" [164].

j. Creation

The creation story is told in a not entirely biblical fashion, to put it mildly. Flowers and herbs sprouted from the blood of Eros and the virginal daughters of Pronoia (not mentioned before). Beasts, reptiles, and birds were created by the powers from the waters and from their seed [165]. But it was Sophia who fashioned the sun, the moon, and all the stars [166]. Two things are evident. The primal god has nothing to do with creation (the story has an evolutionist twist); and earthly beings have an origin that is as mysterious (bloody) as it is chaotic (watery). At this point one would expect the creation of the first human beings, but no! first something else happens.

To return to Light-Adam. He remained on earth only two days, and then wanted to go back to the Pleroma. "And immediately darkness came upon the whole world" [167]. However, he was held up at the firmament because, having dwelt upon the earth, his light was no longer pure. For the umpteenth time it becomes clear that any contact with matter betokens a defilement. Frustrated, Light-Adam started his own creational work, by fashioning an aeon consisting of six other aeons, "sevenfold more exquisite than the heavens of Chaos and their worlds". These new worlds have their place between the firmament and the cosmos. They form, one could say, a kind of counter-cosmos for those here below who "belong to poverty" [168]. All this makes the constitution of the cosmos an incredibly intricate affair in which many creational powers took part.

k. The origination of mankind

And now at last we are at the creation of man! The idea of this originated with the Demiurge. "Let us create (someone) from the earth according to our body ... that he may serve us." But how stupid and ignorant this Demiurge and his cronies were! They did not realize that they were going to create 'the one against themselves' who would destroy their work. Sophia/Zoê anticipated their plan by creating her own man first. She let fall 'a drop of light' on the waters.

The following passage is obscure to a degree. In the water an androgynous being appeared. This body then became 'patterned' as a female body, and this proved to be a mother. She is a virgin mother without a husband and is called 'Eve of Life' which is not interpreted as 'mother of all that lives' but as 'instructor of life' [169]. The virginal Eve gave life to a being that, as will be self-evident, was androgynous too, although he is called 'a man'. As the son of the 'instructor' "he was found to be wiser than all of them (the powers)" [170].

Androgynous Eve and her androgynous 'son' are the ideal prototypes of mankind. Androgynity was seen by the Gnostics as a hallmark of the Pleroma, that is, of perfection; as explained before, the existence of sexual gender was considered a degeneration, even a mutilation. Sexuality, apparently, plays no part in the origination of Eve and her son, but the creation of earthly Adam is related with the usual sexual imagery. "Each one of them (the powers) cast his seed on the midst of the navel of the earth." Then a body was formed by the seven rulers in likeness of themselves. This expresses the accordance of the (macro-)cosmos and the microcosmos that is man.

The new being received the name of Adam. But as things stood, there was no spirit (pneuma) in him; he was still 'like a miscarriage'. Cosmic powers are incapable of providing pneuma; it is not in them. The Demiurge then remembered Sophia's prophecy that his own creation would destroy him, and he took to his heels [171]. What is going on all the time is essentially a battle between Knowledge and Ignorance.

So far Adam is no more than a great doll; having originated from the seed of the Rulers and the earth he is only matter. "But on the fortieth day Sophia sent her breath into Adam, who was without a soul." This 'breath' is not the soul but the animal life-force, so that Adam was able to move his limbs now. However, he was not yet capable of standing upright, that is, he was still animal-like. It set the anguished Rulers' minds at rest that he was not able to rise. They took him and deposited him in Paradise. Just as the creation of the cosmos was accomplished in many stages, Adam's creation too was no simple thing! Sophia sent her daughter Zoê who is identified here as Eve, the instructor, to Adam, and she made him rise [172]. The reader does not need much biblical knowledge to see that the story of Gen. 2 is reversed here : Eve comes first, and then Adam. This is the old myth that the female principle is the original one.

The angry Rulers, the Archons, tried to rape Eve, because, once polluted, she would be unable to return to heaven. But she escaped their hands and tried to hide herself in the tree of knowledge, leaving only "her likeness there stealthily beside Adam". The deceived Rulers now played their ignoble game with the likeness thinking it was the true Eve, defiling her abominably but not realizing that "they had defiled their own body". Sexual lust and depravity are, in the Gnostic view, constitutive elements of the cosmos. The 'likeness', however, was real enough to bear sons to the Rulers, one to each of them, seven in all, with Abel as the son of the Demiurge himself [173]. In consequence, Abel is not Adam's son.

Next the Rulers forbade Adam and (likeness-)Eve to eat from the tree of knowledge.; they wished to keep them barren of true Knowledge. But now Light-Adam, "the one who is wiser than them all (the Rulers)" reappears and exhorts them to eat the fruit of the tree. Now what was the result? They indeed received knowledge; "the light of knowledge shone for them". What it revealed them was, first, that they were "naked with regard to knowledge", that is, that they as yet knew nothing at all, second, that they became enamoured of one another (carnal knowledge made its entry), and, thirdly, that their makers, the Rulers, were beastly monsters.

Furious as they were, the Rulers then cursed all and everything, the man, the woman, her sons, the earth and its fruits. "And everything which they created they cursed. There is no blessing for them (= they were incapable of blessing, they could only curse - F.). It is impossible that good be produced from evil." But they proved unable to curse the Instructor, because their eyes were blinded. Then they cast Adam and his wife out of Paradise [174]. Since the Rulers of the world are wicked, it can never be a good place.

The Rulers created many demons upon the earth in order to serve them. "They taught men many errors with magic and potions and idolatry, and shedding of blood, and altars, and temples, and sacrifices, and libations to the demons of the earth ... All the men who are on the earth served the demons from the foundation until consummation (of the aeon) ... Thus the world came to be in a distraction and an ignorance and a stupor" [175]. The 'conditio humana' is epitomized in this one word : Ignorance.

1. The Father intervenes

In their stupidity the Rulers had not reckoned with the primal godhead, the immortal Father of all, the Boundless One. He knew that things had gone wrong down here, but he sent "little guileless spirits, down to the world of destruction". These must be thought of as particles of Light and Knowledge. "They are not strangers to Knowledge." "Whenever they appear in the world of destruction, they will first reveal the pattern of indestructibility for a condemnation of the Rulers and their powers." This means that they have come to impart superior knowledge of the unchangeable and eternal Pleroma in order to enable the chosen ones to ascend to this sphere. "These will enter into the holy place of their Father, and they will rest themselves in a repose, and eternal, ineffable glory, and a ceaseless joy ... (And) they will pass judgment on the gods of Chaos and their powers" [176].

m. The Apocalypse

The last paragraphs of this document are devoted to the Apocalypse, the final catastrophe. The gods of Chaos will then be wiped out, and their whole cosmos will crumble down. Nothing will remain. Then comes the final triumph of the Light that will blot out the darkness as if it had never existed. "And the glory of the unbegotten (= the primal godhead) will appear and it will fill all the aeons." But those who are not perfect will never enter the Pleroma [177].

n. Conclusion

Is it really necessary to explain how utterly dualistic this tract is? All the paraphernalia of Gnostic dualism are there, above all the division of the Pleroma and the cosmos, which is equivalent to that of light and darkness, order and chaos, life and death, and the separation of the elect and the rest. One of the milder features of this tract is that the ignorant are allowed to live on in blissful ignorance. But there is hardly another tractate in which 'matter' is spoken of in such harsh terms.

5. On the Soul

a. The Fall of the soul

The 'Expository Treatise on the Soul' [178] presents a graphic demonstration of the Gnostic abhorrence of the body and of the dualistic split in the human person [179]. It begins by stating that the soul not only has a feminine name ('psuchê' in Greek) but is really female in nature and even has a womb. As long as she dwelt with the Father (the prime godhead) she was virginal and androgynous in form [180]. But this serene existence came to an end when "she fell down into a body"; she was even passed on from one body to another [181]. 'Robbers', that is the demons of the lower world, defiled her. She lost her virginity, became entirely sexual, and lived like a prostitute (this reminds us of Simon the Magician's Helen of Troy [182]). It is all too clear : contact with the body means depravity and wantonness, in short a Fall.

But then the fallen soul repents, without, however, as yet abandoning her way of life. The adulterers "compel her to live with them and render service to them upon their bed, as if they were her masters ... They deceive her for a long time, pretending to be faithful, true husbands, as if they greatly respected her" [183]. I ask myself whether this can be a portrait of ordinary marriage. The men mentioned do not behave as if they were visiting a harlot. But ordinary marriage was seen as something inferior by most Gnostics. This idea is perhaps corroborated by the fact that "her (the soul's) offspring by the adulterers are dumb, sickly and blind. They are feeble-minded" [184]. This reads like a description of non-Gnostics who have no 'Knowledge'.

b. The healing of the soul

Repenting even further, the soul implores the Father to save her : "Restore me to thyself again" [185]. Then follows a revealing passage. "The womb of the (female) body is inside the body, like all other internal organs, but the womb of the soul is around the outside like the male genitalia, which are external". But once again she repents. "The Father will have mercy on her and he will ... turn her womb inward again, so that the soul will regain her proper character." What does this curious anatomical talk signify?

We are much helped by the remark that the Father "will make her womb turn from the external domain" [186]. This 'external domain' is the nether world, the domain of exclusiveness ('womb outside'). When the womb is turned inward again, pleromic inclusiveness is restored to the soul. A soul within a body can never enjoy its proper character, which is spiritual; she is exposed to all kinds of material and physical influences, above all to sexuality and bearing offspring. It deserves attention that so far the talk is solely of 'soul', and not of 'pneuma'.

c. The celestial wedding of the soul

Once returned to the Pleroma, the soul is "cleansed of the external pollution which was pressed upon it". Because she wants to have a child, the Father sends a bridegroom to her who is none other than his 'first-born' (not mentioned earlier). In the beautifully adorned bridal chamber bride and bridegroom unite. A flaming arrow is fired at ordinary marriage. Theirs is "not like the carnal marriage ... As if it were a burden, they leave behind them the annoyance of physical desire" [187]. The pleromic inclusiveness is indicated by the fact that "they become a single life" [188].

During their intercourse the soul receives the seed which should not be understood as male semen but as 'the life-giving Spirit, the Pneuma'. This makes the soul really perfect at last. "She received the divine nature from the Father for her rejuvenation, so that she might be restored to the place where originally she had been." Since it is also stated that the soul "bears good children and rears them", which is "the great perfect marvel of birth", we may safely assume that here the Gnostic rebirth is pictured. Realizing, 'knowing', that one possesses a pneuma, a spark of the celestial light, is "the ransom from captivity. This is the upward journey of ascent to heaven. This is the way of ascent to the Father" [189]. But "no one is worthy of salvation who still loves the place of deception (= this world)" [190].

6. The First Apocalypse of James

The 'First Apocalypse of James' [191] is one of four 'apocalypses' in codex V; it is supposed to have "emerged out of Syrian Jewish Christianity" [192]. In it the apostle James, on the day before the passion began had a conversation with Jesus, and later, after the resurrection, another one on a mountain called 'Gaugelan'. Jesus' words sound strikingly anti-Judaistic. "Leave Jerusalem", he says to James, "for it is she who always gives the cup of bitterness to the sons of light (= the Gnostics). She is a dwelling-place of a great number of archons." This signifies that the Holy City is the capital of the lower, condemned world. There is no redemption in it. James is informed that "your redemption will be preserved from them (the Jews) (= that the Jews will have no part in it - F.)" [193].

The archons of the cosmos are brought up in arms against Jesus [194]. But "I (Jesus) shall appear as a reproof to the archons" [195]. James is told that he too will suffer; in fact, he is portrayed as a prototype of the Gnostic believers. "A multitude (of Archons) will arm themselves against you that (they) may seize you." When they have laid hold of him, they will ask him : "Who are you and where are you from?" James then is to speak the magic formula : "I am from the Pre-existent Father, and a son in the Pre-existent One". And when they ask : "Where will you go?", he has to answer : "To the place from which I have come, there I shall return" [196].

This means, of course, that James will disclose to the archons that he is a member of a special race that has its origin in the Pre-existent One. This highest divinity has 'in him' Sophia, the imperishable Knowledge, who is in the Father (= the Pre-existent One) and who is the mother of Achamoth" [197]. Armed with this superior Knowledge James obviously stands on a higher plane than the other disciples whom he rebukes, because they think they 'know', although they don't [198]. With this the message of the New Testament is virtually enervated.

7. The Second Apocalypse of James

In the Second Apocalypse of James [199] the high position assigned to James in the order of salvation is accentuated still more forcefully. Speaking to 'the multitude of the people', he announces that he has "received revelation from the Pleroma of Imperishability" and is "rich in Knowledge (and has) a unique understanding, which was produced from above ... That what was revealed to me was hidden from everyone" [200]. This is the favourite Gnostic tenet that a secret doctrine exxists that makes the greater part of the Bible seem superfluous. The Saviour himself orders him to proclaim this doctrine [201].

James thus becomes the guide of the chosen. "Those who wish to enter (the Pleroma), and those who seek to walk in the way that is before the door, open the good door through you; they enter, and you escort them inside, and give a reward to each one who is ready for it." The others are rejected. "You are not a redeemer or a helper of strangers. You are an illuminator and a redeemer of those who (are) mine (= of Jesus), and now of those who (are) yours" [202]. James virtually usurps the place here that Jesus Christ occupies in the Gospels; this is strongly stressed by the fact that he is flatly called 'redeemer'.

James did what he was told and proclaimed the message. But the priests (obviously the Jewish ones) would not listen and decided to kill him. He was led outside the town and stoned; he died while he was praying to his God and his Father "who saved me from this dead hope (= the Jewish and orthodox doctrines - F.)" [203]. This account shows a strong resemblance to the passion of Jesus who also preached the message from above and also died praying, as well as to the martyrdom of Stephen who was stoned to death and equally died with a prayer on his lips. Acts, however, does not mention a martyrdom of James. But Josephus reports that James was stoned to death on the orders of the High Priest Ananus [204].

8. Authoritative Teaching

In the short tract 'Authoritative Teaching' [205] we find some of the usual Gnostic-dualistic topics. It begins by stating that the soul, 'the invisible soul of righteousness', is of pleromic origin [206]. But then, it is not related how, the Fall occurs; "the spiritual soul was cast into the body". When the spiritual and the material have to go together, then, in Gnostic view, the spiritual invariably becomes the victim and has to be liberated. "The body came from lust, and lust came from material substance." As always, Spirit and matter are dualistically opposed. The soul "became a brother to lust, and hatred, and envy, and (became) a material soul" [207].

Once having fallen so deeply, the soul goes from bad to worse. She is behaving like a prostitute and abandons modesty. "She does not remember her brothers and the father (= the aeons of the Pleroma and the primal godhead - F.), for pleasures and sweet profits deceive her" [208]. Then comes a revealing passage. "Having left Knowledge behind, she fell into bestiality. For a senseless person (i.e. a non-Gnostic) exists in bestiality, not knowing what it is proper to say, and what it is not proper to say" [209]. The dualistic rift between Gnostics and the others could not be more clearly expressed, for Gnostics know "what it is proper to say", a gift which makes them fully human, or rather, divine, whereas the ignorant are subhuman, and, indeed, no more than dumb beasts.

Those who are going to be saved must "leave behind the things that had come into being (= creation, the cosmos), and despise them with a lofty, incomprehensible Knowledge, and flee to the one who exists (= the first godhead)". They will live in conflict with the world and the ignorant. "We are to be victorious over their ignorance since we have already known the Inscrutable One from whom we came forth ... And we ignore them (the ignorant) when they curse us" [210].

But not even with the elect all is well. "Our soul is indeed ill, because she dwells in a house of poverty (= the body), while matter strikes blows at her eyes, wishing to make her blind". She has, however, a medicine which is the light from above. "Her light may conceal the hostile forces that fight with her, and she may make them blind with her light, and enclose them in her presence" [211].

To paint the situation in which the Gnostic finds himself in this world, grappling with ill-disposed powers, the author uses a simile that will turn up, ages later, in an unexpected place, namely in Luther's theology. A fisherman casts his baited hook into the water; a fish eats the bait and swallows the hook too. The fisherman then lifts the fish out of the water so that he may eat it. The author calls this 'the ruse of the food' [212]. And he continues in the same vein. "We exist in the world like fish. The adversary spies on us, lying in wait for us like a fisherman, wishing to seize us, rejoicing that he might swallow us ... He wishes to bring us out of freedom and take us into slavery. For whenever he catches us with a single food, it is indeed necessary for (us) to desire the rest. Finally, then, such things (= the worldy things) become the food of death" [213].

But the knowing soul "looks for those foods that will take her into life, and leaves behind the deceitful foods. And she learns about her light, as she goes about stripping off this world ... (And) her bridal clothing is placed upon her in beauty of mind, not in the pride of flesh ... She did not realize that she has an invisible spiritual body ... They did not realize that she knows another way which is hidden from them. This her true shepherd taught her in Knowledge" [214].

"The ones who are ignorant do not seek after God." In all probability orthodox Christians are the butt in the following passage. "They are more wicked than the pagans ... Indeed, they are sons of the devil ... They have not heard that they sould inquire about his (God's) ways ... The senseless man hears the call, but he is ignorant of the place to which he has been called" [215]. But "the rational soul learned about God ... She came to rest in him who is at rest ... She has found what she has sought after" [216].

9. The Concept of our Great Power

The short essay on the Concept of our Great Power [217] originated perhaps before or during the latter part of the fourth century [218]. A remarkable feature of it is that "in good apocalyptic fashion history is divided into several main periods : the fleshly aeon which was ended by the Flood, the natural or psychic aeon during which the Savior appears, and the indestructible aeon of the future" [219]. A similar threefold division of history will be found in Joachim da Fiore's theology of history in the twelfth century. This is a difficult tract couched in mystical and obscure terms.

The first, 'fleshly' (= material) aeon is washed away with the Flood. The second, the psychic aeon is not conspicuously better. "It begot every work : many works of wrath, anger, malice, envy, hatred, and so on" [220]. But it is exactly in this aeon that the Saviour will appear. "The man will come into being who knows the great Power (= the first godhead) ...; he will proclaim the aeon that is to come ... And he opened the gates of the heavens with his words" [221]. This is a deviation from Christian orthodoxy, for according to its doctrine Jesus Christ opened the gates of heaven, not with his words, but through his death on the cross. This event is not even mentioned.

"The archons raised up their wrath against him. They wanted him to hand him over to the ruler of Hades (= Satan)." Using Jesus as their tool, they tried to execute their plan, but Satan was unable to lay hands on him. "Who is this? His word has abolished the law of the aeon (the cosmos) ... And he (Christ) was victorious over the command of the archons, and they were not able by their world to rule over him" [222].

But the Demiurge, the supreme Archon, counter-attacked in great force. "The wrath of the archons burned. They were ashamed of their dissolution." They created enormous havoc on the earth. Even the mountains were overturned. "Then, when the times were completed, wickedness arose mightily" [223]. The height of this wickedness was that an anti-Christ was installed. "He reigned over the whole earth and (over) all those who are under the heaven ... He will perform signs and wonders. Then they will turn from me (the true Saviour), and they will go astray" [224].

Judaism comes under fire. "Those men will follow after him who will introduce circumcision." The anti-Christ is strongly opposed to those "who are from the uncircumcision who are the (true) people (= the Gnostics who, in this case, obviously are no Jews - F.)". During the apocalyptic scenes which herald the end of the cosmos, the Saviour will "withdraw with everyone who will know me" and bring them "into the immeasurable light, (where) there is no use of the flesh". Then he will return "to destroy all of them (the ignorant) ... When the fire has consumed them all, and when it does not find anything else to burn, then it will perish by its own hand" [225].

The holy ones, on the contrary, "will be in the aeon of beauty ... since they are ready in wisdom ... And they all have become as reflections in his light ... And they have found rest in his (the godhead's) rest" [226].

10. The Apocalypse of Peter

Short as it is, the Apocalypse of Peter [227] is in many respects an important text. It was probably written in the third century, when the "distinction between (Christian) orthodoxy and (Gnostic) heresy was rather clearly drawn" [228]. It is addressed to a Gnostic community which saw the apostle Peter as its originator. In any case, he is the recipient of a revelation communicated by the Saviour as "he (Peter) was sitting in the Temple" [229].

This Gnostic community is shown as being embattled on all sides. Already during the revelation, "I (Peter) saw the priests and the people running up to us with stones, as if they would kill us". This refers to the enmity of the Jewish establishment. The Jews "are blind ones who have no guide" [230]. "Many will accept our teaching in the beginning. And they will turn away again by the will of the Father of their error (= the Jewish God)." They will become prisoners, "since they are without perception (= without Knowledge). And they praise the men of the propagation of falsehood (= the orthodox creed) ... And they will cleave to the name of a dead man (= Jesus of Nazareth)" [231]. This whole passage blatantly reveals the dualistic opposition of the Gnostics to Judaism and still more to the Roman-Catholic Church, in particular its hierarchy. The text speaks of persons "who are outside our number who name themselves bishops and also deacons, as if they had received their authority from God ... Those people are dry channels" [232].

It is, however, fairly possible that also some rival Gnostics are envisaged. There are those who "think that they will perfect the wisdom of the brotherhood which really exists, which is the spiritual fellowship with those united in communion, through which the wedding of incorruptibility shall be revealed ... These are the ones who oppose their brothers saying to them, 'Through this (= their specific doctrine) our God has pity, since salvation comes to us through this'" [233].

This Gnostic community apparently lives amidst a sea of hostility. But their consolation is that they know they are immortal, whereas 'the others' are destined to eternal death. This time the dualistic opposition between the two races of mankind is typified by that between death and immortality. "Every soul of these ages has death assigned to it in our view, because it always is a slave, since it is created for desires and their eternal destruction in which they are and from which they are. They (these souls) love the creatures of matter which came forth with them. But the immortal souls are not like these" [234].

The problem, however, is that Gnostics too die so that their alleged election will come to naught. "Indeed, as long as the hour is not yet come, (the immortal soul) shall resemble a mortal one ... It shall not reveal its nature, that it alone is the immortal one". But the outcome will be different. "That (immortal soul) which comes to be in the Eternal One is in the One of the life and the immortality of the life which they resemble (i.e. the pleromic life - F.)" [235].

A third dualistic feature in this tract is the distinction of Christ and Jesus, a distinction with a docetist character. Peter is described as witnessing the crucifixion of Jesus (according to the canonic Gospels he was not present on Golgotha). He felt upset and confused because he thought that his Lord, the Saviour, was hanging on the cross. "Is it yourself whom they take? ... Or who is this one, glad and laughing on the tree? And is it another one whose feet and hands they are striking?" [236]. The scene is rather difficult to imagine but Gnostic authors are not easily discomfited when it comes to distinguishing between Christ (the Saviour) and Jesus. In no case Christ must suffer on the cross. First of all, there is an entirely human, physical person "into whose hands they drive the nails"; this is "his (Jesus') fleshly part which is the substitute". But "the one whom you saw on the tree (the cross), glad and laughing, this is the living Jesus". Obviously this Jesus, the real Jesus, is incapable of suffering.

This Jesus is seen as identical with the celestial Saviour. "I (Peter) saw someone about to approach us, even him was laughing on the tree. And he was (filled) with a Holy Spirit, and he is the Savior." Then the essential distinction is made apparent. "He whom they crucified is the first-born, and the home of demons, and the stony vessel (?) in which they dwell, of Elohim, of the cross which is under the Law" [237]. The one who died on the cross, the 'dead man', was mentioned earlier in this tract as 'the first-born of unrighteousness' [238], in all probability the son of the Demiurge. "But he who stands near him is the living Savior ... who stands joyfully looking at those who did him violence ... He laughs at their lack of perception, knowing that they are born blind ... But what they (his hangmen) released was my (the Saviour's) incorporeal body ... I am the intellectual Spirit filled with radiant Light" [239].

11. The Trimorphic Protennoia

We shall conclude our study of the contents of the Nag Hammadi Library with a short disquisition on the 'Trimorphic Protennoia', one of the best organized of them all [240]. The 'Protennoia' is the 'First Thought', namely of the Father; she is nobody else than Barbelo [241]. The First Thought is called 'trimorphic', because she appears in three forms, Father, Mother, and Son [242], an outstanding example of the Gnostics' predilection for inclusiveness. Although she has three names, or shows three aspects, she is essentially one : "I am the invisible One within the All, and exist alone"; In fact, she is Sophia, wisdom, and knowledge, since "I know the All ... Whenever I wish, I shall reveal myself" [243]. As the first-born of the Father, she is certainly not much different from him.

Her first manifestation is that of father, or Voice. "Within my Thought, it is I who am laden with the Voice." This means that she has to proclaim "the knowledge of the everlasting things ... I revealed myself within all these who know me (= the Gnostics) ... (It is Light) dwelling in Light". It is this wisdom that redeems. "It is we (who have separated) ourselves (from the) visible (world) since we (are saved by the) hiddden (wisdom mediated by the) ineffable, immeasurable Voice" [244]. The dualistic opposition of the Gnostics to the created world comes to the fore here.

The second manifestation of the Protennoia is that of Son, "that is, the Word who originated through that Voice"; he too "revealed the everlasting things and all the unknowns were known ... He revealed himself to those who dwell in darkness, ... and he taught irreproducible doctrines to all those who became Sons of the Light" [245]. This "Perfect Son revealed himself to his Aeons who originated through him" [246].

Thirdly, there is the Mother, a Sound. "I am the Mother of the Voice, speaking in many ways, completing the All. It is in me that Knowledge dwells, the Knowledge of things everlasting ... It is I who lift up the Sound of the Voice to the ears of those who have known me, that is the Sons of the Light" [247]. "O, Sons of the Thought, listen to me, to the Sound of the Mother of your mercy, for you have become worthy of the mystery hidden from the Aeons" [248]. The Mother is a curious sample of inclusiveness. "I am androgynous. (I am both Mother and) Father since I (copulate) with myself ... I am the Womb (that gives shape) to the All by giving birth to the Light" [249].

The Protennoia would not be a Gnostic document if the luminous celestial world was not offset against a lower, dark underworld. "The great Demon began to produce aeons in the likeness of the real Aeons, except that he produced them out of his own power ... The Archigenitor of ignorance reigned over Chaos and the underworld" [250]. He is "the Tyrant and the Adversary, and the one who is King and the real Enemy" [251].

However, he and his cronies are doomed to extinction through the power of the Protennoia. An apocalypse is shortly described. "The thrones of the Powers were disturbed since they were overturned, and their king was afraid ... The consummation of this Aeon (that is, the cosmos) and of the life of injustice (has approached and there dawns the) beginning of the (Aeon to come) which (has no change forever)" [252]. But those who 'know' will be saved. "I (Protennoia) gather (together) all (my fellow-)brethren within my (eternal kingdom). And I proclaimed to them the ineffable (Five Seals = the Knowledge) in order that (I might) abide in them and they might also abide in me ... My seed, which is mine, I shall (place) into the Holy Light" [253].

The text closes with the comment that this is "a Sacred Scripture written by the Father with perfect Knowledge".

NOTES TO CHAPTER I

1. NHC 1.3.
2. Peel, Gnosis 60/61 : "Obgleich mehrere Persönlichkeiten mit Namen 'Rheginus' aus der späthellenistischen bzw. römischen Zeit bekannt sind, kann keiner davon mit den Adressaten unseres Briefs identifiziert werden."
3. The date of the letter is discussed in Peel, Gnosis 23-27.
4. NHL 50. Layton, Treatise on Res. 20 : "About the date of the composition little can be said." For that of the original composition in Greek this scholar suggests the late second century.
5. An extensive synopsis is to be found in Peel, Gnosis 45-56.
6. NHC 1.3.46-47.
7. NHC 1.3.47.
8. NHC 1.3.48.
9. NHC 3.1.48.
10. NHC 1.3.44.
11. NHC 3.1.45.
12. NHC 1.3.45.
13. NHC 1.3.45.
14. NHC 1.3.44.
15. NHC 1.3.44.
16. Peel, Gnosis 120-122.

17. NHC 1.3.44-45.
18. NHC 1.3.44.
19. NHC 1.3.47.
20. NHC 1.3.46.
21. NHC 1.3.46.
22. NHC 1.3.48.
23. NHC 1.3.47-48.
24. NHC 1.3.45-46.
25. 2Tim.2:18.
26. NHC 1.3.49.
27. NHC 1.3.45.
28. NHC 1.3.47.
29. NHC 1.3.48-49.
30. NHC 2.3.
31. NHL 131.
32. NHC 2.3.52.
33. NHC 2.3.53.
34. NHC 2.3.53.
35. NHC 2.3.54.
36. NHC 2.3.75.
37. NHC 2.3.53.
38. NHC 2.3.54.
39. NHC 2.3.54.
40. NHC 2.3.61.
41. NHC 2.3.61.
42. NHC 2.3.71.
43. NHC 2.3.70.
44. NHC 2.3.68.
45. NHC 2.3.70.
46. NHC 2.3.71.
47. Mahé, Le sens 136.
48. NHC 2.3.71.
49. NHC 2.3.71-72.
50. NHC 2.3.71.

51.	NHC 2.3.59.
52.	NHC 2.3.55.
53.	Ménard, Évangile 35.
54.	NHC 2.3.71.
55.	NHC 2.3.71.
56.	NHC 2.3.52.
57.	NHC 2.3.52-53.
58.	NHC 2.3.55.
59.	NHC 2.3.58.
60.	NHC 2.3.56; Ménard, Évangile 17.
61.	NHC 2.3.54.
62.	NHC 2.3.65.
63.	NHC 2.3.83.
64.	NHC 2.3.59.
65.	NHC 2.3.63.
66.	NHC 2.3.59.
67.	NHC 2.3.82.
68.	Ménard, Évangile 148.
69.	NHC 2.3.63-64.
70.	NHC 2.3.77.
71.	NHC 2.3.74.
72.	NHC 2.3.55.
73.	NHC 2.5.3. See Ménard, Évangile 20-22.
74.	Ménard, Évangile 19.
75.	NHC 2.3.57.
76.	Ménard, Évangile 20.
77.	Eph.5:23-33; Grant, Mystery 129/130.
78.	Grant, Mystery 131.
79.	NHC 2.3.68.
80.	NHC 2.3.70.
81.	NHC 2.3.70.
82.	NHC 2.3.61. See Grant, Mystery 135.
83.	NHC 2.3.75-76 and 86.
84.	NHC 2.3.82.

85. Grant, Mystery 137.
86. NHC 2.3.82.
87. NHC 2.3.64.
88. NHC 2.3.69.
89. Grant, Mystery 138.
90. NHC 2.3.86.
91. NHC 2.4; NHL 2.4. Barc, L'Hypostase (see Bibliography); this scholar assumes that two editors have been at work on the original text which would explain certain contradictions (pp. 45-48).
92. NHL 152.
93. Bullard, Hypostasis 42, writes that, "while hypostasis does mean 'nature' or 'essence', 'origin' is also a legitimate meaning". He adds that, according to Heinrich Dörrie, 'becoming' or' realization' as the rendering of the Greek term, has also been in use.
94. NHC 2.4.93-94.
95. Bullard, Hypostasis 3 : "It will be noticed that of the various Gnostic sects described by the Church Fathers, the Ophite groups seem to have a closer relation to the ideas of this treatise than the others, though on occasion notions distinctly Valentinian are evident."
96. NHL 153.
97. NHC 2.4.88.
98. NHC 2.4.86.
99. NHC 2.4.87.
100. NHC 2.4.94.
101. NHC 2.4.87.
102. NHC 2.4.87.
103. Bullard, Hypostasis 51.
104. NHC 2.4.93 : "within limitless realms dwells Incorruptibility. Sophia who is also called Pistis ...".
105. NHC 2.4.94.
106. Bullard, Hypostasis 103.
107. NHC 2.4.87.
108. NHC 2.4.94.
109. Bullard, Hypostasis 106.
110. NHC 2.4.87.
111. NHC 2.4.94.
112. NHC 2.4.95.

113. Bullard, Hypostasis 105.
114. See also Bousset, Hauptprobl. 353. Orig., Contra Celsum 6.31 (655).
115. Is.46:9.
116. NHC 2.4.94. The opera-minded reader will probably remember that in Carl Maria von Weber's 'Der Freischütz' (libretto by Friedrich Kind) the wicked Kaspar, when founding the magic bullets, calls up a demon named 'Samiel'.
117. Bullard, Hypostasis 107.
118. NHC 2.4.95.
119. NHC 2.4.95.
120. The role and significance of Sabaoth in this tract is discussed by Francis Fallon, The Enthronement (see Bibliography).
121. NHC 2.4.95.
122. Bullard, Hypostasis 110.
123. NHC 2.4.95.
124. NHC 2.4.96.
125. NHC 2.4.87.
126. NHC 2.4.88.
127. NHC 2.4.88-89.
128. NHC 2.4.89.
129. Bullard, Hypostasis 85.
130. NHC 2.4.89-90.
131. NHC 2.4.90.
132. Bullard, Hypostasis 89.
133. NHC 2.4.91.
134. NHC 2.4.91.
135. Bullard, Hypostasis 92.
136. NHC 2.4.91.
137. Bullard, Hypostasis 92.
138. NHC 2.4.91-92.
139. NHC 2.4.92.
140. NHC 2.4.92.
141. NHC 2.4.93-96.
142. NHC 2.4.96.
143. NHC 2.4.97.

144. NHC 2.5. and 13.2.
145. NHL 161.
146. NHC 2.5.97-98.
147. NHC 2.5.98.
148. NHC 2.5.98-99.
149. NHC 2.5.98.
150. NHC 2.5.98-99.
151. NHC 2.5.99.
152. NHC 2.5.100.
153. NHC 2.5.101-102.
154. Is. 43:10.
155. NHC 2.5.103.
156. The role and the significance of Sabaoth in this tract is discussed by Fallon, Enthronement 89-132.
157. NHC 2.5.103-104.
158. Is.6.
159. NHC 2.5.104-105.
160. NHC 2.5.105.
161. NHC 2.5.106.
162. NHC 2.5.107-108.
163. NHC 2.5.108-109.
164. NHC 2.5.110.
165. NHC 2.5.111.
166. NHC 2.5.112. Here the text closely resembles that of Gen. 1:16-18, with this difference that there it is God who makes them, like everything else.
167. The Gospels of Mark (15:33) and Luke (24:44) use exactly the same words for what occurred at the death of Jesus.
168. NHC 2.5.112.
169. NHC 2.5.112-113.
170. MHC 2.5.113-114. A fine sample of Gnostic inclusive language is given in 114 : "I (Eve) am the mother, I am the woman, and I am the virgin. I am the pregnant one. I am the physician, I am the midwife. My husband is the one who begot me, and I am his mother, and he is my father."
171. NHC 2.5.114-115.
172. NHC 2.5.115-116.

173. NHC 2.5.116-117.
174. NHC 2.5.119-121.
175. NHC 2.5.123.
176. NHC 2.5.126.
177. NHC 2.5.127.
178. NHC 2.6; NHL 2.6, introduced and translated by William C. Robinson Jr.
179. The interested reader should not fail to consult the informative edition with commentary by Maddalena Scopello, L'Exégèse de l'âme (see Bibliography). He or she will find yet another commentary in Sévrin, L'Exégèse de l'âme (see Bibliography).
180. William Robinson, Exegesis, NT, 1970, 111 : "(Her) virginity consisted in an asexual androgynous union with her brother, and consequently the defilement consisted in (as well as resulted from) her becoming female, sexually differentiated".
181. NHC 2.6.127.
182. See Vol. VII, Ch. III.1d.
183. NHC 2..6.128.
184. NHC 2.6.128.
185. NHC 2.6.128-129.
186. NHC 2.6.131.
187. NHC 2.6.132.
188. NHC 2.6.132.
189. NHC 2.6.134-135.
190. NHC 2.6.136.
191. NHC 5.3; NHL 5.3, introduced and translated by William R. Schroedel. Edited by Douglas M. Parrott. Commentaries on both the First and Second Apocalypses in Armand Veilleux, La première Apocalypse de Jacques (NV V.3). La seconde Apocalypse de Jacques (NH V,4). Texte établi et présenté par --. Bibliothèque copte de Nag Hammadi. Section 'Textes' 17. Québec, 1986.
192. NHL 242.
193. NHC 5.3.25.
194. NHC 5.3.22.
195. NHC 5.3.30.
196. NHC 5.3.33-34.
197. NHC 5.3.34.
198. HNC 5.3.42.

199.	NHC 5.4; NHL 5.4, introduced and translated by Charles W. Hedrich. Edited by Douglas M. Parrott.
200.	NHC 5.4.45-47.
201.	NHC 5.4.52.
202.	NHC 5.4.55.
203.	NHC 5.4.61-62. Funke, Zweite Ap.. 2.4. Exkurs 'Die beiden 'Väter' und die theologischen Tendenzen der Schrift', points to the occurence of two gods, two Fathers, in which he sees a strong resemblance to Marcionite doctrine.
204.	Jos., Ant. 20.200.
205.	NHC 6.3; NHL 6.3, introduced and translated by George MacRae. Edited by Douglas M. Parrott.
206.	NHC 6.3.22.
207.	NHC 6.3.23.
208.	NHC 6.3.23.
209.	NHC 6.3.24.
210.	NHC 6.3.26-27.
211.	NHC 6.3.28.
212.	NHC 6.3.29-30.
213.	NHC 6.3.30.
214.	NHC 6.3.32-33.
215.	NHC 6.3.34-35.
216.	NHC 6.3.34-35.
217.	NHC 6.4; NHL 6.4, introduced by Francis E. Williams. Translated by Frederik E. Wisse. Edited by Douglas M. Parrott.
218.	NHL 284.
219.	NHL 284.
220.	NHC 6.4.39.
221.	NHC 6.4.40-41.
222.	NHC 6.4.41-42.
223.	NHC 6.4.43-44.
224.	NHC 6.4.45.
225.	NHC 6.4.46.
226.	NHC 6.4.47.
227.	NHC 7.3.; NHL 7.3, introduced by James Brashler. Translated by Roger A. Bullard. Edited by Frederik Wisse.

228. NHL 340.
229. NHC 7.3.70.
230. NHC 7.3.72.
231. NHC 7.3.73-74.
232. NHC 7.3.79.
233. NHC 7.3.79.
234. NHC 7.3.75.
235. NHC 7.3.76.
236. NHC 7.3.81.
237. NHC 7.3.82.
238. NHC 7.3.78.
239. NHC 7.3.82-83.
240. NHC 13.1; NHL 13.1. Introduced and translated by John D. Turner. Also Janssens, Prôtennoia (see Bibliography).
241. NHC 13.1.38. Janssens, Prôtennoia 59 : "The name 'Protennoia' appears only here."
242. NHC 13.1.37.
243. NHC 13.1.35.
244. NHC 13.1.36-37.
245. NHC 13.1.37.
246. NHC 13.1.38.
247. NHC 13.1.42.
248. NHC 13.1.44.
249. NHC 13.1.45.
250. NHC 13.1.40.
251. NHC 13.1.41.
252. NHC 13.1.44-45.
253. NHC 13.1.50.

CHAPTER II

THE MARCIONITE CHURCH

1. What we know of Marcion's life

a. Uncertainties and some facts

Harnack, in his famous book on Marcion, stated categorically : "For a biography of Marcion the sources are lacking" [1]. What a pity this is! For among the Gnostic prophets and teachers Marcion doubtless was one of the greatest. He created a great theological system the influence of which was immense and long-lived. How fascinating it would be, if we knew something more about the fortunes, the personality, and the character of this man who was such an important figure in the history of religions. But let us not complain; when all is said and done, we know him better than almost all other prominent Gnostics [2].

The dates of Marcion's birth and death are unknown, but that he lived in the second century A.D. is a certainty. The oldest source is to be found in Irenaeus. This Father of the Church relates how Polycarp, the venerable bishop of Smyrna, came to Rome during the pontificate of Anicetus (ca. 154-165), to die a martyr's death there on February 23, 155. During his stay in the imperial city, which must have been short, he is said to have brought many Valentinians and Marcionites back to the Church. Since Polycarp was installed as bishop of Smyrna by the apostles themselves, and, at the time of his death, was the only Christian living to have known them personally, he could claim to be better acquainted with the apostolic creed than Valentinus or Marcion.

Irenaeus then adds the anecdote that Polycarp once met Marcion who asked the bishop : "Do you know me?". Polycarp retorted : "Yes, I know you, you are the first-born of Satan" [3]. Although it by no means follows that this encounter took place in Rome, the conclusion is that we can safely assume that Marcion 'flourished' in the middle of the second century A.D. In consequence, he was a contemporary of Basilides and Valentinus [4].

If we are to believe Clement of Alexandria, Marcion knew both Basilides and Valentinus personally; "he went about with them as an older man with younger ones" [5]. Moreover, from what Clement wrote we can conclude that Marcion was already active in the days of the Emperor Hadrian (117-138) [6]. On the strength of this report Harnack believes that Marcion must have been born about A.D. 85; if this is correct, then Basilides and Valentinus were some twenty years younger [7].

All the sources agree that Marcion came from Pontus; he was a native of the harbour town of Sinope, on the southern shore of the Black Sea [8], which is now the languishing Turkish town of Sinop with some fifteen thousand inhabitants. Then it was flourishing, situated as it was on a small peninsula with good natural harbours on both sides. This deserves attention, because Marcion was a shipowner himself [9], and, as we shall see, an opulent man. His father was the bishop of his native town, a very stern man, so it seems [10].

b. Banished from Sinope

As a young man, Marcion is said to have felt drawn to a life of monastic chastity, but Epiphanius adds that his reputation in the town was dubious. This ancient author does not expatiate on this, but he reports a story to the effect that Marcion had seduced a virgin [11]. His father, who was very strict in things religious, excommicated him, in spite of the urgent entreaties of his son and of a promise by the young man to do penance [12].

How should we interpret this story? It is often supposed to be a malicious attempt by the early fathers of the Church to put the founder of the most important Gnostic sect in a bad light. However, it is not impossible in itself that the story is true. Amann, for one, finds attempts to explain this event in an allegorical way somewhat too refined [13]. On the other hand, some elements might plead for a non-literal reading of the violation story, in the sense that the 'virgin' in question was not some girl but the Church of Sinope which was disturbed by heretical opinions of young Marcion [14]. This hypothesis is lent some force by a phrase of Pseudotertullian that "they (the heretics), by their heretic adultery, have defiled the virgin handed down by Christ (= the Church)" [15]. If this explanation is correct, then Marcion must have developed his deviant opinions early in his life [16]. Whatever the reason may have been, he left Sinope forever.

c. Marcion in Rome

One of our sources, Papias, bishop of Hierapolis in Phrygia in the second century, writes that Marcion left Sinope armed with 'writings or letters' from 'his brothers who were in Pontus' [17]. This can hardly mean anything else than that he had a number of adherents in his home country, although it is said that his friends were 'believers in our Lord'. With these letters of recommendation he went to the Greek coastal towns of Asia Minor. But because Marcion vented 'deviant opinions', the bishop of an unnamed city wanted to have nothing to do with him. Perhaps this city was Ephesus or Smyrna [18] or some other city, we don't know. Rejected for the second time, Marcion travelled on to Rome. Harnack assumes that he arrived in the imperial city in A.D. 138, or thereabout, when Antoninus Pius had just become emperor [19] and Hyginus was bishop of Rome [20]. The Church of Rome apparently as yet knew nothing of Marcion's misadventures in Pontus and Asia. He was made welcome and was incorporated into the local Christian community. The fact that he made a handsome donation of two hundred thousand sestertii to the Church may have made his welcome even warmer [21].

d. His breach with the Church

Perhaps made prudent by his experiences at home and in Asia Minor, Marcion for some time to come kept a low profile. But he did not sit still. Harnack supposes that in the years between 138 and 144 he wrote his own New Testament and his book of antitheses, if he had not already done so in Asia Minor [22]. After a couple of years, however, he appeared before the presbyters of the Church of Rome in order to have a disputation with them (the bishop of Rome is not expressly mentioned). He seems to have started from a passage in Luke : "There is no such thing as a good tree producing worthless fruit, nor yet a worthless tree producing good fruit" [23]. In all probability this refers to the existence of two gods, one good, one evil, which forms the basis of Marcion's dualistic ideology [24].

He then asked what the following text might mean : "No more do they put new wine in old wine-skins nor do they sew a patch of unshrunk cloth onto an old coat" [25]. Did the elders suspect at once what was on the air? That Marcion was ready to bring forward a new doctrine? Anyhow, they calmly explained to their questioner that the 'old wine' and the 'old cloth' referred to the scribes and Pharisees who proved unwilling to accept Jesus' teaching. A long palaver followed; Harnack called this 'the first Roman Synod' [26].

When Marcion began to defend his theses, the debate grew more and more heated. Finally, he vehemently cried : "I break away from your Church, and I shall forever hold it to be schismatic" [27]. One infers that his retreat from the orthodox Church was peaceful enough since his gift of money of a few years back was restituted to him in toto [28]. He now definitively left the Church, "rescinding what he had first believed" [29]. The date of this memorable event is known almost to the day; it must have occurred in the second half of the year A.D. 144 [30]. For the Marcionites it always remained a day to celebrate. Just as they considered Jesus' baptism in the Jordan as his 'epiphany', so they saw Marcion's leaving the Church equally as an 'epiphany' [31].

This important event has been compared more than once with Luther's rupture with the Church, the more so since Marcion, just like the German Reformer, appealed to Paul's theological insights. Blackman even speaks of the first 'protestant' schism [32]. Of the rest of his life very little is known. He used the years that remained to him for elaborating and spreading his doctrine in a way that clearly was highly successful. Hardly more than six years later Justin the Martyr said that it had already spread 'over the whole human race' [33]. "A rival to the Catholic Church had sprung into being, and for a few years it must actually have seemed possible that Marcion's Church would have become the dominant Church" [34]. Marcion's death must have occurred around A.D. 160.

e. Marcion's dualistic tendencies

Marcion was doubtless one of those religious people who strive on strong contrasts; temperamentally he would have been a dualist. But it was not, as one would perhaps surmise, the opposition between God and the world on which his attention was focused, or on that between good and evil, but on something quite different. What intrigued him more than anything else was "the opposition between the supreme, unknown God, the father of Jesus Christ, and the God of the Old Testament". Bousset, whom I am quoting here, thinks that Marcion transferred "the absolute oriental-Persian dualism with its opposition of a good and a bad god" to the opposition between the Old and the New Testaments [35]. But we don't know at all whether Marcion was acquainted with Zoroastrian and Zervanite doctrine.

Are we in a position to speculate on the psychological origin of Marcion's dualism? If we knew more about his life and character, this would be an interesting subject for discussion, but for a psychological reconstruction the relevant data are sorely lacking. Some time ago I had a discussion with Stefan van Wersch, the author of a remarkable book on the course of the Gnosis throughout the centuries [36]. He contended that Gnostic dualism always has its origin in a conflict with the father of the founder. I did not deny that a conflict of this kind may play an important part in the origination of an ideology of this type, but I doubt whether it is the decisive factor. In my opinion, Van Wersch's thesis is reductionist in the sense that it neglects other factors of a more general, ideological, 'ideengeschichtlich', or historical nature.

Furthermore, in the study of dualism in Antiquity we are severely handicapped by the fact that we have very little (auto)biographical material to go on. The first really authentic ego-document is the 'Confessions' of Saint Augustine (around A.D. 400). There are only two ancient dualists of whose dualism something in the biographical line can be said, Plato and the apostle John [37]. In both cases we find elements of a personal character which go at least some way to explain the origin of their dualism. But in neither case is there any allusion to a conflict with the father.

However, in Marcion's early life we do detect, indeed, a clash with his father; so much I willingly concede to Van Wersch. Marcion, as we saw, was expelled from the Sinopian Church because of his violation of a virgin; the man who excommunicated him was his own father, the bishop of the town. But, as we have just seen, there is some reasonable doubt with regard to that violation. Did the young man actually assault a girl? In that case we could imagine that he took it ill of his father to punish him so severely, and in reaction began to develop a deviant doctrine. But it is equally possible that the violated virgin was the symbol of orthodox, 'unadulterated' ecclesiastical doctrine. If this is correct, then he was expelled because he was an heretic. In that case we have it the other way round. First there was the deviation and then only the clash with his father. This last explanation is seconded by the circumstance that Marcion, on leaving the town of his birth, took letters of recommendation with him. This would mean that he had already formed a group of followers in and around Sinope.

This disquisition on Marcion's personal circumstances does not make us any the wiser. Once we have explained Marcion's ideology more fully, we must see whether we can adduce factors of a more general character.

2. Cerdo, the forerunner

a. What we know of his life

In contrasting the celestial god of love and the Demiurge, Marcion had a forerunner, a certain Cerdo. Of his life and activities next to nothing is known; his writings, if there were any, have not been preserved. In all probability he was a native of Syria [38]. According to Irenaeus, he arrived in Rome during the pontificate of Hyginus, around A.D. 140, that is, he came there before Marcion. This author adds that he made a confession of faith [39]. Could this be taken to mean that he, on his arrival in the imperial city, was not yet a Christian? Like Marcion, he was a past-master in dissimulation : he paraded as a true believer, but secretly he taught quite other things. Finally, he was detected and excommunicated [40].

b. His doctrine

It is an undisputable fact that Cerdo's doctrine was essentially different from that of the Catholic Church. There existed, he said, not one but two gods, one good, the other bad. The evil god was the creator of the world, the instigator of Mosaic Law, and the one who had inspired the prophets. The good god was the father of Christ who came into this world. Christ's body, however, was only an appearance, with the consequence that his birth as well as his passion and death were no more than illusions. It is true that he rose from the grave, but this does not mean that there would be either a resurrection of the body or immortality.

The New Testament was absolutely worthless in his eyes (to say nothing of the Old Testament) with the exception of Luke and the Letters of Paul, with the proviso, however, that he eliminated those passages in Luke that did not suit him as well as a number of Pauline Letters and certain passages in others [41]. If this description of Cerdo's doctrine is correct, then we have before us one of the rare instances of absolute dualism, in this case of two equivalent and totally opposed gods.

But is it correct to view Cerdo as the forerunner of Marcion? The problem is that Marcion's Church did not refer to or even mention a Cerdo as the forerunner or teacher of its founder; it remained completely silent about him. On the other hand, Cerdo and Marcion were in Rome in the same years; it seems improbable that the two would not have met. This much even Harnack admits, although in general he is ready to fall over backwards to defend the absolute originality of his hero. It could be that ancient Marcionites did the same. Perhaps Cerdo did indeed influence Marcion to a certain extent and in certain respects, although the Marcionites preferred to pass this over in silence [42]. But we shall probably never know exactly what the relationship Cerdo-Marcion was.

3. Marcion and the scriptural tradition

a. The New Testament distorted by Judaizers

Marcion in all sincerity thought that the scriptural tradition of the teaching of Jesus Christ was one great tragedy. In his opinion, not long after Jesus' death Judaizers in the early Christian fold had begun to distort the original teaching since they had no use of a new religion that would supplant the Jewish one. Among these Judaizers were the apostles themselves, Jesus' own disciples; they had added elements taken from Mosaic Law to the words of the Saviour [43]. They had not even understood the truth [44].

Obviously they wanted to stick to what they knew best, the Jewish faith, and, in consequence, tried to tune down the novel sayings of Jesus. Marcion suspected them of deliberately twisting the Gospel message [45]. The main culprit was nobody less than Peter himself, that 'man of the Law' [46]. Lots of pseudo-apostles made their way into the Church, preaching the necessity of circumcision and of celebrating the Jewish feast-days [47]. All this led Marcion to a very sad conclusion : the writings that form part of the New Testament, but in particular the Gospels, are simply not be trusted; what Jesus really wanted to convey to the world was "wiped out by a flood of falsifications" [48].

b. Marcion and the Gospel of Luke

We should, nevertheless, not give up our attempts to accurately reconstruct the message of Jesus. In Paul's Letter to the Galatians Marcion found it stated that there was a Gospel which was no human invention and which was revealed to its author by Jesus himself [49]. Marcion inferred from this that there existed one Gospel that was, at least more or less, free from Judaistic distortions and accretions; he decided that this must be the Gospel of Luke. "Out of the authors whom we possess, Marcion is seen to have chosen Luke as the one to mutilate" [50], with which 'to mutilate'; Tertullian who is quoted here, means by 'mutilate' to appropriate it for his own (Marcion's) end. The other three Gospels were falsified by the Judaizers beyond recognition, but Luke's was adulterated only to some extent.

We do not know why Marcion finally opted for Luke. John and Matthew were certainly much too Jewish to his taste, but, as Harnack writes, Marc might have been his choice too. This scholar believes that the Gospel of Luke was the first to have come to Marcion's native country, Pontus, and may have been the only one he knew in his youth; another reason could have been that Luke was an intimate of Marcion's great favourite, the apostle Paul [51]. If I am allowed to venture a guess : the fact that Luke was not a born Jew but a proselyte, who, for this reason, could not be accused of 'judaizing' may have also appealed to him .

All this does not mean that Marcion was ready to accept all that this Gospel said at its face-value. Far from it! First of all, although he found the name 'Luke' a trustworthy label, he did not believe that Luke was actually the author. For hadn't Paul expressly stated that this author had received his Gospel through a revelation directly from the Lord [52]? This is yet another instance of the importance attached by the Gnostics to personal revelations and esoteric knowledge. Because Marcion assumed that the text of Luke had been tampered with, he set himself to revising it. Blackman thinks that Marcion began his task of text criticism by first of all expurgating the Pauline Epistles (which had also been manipulated), "and thence obtained the criterion to judge the Gospel itself" [53]. What resulted was a clipped version of Luke's Gospel. One sees that the German professors who, from behind the writing-desks, know exactly what Jesus said or did not say, had an august patron-saint.

From Harnack's careful reconstruction of the Marcionite Gospel we are fairly well informed about what had to be crossed out. The so-called 'infancy gospel' in Chapters 1 and 2 had to go to the last word. From Chapters 3 and 4 not much was retained either : Jesus' baptism, his genealogy, and his temptation by Satan were all struck out. The Marcionite Gospel began with Luke 3:1 : "in the fifteenth year of Tiberius Caesar', and, omitting everything in between, continued straight-away with 4:31 : "God descended into Capernaum" (which, of course, is a Marcionite emendation, Luke's own text being : "He (Jesus) went down to Capernaum").

From this point onward the narrative proceeds more or less evenly, although every now and then a few words or one or two phrases in the original are deleted. There are also some longer omissions : curiously enough the parable of the Prodigal Son in Chapter 15, the last journey to Jerusalem, and the triumphal entry into that city, together with Jesus' lament over it [54], and further the parable of the vineyard [55], with Jesus' prophecy regarding the fate of the Temple [56]. This seems rather arbitrary but Marcion will have had his reasons. Anyhow, he considered the rump-Gospel that resulted from his revision as the only authentic one [57].

c. Marcion and the Pauline Letters

What appealed to Marcion in Paul was his rejection of Judaizing. We must never for a moment forget that he (Marcion) was fundamentally anti-Jewish. He abhorred the whole of the Old Testament which, of course, is Jewish to the core. With regard to Paul whom he considered an anti-Jewish Jew, 'he must discover the original teaching of his master, that is, he must become a textual reviser, and eject from the text of the Pauline Epistles every interpolation" [58]. For the Judaizers had busied themselves even with these sacred texts. Here too quite a lot was jettisoned, for instance all references to the Old Testament. To quote only one example, Eph. 2:20

reads : "You (the Christians) are built upon the foundation laid by the apostles and prophets"; Marcion struck out the prophets, because Jewish prophets are swindlers [59].

d. A New Testament that was free of Judaism

With the cleansed Gospel of Luke and the revised Pauline Letters in his hand, Marcion believed that he was now in possession of an entirely trustworthy body of scriptural texts. After his thorough revision it was now free from Judaism. All links with the Old Testament and the Jewish religion had become severed; it was almost a necessity, as Harnack writes, that the revised Gospel had to be inimical to Judaism [60]. It will not surprise us that Marcion eliminated the whole of Rom. 9; he had no need of phrases like these : "They (the Jews) are God's sons; theirs is the splendour of the divine presence".

4. The 'Antitheses'

Marcion's truncated New Testament was not an original creation, in so far that he constructed it from existing material. He was, however, the author of a new work, the so-called 'Antitheses'. This work is not extant, alas. In spite of our possessing a fair number of quotations, it has not proved possible to reconstruct the book, not even in its outline [61]. It must have been Marcion's only work, and the only one in all Antiquity with this title. No other author has made it so abundantly clear, right from the outset, that he intended to point out oppositions, even of a dualistic nature. Tertullian dubbed it 'a juxtaposition of opposites' [62].

5. The separation of Law and Gospel

"The separation of Law and Gospel is the primary and principal object of Marcion" [63]. The Law is the Old Testament and Judaism; the Gospel

(Marcion's own, expurgated Gospel) is the New Testament and Christianity. His "one purpose was the setting up of an opposition between the Old Testament and the New" [64]. This dualistic opposition was the starting-point of Marcionite ideology. "The religious principle", thus Harnack, "which condenses every higher truth in the opposition of Law and Gospel, is also the explanatory principle of all that is and happens" [65]. The consequence is that whole of the Old Testament was thrown overboard. Harnack supposes that this radicalism must have been painful even to Marcion himself [66].

6. Marcion's ditheism

As is to be expected, the next stage was the positing of two gods, a god of the Old Testament and another of the New. "From the adversity of principles between those two documents they (the Marcionites) may argue further for a diversity of gods. It is precisely this separation of Law and Gospel which has suggested a god of the Gospel, other than and in opposition to the god of the Law" [67]. And a fierce opposition it was at that! "Between (those two gods) he sets up a great and absolute (= dualistic) opposition, such as that between justice and kindness, between Law and Gospel, between Judaism and Christianity" [68].

It would not be suprising if the reader were inclined to think here of the Zoroastrian opposition between a god of light and a god of darkness. But Marcion passes over this particular dichotomy. Tertullian was astonished that his opponent did not refer to this Iranian tenet of faith. "You (Marcion) ought rather to have shown that there is one god of light and another of darkness; after that you would have found it easier to persuade us that there is one god of kindness and another of severity" [69]. Was Tertullian thinking here of the opposition between God and Satan, an opposition that he would have understood better? Anyhow, he seems a forerunner here of modern scholars who at every mention of dualism look in the direction of Iran.

However, the opposition between the two gods is not one of light and darkness, but is characterized by Tertullian in the following terms. "Marcion sets up unequal gods, the one a judge and warlike, the other mild and peaceable, solely kind and supremely good" [70]. This is vintage dualism, radical and absolute. It fits my definition of dualism to a T, for we are in the presence here of two beings (or principles), that cannot be reduced to each other, with no intermediate link between them, one of which is considered inferior in quality to the other. Blackman is of the opinion that "considered as an intellectual theory this dualism is grotesque, and Christian apologists may have felt that their own doctrine had nothing to fear from it. Monism is ultimately always more satisfying to the intellect than dualism" [71].

But if Marcion really was so harmless, why then did minds as powerful as Irenaeus or Tertullian (not to mention many others) engage him in conflict? And why is this dualism 'grotesque'? Did anyone ever say the same of Zoroastrian or Zervanite dualism to which it bears such a strong resemblance? Monism, moreover, creates problems of its own, as I have often argued; it must be sharply distinguished from monotheism. I for one would never define the Jewish and Christian theological systems as monistic.

Against Marcion's metaphysical dualism [72] Tertullian, just like Anselm of Canterbury many centuries later, adduces an ontological argument. He argues that "God is the supremely great, firmly established in eternity and unbegotten, uncreated, without beginning, and without end ... God is supreme greatness in both form and reason and power and authority ... It has nothing to equal it, that is, there exists no other thing supremely great ... Therefore, that which is supremely great is of necessity singular, as having no fellow ... If God is not one God, he is no god" [73].

This comes dangerously near to a petitio principii. Perhaps Tertullian himself felt the flaw in his argument since he goes on to adduce the presence of several mighty kingdoms in the world as an example of the possibility of the existence of more than one supremely great entity. But, he says, if there are two gods, why then not three or four or still more [74]?

Perhaps Tertullian should have started with demonstrating the metaphysical impossibility of polytheism (or, as in Marcion's case, of ditheism). But we shall leave him to his own devices, since we are not occupying ourselves with him but with Marcion. It is enough to state how much Marcion's dualism bothered this great scholar!

7. The nature of the Demiurge

Of the New Testament god - his god - Marcion stated that he was 'supremely good'. But does this imply that the other god was supremely evil? It seems that Marcion did not call him so; he spoke of him as a 'judge'. A judge must be just and exercise justice, but he is also severe and strict, often harsh, and he is out to punish. He is not lovable nor does he love. However, he is not necessarily bad nor is he the principle of evil; Marcion made room in his system for Satan as the instigator of evil. This god of Justice has the world as it is for himself alone; he made it, he is the Demiurge, the creator-god. His counterpart, the god of Love, did not intervene in the Demiurge's work. The Justice-god is the ruler of this world and also 'the particular God of the Jewish nation' [75]. The Demiurge, this means, is identical with Jahve, the God of Israel.

From a theological viewpoint it is a very remarkable thing that the two gods are unequal in quality. More than once Tertullian speaks of a superior, or more sublime, god, and an inferior one [76]. The two are far apart : "(They) are separated from one another by an infinite intermediate space" [77]. The god of Love has a place in the universe far above the other one [78], which implied that Jesus, when descending to the earth, had to pass through the Demiurge's heaven [79]. We have to imagine the reciprocal positions of the two gods in a spatial context.

Marcion portrays the Demiurge, the god of Justice, as fickle and unstable. He regrets his own decisions and comes back on them. Tertullian, quoting Marcion, cites many examples of this inconsistency : for instance that labour on sabbath days was forbidden, but that, notwithstanding this, the Israelites carried the Ark during eight consecutive days around the walls of Jericho, a period must have included a Sabbath [80] (a very fine example of close reading, by the way!). The Demiurge is "changeable, variable, teaching one thing, doing another [81]; ... he is unstable, inconsistent and untrustworthy, cancelling appointments he himself has made" [82].

Marcion agrees with other Gnostics in assuming that his Demiurge is ignorant; he simply does not realize that there is yet another, superior divinity. "He was unaware of the existence of any other god, and in fact was then and there swearing that besides himself there is no other god at all [83]; ... he did not know that there was a god above him" [84]. More than anything else this fundamental ignorance proves the Demiurge's inferiority, if we look at it from a Gnostic point of view.

8. Matter as a third principle

The question obviously arises whether such an inferior divine being is really a god. But Marcion asserts, or at least does not deny, that the Demiurge is a god [85]. But he is a lesser god, he suffers 'from sort of diminution' [86]. The two gods are, although both of them divine, unequal [87]. The inferiority of the Demiurge becomes especially apparent in his use of matter as the material with which to fashion the world. It is important to realize that just as the Demiurge is not the principle of evil, he is not identical with matter. Marcion saw matter as pre-existent, as something uncreated. "(The Demiurge) has constructed his world of some subjacent material, unbegotten and uncreated, and co-temporal with the god" [88]. Tertullian says that Marcion concurs with the Stoics in this [89].

This leads to the inescapable conclusion that Marcion not only acknowledged two independent gods but also three uncreated entities : his two gods and matter. With respect to quality these three form a descending line : the superior god is good, the inferior god is neither good nor really bad, and matter is bad. "The good (god) is the unknown whom he (Marcion) proclaimed as the Father of the Lord (Jesus); the Demiurge is just, he also calls him malicious; besides them there is matter which is bad and intent upon other evil" [90]. Eznik adds that the Demiurge "created all that he made in collaboration with matter" [91]; no mention is made of the good god in the creational process.

9. The creation of the world and mankind

The character of the Demiurge deserves no praise, as we have already seen, and since matter is bad in itself, the collaboration must necessarily result in a repellent finished product. This product is the world and all that it contains. The main proof of the malignant nature of the Creator is the existence of the world as such. "The Marcionites consider nature to be evil, because it has been made out of matter that is bad by the just Demiurge" [92]; "Marcion is so ungrateful that to him creation is bad" [93]. The Demiurge manages his handiwork in a most malicious way. One of the Pseudoclementine Homilies recites his sins : he lies, he deceives, he tempts, he makes deaf and blind, he is misleading, he works evil. And the author concludes : if the Creator is like this, how can man be good? [94].

Harnack shows us in which respect the malignity of the Creator, with regard to the creation of man, becomes apparent. He created man as a feeble being, helpless and mortal, and allowed him to be seduced. He tolerates sin, death, and the devil (who was created by him), and all kinds of evil. He punishes transgressions out of all proportions. He is hard, cruel, bellicose, bloodthirsty. He wreaks the sins of the fathers on the children and makes the innocent suffer for the guilty. He makes the rebellious obstinate. He was jealous enough to keep the first couple away from the tree of life. He is prejudiced in favour of his admirers however bad these may be, and allows them to commit fraud and violence against their enemies. Harnack adds that all this is compatible with the 'justice' of the Demiurge, if only we see him as an oriental despot whose will is law. Subjection to his rule is the supreme virtue; those who oppose him are eo ipso without rights and will be crushed [95]. All texts in the Old Testament that speak a different language are consistently overlooked [96].

Man is a creation of the Demiurge, not of the good god. The Creator fashioned the human body out of matter (which is bad); he imparted his own substance to man, insofar as he gave him a soul, but this substance is of a highly doubtful quality. Man is a failure in a double sense, first as a consequence of his origin, and then because he lost his privileged state and was thrown out of paradise [97]. But as always in Gnostic ideology, the Fall was not the fault of man but was caused by the Demiurge's jealousy. He refused to allow that beings whom he had created should enjoy the fruits of the tree of life [98].

10. The Law and the prophets

After the Fall the Demiurge - who, of course, is identical with Jahve - tried to win back mankind. This he attempted to do through Abraham and his progeny. To control this progeny, the Jewish nation, he made Moses promulgate the Law. It was formulated 'because of its Author's (the Demiurge's) hardness' [99]. Of this Mosaic Law Marcion had not much good to say. In particular the practice of sacrifice came under his fire; he found this foolish and dishonourable. But, as Tertullian concludes with an audible sigh, "as far as I know, the whole of Old Testament is a matter of scorn to every heretic" [100].

That Marcion detested Mosaic Law does not mean at all that he advocated lawlesness and proflicacy. He did not plead moral antinomianism, far from it, rather the contrary. He was a convinced moralist and strongly inclined to puritanism. In fact, he preserved certain parts of the Law as valid and declared them good, holy, and spiritual. To give a few instances : "Those who have sinned under the Law will be judged by the Law. It is not by hearing the Law, but by doing it, that men will be justified before God" [101], or still more remarkable : "In the Law you see the very shape of knowledge and truth" [102], and, "the Law is in itself holy" [103]. These Pauline texts, and others, were left intact in Marcion's Gospel [104]. Harnack explains the somewhat surprising presence of such texts in

Marcion by contending that he (Marcion) had no problem with justice as such but only with the way it was administered by the Demiurge [105].

Marcion's attitude to prophecy is similar to that towards the Law. Prophecy in itself is quite legitimate and instructive, but he would have nothing to do with Jewish prophets. They were all blind and preached the wrong god, the Demiurge [106]. Marcion's conception of the Old Testament as a whole is somewhat ambivalent. It is the work of the Demiurge and such highly objectionable; on the other hand, he does not deny that it also contains salutary instructions [107].

He had his own idea of the predictions of the Messiah. Some of these, he thought, were already fulfilled, in David or others. In his opinion, the words of Ps. 72:7 : "You are my Son, this day I have begotten you", refer to David, not to Jesus [108]. Marcion did not doubt that there would appear a Messiah, but he is not incarnate in Jesus Christ. He is still to come, just as the Jews believe to this day; he will be a belligerent hero who has come to reinstate the wordly kingdom of the Jews - an idea that for the peace-loving Marcion went against the grain [109].

11. Marcion and the Jews

Behind these depreciatory and at best ambivalent judgements is Marcion's wholly negative attitude respecting the Jewish people; he could not imagine a worse lot. For it was they who had acknowledged and proclaimed the Demiurge. To understand this attitude, we must realize why Marcion had no need of the Old Testament, of the religion of Israel with almost all that it implies, and of the Jewish people as the bearer of that religion. He wanted a totally new beginning; his special brand of Christianity must not be connected with any previous religion, and least of all with Judaism. His rejection of the Jewish religion was total and dualistic in nature. To him, "the Old Testament was not a body of literature which had a message for future as well as for past generations ... (He) started from the axiom that Christianity had no forerunners, and worshiped a God who entered in no dealings with mankind previous to the fifteenth year of Tiberius Caesar" [110].

12. Marcion's rejection of history

In doing away with the whole of the religious history of mankind, and in contending that real religion had begun only one and a half century earlier, Marcion remained in keeping with one of the most important tenets of Gnostic ideology, viz. that religion must be not be rooted in or based on history but in mythology. "The Old Testament is not a book of mythology nor a book of philosophy or of systematic theology. It is a book of history, i.e. a record of Divine contacts with man in and through past events" [111]. Behind Marcion's rejection of the Old Testament stood his equally radical and dualistic rejection of history, and, by the same token, of the New Testament.

Here lies his profound difference with the Roman-Catholic Church. "It asserted for its own part that Christianity was the highest development of Judaism ... Christianity claimed to be a historical religion ... The retention of the Old Testament within the Christian canon served to attest the continuity of Christianity with the past." To orthodox Christians the Old Testament was (and is) not 'a devotional book or great literature' [112]. The Church was forced to stress strongly the historicity of the Old Testament and its organic connection with the orthodox creed, because, as Blackman says, "a large number of Greek-speaking converts had no understanding of the Old Testament and felt no obligation to retain it. It remained to them a book of Jewish fables. These were a field ripe for Gnostic and Marcionite sickles to harvest" [113]. This may explain the success of the Marcionite doctrine.

13. Mankind a sorry lot

It is necessary to speak once again of the Demiurge's creational work in order to throw into relief the soteriological role of Christ. As we saw, the

Demiurge made a bad job of creation. It goes without saying that mankind, as part of creation, is not a whit better than creation itself (or than the Demiurge). It must not surprise us that of all the Demiurge's institutions Marcion most of all loathed sexuality and procreation, for this is where man becomes creative himself. "Marcion's god expresses disapproval of marriage, as an evil thing, and as a traffic in unchastity" [114]. Marcion ridiculed pregnancy, child-bearing, and the rearing of the baby [115]. If all this is evil, it is the Demiurge who is responsible for it. "The Creator's very essence is seen to be capable of sin, since it was the soul, which is the breath of god, that sinned when man sinned, and the corruption of the derivative (= the human being) cannot escape being referred back to the original whole (i.e. man cannot be better than his Creator, the Demiurge - F.)" [116].

14. The unknowable god

To understand the part of Christ in the work of salvation, it is necessary to realize that the god of Christ, the supreme and superior god, was totally unknown to mankind until Jesus came. The one who was known is the inferior god, the Demiurge; people knew him through his works, i.e. through creation. The supreme god is fully the 'deus absconditus et ignotus' of the Gnosis. He is "a new god, unknown and unheard of in the old world, in the old time, under the old god [117] ... In boasting of their god as 'new', they (the Marcionites) mean new in men's knowledge of him" [118]. He is "a god by nature unkown, one not revealed except in the Gospel (i.e. of Marcion - F.), one not capable of being known by all" [119].

The reason of his remaining unknown for so long is that he created nothing material; he cannot be inferred from the works of creation. Marcion's god is "a leisured god ... who has never done anything" [120]. He did, however, create what is invisible [121]. The supreme god has his creation just as well, his own world and his own heaven, "all invisible and hermetically separated from the visible world" [122]. This superior world does not manifest itself in the lower one [123]. There is simply no connection. "There was no possibility of it being brought to light in this (= the lower) world" [124]. This too is utterly dualistic. The Marcionite supreme god not only is unknowable and hidden, but also 'different, the other'; many adherents call him 'the alien' [125]. Their favourite name for their god was 'the good alien'; Harnack remarks that from the viewpoint of this god human beings were 'aliens' too [126].

15. Redemption

This supreme god is "above all dominion, above every beginning, above all power" [127]. At the same time, he is all good, 'supremely good' [128]; in fact, he is 'primary and perfect goodness himself' [129]. Because of his goodness he wanted to reveal himself in order to redeem mankind by this self-revelation [130]. "He is the father of mercies ..., since he undertook to deliver the human race" [131]. "Sufficient to our (the Marcionites') god is this single work, that he has by his great and particular kindness set man free" [132]. For this work the supreme god has no need of a chosen people and still less of matter. The redemption has to be universal [133].

The great question now is from what mankind has to be delivered. From sin? Yes, but not directly. We know that the concept of sin did not play a great role in Gnostic ideology. Marcion did not deny sin but saw it caused by the Law. It is the Law that makes people sinful. In order to deliver mankind from sin it is first of all necessary to destroy the Law [134]. This is what Jesus accomplished. It is true that Marcion read in the Gospels that Jesus said that he had come not to abolish the Law but to complete it [135], but he "raged and stormed to discount this saying" [136]. With the freedom Gnostics used to take with Bible texts, Marcion taught quite the contrary : that Jesus came "to overthrow the Creator and destroy the Law and the prophets" [137]; he "dissolved the Law and the prophets, and all the works of the Demiurge" [138]. Jesus announced the end of everything that came before him in the Sermon on the Mount [139].

16. The role of Christ

a. Marcion's docetism

Christ the Redeemer appeared on earth so to speak out of nowhere. Since Marcion discredited the Old Testament, his coming had not been announced by the prophets; nobody could have known anything about him beforehand. The story of salvation did not find its fulfilment in him; there is no story of salvation. Jesus was not born from Mary, since birth is something despicable; even a virgin birth did not escape from this taint. Mary was not 'overshadowed by the Holy Ghost', since the supreme godhead does not manifest himself in this world. Marcion consequently stuck to his dualistic principles! And since matter is bad, Christ could not possess a proper physical body.

This does not mean that he was a kind of spectre, so that one could look right through him. He certainly looked like and acted and felt as a human being, with this proviso that his was a 'phantasma' of a human body [140]. As Harnack explains, "the identity with a physical body that is brought forth in a natural way was only apparent because the physical substance was failing" [141]. The problem was that Jesus could not "hold converse among men except by means of a copy of a man's substance" [142].

But still more important is the theological problem. It is perfectly possible that it was Marcion who stated : "If Christ had been born and taken on a human body, he would have stopped being God by laying down what he was (= his divinity) and assuming what he was not (= humanity)" [143]. All this is, of course, sheer docetism. However, I don't believe Marcion was greatly interested in the theological niceties of his presentation, as long as he could manage to keep his Christ away from contact with matter.

b. Christ an emanation from the supreme god

Marcion had no doubt that his Christ was divine, a god, just as much as his supreme god. He acknowledged no great difference between this godhead and his son Christ [144]. Marcion was a modalist. This signifies that he stuck to the letter of the trinitarian dogma but not to its spirit. Modalists pleaded for the essential unity of God, or should we say, for his uniformity? For to them the Father, the Son, and the Holy Ghost were not three distinct persons, but only three modes through which the godhead expressed or manifested himself. "Marcion hardly differentiated between the good God and Jesus his Son. Jesus is the good God, human in appearance, just as the good God is Jesus stripped of his lendings and returned to his original state" [145].

c. Did Marcion's Jesus preach a new god?

As we have seen, the god preached by Jesus remained totally unknown until the fifteenth year of the reign of the Emperor Tiberius. But did Jesus really proclaim that his god was a new one? It was a formidable difficulty for Marcion that the Bible, even his favourite Gospel of Luke or the Pauline Letters, never drew a distinction between a God of the Old Testament and one of the New Testament. This is what Tertullian categorically stated in the following words : "Nowhere in any sense is a different God revealed by Christ". And he added : "I am surprised that in this alone Marcion's adulterating hand lost its cunning".

In other words, Marcion's Jesus never says in so many words that he brought a totally new God. Perhaps he shrank away from this last consequence of his radical doctrine, in the sense that he preferred believing it in foro interno to proclaiming it openly. This was Tertullian's opinion : "Even robbers have their fears. No evil act is exempt from fear" [146]. Harnack thinks that the Gospel tradition was too strong to allow Marcion to ascribe to Christ the unambiguous proclamation of two gods. "He left the consequence to his hearers" [147].

d. The act of redemption

The supreme means by which Christ redeemed mankind was his death on the cross. "The death of the good one became the salvation of man" [148]. This implies that Christ really suffered and died; he did not, as in other gnostic systems, take his leave before the passion began. Of course, Christ, as God, is impassible, but his body could really suffer. Usually, as Blackman writes, "it was the passion rather than the birth of Christ which formed the main-stumbling block (for most Gnostics), since it contravened the doctrine of divine impassibility". However, the cross was not Marcion's particular problem; instead, he directed his fire on the birth, because his Christ must have no human prehistory, neither in the prophecies nor in his actual biography. "To admit that he had been born would imply that he really belonged to the Creator (= the Demiurge)" [149]. It was the Demiurge who brought Christ on the cross. "When the Demiurge saw that he (Christ) was abolishing the Law, he laid an ambush for him ... But his death did not really harm him" [150].

By his death on the cross Jesus paid the price for the redemption; we must, indeed, not forget that mankind did not belong to him but to the Demiurge. So he had to ransom it. "If Christ had come from the Demiurge, he would have rightly loved what was his; but since he came from another god, his love was all the greater because he redeemed what was alien to him" [151].

e. A dramatic scene

Probably referring to Marcionite mythology of a later date, Eznik of Kolb describes a dramatic scene that occurred between the Demiurge and Jesus. After his death Jesus, looking god-like, descended to the Demiurge and called him to account. "When the ruler of the universe saw Jesus, he acknowledged that there was yet another godhead than he." Jesus accusingly asked him : "Did you not write in your Law, 'Who kills must die? And who sheds the blood of someone, the blood of him will be shed too?'" [152].

The Demiurge admitted this. "Then Jesus said to him : 'Surrender yourself into my hands, that I kill you ... For I am endlessly more just than you'." The Demiurge realized that he had stumbled into his own pitfall and began to implore forgiveness; to excuse himself he said that he never knew that Jesus was God. Finally Jesus let him go.

Jesus now turned to the apostle Paul and revealed what price he had paid. "Then he dispatched him to preach that we have been ransomed for a price, and that everyone who believes in Jesus has been sold by the just god (the Demiurge) to the good god" [153]. This refers to Paul's being "caught up as far as the third heaven, (where he) heard words so secret that human lips may not repeat them" [154].

f. Who will be saved

The price Jesus paid is valid not only for the generation of the past and for those who lived in Jesus' own days but also for those to come. No longer will people be saved by the works of the Law. "The good one wrested those who were bad from the evil one and changed them through faith and made them good by believing in him" [155]; "the good one saves those who have faith in him" [156].

All this sounded new and optimistic enough, but Marcion's reality was different. We have seen that he contrasted the universality, the all-embracing love of the supreme god with the narrowness of the Demiurge. But when it came to the consequences, he could not rid himself of his dualistic abhorrence of the Jewish people. Not all men will be saved, and certainly not the Jews and Christians who belong to the Demiurge - for them there is no hope. "The majority are not to be saved" [157]. Jews are incorrigible; they prefer to stick to the Demiurge. "They cast out the devil by Beelzebub, using the power of the Demiurge" [158]; they even kill their own prophets [159]. They killed Jesus too, acting in the spirit of their over-lord, the Demiurge. The Christians could have known better but most of them had already relapsed into the old ways. Had it been different, it would not have been necessary for a Marcion to proclaim the unknown god with such vehemence. The consequence is that only those souls will be saved who have learned Marcion's lessons.

After his death Jesus descended 'ad inferos', to the underworld where the just dwelled who died before Jesus' redeeming act. On this point Marcion agreed with the orthodox creed. But soon enough they parted ways. But those whom Jesus took upwards with him were not exactly the just according to Old Testament standards; the redeemed counted amongst others, Cain and those similar to him, the Sodomites and the Egyptians. But Abel, Henoch, Noah, the patriarchs, the prophets, all those who were just in Jewish eyes, did not obtain salvation. "Because they knew that God (the Demiurge) had always tempted them, they now too suspected a temptation, they did not rush towards Jesus", with the consequence that they had to stay where they were [160]. Marcion did not concur with Gnostic antinomian authors who glorified Cain and the Sodomites, but he was quite ready to declare them saved. Judas, however, is not mentioned at all.

"There will be no resurrection of bodies, only of souls [161] ..., for the body, taken from the earth, cannot possibly partake (in salvation)" [162]. Nothing else was to be expected. "According to him (Marcion) the flesh does not rise again" [163].

g. A Marcionite act of faith

To those who are saved the good god grants 'the true substance of angels' [164]. But for the Marcionites who are still living in this world, this view is based on an act of faith. Marcionites, it was believed, will be released, but only in the future. For the present they remain under the sway of the Demiurge. "The Marcionite still gets malaria; ... he is exposed not only to the Demiurge's lightnings, with his wars and pestilences and other chastisements, but even to his scorpions" [165]. Worse still, they will be persecuted by pagans, Jews, and false Christians, acting on the instruction of the Demiurge.

17. The day of reckoning

But the day of reckoning will come. In the end "Jesus will judge evil by refusing consent, and condemn it by forbidding it" [166]. In the view of Marcion Jesus will not return as the eternal judge in order to punish. Rather he will leave the obdurate evil-doers to their fate. He judges, as Harnack explains, 'prohibendo', by excluding the latter from the blissful future [167]. Thus the great distinction is made : a minority will join Jesus for all eternity; the majority will be "apprehended by the fire of the Demiurge" [168]. This fire will also consume the whole cosmos.

To sketch the apocalypse of the world, Marcion made a wilful use of 1 Cor. 15:24-26 : "When he (Christ) has abolished every kind of domination, authority, and power, he is destined to reign until all his enemies have been put under his feet". As so often, Marcion rearranged the biblical text so that it might suit his own purpose. This purpose was to show that the Demiurge destroyed the fundaments of his work with his own hands. "They (the Marcionites) say that the Lord of the world destroys himself and his creation forever" [169]. In the end only the good god will remain.

18. Marcion's Gnostic dualism

a. Marcion's dualism

Let us pause now for a moment to consider how Gnostic and how dualistic Marcion's doctrine is. With regard to his dualism there cannot be the slightest doubt. In Marcion we encounter one of the most radical dualisms of all Antiquity. "Dualism ... is the very heart of Marcionite thought and connects it in an organic way with the world of Gnosticism" [170]. First and foremost, there is the absolute distinction between his two gods, the supreme one and his inferior counterpart, the Demiurge. The supreme god is not only unknowable, as in all other Gnostic systems, but at the same time utterly unknown, until he appeared in the person of Christ during the reign of the Emperor Tiberius.

A constitutive element of this metaphysical Marcionite dualism is the distinction between the divine and physical principles. His ditheism was the starting-point of his whole system. It put him at an unbridgeable distance from both Judaism and orthodox Christianity. But even in Gnostic ideology his radicalism must be termed exceptional. Marcion's supreme divinity is so purely spiritual that he has nothing to do with the cosmos and its creation and is wholly alien to it; he can not even be known from creation, since this is not his handiwork. He is so far distanced from all that is matter and created that, when his emanation Christ appears, he has had no previous human existence, no birth, no youth; almost the only event mentioned is his death on the cross. His body is presented as real but is nevertheless not fully physical and human.

The reader will not be surprised to find the usual opposition between soul and body (there is no resurrection of the body), and that between the elect and the massa damnata. In the last case the opposition is sharper than, for instance, in Valentianism, because here there is no middle group of psychics who may choose either way. Marcion did not use the terms 'hylics' and 'pneumatics' either. The rejection of the Old Testament is more accentuated than elsewhere.

What is new in him is his radical rejection of marriage and procreation. As far as I know, all other Gnostic sects, with the exception of Manichaeism saw these as necessary evils (and Mani allowed the Auditores to marry). It is arguable that Marcion, as so often, radicalized Paul's opinion on this point. The apostle did not reject marriage as an institution but he saw the celibate state (if only in the service of God's Kingdom) as more commendable. But he also wrote : "It is a good thing for a man to have nothing to do with women" [171], and "I should like you all to be as I am myself" [172]. He himself always remained single.

Beyond any doubt Marcion radicalized the Pauline opposition between Law and grace. Always ready to stretch Paul's sayings to the utmost, and conveniently forgetting that the apostle had also had some good words to say of the Law, he clamped down on this phrase : "Their unbelieving minds are so blinded by the god of this passing age, that the gospel of the glory of Christ, who is the very image of God, cannot dawn upon them and bring them light" [173]. This refers to people who feel unable to accept the message of Jesus Christ, that is, the unbelieving Jews, but doubtless Marcion was also thinking of orthodox Christians. And with 'the gospel' Paul meant what the Church meant by it, but Marcion had his own gospel in mind. It must have sounded like music in his ears that Paul said that the unbelievers (by whom Marcion also understood the Christians) were 'on the way to perdition' [174].

Some words must be said on the sources of Marcionite dualism. Bousset was of the opinion that Marcion found his inspiration in Iranian dualism. "Marcion transferred, strictly speaking, the absolute Persian-oriental dualism and the opposition of the good and the bad god to the opposition between the supreme and unknown god, the father of Jesus Christ, and the god of the Old Testament. For him the god of the Old Testament became Ahriman, Satan" [175]. But Marcion never equated his inferior god, the Demiurge, with Satan, and still less with Ahriman. Marcion's ditheism is not a copy of Iranian Zoroastrianism and Zervanism. There the contending gods are on an equal footing; this is not the case here, they are not contending nor are they equal. Whereas in the Iranian doctrine the two gods will continue to exist in all eternity, coeval and coeternal as they are, the Marcionite Demiurge is condemned to disappear into nothingness, as the consequence of his wickedness. This is a remarkable variation on a well-known theme. Monistic systems not rarely develop soon enough into dualistic ones; here an initially thoroughly dualistic system finally changes into a monistic one.

In the extant Marcionite texts no pointers to Zoroastrianism or Zervanism are to be found. Any suggestion of affinities between Marcionism and the Iranian religion must remain highly conjectural [176]. Bousset fell victim here to an idiosyncracy that is common to scholars : if they but hear the word 'dualism', they turn their eyes in the direction of Iran. But this 'Iranian connection' is a much too facile solution for the question of the origin of dualism. Zoroaster did not 'invent' it. There is far more reason to locate the source of Marcionite dualism in ideologies which, far more than

Zoroastrianism, prevailed in the region where Marcion lived : Jewish apocalyptics and mysticism [177], Gnostic ideas [178], and even Hellenic and Hellenistic philosophy [179]. In all of these, more or less strong tendencies of dualism are discernible. As I have argued, the whole mental climate of the period tended to dualism; it was easier then to be a dualist than to steer entirely free of it. Contempt for matter and the body did not originate with Marcion, neither was he the first to scorn of sexuality.

Summarizing our disquisition on the origin of Marcion's dualism we may reasonably assume that he was a man of a radical temper, prone to sharp distinctions. What he heard everywhere about him was 'gefundenes Fressen' for him : dualistic impulses came from all sides. But when all is said and done, it was Paul's doctrine in which he found the greatest support for his own dualism.

b. Marcion and the Gnosis

Regarding Marcion's attachment to the Gnosis, the situation seems somewhat different. In the eyes of Harnack he was no Gnostic at all but a radical Christian who did no more than develop the ideas of Paul [180]. But if Simone Pétrement is right in arguing that the decisive hallmark of the Gnosis is the existence of two separate gods, or rather the separation of the supreme god from everything else, in particular the cosmos [181], then Marcionism is Gnostic to the core. "The basic and cosmogonical ditheism of Marcionite thought ... really expresses the very essence of the Gnostic sentiment" [182]. Other well-attested elements of the Gnostic doctrine are the occurence of a Demiurge and the attribution of creation to him, the rejection of all that is material, physical, and sexual, and the fact of there being two sets of people, one to be saved, the other to be doomed.

It will perhaps have struck the reader that Marcion's system is far less complicated and much simpler than many we have studied so far. There is, for instance, no Pleroma, nor are there Archons in the Pleroma; Marcion wanted his godhead to be absolutely alone. But the Demiurge is solitary too. In many Gnostic systems he has Rulers or angels at his disposal or he has a son; nothing of this is the case here. There is also no distinct Saviour, sent down by the primal godhead in order to redeem (part of) mankind. The Redeemer, Christ, is virtually identical with the godhead himself.

Along this road we come to the most suprising difference from other, more conventionally Gnostic systems. Knowledge does not play a role; it is not even mentioned. In consequence it is not the redemptive power, as it is in other Gnostic systems. Redemption is effected by the cross; this is a fundamentally un-Gnostic element. On this point Marcion came much nearer to the Roman-Catholic Church which he abhorred than to Valentinus, Basilides, e tutti quanti. It is surely a tricky task to define what is Gnostic (or not). A position such as taken by Simone Pétrement is doubtless defensible. But when all is said and done, I remain stuck with a profound doubt : should a system in which Knowledge is not the means of salvation be called Gnostic?

19. The Marcionite way of life

The Marcionite community was above all characterized by its austere, puritanical way of life. Since matter was seen as the principle of all evil, the body too was bad and the cause of sin. The worst sin of all consisted in procreation; this was so utterly objectionable because putting children into this world meant helping the Demiurge prolong his reign. The consequence was ruthlessly drawn : no marriage, no children! This was the only way to frustrate the designs of the Demiurge. "He (Marcion) said that marriage meant ruin and would lead the disciples to a more than dog-like life; he intended to grieve the Demiurge in this way, if he could keep away (from him) those were to be born or to be generated by him" [183]. "Marriage is fornication and ruin" [184]; they (the Marcionites) do not wish to replenish the world that was created by the Demiurge" [185]. In consequence, no marriages were contracted in the Marcionite Church. Married people could not be baptized, only celibates and eunuchs; Marcionites who were wedded had to wait for baptism until the partner died or until divorce [186].

Who would be surprised now to hear that the Marcionites practised vegetarianism [187]? However, Marcion allowed his followers to eat fish, this being 'a holier kind of food (i.e. than meat)' [188]. Very probably fish was permitted and considered holier, because the risen Christ only ate fish [189]. As fundamentalist vegetarians they disliked the idea of having to eat at all : "They incriminate the use of food as if it were something shameful" [190]. Not eating at all was, of course, impractical since the Marcionites had no intention to do away with themselves, but the only alternative was 'continuous fasting' [191]. In particular, the Sabbath should be a day of abstinence [192] - this contrary to Jewish and Christian usage. Without doubt there is an element of antinomianism in this.

20. The Marcionite Church

"The aim of Marcion was to found not a school, but a Church". Thus writes McLean, adding that he (Marcion) took the orthodox Church as his model [193]. We are, therefore, fully entitled to speak of a Marcionite Church. This is exceptional in the history of the Gnosis, since all other groups were so loosely organized that we cannot think of them as established, well-defined, and hierarchically led Churches. It was one of the two cases in which the expanding Catholic Church was confronted with a similar organization, the other one being Mani's Church of Justice. Tertullian grudgingly admitted as much : "That gospel (i.e. of Marcion) too had its churches; but they are of its own, of late arrival, and spurious ... Even wasps make combs, and Marcionites make churches" [194].

But naturally Marcion himself did not see it like this. In his opinion his Church was the authentic one; the other was corrupted and had deviated from Jesus' teaching. If there should be talk of 'our holy Mother the Church', this should apply exclusively to his own Church. In proof of this, he referred to a passage in Paul's Letter to the Galatians (4:24-26), where the apostle writes that "Abraham had two sons, one by a bondmaid, and the other by a free woman". Paul explained that the offspring of the bondwoman was the synagogue, viz. Judaism, whereas the other was "our mother, the heavenly Jerusalem". But in Tertullian who is obviously quoting the Marcionite Gospel we read about "our holy Mother the Church in whom we (the Marcionites) have expressed our faith" [195]. If this is correct, then Marcion changed the Pauline text somewhat, for the words 'our Mother' in Galatians refer to 'the heavenly Jerusalem', whereas Marcion applies them to his own Church, while the phrase 'the Church in whom we have expressed our faith' was added by him. His intention is clear : he wanted to apply this text to his own Church. In his view the Catholic Church, as the continuation of Judaism, was the son of the bondwoman.

Candidates became full members of the Marcionite Church by baptism [196]. If we remember that at baptism a vow of celibacy was demanded, we must expect that the great mass of Marcionites consisted of cathechumens, because they were married. The Marcionites celebrated the Eucharist. Marcion, says Tertullian, did not reject "the Creator's bread by which he makes manifest his body" [197]. However, in the chalice there was not wine but water [198], which is a considerable deviation from orthodox practice [199]. Tertullian conceded that in the Marcionite Church too there was "rendering of glory and benediction and praise and hymns", and even "the sacraments of the Church and the pureness of sacrifices" [200]. What struck orthodox Christians as strange was that cathechumens were admitted to the mysteries, and even pagans [201].

There was still more that brings the organization of the Catholic Church to mind. In the Marcionite Church too there were bishops, priests, and deacons, with the ensuing distinction of clergy and laypeople. There was, therefore, a hierarchy, although the distinctions were probably less rigid than in the Catholic Church [202]. Women played a role in the liturgy : they baptized, they taught, they exorcized, but there were no female priests. Harnack wondered at this : if gender had lost its significance for the redeemed, why then could Marcionite women not become priests [203]?

21. The interior history of the Marcionite Church

a. Apelles

Rhodon, an Asiatic who lived in Rome towards the end of the second century, wrote a book 'against Marcion'; this book is lost but Eusebius preserves some scraps of it. This Rhodon, as quoted by Eusebius, wrote that "in his time the (Marcionite) sect split up into several schools of thought" [204]. One thinks in this connection of Apelles, Marcion's most important disciple. Very little is known of his life [205].

Initially this Apelles seems to have flourished in the Marcionite Church, but later he fell out with his master. Tertullian says he had a relation with a woman, and thus "abandoned the cause of chastity" [206]. This may be slander. But it may equally be true. We shall never know. Anyhow, doctrinal differences will have played their role. Apelles left Rome and went to Alexandria whence he returned to the imperial city in later years. In Alexandria, or back in Rome, he associated with a woman called Philumenê [207]. This woman was a visionary [208] whose visions were duly noted and published in a book called 'Phanerooseis', or 'Revelations' [209]; it is lost in its entirety. Apelles himself composed one or more works under the title 'Syllogisms', main thesis of which is that all that Moses wrote of God was wrong [210]. This too is lost.

b. A religious dispute

Apelles obviously had his own ways, for he is mentioned as the head of a separate sect, the Apellicians [211] or Apelleians [212]. This looks like a schism in the Marcionite Church; other communication confirm that this was the case. Several ancient authors state that he seceded from Marcion [213] and even turned against his master [214]. At the end of his life, when he was already an old man, Apelles had a discussion with the Rhodon who was mentioned above, an orthodox Catholic, and a staunch adversary of the Marcionite doctrine. Harnack dubs it "the most important religious dispute in the ancient history of the Church that we possess". He thinks it took place towards the end of the reign of the Emperor Marcus Aurelius (161-180). It seems that the Gnostic age inaugurated the long standing custom of holding religious disputes; we have already heard that Marcion himself broke with the Church after a similar debate with its elders.

After relating that Apelles prided himself somewhat on his great age and on his strict conduct of life, Rhodon reports a sort of declaration of intent by him. Perhaps sensing that his opponent would take him to task on specific points of doctrine, and would quote Scripture against him, Apelles declared there was no need at all to get involved in detailed arguments; instead, everyone should stick to his own creed. He went on to say that those who confessed faith in the crucified one would be saved, if only they were found to have done good deeds.

Perhaps Rhodon had not much to object against this statement, but his adversary then brought other, more controversial points to the fore. He categorically stated that there existed only one principle - "just like we say ourselves", wrote the astonished Rhodon [215]. According to Filastrius, Apelles said that he had no need to learn from Marcion that there were two principles. "I proclaim only one principle that I acknowledge as God" [216]. And according to Epiphanius, he emphatically declared that there were neither three principles nor two but only one, and that this was a good and holy God [217]. What this means is evident : Apelles rejected the radical metaphysical dualism of Marcion.

Pressed by Rhodon, who probably could not believe his ears, to be more specific about this single principle, Apelles shrouded himself in fog. He said that, although he could not defend his position intellectually, he instinctively believed it to be true. He added that the prophecies (the Old Testament) confute themselves, because they tell absolutely nothing that is true; it is all lies and contradictions. Rhodon adjured him to tell the truth, but he retorted that, although he did not **know** how there could be one uncreated God, he believed it. At this, his opponent broke out laughing and accused him of being a teacher who had not mastered his own subject [218].

Both Rhodon and Apelles revealed themselves here as worthy representants of their respective doctrines. As a good Catholic, Rhodon was sceptic about religious intuition and preferred to appeal to Scripture. Apelles, as a good Gnostic, invoked his inner light and was distrustful of systematic theology. Everything that appertained to God, he averred, was intrinsically obscure [219]. This implies that there is nothing in the world that can lead to the knowledge of God; even the Old Testament is valueless in this respect. The only sure thing we have is the inner light [220].

c. Creation

Eusebius has no more to report on this dispute, but from other sources we can glean some additional information about Apelles' ideas. The good God may be his one and only principle, but there is also a Demiurge who, just like Marcion's Creator, is just. There is also a third being, the one who spoke to Moses. And a fourth, the instigator of evil. We should not think of the three lesser beings as gods; Apelles calls them 'angels' [221]. Tertullian [222], however, and Epiphanius [223] do not mention these three lower divinities, but only one, who, incidentallly, is called 'god' by Epiphanius. Perhaps the above mentioned three 'angels' should be seen as aspects of the one God who, at the same time, is the Creator [224].

Apelles thought more mildly of creation than Marcion. According to him, the Demiurge fashioned the cosmos after the model of the higher (= divine) world, but since the result was not really perfect, "repentance was mixed into the world" [225]. This does not necessarily mean that the world was evil but rather that it was leavened with melancholy, since it was not what it should have been.

d. The Bible

Apelles was wholly negative about the Old Testament : "He rejected the Law and the prophets" [226]. "There is", he found, "absolutely no divine wisdom in the writings of Moses; they contain nothing of the work of the Holy

Spirit" [227]. The Old Testament is the work of man, he thought, and entirely mendacious [228]. In this respect, Apelles was just as anti-Jewish as his master. With regard to the New Testament he was less fastidious, but all the same he too was selective. "He made his choice in the Gospels and in the Letters of the Apostle (sc. Paul) and took from them what pleased him" [229].

e. Christ

The Christ of Apelles is the Son of the first god. Appearing 'at the end of the times' [230], he descends from on high to the earth, which means that he is essentially non-human and must be thought of as an aeon, an emanation from the first principle. During his descent downward he assumed an aerial and sidereal body [231]. This means, we are told, that Christ possessed a body made of the four elements [232]. Contrary to Marcion, Apelles said that Christ had a real body, a solid one, although he had not gone through the process of birth; he was not born from the virgin Mary nor from the seed of a man [233]. He based this on the authority of his companion Philumenê who had seen this in the spirit [234].

Apelles attached a great importance to this idea. By stressing the reality of Christ's physical part he sought to evade the objection that could be levelled against Marcion who was a docetist : if Christ had a body only in appearance, how could he have suffered? Wasn't his passion a sham [235]? But by arguing as he did Apelles worked himself into a curious dilemma. His Christ might be really physical but in no case he must adopt his flesh from earthly matter, for this was not held in high regard by him. This dilemma was expressed with great precision by Pseudotertullian who wrote that Christ's body, according to Apelles, neither was a phantasm, as the docetists taught, nor really substantial, as was maintained in the Gospels [236]. It is not easy to detach oneself from a dualistic position!

All the deeds that Christ performed, taught Apelles, were real, just as his passion was real and just as he was really crucified, and not in appearance. In his system there is no laughing Saviour. He rose from the grave and showed himself to his disciples [237]. However, when his redemptive work was completed, he returned to heaven and restored to the spheres the physical elements out of which his body was made. When he finally came back to his father, he was once again a pure spirit [238]. In this way Apelles managed to keep open the dualistic distance between spirit and body which is equivalent to the chasm between the upper and nether worlds.

f. The role of Knowledge

Harnack states categorically that, for Apelles, the work of redemption consisted in the death on the cross which Christ really underwent. But, to be sure, I nowhere found this expressed in so many words. Perhaps rather the contrary. "Christ descended to save those who come to the knowledge of him." Of course, this text recorded by Epiphanius, may imply knowledge of the crucifixion and of its significance, but it seems more probable that the knowledge meant is knowledge of higher things. "He (Christ) taught us the things from above, to despise the Demiurge, and to renounce his works" [239]. It seems to me that the accent is on Knowledge rather than on the cross.

g. The saving of the souls

Only souls will be saved; the bodies will be left behind. The prototype is Christ's shedding his material part before he reached heaven. Likewise the redeemed will have to restore the elements from which they are made to the spheres [240], thereby "loosening the bond of the body" [241]. Only thus can the soul "surge back to the place where it came from" [242]. This last phrase proves that Apelles believed in the pre-existence of souls, a widespread conviction among Gnostics.

His female companion Philumenê taught him that even souls are male or female, and that their gender determines their sex on earth [243]. In all probability souls are emanations of the godhead. They were tempted away from their heavenly abode by the fire-angel who used 'terrestrial food' to lure them away. It is not explained what this food was. What is stated explicitly is that this 'angel of fire' is the God of Israel who enveloped the souls with 'sinful flesh'. This is the Fall, quite a different story from that told in Gen. 3. In his rejection of the institution of marriage Apelles follows Marcion.

h. Apelles' dualism

The great difference between Marcion and Apelles is that the last mentioned did not acknowledge two coeval eternal principles. He has only one. But all the important dualisms are there : that between the first godhead and the Demiurge, the God of Israel, that between the celestial world and the cosmos, and that between body and soul. Whether the dualism between those who 'know' and those who are ignorant forms part of his system too, and whether those who do not 'know' are doomed, does not become clear.

22. Marcionism seen as a threat to the Roman-Catholic Church

a. Orthodoxy at war

To return now to Marcion himself, and more particularly to the Church he founded, the sole fact that so many Fathers of the Church took up arms against him and his doctrine proves that he was fairly successful. All polemical talents in east and west were mobilized to refute him. He was kept under a continuous barrage from ca. A.D. 150, when Justin the Martyr fired the first shots, until the closing volleys of Tertullian around 300. There is a resounding echo of these fireworks in later writings such as those of Epiphanius in the fourth century. The Fathers did not mince matters, expressing themselves, even such otherwise mild men as Clement and Origen, in bitter and contemptuous words. This again shows how dangerous Marcionism was judged [244].

Already around A.D.150 Justin the Martyr was convinced that it was only 'with the help of demons' that Marcionism spread so rapidly [245]. And some seventy years later Tertullian complained that "the heretic tradition of Marcion filled the whole earth" [246]. Epiphanius gives an impressive list of Roman provinces where Marcionite communities existed : not only in Rome where it all began, and in Italy, but also in Egypt and Palestine, in Arabia and Syria, in Cyprus and the Thebais, and even outside the Empire, in Persia. His catalogue is not complete since he adds that such communities were also to be found in other regions [247].

In contrast to other sects of the time, Marcionites did not keep aloof; their churches were open to everyone, even to pagans. This openness, together with the seriousness the Marcionites displayed, impressed many people, even Roman-Catholics. Add to this that the Marcionite ritual in many respects resembled that of the orthodox Church, and it will not amaze us that many Catholics did not see much difference between their services and those of Marcionites [248]. Furthermore, the Marcionites too had bishops and presbyters, just like the Roman-Catholic Church.

"During the generation living between 150 and 190 the danger this Church represented for Christianity was the greatest", to quote Harnack; "in this period it, and it only, was the real counter-Church" [249]. But on the whole, the Roman-Catholic Church made far more converts than its Marcionite counterpart. The Marcionites committed the tactical error of concentrating on orthodox Christians, without bothering much about pagans, as the great Church did. Anyhow, the danger to the Catholic Church seems to have been warded off around 250, whereas in Rome, where there were still Marcionites living at that time, they were no longer seen as a risk.

The Roman Empire, it must be pointed out, was not interested in theological niceties and treated Catholic Christians and Marcionites alike as enemies. "Today all heretics, to wit Manichaeans, Marcionites, Gnostics, and all those who are no Christians, are comprehended by all (i.e. pagans) under the name of Christians" [250]. In consequence, there were many Marcionite martyrs [251].

b. A longer life in the east

In the east they enjoyed a longer span of life. Marcionites suffered in the persecutions of the Emperors Valerian (253-260) and Diocletian (284-313/316) [252]. When the Emperor Constantine the Great in January 313 decided to make an end of the age-old imperial policy of persecuting the Christians, the Marcionites profited as much as anybody. In the village of Deir Ali, three miles south of Damascus, an inscription was found (the oldest inscription on a church we have, writes Harnack) which said that this was a temple of the Marcionites; it is dated, and so we know the year was 318/319 [253].

Syria was one of the regions where they prospered, Palestine another, and also Cyprus where they seem to have been extremely numerous. But soon the Roman authorities began to frown upon them, since they came to understand that Marcionites were schismatics or heretics, and, in any case, did not follow the line of official orthodoxy. Not long after the liberating measures of Constantine the government began to persecute the sect; Constantine (who, by the way, was not a baptized Christian) forbade their gatherings, even in private houses, closed their temples, and confiscated their books [254]. This, slowly but surely, suppressed the Marcionite communities, at least in the cities. In the country, where the Roman arm was not so long, they managed to hold their own for a long time. Bishop Theodoretus of Cyrus who was the very last Greek author to polemize against the sect, boasts that he has converted thousands of Marcionites in eight villages somewhere in the Euphrates region; this happened in the first half of the fifth century [255]. In about the same period Eznik of Kolb deemed it necessary to combat them in Armenia.

A slightly unsavoury anecdote related by Theodoretus proves that in his lifetime there existed still deeply convinced Marcionites. He knew a man, he wrote, of some ninety years old who, when he got up in the morning, used to wash his face with his own saliva (sic). Asked why he did this, he responded that he did not want to have anything to do with the Demiurge's works; since water belonged to these works, he would not utilize it. Then some people who stood around him said : "How then can you eat and drink and clothe yourself and sleep and fulfil the customary mysteries?" (what they meant was that in the Marcionite ritual bread and water was used - F.). His answer was that he was "forced to do this, since he had to live" [256].

c. What made Marcionism so attractive

Harnack asks himself what made the Marcionite doctrine so attractive to numerous people; he adds that our sources offer nothing to inform us on this point. Perhaps it was, he thought, the concept of the existence of an exclusively good god (which means that he in no way could be made responsible for evil - F.), together with the rejection of the Old Testament, then again an ascetism that promised to make ordinary people superhuman, and, finally, the grim abhorrence of the 'world'.

Let me add that the fierce dualism in Marcion's doctrine was also a source of attraction. Ethical dualism has the great advantage of strictly separating good and evil from each other. Whereas in ordinary life they are almost inextricably intermingled, in ethical dualism each has its own domain, its own 'chasse gardée'. From a superficial viewpoint this seems to make life much more tolerable. At the same time, this dualism in the long run proved the undoing of Marcionism. Most people are much too realistic to believe that there can be good without evil, and too much down-to-earth to despise the 'world'. Instead of a dualistic vision they prefer a 'holistic' one. This was offered them by the Catholic Church that proclaims its 'holism' in its proper name, Catholic = 'kat'holên (gên)', over the whole (earth). For these reasons the Marcionite Church finally proved no match for the Roman-Catholic one.

23. The relationship of the Catholic and Marcionite Churches

It will be evident that the relationship of the two Churches was dualistic in nature. What obtains here is that it was a relative dualism; the Marcionite

Church, with regard to organization and hierarchy, to a certain extent was dependent on the Catholic one. But Marcion virtually saw the latter as a non-Church, hardly different from Judaism. Because the Catholic Church stuck to the Old Testament, the book of a false god, it was in Marcion's view just as reprehensible as Judaism.

Harnack had idiosyncratic ideas on the relationship of both Churches. His admiration for Marcion and his originality in theology knew no bounds; it reached its pinnacle when he discussed the impact Marcion was supposed to have had on the Roman-Catholic Church. One could even say that, in the view of this great German scholar, there really was no such Church before ca. A.D. 150. In his opinion what used to be called orthodox Christianity consisted at that time of loosely connected and loosely organized communities that were none too sure of their peculiar theology. Only the Old Testament existed in a scriptural form. About the composition of the New Testament there was much confusion. Some local Churches, but by no means all of them, acknowledged the four Gospels, but nobody considered that the Pauline Letters, for instance, were as canonical as the Gospels. "From where could the authority to create a New Testament have come?"

Marcion, to follow Harnack's argument further, saw the necessity of uniting the dispersed Christian communities into a definite organization. In other words, he initiated the concept of a universal, really 'catholic' Church. In this way he saved Christianity from dissolving into the ideological currents of that age (mainly Gnostic) or from merging with Judaism. Furthermore, he was the first to establish a real biblical canon, albeit an extremely short one, and to make a very clear distinction between what was canonical and what was not. He pointed out how important Paul's theology was, in particular his soteriology, his doctrine of redemption.

In all these respects, thought Harnack, the Roman-Catholic Church was the imitator; to a certain extent it may be seen as an epiphenomenon of the Marcionite Church. The orthodox Church threatened to be swamped by triumphant Marcionism. In order to defend itself, orthodox Christianity "had to adopt - and, indeed, did adopt - everything of Marcion, with the exception of the basic religious concept" (by which Marcion's ditheism is meant). His influence was "the decisive impulse for the creation of the Catholic Church". To remain on an equal footing with Marcionism this Church too had to come forward with a biblical canon of its own. Finally, it had to acknowledge the significance of Pauline theology and make it is own [257].

However, in one more important respect the Roman-Catholic Church did not follow Marcion : it did not reject the Old Testament. Greatly as Harnack admired Marcion, he found his antinomianism with regard to almost every biblical book a mistake, at least to a certain extent. "To reject the Old Testament in the second century A.D.", he wrote, "was an error that the great Church was rightly averse to." This rejection he went on to say, meant cutting off every link with the Christian religion. This severing was so unhistorical and, at the same time, so confusing in respect of religion, that the Church instinctively and rightly took into the bargain all the difficulties that the integral reception of the Old Testament might bring with it. Anything was better than the historical vacuum for which Marcion's action was responsible [258].

Nowadays nobody fully accepts Harnack's bold theses. On the other hand, there is no denying that Marcion exercised a certain influence on the shaping of the Catholic Church, just as the Reformation left its traces in the Catholic world. But I do not believe that his influence on the structuring of Roman-Catholicism has been really great. Apart from the fact that "Marcionism failed to win the whole Mediterranean world and become the dominant, universal Church" [259], it did not give the great Church its structures, but took them over from its rival.

Greater, perhaps, was Marcion's influence on the development of the biblical canon, that is to say, on that of the New Testament, since the Old Testament was rejected in its entirety by him. That Pauline Letters were in use in the earliest Church is proved by 2 Peter 3:15-16, where its author mentions them. In the first half of the second century a large part of the New Testament was judged to be as normative as the Old Testament. However, the Marcionite canon undoubtedly was the first of its kind and may have incited the Catholic Church to become more precise on this point. The existence of so many apocryphal Gospels, Acts of Apostles, Apocalypses, and Apostolic Letters played its role too. In conclusion, we may state with Blackman that "it is extravagant to pronounce him (Marcion), as Harnack does, the creator of the Catholic canon" [260].

Greater still may have been Marcion's influence when he stressed the importance of Paul's soteriology. But Blackman rightly says that "other elements in Marcion's version of the Gospel would have filled the Apostle with horror - Marcion's docetism, dualism, and his rejection of the Old Testament" [261]. On these points he surely did not do justice to Paul's theology. For this reason, some modern scholars think that "Marcion did not find his main thoughts in Paul, but rather assimilated Pauline theology to them" [262].

For us, however, the interest in Marcion that is displayed in this chapter, and the space devoted to him, his doctrine, and his Church, is the consequence of his radical dualism, in which the great Church, sure enough, did not follow him.

NOTES TO CHAPTER II

1. Harnack, Marcion 3*.
2. All the sources relating to Marcion, his doctrine, and his sect have been neatly assembled by Harnack, Marcion, in which the pages with the sources are marked with an asterix.
3. Ir., Adv.haer. 3.3.4.
4. Harnack's commentary Marcion 3/4.
5. Clem.Al, Strom. 7.107.1.
6. Clem.Al., Strom. 7.106.1.
7. Harnack, Marcion 15*.
8. Epiph., Panarion 3.42.2.
9. Eus., Hist.eccl. 5.13.2; Pseudotert., De praescript. 30.1; Tert., Adv.Marc. 5.1. Eus. reads 'nautês' = sailor, but Tert. has 'nauclerus' = master of a ship.
10. Epiph., Panarion 42.1.

11. It is possible that Epiph. found this story in the lost 'Syntagma' of Hippolytus, Harnack, Marcion 24*. It is also mentioned in Eznik of Kolb, Wider die Irrlehren 4.16 (written 441-449).
12. Epiph., Panarion 42.1.
13. É. Amann s.v. 'Marcion', Dict.théol.cath. 9.2, 2016. Paris, 1927.
14. Harnack, Marcion 23 and 26*.
15. Pseudotert., De praescript. 44.
16. Hranack, Marcion 24 and 28*.
17. Papias, Prologus 2.
18. Harnack, Marcion 13/14.
19. See Harnack, Marcion, 27* note 1, and 29*/30*.
20. The report of Epiph., Panarion 42.1 that M. arrived in Rome 'after the death of Hyginus', i.e. after A.D. 142, can hardly be correct.
21. Tert., Adv.Marc. 4.4; Pseudotert., De praescript. 30.
22. Harnack, Marcion 26. The statement by Epiphanius, Panarion 41.1, that M. went straight to the elders of the Church but was turned away by them does not tally with their acceptance of the money gift.
23. Lc. 6:43.
24. Tert., Adv.Marc. 2.
25. Mt. 9:16-17; Lc. 5:36-37.
26. Harnack, Marcion 26.
27. Epiph., Panarion 42.2.
28. Tert., Adv.Marc. 4.3; Pseudotert., De praescript. 30. Harnack, Marcion 27*, categorically states that "this dramatic scene is in no way credible". As so often I wonder at the clairvoyance of German scholars. They always exactly know, for instance, what Jesus said or rather what he did not say. How does Harnack know that these words were not spoken? Was he present perhaps? I see absolutely no reason why Marcion could not have flown into a rage after a hot discussion and have uttered this phrase. It seems perfectly natural, the more so since Harnack himself admits that the proceedings of the Synod had taken a dramatic turn.
29. Tert., De carne 2.
30. This statement is based on a communication by Tert., Adv.marc. 1.19, in which he says that between Christ and Marcion 115 years and 6 1/2 months elapsed. Harnack, Marcion 20*/21*, has studied this in depth and thinks that we must start from the fifteenth year of the Emperor Tiberius = A.D. 29. According to Lc. 3:1, Jesus began his public life in that year. If we take this as the starting-point, then we arrive at the second half of July 144. "This can only be the year of the complete breach of Marcion with the Church and the foundation of his own Church based on a new biblical canon, Harnack, Marcion 20*. This chronology has been the subject of critical discussion, but Blackman, a

modern scholar, believes that Harnack's is "still the best reconstruction", Marcion 21.

31. Harnack, Marcion 21*.
32. Blackman, Marcion 3; Harnack, Marcion 27.
33. Just., Ap. 1.26.
34. Blackman, Marcion 3.
35. Bousset, Hauptprobl. 109.
36. See Bibliography.
37. For Plato see Vol. III, Ch. III.22, and for John Vol. VII, Ch. IV.5b.
38. Epiph, Panarion 41.1; Filastrius, Div.haer. 44.
39. Ir., Adv.haer. 3.4.3; Cyprianus, Ep. LXIIII.2. G. Bardy Dict.hist.géogr.eccl. 12, 162 (Paris, 1953) says that his coming to Rome is the best attested fact in his life.
40. Ir., Adv.haer. 3.4.3.
41. Pseudotert., Adv.haer. 6.1; Epiph., Panarion 41.1; Filastrius, Div.haer. 44,45.
42. Harnack, Marcion 33*-39*.
43. Ir., Adv.haer. 3.2.2.
44. Ir., Adv.haer. 3.13.2.
45. Tert., Adv.Marc. 4.3.4.
46. Tert., Adv.Marc. 4.11.1.
47. Tert., Adv.Marc. 4.3.4.
48. Tert., Adv.Marc. 4.3.5.
49. Gal. 1:12.
50. Tert., Adv.Marc. 4.2.4.
51. Harnack, Marcion 41/42.
52. Gal. 1:12.
53. Blackman, Marcion 43.
54. Lc. 19:28-46.
55. Lc. 20:9-18.
56. Lc. 21:1:17.
57. See for this passage first and foremost Harnack's founding text, Marcion 52-61; useful and shorter Blackman, Marcion 45-47, and Ernest Evans' Appendix 2 in his translation of Tert., Adv.Marc., vol. 2, 643-644. The texts in this book from Tert., Adv.Marc., are borrowed from Evans' translation.
58. Blackman, Marcion 43.

59. See Harnack, Marcion 45-51; Blackman, Marcion 44-45; Evans 644-646.
60. Harnack, Marcion 36.
61. Harnack, Marcion 74.
62. Tert., Adv.Marc. 4.1.15. The remains of the Antitheses have been assembled by the indefatigable Harnack, Marcion, Beilage V, 256-313.
63. Tert., Adv.Marc. 1.19.4.
64. Tert., Adv.Marc. 4..6.1.
65. Harnack, Marcion 30.
66. Harnack, Marcion 31.
67. Tert., Adv.Marc. 1.19.4-5.
68. Tert., Adv.Marc. 4.6.3.
69. Tert., Adv.Marc. 2.29.4.
70. Tert., Adv.Marc. 1.6.1.
71. Blackman, Marcion 66.
72. According to Blackman, Marcion 71-73, Marcion's dualism should not be termed 'metaphysical'. "His dualism was not offered as a new theory of the universe nor as a contribution to the philosophy of religion. It was the expression of what were to him the fundamental facts of life ... (He) saw two principles at work in the universe. The first is the principle of Justice and Law, inherent in the universe and in fact the originator of it ... The second principle intervenes and overrules Justice; we may call it Grace and Redeeming Love." It may be correct that Marcion started from 'the fundamental facts of life', but what other label must we attach to the end-product, the two principles governing the universe, than 'metaphysical'?
73. Tert., Adv.Marc. 1.3.2-5.
74. Tert., Adv.Marc. 4.4.1.
75. Tert., Adv.Marc. 4.33.4.
76. Tert., Adv.Marc. 1.11.9; 2.2.3; 5.18.11.
77. Ir., Adv.haer. 4.33.2.
78. Ir., Adv.haer. 1.27.2.
79. Tert., Adv.Marc. 4.7.1.
80. Tert., Adv.Marc. 1.21.1.
81. Tert., Adv.Marc. 4.27.1.
82. Tert., Adv.Marc. 2.7.3.
83. Tert., Adv.Marc. 2.27.1.
84. Tert., Adv.Marc. 1.11.9.
85. Tert., Adv.Marc. 1.7.2.

86. Tert., Adv.Marc. 1.1.3.
87. Tert., Adv.Marc. 1.6.1.
88. Tert., Adv.Marc. 1.15.4.
89. Tert., Adv.Marc. 5.19.7.
90. Theodoret., Haer.fab. 1.24 (315).
91. Eznik of Kolb, Wider die Irrlehren 4.1.
92. Clem.Al., Strom. 3.12.1.
93. Clem.Al., Strom. 4.7.45.5.
94. Hom. 2.43.
95. Harnack, Marcion 100.
96. Harnack, Marcion 101.
97. Harnack, Marcion 105.
98. Ir., Adv.haer. 3.23.6.
99. Tert., Adv.Marc. 2.19.1.
100. Tert., Adv.Marc. 5.5.10.
101. Rom. 2:12-13.
102. Rom. 2:20.
103. Rom. 7:12.
104. Harnack, Marcion 108/109.
105. Harnack, Marcion 111.
106. Harnack, Marcion 113/114.
107. Harnack, Marcion 116.
108. Tert., Adv.Marc. 3.20.3.
109. Harnack, Marcion 117.
110. Blackman, Marcion 118.
111. Blackman, Marcion 119/120.
112. Blackman, Marcion 119/120.
113. Blackman, Marcion 120.
114. Tert., Adv.Marc. 1.29.5.
115. Tert., Adv.Marc. 1.11.7; see also 4.21.10.
116. Tert., Adv.Marc. 2.9.1.
117. Tert., Adv.Marc. 1.8.1.
118. Tert., Adv.Marc. 1.9.1.
119. Tert., Adv.Marc. 5.16.3.
120. Tert., Adv.Marc. 5.4.3.

121. Tert., Adv.Marc. 1.16.1.
122. Tert., Adv.Marc. 1.15.1-2.
123. Tert., Adv.Marc. 1.15.2.
124. Tert., Adv.Marc. 1.15.2.
125. Harnack, Marcion 265*.
126. Harnack, Marcion 119.
127. Ir., Adv.haer. 3.7.1.
128. Tert., Adv.Marc. 4.36.3.
129. Tert., Adv.Marc. 1.23.3.
130. Harnack, Marcion 121.
131. Tert., Adv.Marc. 5.11.3.
132. Tert., Adv.Marc. 1.17.1.
133. Harnack, Marcion 122.
134. Tert., Adv.Marc. 1.2.2.
135. Mt. 5:17,18.
136. Tert., Adv.Marc. 5.14.14.
137. Tert., Adv.Marc. 4.36.11.
138. Ir., Adv.haer. 1.27.2.
139. Ir., Adv.haer. 4.13.1.
140. Tert., Adv.Marc. 4.8.3.
141. Harnack, Marcion 125.
142. Tert., Adv.Marc. 3.10.2.
143. Tert., De carne 3.
144. R.S. Wilson, Marcion VIII : "Marcion, from his own experience, decided that God was very like Jesus Christ; in fact, so like that the two could be differentiated in name only."
145. É. Amann s.v. 'Marcion', Dict.Théol.Cath. 9.2.,2021. Paris, 1927.
146. Tert., Adv.Marc. 4.17.12.
147. Harnack, Marcion 127.
148. Adamantius, Dialogus 2.45.
149. Blackman, Marcion 100.
150. Adamantius, Dialogus 2.45.
151. Tert., De carne 4.3.
152. Gen. 9:6.
153. Eznik of Kolb, Wider die Irrlehren 4.1.8-9.

154. 2Cor. 12:2-4.
155. Adamantius, Dialogus 2.37.
156. Adamantius, Dialogus 2.31.
157. Tert., Adv.Marc. 1.24.2.
158. Tert., Adv.Marc. 4.26.10-11.
159. Tert., Adv.Marc. 5.15.1.
160. Ir., Adv.haer. 1.17.3; Theodoret., Haer.fab. 1.24; Epiph., Panarion 1.42.4.
161. Epiph., Panarion 1.42.4.
162. Ir., Adv.haer. 1.27.3.
163. Tert., Adv.Marc. 3.9.4.
164. Tert., Adv.Marc. 3.9.4.
165. Tert., Adv.Marc. 1.24.7.
166. Tert., Adv.Marc. 1.27.1.
167. Harnack, Marcion 139.
168. Tert., Adv.Marc. 1.28.1.
169. Eznik of Kolb, Wider die Irrlehren 4.10.
170. Bianchi, Marcion 141.
171. 1Cor. 7:1.
172. 1Cor. 7:7.
173. 2Cor. 4:4.
174. 2Cor. 7:3.
175. Bousset, Hauptprobl. 109.
176. In a recent work Hoffmann, Marcion (see Bibliography), the author presents a 'Hellenistic matrix' as the general context into which Marion's system must be placed (Chapter 1). However, in this Hellenistic matrix, he writes (p. 5), Irano-Babylonian and Jewish influences were active, creating in Pontus "a religious climate of a distinctly pluralistic variety". In that country, "where the Asiatic influence was especially strong owing to the Iranian-Babylonian provenance of the inhabitants, this religious syncretism naturally assumed the character of theological dualism." But Hoffmann does not speak here of Zoroastrianism and Zervanism but of Mithraism. This ideology must have been powerful in Pontus, as the often used royal name 'Mithridates' proves (p. 11). But then he adds that "Anatolian Mithraism was limited in its appeal, and attracted chiefly members of the military class" or the court (p. 12). Now Marcion was neither a soldier nor a courtier. Hoffmann weakens his own argument by stating (p. 13) that "the cosmogony of Mithraism is obscure, but bears some resemblance in its Anatolian variety to that of Zoroastrianism". He suggests further (p. 23) that "Marcion's understanding of baptism was not altogether unlike that which obtained in the

Hellenistic mysteries, and especially in the cult of Mithra". He does not mention the term 'dualism' in this context, which is no wonder since Mithraism is a sacrificial cult rather than an elaborate theology. Anyhow, Hoffmann's remarks with regard to a possible link between Marcion and Iranian dualism are not very conclusive, to say the least of it.

177. See Vol. VII, Ch. VI.4b and c.

178. See, apart from this volume, Vol. VIII.

179. See Vol. III, Ch. III, and Vol. VI, Ch. III.

180. Bianchi, Marcion 141.

181. As she did in the Introduction of her book 'Le Dieu séparé' (see Bibliography).

182. Bianchi, Marcion 142.

183. Hipp., Ref. 10.9.4.

184. Ir., Adv.haer. 1.28.1.

185. Clem.Al., Strom. 3.3.12.1.

186. Tert., Adv.Marc. 4.11.8.

187. Eznik of Kolb, Wider die Irrlehren 4.12.

188. Tert., Adv.Marc. 1.14.4.

189. Eznik, Wider die Irrlehren 4.12.

190. Theodorus of Mopsuesta, Commentarium in 1 Tim. 4.1. sqq, quoted by Harnack, Marcion 278*.

191. Tert., De ieiuniis 15.

192. Epiph., Panarion 42..3.3.

193. N. McLean s.v. 'Marcionism'. Enc.Rel.Eth. 8, 408. Edinburgh, 1915.

194. Tert., Adv.Marc. 4.5.3.

195. Tert., Adv.Marc. 5.4.8.

196. Tert., Adv.Marc. 1.14.3. During the third century A.D. a conflict raged in the Catholic Church with regard to the rebaptism of repentant heretics, among them Marcionites. The African Church, in particular its spokesman Saint Cyprian, argued that sectarian baptism was not valid so that converts from heresy had to be rebaptized, or rather, to be baptized. Contrary to this opinion, Pope Stephen I (254-257) decreed that such converts need not be (re)baptized; only an imposition of hands was necessary (as a sign of reconciliation), S.Stephani decretoriae sententiae II.

197. Tert., Adv.Marc. 1.14.3.

198. Epiph., Panarion 42.3.

199. According to Roman-Catholic theology, a consecration of water instead of wine is not valid.

200. Tert., Adv.Marc. 3.23.6-7.

201. Epiph., Panarion 42.3.4.
202. Tert., De praescript. 41.
203. Harnack, Marcion 147.
204. Eus., Hist.eccl. 5.1.3.
205. The ancient sources referring to Apelles are to be found in Harnack, Marcion, Beilage VIII. See also the article by G. Bareille s.v. 'Apelles', Dict.théol.cath. 1,1455-1457. Paris, 1923.
206. Tert., De praescript. 30 and 41.
207. Pseudotert., De praescript. 30, adds that she was 'a frightful prostitute'. Could he have been thinking here of the association of Simon the Magician with the harlot Helen (see my Vol. VII, Ch. III.1d)?
208. Eus., Hist.eccl. 5.13, calls her 'demoniacal'.
209. Pseudotert., De praescript. 30; Theodoret., Haer.fab. 1.25. mentions this book as 'Prophecy'.
210. Pseudotert., De praescript. 41; Origenes, In Genesim homilia 2.2., says : "There was no divine wisdom in these writings". Only one fragment survives in Ambrosius, De Paradiso 5.28.
211. Tert., De carne 8.
212. Epiph., Panarion 44.1.
213. Pseudotert., Adv.haer. 6.
214. Epiph., Panarion 44.1.
215. Eus., Hist.eccl. 5.13.5.
216. Filastrius, Adv.haer. 19.1-2.
217. Epiph., Panarion 44.1.
218. Eus., Hist.eccl. 5.13.6.
219. Eus., Hist.eccl. 5.13.5.
220. See for this whole passage Harnack, Marcion 183/184.
221. Hipp., Ref. 7.38.
222. Tert., De praescript. 51.
223. Epiph., Panarion 44.1.
224. G. Bareille s.v. 'Apelles', Dict.théol.cath. 1.2, 1456. Paris, 1923.
225. Pseudotert., Adv.haer. 6.
226. Pseudotert., Adv.haer. 6.
227. Origenes, Homilia in Gen. 2.2.
228. Pseudotert., Adv.haer. 6; Hipp.. Ref. 38.
229. Hipp., Ref. 7.38.
230. Epiph., Panarion 44.2.

231. Pseudotert., Adv.haer. 6.
232. Filastrius, Adv.haer. 47; Epiph., Panarion 44.2.
233. Epiph., Panarion 44.2; Hipp., Ref. 7.10.20.2.
234. Tert., De carne 6.
235. Harnack, Marcion 189.
236. Pseudotert., Adv.haer. 6.
237. Hipp. 7.38.4-5; Epiph., Panarion 44.2.
238. Epiph., Panarion 44.2; Hipp., Ref. 7.38.5.
239. Epiph., Panarion 44.2.
240. Epiph., Panarion 44.2.
241. Hipp., Ref. 7.38.5.
242. Epiph., Panarion 44.2.
243. Tert., De anima 36.
244. É. Amann s.v. 'Marcion. Histoire du Marcionisme'. Dict.de théol.cath. 9.2, 2026. Paris, 1927.
245. Just., Ap. 1.26.
246. Tert., Adv. Marc. 5.19.2.
247. Epiph., Panarion 42.1.
248. Harnack, Marcion 144/145.
249. Harnack, Marcion 154.
250. Epiph., Panarion 21.6.6.
251. Eus., Hist.eccl. 5.16.21.
252. Eus., Hist.eccl. 5.14.40, 5.16.21, 7.12.
253. Harnack, Marcion 341*-344*.
254. Eus., De vita Constant. 3.64-66.
255. Theodoret., Ep. 81C, 113C, 145B.
256. Theodoret., Haer.fab. 1.24.
257. R.S. Wilson, Marcion VIII, remained true to the line taken by Harnack by stating that Marcion "compelled the church to make up its mind as what exactly is believed, and so to take the important step of formulating a creed and a canon."
258. Harnack, Marcion 211-217. Further on Harnack wrote that the problem posed by Marcion cropped up again in the sixteenth century when Luther on his part saw an opposition between law and Gospel (pp. 218/219). In Harnack's opinion Marcion's stance still forms a challenge for Christianity. He sees the Roman-Catholic Church obviously as hopeless in this respect, but he expects an answer from Protestantism. This answer should not be the total rejection of the Old Testament but

the denial of its canonical status (p. 223). In other words, the Old Testament must be relegated to the position of an ordinary human book with a religious impact.

259. Blackman, Marcion 126.
260. Blackman, Marcion 126.
261. Blackman, Marcion 107.
262. Blackman, Marcion 110.

CHAPTER III

MANDA, THAT IS, KNOWLEDGE

1. Mandaeans forever!

"The reader may be astonished that such an insignificant sect (as the Mandaeans) that, apart from its sacraments, has nothing special, has attracted the attention of a fascinated scholarship for so long" [1]. Thus wrote Puech. But there is an easy explanation for this spell. All Gnostic-dualistic sects perished already in Antiquity, with the one exception of the great and important religion of Mani that, however, was not to survive the Middle Ages. To this rule of general extinction there is one notable exception, that of the sect of the Mandaeans. Kurt Rudolph, the great expert on Mandaeism, describes them as "the last living representative of this gnostic religion, which played an important role in the first centuries after Christ" [2]. Their Gnostic origin is expressed by the term with which they refer to themselves : 'mandayye' ('Mandai') = those who know, for the word 'manda' means 'knowledge [3].

We find them to-day, to the number of some fifteen thousand, mainly in Lower Iraq, but also in Baghdad and in Kurdistan; there are other Mandaean settlements in Iran, east of Lower Iraq, along the river Karun in the south-western province of Khuzestan [4]. The great majority of the Mandaeans live, therefore, in a geographical continuum, although they are separated by the frontier between Iraq and Iran. Their favourite professions are those of silversmiths, blacksmiths, and boatbuilders; they dwell preferably along waterways. They do not resemble other Iraqis; their complexion is much lighter. One wonders how they, being so different in exterior and religion, fare under the repressive regime of Saddam Hussein, in particular if we take into account how he is treating the Shi'ites in Lower Iraq whose only fault is that they are not Sunnites like himself. The forty-eight plates in Rudolph's book 'Mandaeism', together with those in Lady Drower's book 'The Mandaeans', give us a first impression of what these people look like, and of their rituals. These illustrations demonstrate specifically the central place of baptism in their cult; in fact, they are known as 'Subba' = Baptists [5]. Formally, however, they refer to themselves as 'Mandai' [6].

2. The Mandaeans discovered

Totally unknown to the western world during the Middle Ages [7], Mandaeism was 'discovered' by Portuguese missionaries visiting the east in the seventeenth century. They brought back to Europe a number of Mandaean texts to Europe, but for the time being scant attention was paid to them. It was only in the nineteenth century that Mandaean documents began to be published. Really satisfying text editions and translations had to wait until this century; these publications made possible expert study on Mandaeism [8].

3. The origin of Mandaeism

a. The Jordan region

Where do the Mandaeans hail from? Certain elements in Mandaean literature and mythology point westward [9], more particularly allusions to 'Yardna' in which one easily detects the name of the river Jordan. Mandaeans call all streaming water 'Jordan'; only such water is appropriate for baptism [10]. In hearing the word Jordan one's eyes turn, of course, to the actual river of that name; the frequency of its use in Mandaean texts at least suggests that there is a connection between it and the Mandaean sect far to the east. "As long as there is no better explanation", writes Rudolph, "one cannot brush aside the suggestion that there is a historical recollection in the use of Jordan by the Mandaeans" [11]. Later this scholar was ready to express himself in a more emphatic way. He then stated that 'clear connections with the baptismal sects in the eastern Jordan regions and with early Syrian Christianity, as well as several striking West Syrian elements in the Mandaean language and in Mandaean mythology ..., confirm our thesis that the Mandaeans originated in the West" [12].

Rudolph was thinking of the West-Syrian region as the birthplace of the Mandaean sect. Many other scholars agree with him in this, arguing for an origin in pre-Christian days; others plead for a Judaeo-Christian origin, whereas still others see it as an offshoot of Babylonian folk religion. Finally, Drower proposes a Persian 'Heimat'. An 'embarras du choix' between far distant locations! The two greatest experts differ widely, since Rudolph is for West-Syria and Drower for Iran. Shall we ever know?

Wherever the Mandaeans may hail from, in the third century A.D. we find them in Mesopotamia. Further back in time their history they cannot be traced, which does not mean that Mandaeism would not be older than the third century. The rise of Christianity just as that of the Islam later on, presented a great problem for them, so that it is possible that they found a refuge in the marshes of the Euphrates-Tigris estuary. Some of them emigrated to the adjoining region of Iran [13].

b. A connection with John the Baptist?

It is an old idea that the Mandaeans descend fom the followers of John the Baptist; their 'discoverers', the Portuguese priests, accordingly called them 'Christians of St. John' [14]. This seems to be an erroneous idea since Mandaean texts do not mention the Baptist as the prophet or founder of the sect [15]. Rudolph categorically states that "John and his group of disciples, according to what is said in the sources, do not have a relationship to the Mandaeans" [16] nor is his name pronounced during the baptismal ritual [17].

All the same, Lady Drower, in the days of the British mandate in Iraq, "sometimes saw a board (viz. on a silver-shop in Baghdad) announcing the proprietor to be a 'St. John Christian'". When asked about their faith the Mandaeans will reply : "John is our prophet like Jesus or Muhammad is yours". Lady Drower, however, adds that "John the Baptist (Yuhana, or Yahya Yuhana) could not with accuracy be described as 'their prophet'" [18]. Nevertheless, in Mandaean teaching John occupies a place of his own, as a great teacher and priest; "he was a Nasurai [19], that is an adept in the faith, skilled in the white magic of the priests and concerned largely with the healing of men's bodies as well as their souls" [20].

c. Mandaeans and Christ

Just as the name of John the Baptist in the term 'St. John's Christians', should not made us think of him as the founder of the Mandaean sect, the word 'Christian' must not lead us astray. Although, as Loisy writes, "the great persecutor of Mandaeism was Islam, their great hatred, nevertheless, was directed towards Christianity" [21]. Mandaeans show very little sympathy with Christianity. It would be entirely wrong to consider Mandaeism a derivative from early Christianity. The Mandaean sources speak in the most unfriendly way of Christ who in the texts is referred to as 'Yshu Mshiha' = Jesus Messiah. He has no divine origin nor was he conceived by the virgin Mary. Instead, his mother is 'Ruha' who may be characterized as 'the Breath of Physical Life'; she is also the mother of the seven planets [22]. He was, however, born from Mary, after having entered her womb as an almost fully-developed foetus of nine months old.

He became the false prophet of the Jews who distorted the Torah and deceived his people by saying : "I am the true God sent down by my Father ... I am the Father, I am the Son, I am the Holy Ghost" (in the New Testament Jesus never said anything of this kind). He held the Jews captive by magic and deceit [23]. All evil in the world stems from him [24]. In short, Jesus "was a rebel, a heretic who led men astray, betrayed secret doctrines, and made religion easier (i.e. flouted the elaborate and difficult rules of purification - F.)". He occupies "the first rank among the prophets of error" [25]. "The references to Christ ... are, in fact, entirely polemical" [26].

d. Mandaeans and Christianity

Mandaean sources show no higher regard for Christianity itself. The Christian Church was founded by Ruha [27]. Christians disagree among each other and, in consequence, are liars [28]. Christian baptism is a sacrament of indignity [29], the Eucharist 'the bread of shame' [30]. "They (the Christians) leave their homes and become monks and nuns. They withhold their seed from one another, the women from the men and the men from the women". Nothwithstanding their being abstinent, they become pregnant by liliths (= female demons), that is, from their seed come "spirits and fauns who swoop down on human beings" [31].

While their celibacy counts against the inhabitants of the monasteries, Christian lay-people are accused of profligacy. At the instigation of Christ (sic), "men run after the women, women after the men ... He (Christ) brings fornication, adultery, whoredom, lechery, and passion over men and women, over young men and virgins" [32]. Enough to show that, first of all, the Mandaeans must not be seen as some sort of Christian sect, and, second, that their attitude to Christianity should be considered dualistic.

e. Mandaeans and Jewry

Not that Judaism comes off much better. This is all the more remarkable, thinks Rudolph, since Mandaeism is rooted in it [33]; however, he admits that this root may have been a heretical Jewish sect [34]. Elsewhere this scholar states that Mandaeism is a split off from official Judaism [35]. He duly enumerates the Jewish elements occurring in Mandaean religion [36]. At the same time, he admits that "evidently a large part of the Old Testament stories have mostly been distorted (by the Mandaeans) in an absurd way" [37]. When I read that "in no account one can speak, in Mandaeism, of a strict Jewish monotheism" [38], then I can only assume that the Jewish sect from which Mandaeism is supposedly derived, must have been exceedingly heretical indeed [39]!

If Judaism really is the religious backdrop of the Mandaeans, they did not prove very grateful to their spiritual ancestors. "It is clear that Mandaeism considered the Jewish Bible more or less as Marcion considered it, not as a really divine book but as a false revelation, the work of an inferior god" [40]. Rudolph blandly writes that "the abysmal hatred against Judaism that penetrates all layers of Mandaean literature ..., is very characteristically Mandaean" [41].

Quite another, in fact antinomian story is "the assertion (by the Mandaeans) that the Egyptians were (their) co-religionists", and that the ancestors of the Mandaeans came from Egypt. Lady Drower says that 'yearly a ritual meal is eaten in memory of the Egyptian hosts who perished in the waters when following the wicked Jews" [42]. Jewish origin or not, the attitude of the Mandaeans towards the Jews is as inimical and dualistic as their idea of the Christians. I feel that Loisy is correct in stating conclusively that, "with regard to the Jewish origin (of Mandaeism), we know that Mandaean religion fundamentally contradicts it, since it is essentially dualistic and not monotheistic" [43].

4. The myth of Mandaean origin

Like all Gnostics, the Mandaeans were not interested in history, not even in their own history [44]. Their literature does not inform us about their origin, earliest history, and migrations. There is a Mandaean legend [45] which says that the Subba are 'the true children of Adam and Eve' and originally lived in Serandib = Ceylon. Their descendants came in the ark of "Noh' (= Noah) to Egypt. In addition to his three well-known biblical sons, Noah had a fourth, called Sam. Sam and his wife became the progenitors of the Mandai.

Six thousand years later the Beni Israiil (= the Jews) had a king with the name of Musa (= Moses). This Musa was against the Mandai and quarrelled with them in Egypt. Thereupon a Mandai chief led his people out of Egypt, dry-shod through the Red Sea (the Mandai in the role of the Jews!). Sixty thousand Mandai travelled and travelled until they reached the Tura dMaddai, a mountain in the east. Musa pursued them but was incapable of passing this mountain.

This legend accords with the so-called 'Haran-Gawaita legend', a find of Lady Drower, dating from the time after the Arab conquests. It polemizes against Islam but far more against the 'Yuhataiia", a term which is used indiscriminately for both Jews and Babylonians. For neither of them had the Mandai much sympathy so that there even is a Mandaean legend in which Nebuchadnessar is the king of the Jews (sic) [46]. The Mandaeans finally found a refuge from their enemies in the mountains of the Madai. There lay a paradisiacal land called 'Parwan', where Yahya Yuhana (= John the Baptist) was born. In this text there is no mention of Christ's baptism by John. John went to Jerusalem, a city founded by Ruha whose servants most of its inhabitants were; however, there was also a community of Mandai there [47].

What strikes the eye in this story is how inimical it is to the Jews. What would they think of being lumped together with their arch-enemies, the Babylonians? There is an anti-biblical point in the communication that Noah had an extra-son in Sam; whereas, according to Gen. 10, all mankind descends from the three sons (who, by the way, are in this legend named Ham, Yam, and Yafet, instead of Sem, Cham, and Japhet), the Mandai are endowed with an ancestor of their own. The land of the 'Maddai' may be identified with Media which locates the Mandai far into the east.

5. The mental roots of the sect

More important than the ethnic birthplace is the question of the mental roots of Mandaeism. Jewish influences have already been mentioned; there were also Christian ones. Some impulses may have come from Iran, some from Mesopotamia, and last but certainly not least, there is the strong Gnostic impact since, when all is said and done, the Mandaean religion is a branch of the Gnosis.

6. The religious literature of the Mandaeans

Mandaean is a Semitic language, one of the East Aramaic languages to which also Syrian and Aramaic belong. Mandaean laymen who are native Arab speakers cannot read it; this is the privilege of the priests who do not feel inclined to share their knowledge of the sacred language with others. Drower suggests that the priestly prestige is based on this knowledge. Add to this that, as in many other cultures, writing is seen as "a magic act ..., conferring merit on the writer" [48]; the more mysterious and mystic the text, the greater the merit. Therefore, in century after century priests copied the holy books by hand without ever having them printed. "Pious Mandaeans ... believed the possession of holy books ensured protection for them in this world and the next" [49]. This explains why Mandaeans are unwilling to part with their treasures or even let outsiders browse through them.

Mandaean religious literature is voluminous and varied. The largest book is the 'Ginza Rba' = the Great Treasure, also called 'Sidra Rba', the Great Book, or Book of Adam, here to be quoted as 'Ginza'. A second important, although less bulky work, is the 'Drasha dYahya', the Book of John (although this book bears the name of John the Baptist, only a few passages deal with him [50]). Both works are collections of diverse materials, mostly legends and tractates of a mythological and cosmological nature. Then there are a number of ritual books with liturgies and hymns, the Diwans which deal with cult, belief, and language, and with astrology and magic.

The fact that these books are collections already suggests that they must have been long in gestation. When this process began is not known, but some parts are very old. The definitive editing took place after the Arab invasion into Mesopotamia, probably in the seventh or eighth century. The immediate cause seems to have been the wish to have a book similar to the Koran, "in order to gain status as 'people of the book'" [51].

The first translation of the Ginza into a European language appeared in 1913. Its authoritative translation, into German, is by Mark Lidzbarski, published in 1925; a new edition of it is being prepared by Kurt Rudolph. Already earlier, in 1915, Lidzbarski had published his version of the Book of John, equally in German [52]. Lady Drower, one of those indefatigable British travellers, many women among them, whom nothing can deter, procured a translation of the Canonical Prayerbook of the Mandaeans (Leiden, 1959). So there is much easily obtainable textual material - which does not mean that the texts themselves are mere child's play.

7. Two worlds

Before we begin to study Mandaean mythology, we must take to heart some cautionary words by Rudolph. He wrote that "it is very difficult to get a clear picture of these religious ideas from Mandaean literature. It is known that this literature is in a badly confused state. It has therefore not yet been possible to reconstruct the evolution of Mandaean ideas from their earliest beginnings with any certainty" [53]. There are, this means, earlier and later strata in this system. With this proviso in mind, let us begin our disquisition.

The first and most decisive element in Mandaean mythology is that, as in other Gnostic systems, there are two sharply separated worlds. The upper one is that of the Pleroma, although in Mandaean it is not called so. It is the Lightworld. This world is dualistically opposed to a lower world, our world. This dualism is the prop and mainstay of the Mandaean mental concept. While in the upper world there is nothing but Life, Light, and Goodness, in the lower world Death, Darkness, and Evil reign supreme. "There is Death and there is Life, there is Darkness and there is Light, there is Error and there is Truth", in this way a Mandaean text summarizes the basic dualism of this ideology [54].

However sharp the dualism of the two worlds may be, it is not absolute or radical, in the sense that they are equal and coeval. The Lightworld has a temporal or ontological precedence over that of Darkness. "The uthras (the luminous spirits) are older than the Darkness ... The Good is older than the wickedness of the place of Darkness; softness is older than the rebellion of the place of Darkness" [55]. This must not be taken to mean that the lower world emanated from the higher world. "Two kings there were, two natures were created : a king of this world (= the lower one), and a king from beyond the worlds" [56].

Whatever its relationship to the upper world, there can be no doubt that the lower world is an original phenomenon as well as the fierce opponent of the Lightworld. "See and comprehend that between the Darkness and Light there can be neither kusta (= the ritual hand-clasp of friendship) nor laufa (=the ritual meal for the dead) but only hate, jealousy, and division. For Darkness is the opponent of the Light, for they (the two worlds) are right and left, Ruha (the spirit of the underworld) and soul, sun and moon, day and night, heaven and earth, and they (these worlds) are called Adam and Eve" [57]. We shall meet Ruha shortly. The last words introduce us to one of the most essential Mandaean dualisms, that between man and woman; we shall have to come back to this.

8. Mandaean theogony

a. The first principles

By far the greater part of Mandaean theogony and cosmogony is contained in Book III of the Right Ginza [58]. We must not be deterred by the fact that in the text no uniform descriptions are to be found. There are no less then three theogonies; what connects them is that the catchword is not creation but emanation - which is usual in Gnostic systems [59].

The Lightworld is pre-existent. Before anything else, there was 'pira', the 'great fruit', which is equivalent to the universe. "The fruit was in the fruit", all three say [60], which means that the universe (the Pleroma) is uncreated and self-contained. This 'fruit' is the first primeval principle. The second original principle is 'ayar', the ether or air [61]. We must not think here of the atmosphere of our globe but of a higher, purer and rarer atmosphere [62]. "The ether is in the ether" equally indicates its autonomous and independent status [63].

All three sections acknowledge yet another principle, probably the same in all of these, but with different names. In the first it is 'Mana rba', the 'great soul', the 'Mana of glory'; it is the source of Light [64]. In the second theogony it is 'Jura rba', the "great radiance, the radiance of which stretches far and wide; before it was nobody" [65]. In the third it is 'Malka rba', the 'great King of Light'; from him an uncreated and autonomous being, the ether, proceeds [66]. In all three texts, therefore, there is a pre-existent source of light which makes the Pleroma into a Lightworld.

b. The manas and uthras

The first theogony teaches us that from the first principles emanations proceed with which the Lightworld is peopled. From the Pira or fruit 'piras' and 'skinas', celestial beings without number come forth, and from the great Mana the manas, or individual souls. "Their light is too great to be told with (human) lips" [67]. All three theogonies agree that 'the Jordan' is an emanation too, the "living water ..., the smell of which is sweet" [68]. Still other 'Jordans' sprang from this mother-Jordan; they are "without end and number" [69]. The second and third theogonies add the important information that the 'uthras' also emanate [70]. The uthras are "the spirits whose function it is to govern natural phenomena" [71]; this word means 'wealth' or 'abundance' [72].

Rudolph says that the three versions all present the same fundamental concept : there is a trilogy of pira, ayar, and mana; there is the connection of Mana (or the Lightking) with Life, there are emanations from these principles [73]. We come one stage nearer to actual creation when we hear that from Mana proceeds the 'First Life', the true 'image' of Mana [74].

Life, in consequence, is something divine and celestial (but must not be understood as biological or natural life). This First Life, not wanting to remain alone, makes the 'Second Life' emanate from itself; this is the 'creative spirit' [75]. This creative spirit makes creation possible.

In its turn Second Life creates uthras, and three of these uthras express a wish to create a world. This idea pleases their father, Second Life, who approves of their plan [76]. But it does not please First Life at all! The wish is now addressed to Mana Rba, the great soul, or first principle. On hearing what the lower uthras are planning, the great Mana creates a controlling agent, Kbar Rba, or Kbar Ziva, and tells him to keep a watchful eye on these opinionated uthras [77]. What happens here is something that we already encountered in other Gnostic systems. In the nether regions of the Pleroma, in this case the Lightworld, a deviation is showing up, and a split is becoming possible, since some lesser entities foster plans that are not in accordance with the intentions of the most supreme beings. In the words of Rudolph, "there is a gradual devolution, a fall, from the first Oneness to the (lower) arbitrary world" [78]. It should be noted that this devolution takes place within the Lightworld.

c. Manda dHayye

Rather unexpectedly, a new being turns up, Manda dHayye, the 'Knowledge of Life'; it is generated by the First Life, that is to say, it is very high in the celestial hierarchy [79]. The great Mana asks Manda : "Does it please you that the Light-uthras abandon the Light and turn their face to the Darkness ..., to the place where no living water is streaming and where no radiance dwells?" [80]. Next to the upper world, as we have already seen, there is a lower world, a dark world, peopled with demons. It is not explained what is the origin of this world; in all probability it has no origin, just as the Lightworld has no beginning.

d. War in the underworld

The great Mana orders Manda to go to war against the 'rebels of Darkness' [81]. Down there Manda goes, to 'the place of the dragons, to the oven of the consuming fire'. There they sit, the monsters, planning evil against the Good [82]. Their sovereign is Ruha, the great she-devil, the demoniacal counter-part of the great Mana; she is an arch-liar and a magician [83]. She has a son, called Ur, who is the King of Darkness. Just as in other Gnostic systems this king proves himself ignorant of the Pleroma; he has to be informed by his mother about the supreme beings. "There exists somebody who is greater than you are, and whose power surpasses all your worlds" [84].

This communication makes Ur, understandably, very angry; he resolves to wage war upon the upper world. "I want to rise up from the place of Darkness ... and throw the mighty from their thrones" [85]. He assembles an enormous host and marches on. But then he encounters Manda, and although he rages like a madman and creates a fearful havoc, he has the worst of it [86]. Manda finally puts his knee on his belly, binds him with a thick rope, and muzzles him [87]. The humbled Ur pleads for mercy [88], but does not get it, although he now acknowledges that "the man who did this to me is greater than the whole world" [89]. Manda then erects an iron wall around his dwelling-place, guarded by watchmen [90].

When Ur complains of his fate, Manda speaks some meaningful words to him. "The good one ascends because of his virtue and views the realm of Light; the bad one, because of his wickedness, is confined to the place of Darkness" [91]. This whole episode forcefully brings out, first, the overwhelming power of Knowledge, and then, the dualism of good and bad which is expressed by the existence of two separate and inimical worlds. It should, however, be noted that, although Ur is defeated, chained, and imprisoned, he is not destroyed.

9. The descent of the Redeemer into the underworld

Lidzbarski called the descent of the Redeemer into the underworld 'the most important part of Mandaean scripture' [92]. It is contained in Book V of the Right Ginza; there we meet Hibil-Ziwa who is portrayed in this book as a son of Manda dHayye, which means that he too is in possession of celestial wisdom. In consequence we may expect a dramatic and dualistic clash with the powers of Darkness.

a. How the world of Darkness is organized

The world of Darkness counts four entrance-halls and three proper hells; in crossing these one gets lower and lower until one reaches the deepest and darkest pit. Pairs of guards watch over the gates to the four halls; in each of these infernal kingdoms an old ruler reigns. In the first hall Ruha lives, the embodiment of evil [93]. In the lowest pit the oldest and mightiest of the kings of hell sits, Krun. He is surrounded by three hundred and sixty six (the number of the days in the year) 'dews', hellish demons in whose name we easily recognize the word 'devil' [94]. One version of the Mandaean cosmogony informs us that Ur too is a dew. Here his father is Gaf, a giant of the underworld, but his mother is Ruha [95].

b. Hibil prepared for his task

At a certain moment a dew - it is not said that it is Ur - begins forcing its way upwards from the regions of Darkness. Now the real threat is that the underworld will invade the Lightworld. Manda brings this to the attention of the great Mana who orders him to go down and do what is necessary to stave off the danger [96]. What is necessary is, of course, that the dualistic separation of the higher and lower realms should remain intact. Manda dHayye then looks for his son Hibil who is an image of himself; thus his father is also his brother - an instance of Gnostic inclusive thinking of which there are all kinds in these texts. Hibil is baptized and brought into the presence of the great Mana and the other superior luminous beings whose aspect frightens him. But Hibil is so carefully prepared for his task that he becomes a mana himself. Finally, Manda hands him 'the hidden mysteries' of the Manas [97]. This 'mystery' is a living being itself, since it exhorts Hibil to descend to the underworld [98]. Doubtless this being symbolizes the secret Knowledge of Life and Death.

c. The descent to Krun

In the following story there are two sections that originally, according to Rudolph, did not belong together : the descent towards Krun, and the descent towards Ruha and Ur. Hibil first reaches the uppermost realm of Darkness where Ruha dwells; here he lives a hidden existence for a thousand myriads of years. Ruha did not know that he was so near [99]. After this incredibly long time Hibil goes on to the second department of the underworld where his long stay remains equally unnoticed, this in spite of the fact that he celebrates rituals here with the luminous beings who accompany him. He allayed his fear by saying to himself that his place was with his Father, Life, and that, for this reason, he need not be afraid of the infernal demons [100]. This portrays the basic condition of life : if one possesses the (secret) Knowledge and performs the right rituals, one need not be afraid of anything. The infernal beings are so stupid and ignorant that they do not recognize a Mandaean, even if they see one.

Down again to the third world, where Hag and Mag, the 'Manas of Darkness', reign; Hibil "knew what was in their hearts" [101]. One world further down Hibil enters that of Gaf and Gafan, the 'Giants of Darkness'. He tells them that they are bound and powerless and bereft of all their magic and their deceit and their hateful liliths [102]. The next lower world is that of the bellicose Anatas and his wife Qin, the Queen and Mother of Darkness. But Hibil and his retinue illumine this dark abode with prayers and hymns which rise up to the great Mana [103].

Hibil has now crossed the four entrance-halls but his most arduous task is still awaiting him. He opens the gates that lead to the three hells proper. The first one is that of Sdum, King of the world. Hibil, who has assumed a beautiful form, approaches him and takes him to account because of that ambitious dew who would penetrate into the Lightworld. But Sdum knows - or pretends to know - nothing of this and remits him to the following hell [104]. There Gew reigns, but interrogated about a certain dew who wanted to fight the Lighworld, he too protests his innocence [105]. Hibil now has to turn to Krun, the sovereign of the deepest and darkest of all hells.

Having entered his abode, Hibil asks that horrifying Krun about the rebellious dew. "What do you know of him?". "Go away!", Krun answers gruffly, "or I devour you". Hibil calmly retorts : "Well, do!". Krun begins to devour him indeed. But having swallowed half of him, he spat him out again, because his intestines were heavily damaged. Life and Light do not agree with the powers of Darkness; they are destructive of them. The roles are reversed now, for Krun admits that "you (Hibil and his retinue) are giants, we are weaklings; you are gods, we are men; you are great, we are small" [106]. At last Krun has become aware of the dualistic difference between the upper and lower worlds!

d. The return of Hibil

Hibil now asks Krun for some sort of talisman by means of which he can return to the Lightworld. The demon hands him a signet-ring in which 'the name of the great Darkness' is engraved [107]. Hibil is now in the possession of the two great secrets of the universe, the 'mystery' of the Lightworld, and the 'name' = the essence, of the realm of Darkness.

Hibil hurries back, but when he reaches the hall of Qin, he asks her for the hand of one of her daughters. Zahrel is given to him, but, as is self-evident, as one of the luminous beings Hibil has no idea of setting up house in the underworld; the whole thing is a ruse by means of which he hopes to worm more secrets out of the demons. With great pomp the wedding takes place; however, Hibil does not consummate the marriage, to the utter astonishment of Qin when she discovers that her daughter is still untouched [108].

It is his mother-in-law, Qin, who betrays the secret of the origin of the demons to Hibil. They emerged from a remote well, but none of the demons knows how deep it is. Hibil is now the only one to know its depth. In this well lies a mirror. When the demons look into it, they know what they have to do. But Hibil takes it away and thus makes them powerless [109]. There is no further talk of Zahrel.

Instead, Hibil now occupies himself with Ruha, who is the wife of her brother Gaf and has been made pregnant by Ur. Hibil assumes the shape of Gaf, visits Ruha, and says to her : "Stand up, we will go to your parents". Ruha takes the bait and, accompanied by Hibil, crosses several halls of the lower world. When they arrive in the topmost hall, that of Ruha herself, Hibil locks the doors and hides the keys. "Where are my parents?", Ruha asks, doubtless somewhat worried. "I will show them to you", is the answer. This whole story of Ruha's parents was nothing but a red herring, for now Hibil asks the great Mystery that is with him : "Make her blind, deaf, confused", and this it does. To make absolutely sure of her, Hibil erects walls around her abode. "And she became as though she did not exist" [110].

Hibil's task in the underworld is now completed. "What we did is in order." Singing hymns and praying he and his party ascend to the upper world; they open 'the gates of Light' and go on to the Father, Manda dHayye [111]. Hibil reports to Manda what he saw and did in the underworld. "And his heart sprang up, his breast swelled with joy by what I told him, and he was full of bounty" [112].

e. What this means

It is time now to pause for a moment and consider what it all means. From the perspective of the subject of our inquiry, dualism, there is a most important remark to be made. The two worlds, the Lightworld and the Realm of Darkness, have nothing in common. They are totally unconnected, and their inhabitants have very little knowledge of each other. The inferior world is not created by the powers of the Lightworld; they do not even know what the origin of the demons is. The two worlds exist side by side, independently of each other, both having their own origin and their own rulers. This signifies that we are in the presence of a case of absolute dualism.

What did that dew that is suddenly seen striving upward intend to do? It is hard to believe that it is out to conquer the upper world single-handed. It rather looks like a reconnaissance-expedition. Perhaps the curious little devil wanted to know how the upper world was shaped, maybe even whether there is such a world at all. However, this already proves too much for the rulers of the Lightworld : knowledge of higher things should not be appropriated by demoniacal (or human) beings.

The luminous beings evidently are afraid of that other world. Hibil is elaborately prepared for his task and needs to be provided with a 'mystery' to help him; he also needs a talisman from Krun in order to travel freely through the lower regions. It is made abundantly clear that pleromic beings are not fit to live in the inferior realms. Manda (Knowledge) does not go down at all. Hibil does not destroy the lower world since he is evidently unable to do this. But by taking away its hidden secrets and by locking up Ruha, he subjects it more or less to the upper world. When Krun exclaims : "You are gods, we are small", he admits that he has become dependent on the Lightworld. This is the result of Hibil's mission. The absolute dualism with which it all began has now been turned into a relative one. I do not believe that we met a similar phenomenon earlier; it really is exceptional.

f. The Ruha version

Then a second 'descensus ad inferos' follows. This second myth in all probability originally stood on its own, but has been artificially linked with the first one. Hibil asks Manda for permission to visit the incarcerated Ruha; this permission is given him, and once again he crosses 'the frontier of Darkness' [113]. Presenting himself to Ruha in the shape of her husband

Gaf, he presses her to curse her parents who, in this version, are Hag and Mag. She no longer wants to see them [114]. For the time being - which time lasts a thousand years - Hibil returns to Manda but then he descends again to Ruha to whom he announces the birth of Ur, the 'Giant of Darkness' [115].

After a second return to heaven, Hibil for the third time in succession joins Ruha and witnesses the birth of her son Ur [116] (chronological sequences are often somewhat muddled in these relations). He then erects seven walls of gold around Ruha's abode [117], and provides these with magic names so that nobody can pull them down. He is not happy with Ruha's offspring. When Ur has grown up, he (Hibil) fashions an 'earth of copper' to sustain Ur since he has become so disproportionally big and heavy. Clearly Hibil is afraid of Ur and of what the giant might do. "When he goes on growing in this way, he will make the whole world burst by his force and his growth." Hibil then runs his hand over Ur's side and, in doing so, makes him powerless. This makes Ur very angry, although he does not know who did this to him. The ignorance and stupidity of the demons form staple themes in these myths. Thus disempowered, Ur tumbles into the black water, until he lands upon the copper earth in which he makes a crack [118].

Next, Ruha intends to crown her son but, like Napoleon, he puts the crown on his head himself. Being King of the Darkness now, he wants to pull these walls down. Together with his mother he speaks "a thousand times thousand endless, and ten thousand times ten thousand endless (spells) but the walls did not melt". Ruha then creates warlike devils for him, but this too is obviously in vain. She hands him a mirror in which he sees not only his parents and their dark world but even the Lightworld, "the light that I see with my own eyes, and that is not ours". Angered by the existence of a higher world, he declares that he wants to fight it, but Ruha warns him against this temerarious plan. However, "I want to fight the Light, not the Darkness" [119].

In his frenzy Ur literally raises hell against the enclosing walls; he screams so loudly that they begin to totter. Since it is evidently possible that he will break out, Life sends Hibil to him. Hibil takes the crown from Ur's head (the giant does not know who Hibil is). In his wrath Ur conjures up myriads of dews but when they see Hibil, they "become as though they had never been" [120]. Hibil takes away the magic means of which Ruha disposes, with the result that she and Ur go off their heads and root up the earth in their excitement [121].

One last great effort! Ur climbs out of the black water and says to Ruha : "I am going to wage war". He makes the black water pound the walls which again threaten to come down. But Hibil comes and binds Ur with a chain, "ten thousand times as heavy as he himself is". He is thrown down on his face, a cloth is spread over him, and at every corner of this cloth four guards are posted [122].

Then at last Hibil is free to return to heaven. He reports to his father : "Rejoice and be of good cheer, for Ur has been thrown down" [123].

g. What this myth means

The great theme of this myth in the Ruha version is the protracted fight between the Lightworld, represented by Hibil, and the world of Darkness, personified mainly by Ur. In this war there is no definite victor, at least not in the sense that one of these worlds is destroyed. They continue existing side by side, condemned to each other as they are. None of the higher powers is really interested in the lower world; Manda himself does descend into it and does not go any further than giving Hibil permission to descend. This must mean that Manda, i.e. Knowledge, has no real grip on the lower world as such; this world is left to its own devices.

All Hibil can do is to keep the demoniacal powers in check, mainly in order to prevent them from attacking and invading the luminous world. It is a remarkable thing that he presents himself to Ruha in disguise; he obviously fears that, as a representative of the higher world, he will not be able to influence her. The fact that Ruha is prepared to curse her parents shows that she is ready to be controlled to some extent. Her being enclosed with golden walls signifies at the same time a protection for herself against the demons and a shield for the Lightworld against her. Yet if Hibil ever thought that he could hold Ur in his hand, he was painfully wrong. It cost Hibil enormous efforts to make the giant powerless.

10. Mandaean cosmogony

a. Ptahil the Demiurge

So far there has been no talk of a cosmos and still less of mankind, but now the time for cosmogony has come. In view of the ambiguous and unfriendly relations between the worlds of Light and Darkness trouble must be expected. We have already seen that plans to create a world originated with Second Life. This forebodes nothing good! Three specially created uthras will assist him. They "descend to the place of Darkness" [124]. Rudolph thinks that this should be taken literally, not in the sense that they actually enter the lower world, but rather in the sense that they make a move towards it. "This expresses the defection from the Pleroma of Life" [125], in other words a Fall. Creation begins under an unfavourable sign!

In some Mandaean texts Second Life has a proper name, 'Yushamin' (Josamin). Although he ontologically belongs to the higher world, he prefers looking downward. And although he is a luminous being, he is spoken of as rebellious and disobedient. It is above all the Book of John that speaks of a great war against him, how he was defeated and locked in, and how he was admonished by Manda and forgiven [126]. Josamin was married and had a son, Abatur, and a grandson, Ptahil. Abatur is the 'Third Life' and Ptahil the 'Fourth Life' [127]. There are also texts according to which three special uthras were created to assist Second Life in his creational work; in these texts Ptahil was created by these uthras. However, this may be, he takes the place of the Demiurge [128]. Here too we have a descending scale, although we are, the battle against Josamin notwithstanding, still in the Pleroma.

b. Ptahil's failure

Rudolph writes that, with regard to cosmogony, there are clearly two conceptions, a dualistic one and a monistic. He believes that the dualistic version is the oldest. In this version the cosmos is brought about against the intentions of the supreme pleromic being [129]. Let me first give this dualistic version.

Abatur, believing he was powerful, conceived a plan to create a world. He had no idea how difficult this would be [130]. He ordered his son Ptahil, the real Demiurge, to take this work in hand : "Create and fashion a world". He gave him the name of Gabriel (in the Old Testament the messenger of God) but told him nothing of the difficulties to be expected [131]. The idea behind there having to be a specially created and appointed Demiurge, says Lidzbarski, is the determination to disconnect the supreme godhead from creation [132].

Unsuspectingly Ptahil the Demiurge descends to the place "where there are no more luminous worlds" and tries to make solid earth out of the primeval waters, but finds nothing but mud. This makes him feel discouraged [133]. Because no solid earth yet, "discord came into his heart" [134]. I think that Ptahil, though a disobedient member of the Pleroma - his disobedience is proved by his (abortive) attempt to create -, is still too 'pleromic' to be capable of creating a material cosmos.

c. Ruha's failed attempt

Less sophisticated help is needed now. Ruha takes a hand, in a way typical for the underworld. Ur, her son, sleeps with his mother; from their incestuous cohabitation seven beings are born. These seven, it goes without saying, are the planets. They rebel against their father [135]. The realm of Darkness is divided against itself; there is no harmony or uniformity in it. Once again mother and son lie together, and once again beings are born, this time twelve (the signs of the Zodiac) [136]. These too Ruha finds repellent; they too repudiate their father [137]. Her problem is that her twofold offspring resemble the beings of the luminous world too closely. They are, in fact, the constellations of the firmament which in Gnostic systems always form the frontier between the upper and the lower worlds [138].

d. Ptahil tries again

Ruha complains to Ptahil of her failure to create in her own way. Now the Demiurge takes over, made the wiser by his misguided first attempt. He bowed down to Light, the supreme being, adored it, and received a 'garb of living fire'. Clothed in this fiery garment, he descended into the muddy waters and succeeded in condensing them so that the dry appeared. He spanned the firmament, caught the still vagrant planets, and assigned them, against their wish, their places and courses on the firmament. In the face of heavy opposition on the part of rebellious lower beings, "he took the heart and would fix it at the heart of heaven" [139]. This means that he put the cosmos, called 'tibil' in Mandaean, definitely in order. But it is clear that it is done in the face of heavy odds. Cosmic forces are basically chaotic and rebellious; they can only be kept under control through the intervention of a superior power.

The planets, having found their master, resign themselves to Ptahil's plans : "We want to be your servants, we want to be your helpers". And the Demiurge accepts them, but only conditionally : "You are my sons. If you do good works, you shall be counted as members of my party" [140]. Ptahil does something unheard of here : he concludes a treaty with the powers of the lower world! This means that he disobeyed his celestial father, for between the upper and nether worlds 'nulla communio' is possible. In consequence of this, he was bound so that he could take no further action. "A curtain was let down between him and his father Abatur" [141]. This means that henceforward he remains consigned to the tibil.

I feel this is the right place to mention that, according to some texts, Ptahil had a son, Jo-Rabba [142]. One text speaks of "Jorabba, Ruha, and the god whom they (the Jews) venerate, and who led them out of Egypt" [143]. Lidzbarski and Rudolph argue that Jorabba is identical with

Adonai, the God of the Old Testament [144]; he obviously has Ruha as a kind of paredra. But he is not acting as Demiurge. In Mandaean texts he has a bad press : the great Mana despised him [145]; he is bellicose [146] and full of malignity [147].

To return now to Ptahil, the Demiurge, it is circumstantially related how he arranges and furnishes the tibil and peoples it with living beings. The 'instrument' at his disposal is not his hands but - and this he has in common with the Creator of Gen. 1 - his voice : he calls into being. Through his voice everything originates, mountains, seas, rivers, trees, plants, fruits, fishes, animals wild and tame, everything without exception.

e. The planets interfere

All this sounds fine enough, but the fact that the 'seven' (planets) and the 'twelve' (signs of the Zodiac) participate in the creational work must make us somewhat distrustful, because they are non-pleromic powers of a lower order. No good can come of this! To give a few instances, Taurus is responsible for the creation of malicious monsters, the Scorpion for that of bad fruit; from Sagittarius comes all Anger, from Aquarius all defects and failure [148]. This explains why so much is wrong in the cosmos.

Yet there are other factors that help to explain the defects of the cosmos. "When the seven (planets) mapped out the Zodiac, they imposed death upon the world as a punishment" [149]. And then there are the twelve 'gates'; these gates are the warring religious factions, all of them false [150]. For instance, "the gates which were created by Christ accuse each other reciprocally of lying ... He distorts the arguments and brings foolishness into the world" [151]. This applies to orthodox Christians as well as to non-orthodox sects. Another example : "From the gate which Adonai (Jahve) created came the whole people of the house of Israel ... They do what it is not permitted to do; ... from the people of the Jews all gates (sects) come forth" [152]. The text is as anti-Christian as it is anti-Jewish. The long litany is wound up in this way. "I taught you about the planets and about the gates they created in the world. I taught you about their works : they were all created defectively : hate, envy, discord" [153].

11. The creation of man

Let us now study the anthropogonic part, the creation of man. Rudolph says that Mandaean anthropogonic myths cannot be so neatly divided into dualistic and monistic myths (as the cosmogonic ones), "because everywhere the body-soul dualism is given expression to - a for the Mandaean religion basically determining feature that must be seen as parallel to the inveterate denigration of the world (= the body)" [154]. Mandaean religion has this in common with all other Gnostic systems.

a. Ptahil the Demiurge

The idea of creating human beings originates in the lower regions of the Lightworld, with Ptahil, a being who would become 'lord of the world'. Ruha and the planets have no inkling of this plan [155]. "The earth will belong to us", the planets emphatically declare, "and nobody else will lord it over the world" [156]. We find here the anti-astrological stance that is typically Gnostic : it is not denied that heavenly bodies have power and can influence human existence, but one of the hallmarks of the redeemed Gnostic is that he is no longer subjected to stellar mechanisms. In this respect, as in many others, the Gnosis stands apart from common opinion in late Antiquity.

b. Adam created

In the lower world Ptahil decides to create 'a beloved son', "so that he will be lord of the world". The planets keep counsel among each other and decide that they themselves will create Adam and Hawwa (Eve), "for he belongs to us". They declare their intention to Ptahil. He feels that he is unable to act against the express wishes of the planets and that he must take action in accordance with them [157]. This means that there will be higher and lower elements in human beings.

Now Adam (there is no mention of Eve as yet) is created, but he is no more than physical, a body without a soul. Whatever the planets may do, they prove incapable of infusing a soul into him [158]. No wonder since they only form part of the lower world. In their despair they turn to Ptahil asking him to help them. Ptahil travels back to the Lightworld and reports to his father Abatur that the creation of his and Abatur's image did not succeed [159].

Abatur goes to a secret spot to fetch a mana, a soul, which he envelopes in a pure turban; he then hands it to his son. But he does not trust his son at all who is even called 'evil' by him. Ptahil must not be allowed to know how "the soul falls into the body". Therefore, Abatur commands three helpers, one of them Hibil, to accompany Ptahil and to take the mana under their wings. They must also see to it that, once Adam has become a living being, the mana, the life-giving principle, is returned to heaven [160]. Having arrived at the spot where Adam was fashioned, they find him still lying lifeless on the ground. The myth does not excel in logicality since suddenly Manda dHayye too appears on the scene. It is finally Manda who turns Adam into a living being - "the lustre of life shone in him" -, and the mana is brought back to heaven. Manda then gets the task to guard Adam's soul from the evil ones [161].

c. Mankind's double origin

The bodily part of Adam is the work of Ptahil the Demiurge and the planets; it is a negative thing, lifeless and powerless. His soul-part comes from above; it is alien in this world and needs special protection. This is downright dualism. The double origin of mankind is clearly brought out in a passage of much later date where there is also talk of Eve. "When Ptahil had created the world, he built his son Adam after his own shape, and after Adam's shape his wife Hawwa was built. Ptahil threw a kind of spirit into him, something from his own spirit; and everyone of the planets threw something of his own mystery into him. Ptahil and the planets who were with him could not erect Adam and his wife Hawwa. Then Ptahil went to his father Abatur, took a hidden mana that was brought to him from the house of life, and threw this into Adam and his wife Hawwa" [162].

As already mentioned, there are also texts according to which Manda dHayye is the one who brought the soul to Adam; some found it obviously unpalatable that Ptahil would have done this. "You (Manda) took the soft manas and gave them a dwelling-place in perishable bodies" [163]. Perhaps there is a ring of reproach in these words. "You took the treasure of life and threw it onto the perishable earth and gave it to beings who are formed of flesh and blood" [164]. Then again it is Hibil-Ziwa, the luminous being, or son of Manda, who brings the soul to the first man [165]. But whoever may be the messenger, one thing is certain : the soul has another and higher origin than the body; it is alien to this world.

d. Mana's dislike of the body and the world

Other passages stress this idea. "The uthras bring the mana to this world, put it into filth, cloth it with a garment of flesh, ... and endow it with default and failure" [166]. Or another passage that closely resembles the soma-sêma similar of Platonism : "I (Mana) went and entered the body and was kept prisoner in the palace (= the body)" [167]. Mana even loudly protests against entering the body. "She does not go in, she cries, wails, and melts in tears ... What did I sin amongst you (the uthras)", she says, "that you stupefy me and take me away out of your midst" [168]. Mana abhors the body, so much is clear!

The task of the soul in its bodily abode is to protect man from the evil influence of the tibil. "When the soul descended from the Lightworld and fell into the body, with it came all the mysteries of the realm of Light : lustre, light, Kusta, Laufa, clarity, peace, all that is there in the place of Light. They formed the retinue of the soul and enwrapped it and filled it with them, so that they would be its helpers against the wickedness and the wrath of the tibil" [169]. The evil influences coming from Ruha and the tibil are song, dance (sic), defamation, falsity, deceit, profligacy, bewitchment, violence, lies, magic, perversion [170].

Mana is not pleased with the world. "I viewed and saw the world : it is ugly and deformed in its shape" [171]. Gnostic contempt of the world is brought out in these words : "I (Mana) despised those who created it" [172]. And Mana complains : "Who made me live in the tibil, who made me sit in the house of my enemies?" [173]. But she will return to where she came from. Its celestial guardian comes, takes off Mana's garment (the body), and clothes her in its own dress (light); Mana is brought into the pleromic treasure-house and is hidden in it. "And Life is victorious" [174].

e. The Mandaeans and the female sex

It is in accordance with the patriarchical constitution of the Mandaean community, writes Rudolph, that Eve does not receive much attention [175]. Just like her husband, she is a product of the Demiurge. We do not find the biblical conception that she was created from Adam [176]. Mandaeans do not place a high value on the female sex. Why are there men and women? The Mandaean answer that this is because there is no order in the world. "Because there is no rectitude, they made you a man and me a woman, or else we would have had but one nature and they would have created it as one mana" [177]. We must make Rudolph's conclusion our own, that "Adam and Eve, man and woman, light and darkness, soul and Ruha must be seen as the dualistic principles of the cosmos; their union is not (or only temporarily) possible because there is no 'order' since the cosmogony" [178]. The 'temporarily' here refers primarily to marital.

Since there are now a man and a woman, we are confronted with the question of their relations. In almost all Gnostic systems this presented a real problem, that of sexuality and marriage. Marriage is not a sacrament with the Mandaeans. How could it be since polygamy is permitted, although not generally practised [179]? When Eve was created, Adam saw that she was naked, which made him feel ashamed. Then Hibil came to Adam and made garments for both of them with which they could cover their nudity [180]. This is exactly the reverse of the Genesis story according to which the first human beings were not embarrassed by their nakedness. I interpret this Ginza text thus that man and woman were immediately confronted by their reciprocal erotic radiation and did not like this.

f. Adakas and Adam

We must now consider a being that was not mentioned before. It (or he) is 'Adakas-Ziwa', the 'lustre of life'. It is extremely difficult to distinguish neatly between Adakas as the bringer of the soul to Adam (yet another messenger!) or Adakas as this soul itself. Sometimes he seems to be identical with Manda. Adakas, as may be expected, has his problems with Ptahil who is also mentioned as the bringer of the soul. As soon as Adam has come to life, he "praises his father Adakas-Ziwa, the mana by whom he was planted" [181]. The word 'father' means that Adakas, the mana, is Adam's (man's) life-giving principle which came from above. Adakas is identified with Adam in so far as he is "the hidden or inner Adam" [182].

This introduces us to the central problem in Mandaeism, the emprisonment of the soul here below and the guarantee of its return to heaven [183]. Adakas, who is the guardian of Adam's soul [184], must see to it that it will go back to its celestial home [185]. "One is your redeemer who will come to you (Adam), Adakas-Mana, your father, who will lead you onto a road that is without heat and terror and trembling" [186]. It is Adakas' specific task to bring Adam's soul back to the Lightworld. "On! Leave, Mana, the trunk into which you were thrown ... Ascend to your real home, to your fine abode of the uthras. Live among the uthras, your brothers; sit there where it is your custom to sit. Return to your home and curse the world of deceit in which you lived ... Your throne be erected ... And Life is victorious" [187]. Thus, in a nutshell, the central thesis of the Gnosis, of all Gnostics, is expressed : that of the return of the soul to where it came from.

g. The Adamites

Just as the earthly Adam was only an image of the celestial Adam, the Adakas-Adam, his and his wife's sons, the Adamites, have their heavenly prototypes. The greatest of these Adamites obviously have an a-sexual origin. "A youthful boy descended to Eve, while Adam lived with her in chastity as one who is celibate." Eve is surprised that all of a sudden she has a child, although she never was pregnant. "Hibil bar (son of) Adam (= Abel, not to be identified with the earlier mentioned Hibil) he is called, the son of Adam (sic) with Eve" [188]. In this version it is unambiguously stated that Eve was not pregnant of Hibil.

In another version it was indeed she who bore the son but not from 'the seed of Adam'. The text takes no trouble to explain this. "This must really be called a miracle!" Its significance is, of course, that Hibil-Abel who is the ancestor of the Mandaeans, is of heavenly provenance and, in consequence, cannot have a sexual origin. "He is a sprig (of the Pleroma) who went into the tibil, revealed himself, and came into the world of the children of man, ... in order to lead men back there (to the Pleroma), to the place from where they came" [189]. "Hibil had a son whose name was Sitil, and Sitil had a son whose name was Anos" [190]. These three great Adamites, Hibil-Sitil-Anos, are, so to speak, the first Mandaeans, the protagonists of the race of Light, because, although living on earth and possessing physical bodies, they are clearly conscious of their heavenly origin and of the Lightworld as their future.

As essentially pleromic beings the three first Adamites are safeguarded against the horrors and terrors of the tibil. "Hibil, Sitil, and Anos, sons of the living, shining, displaying, and luminous tribe (= the uthras) (are) the ones who will not be snatched away by the sword, not burned by fire, not carried off by floods, whose sandal straps will not be wetted by the water" [191].

12. The monistic version

Strictly speaking, monistic versions do not belong here, but I feel it would be in this case intellectually dishonest to omit them.

a. The two worlds are brothers

A transmission from a dualistic to a monistic conception may be found in the suggestion that the two worlds could have a common origin. In spite of all opposition there exists a certain relationship between the two worlds, a kind of osmosis, it seems. "The worlds of Light and the worlds of Darkness are body and image to each other ...; each of them derives a force from the other" [192]. It is not specified what this reciprocal borrowing of force means nor what this force is. When all is said and done, there is a suggestion that the two worlds may have a common, i.e. monistic, origin. "Consider that Light and Darkness are brothers, emanated from one mystery, and one trunk is containing them both in it" [193]. What is this 'one mystery'? In all probability, it is Life. "Life is the origin of Light and Darkness" [194]. "Life sent Death and Darkness to you ...; Death and Darkness have no Light" [195].

This common origin is further demonstrated by the following mysterious words. "Every sign that belongs to Light has in the body a corresponding sign that belongs to Darkness. Whoever is not marked with the sign of Darkness will not be raised up ... and will not be marked with the sign of Life" [196]. Rudolph interprets this in the sense that the Fall must precede salvation : only those who are in need of salvation can be saved [197]. Although the worlds are independent of each other, they nevertheless presuppose each other.

b. A pleromic Demiurge

In some Mandaean creation myths it is not an evil-intentioned Demiurge like Ptahil who fashions the world but a being from the Pleroma. In these cases the perspective for cosmos and mankind is much brighter, of course. Often another term than 'tibil' is used, namely 'arqa' = earth. Or Ptahil is identified with Gabriel, the heavenly messenger [198] : "Ptahil the messenger whose name is Gabriel" [199]. "He will be created and he will receive a charge and he will create the world" [200]. And in yet another text : "Ptahil comes, artfully condenses the earth, spans the firmament, builds the house, and removes the wicked who are brooding on evil" [201].

Sometimes it is not Gabriel-Ptahil who is the Demiurge but Hibil. Rudolph is convinced that this is a earlier version than the dualistic ones. Hibil rearranges the world rather than creating it. Ptahil came first but did not complete his work. "The uthras sent Hibil to arrange this world" [202]. "Hibil made himself known to Ptahil whose thoughts had become confused and all whose works were corrupted ... Ptahil left the world he had made and went to his father Abatur. Abatur was angry with him and put him in the stock until the end of the world" [203]. It is evident that here an older and dualistic myth was patched over to make it less anti-cosmic.

c. About Adam and 'his tribe'

It is perhaps somewhat confusing that sometimes Life itself, the King of Light, is mentioned as the creator. "The high King of Light spoke his word; then everything came into being through his word" [204] - which sounds very biblical. But if the reader becomes confused, Adam was at a loss too. He asks the great Life : "Why did you make the world?" First he seems to utter a reproach. "Why did you send away the tribes (= the Mandaeans) from your midst, why did you bring strife into the tibil? Why do you look for me and for my whole tribe? Why have you brought the whole world into the desert, while there was no guardian for it, while the seven and the twelve in their own world dominate mankind, and while my tribe (=the Mandaeans) is continuously exposed to persecution?" This looks as though Adam is ignorant about the King of Light, and as though he prefers the regime of the planets, oppressive as it may be. But he then realizes that perhaps the King of Light could save him. "If it pleases you, great King of

Light, this world will not be destroyed, and my tribe will not be cut off from you ... The planets, Ruha, and Christ will not hold sway over (the Jordan)." "O Adam", answers the Lightking, "keep calm in your illumination (= Knowledge), and the rest of the good (= celestial peace) may envelop you. Hibil-Ziwa is here, your brothers, the uthras, are here; the whole Jordan is here. You, Adam, will live here (sc. in the Lightworld); your wife Eve will come here, and your whole tribe (the Mandaeans) will ascend after you ... This is the celestial abode that for you, Adam, and for your wife Eve was founded by the great first Life, for the day of judgment, for the hour of redemption, for the great day of resurrection. Then you shall arise, Adam, and you shall go to our own earth (= the Pleroma). Therefore, calm yourself, and let your heart sit on its support. And Life is victorious" [205].

This is an admirable summary of the Mandaean's growth to insight. Initially he is bewildered by the fact that he is living in an incomprehensible and inimical world. Then an 'illumination' comes which makes him realize that there is another, a higher and better world. His life down here may be difficult, he may even be exposed to persecution, but his future is bright. For, redeemed as he is by Knowledge, he will ascend to the Pleroma and side with the uthras.

14. The Mandaean apocalypse

After Adam and his tribe, the Mandaeans, have been saved, the end has come for the world. "Then all generations come to an end, and all creatures will perish. All sources and lakes will dry up, and all streams and brooks will run dry. Mountains and hills are destroyed, topple over, and sink down. Babel and Borsip [206] are laid waste and become as though they had never existed. The land of the Persians and the land of the Romans are destroyed as though they had never existed ... The Earth pronounces sentence on those who spilled the blood of a son of Adam (= a Mandaean) ... All adulterers, thieves, forgers, magicians, witches, priests, sooth-sayers, (etcera, etcetera) will walk into the fire. When the earth goes to ruin ..., and the wicked ones sink all into the depths of darkness, then hail to you, Adam, because you were elected" [207].

15. The rehabilitation of the Demiurge

A speciality of Mandaean theology is what Rudolph calls 'the rehabilitation of the Demiurge" [208]. This rehabilitation does not extend itself to the work of the Demiurge, the tibil, for this will be destroyed. "The tibil will founder forever, and the works of his house will become a prey of ruin ... The wheels (of heaven) will get into disorder; the chain of the dull earth, devoid of light, will be broken ... When the house will be destroyed and the spirit of the seven planets, the figure of the twelve signs, will come to a ruinous end, of them who persecuted this tribe of life (= the chosen, the Mandaeans)" [209]. We have here before us a clear-cut Mandaean apocalypse, which is not essentially different from other Gnostic apocalypses. It is clear that Mandaeans make the usual Gnostic objections against the material world their own.

"On the great day of judgment sentence will be passed on Josamin, Abatur, and Ptahil." These three are, as we saw, the lowest of the pleromic beings who already belong, to some extent, to the cosmic world. But they are not executed. "Later Hibil-Ziwa comes." Hibil-Ziwa, as we have seen, is the Light-giver, a luminous spirit, born from the ether, a full-blown pleromic being therefore [210]; very probably he is a son of Manda dHayye [211]. "He lifts them (Josamin, Abatur, Ptahil) out of this world", with the result that they do not go down with it. First Josamin and Abatur, who did not go down very far into the cosmos - with them it was more intentional than real -, are redeemed; "they are baptized in the Jordan of the mighty First Life" (baptism is the central sacrament of the Mandaeans). "Next they (Josamin and Abatur) fetch Ptahil-uthra out of the nebulous clouds, together with the refuse in which he sits; in that Jordan the dirt is scraped off him, and he too is baptized in it" [212]. Meddling with creation makes one dirty!

15. Mandaean hierarchy, ritual, and sacraments

I will not finish my disquisition on the Mandaeans without saying a few words about their hierarchy, their ritual, and their sacraments. There are two groups of people, the priests and the lay-people. Among the priests there are three ranks : the simple priests, the bishops, and the ethnarch, the head of the community. Today there are not many priests and bishops, while the function of ethnarch has been vacant for a long time. Priesthood is hereditary, which entails that its members are married [213]. There are no real temples or churches but, instead, cult-huts, always with a pool of water on their south-side.

The great sacrament of the Mandaeans is 'masbuta', or baptism. People must be baptized in 'living', i.e. streaming water. Every river or brook is a 'Jordan', connected with the pleromic Jordan. Those baptized are adults. The rite of baptism is followed by a sacred meal consisting of bread and water. The Mandaeans have no eucharistic meal [214].

Then there is the 'masiqta', or 'ascension', a ceremony that is performed for the dying. The body is totally unimportant, because only the soul will go up to heaven. A person on the verge of death is washed with Jordan water, anointed with oil, and clad in a white dress. When he or she is dead, the masiqta is held, a sequence of songs, incantations and prayers, followed by a ritual meal of unleavened bread in which meal only the priests partake. A Mandaean grave is not marked, because it only contains the body [215]. After this dualistic parting shot I conclude this chapter on the only one still existing Gnostic community.

NOTES TO CHAPTER III

1. Puech, Stand 433.
2. Rudolph, Mandaeism 1. This work owes much to that of another prominent expert in this field, Lady Ethel S. Drower, The Mandaeans (see Bibliography). 'Der Mandäismus' (see Bibliography), Einleitung (by Geo Widengren) 1 : "die einzige noch fortlebende gnostische Sekte, die dazu noch vom Hellenismus merklich unberührt ist".

3.   Loisy, Mandéisme 21 : "Cette religion est essentiellement une gnose, ... nettement dualiste."
4.   Drower, Mandaeans 1/2; Rudolph, Mandaeism 1.
5.   The singular is 'Subbi'.
6.   Drower, Mandaeans 1.
7.   The first author to write about the Mandaeans was a Syrian Nestorian who lived in the eighth century, probably around 791. He was Theodore Bar Konaï (or Koni or Kenawi), a monk, maybe, of whom very little is known (see É. Amann s.v. 'Théodore Bar-Koni', Dict.Théol.Cath. 15.1, 228/229. Paris, 1946). Most of what he wrote is lost. Only his 'Liber scholiorum' has been preserved. Jean Baptiste Chabot, provided Alfred Loisy with a Latin translation of the sections concerning the Mandaeans whom Theodore knew and with whose books he was acquainted. The reader will find the essential part of Theodore's notes in Loisy, Mandéisme 19-21.
8.   Rudolph, Mandäer I, 13/14.
9.   Rudolph, Mandäer I, 60/61.
10. Drower, Mandaeans XXI. There is a parallel of this in Catholicism : there an idea is current that Jesus' baptism in the Jordan consecrated all the waters in the world, making them fit for baptism.
11. Rudolph, Mandäer I, 64.
12. Rudolph, Mandaeism 5. Behm, Mand.Rel. 14 : "Die ursprünglichen Sitze der Mandäer und die Uranfänge ihrer Religion, in welcher Form auch immer, müssen in Palästina in der Nähe des Jordan gesucht werden, etwa im Osten des Flusses auf das Haurangebirge zu."
13. Rudolph, Mandäer I, 254.
14. Rudolph, Mandaeism 1.
15. Rudolph, Mandäer I, 66. Theodore Bar Konaï does not mention John the Baptist at all, Loisy, Mandéisme 27. This author, pp. 28-46, relates what Mandaean texts have to say of him.
16. Rudolph, Mandäer I, 80. Behm, Mand.rel. 21 : "Das Bild, das die synoptischen Evangelien von Johannes zeichnen ..., passt nicht mit dem des mandäischen Propheten der Gnosis und des Baptismus zusammen ... Alle Wahrscheinlichkeit spricht vielmehr dafür, dass Johannes ... hier von der täuferischen Gnosis um seiner Taufe willen stillschweigend als ihresgleichen in Anspruch genommen ... worden ist. In das Gewand des mandäischen Offenbarers gehüllt, wurde er so zum Konkurrenten Jesu."
17. Drower, Mandaeans 3.
18. Drower, Mandaeans 2/3.
19. It is, of course, tempting to think of 'Nazoraean' = man from Nazaret, when we hear of a 'Nasurai', and, in consequence, construct a link with earliest Christianity, with Jesus, the man from Nazareth, that is. However, the Mandaeans themselves do not make this connection; they

do not apply the term 'Nasurai' to Christians. Instead, in their language a 'Nasurai', plural 'Nasorayye', means 'observant', that is 'adept in the mysteries of the Mandaean religion', or a highly expert priest. 'Nasuritha' means 'priestcraft' (Drower, Mandaeans 3-5; Rudolph, Mandaeism 1). In the opinion of the Mandaeans both Jesus and John the Baptist were 'Nasoraeans' (Rudolph, Mandäer I, 114). Rudolph, Mandäer I, 155, thinks that there is neither connection with the similar Semitic term for 'Christian', and (Rudolph, Mandäer I, 117/118) nor with Judaeo-Christians. However, he supposes that the term might suggest a historical link with heretical Jewish circles in the country east of the Jordan (Rudolph, Mandäer I, 117). A different opinion is presented by Hans Heinrich Schaeder s.v. 'Nazarênos, Nazooraios', Theol. Wörterbuch zum Neuen Testament 4, 882-884 (Stuttgart (1942). He thinks that 'Nasoraja' is the Mandaean rendering of 'Nasraja', the generic name for Christians in the Syrian speaking region. This agrees with a remark by Drower, Mandaeans 4, that the word for Christian in the Aramaean language is 'Nasara'.

20. Drower, Mandaeans 3. Of all this nothing is to be found in the New Testament.

21. Loisy, Mandéisme 68.

22. Drower, Mandaeism 18, n. 7. Ruha = spirit, cf. Hebrew 'ruah'. For places where Ruha is called Christ's mother, JB 186.11; GR 52,32; in 247.34/35 Christ is created by Ruha **and** the planets.

23. JB 50.146-148.

24. JB 406.19.

25. Loisy, Mandéisme 87.

26. Drower, Mandaeism 3.

27. JB 114.9.

28. GR 134.37-40, 135.1-2.

29. GR 383.12.

30. GR 375.27.

31. GR 50.8-11.

32. GR 52.34-53.7.

33. Rudolph, Mandäer I, 51.

34. Rudolph, Mandäer I, 80. Behm, Mand.Rel. 14 is equally of the opinion that "Mandaismus and Judentum miteinander in der Wurzel verwandt sind und historisch zusammengehören als zwei feindliche Brüder, die sich in Palästina um die Wende unserer Zeitrechnung, jedenfalls noch vor dem Untergang des jüdischen Staatswesens im Jahre 70, in glühender Hass gegenüber gestanden haben". If this is correct, I ask myself why Josephus knew nothing of this. And on p. 18 Behm says : "Wir lernen ihn (Mandaeism) begreifen als ein häretisches Judentum, das im Streit liegt mit Priestern und Ältesten, mit Tempelkultus und Schriftgelehrsamkeit in Jerusalem". But the same may be said of the Essenians and partly even of Jesus who, however, did not reject the Jewish God as

the Mandaeans did : "Zu dem Judengott Adonaj oder El-El und seiner Religionsgemeinde fühlt sich das Mandäertum im schärfsten Gegensatz" (Behm 17). Can a religion that hates and rejects the Jewish God be seen as akin to Judaism in its roots?

35. Rudolph, Entwicklungsgesch.d.Mand.Rel. 72.
36. Rudolph, Mandäer I, 80-90. According to Loisy, Mandéisme 60, Mandaeans do not exhibit, generally speaking, a direct knowledge of the Old Testament. "The textual borrowings, which are not very numerous, will not have been immediate but will have resulted from contact either with Jews or with Christians."
37. Rudolph, Mandäer I, 88.
38. Rudolph, Mandäer I, 87.
39. In fact, Mandaean texts know nothing of a Jewish origin, Loisy, Mandéisme 47.
40. Loisy, Mandéisme 60.
41. Rudolph, Mandäer I, 88; sticking to his idea of a Jewish origin, he adds that this hatred can be explained by the enmity of a heretical Jewish sect against official Judaism.
42. Drower, Mandaeans 10.
43. Loisy, Mandéisme 64. For the relations between Mandaeism and Judaism see the illuminating Chapter III of Loisy's book, 'Le Mandéisme et le Judaisme'.
44. Loisy, Mandéisme 87 wrote that Mandaeism "knew nothing consistent about its own origins."
45. Printed in Drower, Mandaeans 259-263.
46. Drower, Mandaeans, Legend V, p. 284.
47. Drower, Mandaeans 5-8.
48. Drower, Mandaeans 23/24.
49. Drower, Mandaeans 20.
50. Drower, Mandaeans 24.
51. Jorun J. Buckley s.v. 'Ginza', Enc.Rel. 5, 561.
52. There exists a reprint of this, Berlin 1966.
53. Rudolph, Mandaeism 12.
54. I was unable to locate this text in the sources; I found it quoted by Kroll, Gott u. Hölle 273. This scholar gives Mandaean dualism an Iranian background.
55. GR 75.6-9.
56. JB 55.11-13.
57. Equally from ATS, quoted by Rudolph, Theogonie 83, n. 2.

58. The Ginza is divided into a Right Ginza (GR) and a shorter Left Ginza (GL). The Right Ginza contains theogonic, cosmogonic, and anthropogonic material; the Left Ginza is a 'book of the dead'. See Jorun Jacobsen Buckley s.v. 'Ginza', Enc.Rel. 5, 561. My quotations follow the modern page-numbers and line-numbers of Lidzbarski's editions.
59. Rudolph, Theognie 17.
60. GR 65.29; 66.14; 73.9.
61. GR 65.29; 66.14.
62. Drower, Mandaeans 58, n. 13.
63. In the third theogony Ayar appears not as a first principle but as a secondary phenomenon, GR 73.12.
64. GR 66.15.
65. GR 66.15-16.
66. GR 73.11-12; 'King of Light' is a more recent name, Rudolph, Mandaeism 13.
67. GR 66.1-6.
68. GR 66.7-10; 66.16-17; 73.19-22.
69. GR 66.12-13.
70. GR 66.24-26; 73.25-26.
71. Drower, Mandaeans 73.
72. Rudolph, Mandaeism 13. We must be careful not to call these uthras 'gods'; according to the Mandaeans, only false religions have gods, Loisy, Origines 22. This same author gives pp.22-24 a short but very useful synopsis of Mandaean mythology.
73. Rudolph, Theogonie 22; on the same page he prints a useful schedule of the principles and emanations in the three theogonies.
74. GR 66.17-20.
75. GR 66.20-21.
76. GR 67.8-15.
77. GR 67.16-25.
78. Rudolph, Mandaeism 13.
79. GR 142.17.
80. GR 67.25-27.
81. GR 79.15-16.
82. GR 80.1-12.
83. GR 80.31-35.
84. GR 82.5-8.
85. GR 82.24-28.

86.	GR 82.35-84.14.
87.	GR 84.15-33.
88.	GR 85.25-26.
89.	GR 86.24-25.
90.	GR 87.17-23.
91.	GR 87.26-37.
92.	Lidzbarski, Ginza 149. It is related in considerable length in Holl, Gott u. Hölle 270-299.
93.	G. Bardy s.v. 'Mandéisme. Doctrine'. Dict.théol.cath. 9.2. Paris, 1927.
94.	Very probably 'dew' is a borrowing from the Persian where it is 'daeva', see Vol. IV, Ch. IV.8e. Drower gives it as 'daiwa', pl. 'daiwia', Mandaeans 198 and Index.
95.	GR 147.25-148.2, and 165.40-45.
96.	GR 150.30-36.
97.	GR 151.5-153.2.
98.	GR 153.34-154.1.
99.	GR 153.28-33.
100.	GR 154.7-14.
101.	GR 154.15-25.
102.	GR 154.26-39.
103.	GR 155.6-28.
104.	GR 156.4-29.
105.	GR 156.30-36.
106.	GR 157.4-29.
107.	GR 157.30-40.
108.	GR 160.1-161.24.
109.	GR 161.31-162.4.
110.	GR 162.8-163.13.
111.	GR 163.13-30.
112.	GR 164.6-13.\
113.	GR 164.20-34.
114.	GR. 164.35-165.13.
115.	GR 165.27-166.16.
116.	GR 167.18-168.2.
117.	The connection between the first and the second myths is not seamless here, since Ruha was already walled in.

118. GR 168.3-35.
119. GR 170.11-43.
120. GR 171.1-35.
121. GR 172.3-39.
122. GR 172.40-173.28.
123. GR 173.29-33.
124. GR 97.11-12.
125. Rudolph, Theogonie 99.
126. JB 3-9.
127. Rudolph, Theogonie 51.
128. GR 97.13-14.
129. Rudolph, Theogonie 138.
130. GR 97.21-98.6.
131. GR 98.7-21. Lidzbarski, JB XXVII-XXVIII, derives the name of Ptahil from the Egyptian god Ptah; the second syllable is then 'el' = god. "Egypt ranked as the special representative of what is material; in consequence, the creator of the hylic world is from there."
132. Lidzbarski, JB XXVIII.
133. GR 98.22-23.
134. GR 100.6-7.
135. GR 100.15-23.
136. GR 100.21-34.
137. GR 100.37-101.10.
138. Ruha and Ur for a third time slept together, and Ruha gave life to five beings this time, in all probability the five planets that are visible with the naked eye, GR 102.1-21. If this is correct, it is a repetition, for there are already seven planets (= the five + the sun and the moon).
139. GR 103.1-104.22; quotation GR 103.29-30.
140. GR 104.23-105.10.
141. GR 104.23-105.10.
142. JB 184.27.
143. GR 410.16-18.
144. Lidzbarski, JB XXII; Rudolph, Theogonie 170.
145. GL 494.7.
146. JB 182.27.
147. JB 187.3.
148. GR 139.38-140.24.

149. GR 134.13-14.
150. Lidzbarski, Ginza 20, n. 5.
151. GR 134.37-135.8.
152. GR 135.9-26.
153. GR 137.35-40.
154. Rudolph, Theogonie 247.
155. GR 107.3-12.
156. GR 106.26-27.
157. GR 107.28-108.3.
158. GR 108.4-24.
159. GR 108.25-109.3.
160. GR 109.4-110.6.
161. GR 110.13-111.10.
162. GR 242.25-33.
163. GR 361.29-30.
164. GR 362.15-20.
165. GR 275.3-4.
166. GR 96.27-35.
167. GL 508.40-509.2.
168. GL 506.15-24.
169. ATS-text, quoted by Rudolph, Theogonie 266.
170. Quoted from ATS by Rudolph, Theogonie 266, n. 8.
171. GL 487.31-32.
172. GL 487.34.
173. GL 486.22-23.
174. GL 487.5-17.
175. Rudolph, Theogonie 281.
176. Rudolph, Theogonie 287.
177. GR 130.11-14.
178. Rudolph, Theogonie 287.
179. Dower, Mandaeans 59.
180. GR 243.19-23.
181. GR 112.36-37.
182. Rudolph, Theogonie 250.
183. Behm, Mand.Rel. 6.

184. GR 109.29-30.
185. GR 110.4-5.
186. From a hymn quoted by Rudolph, Theogonie 270.
187. GL 455.29-456.5.
188. GR 243.23-28.
189. GR 244.1-8.
190. GR 243.29-30.
191. Quoted from a Qolasha-hymn by Rudolph, Theogonie 299.
192. The source is here the Alf Tristar Suialia (ATS), quoted by Rudolph, Theogonie 95.
193. Another ATS-text, quoted by Rudolph, Theogonie 95.
194. Rudolph, Theogonie 94.
195. GR 253.13-15.
196. ATS-text, quoted by Rudolph, Theogonie 95.
197. Rudolph, Theogonie 95.
198. Rudolph, Theogonie 196-197.
199. GR 284.13-14.
200. GR 89.9-10.
201. GR 143.15-18.
202. GR 352.21-40.
203. GR 243.10-15.
204. GR 15.19-20.
205. GL 437.1-25.
206. Babel and Borsip = Babylon and Borsippa; Borsippa is an ancient Babylonian town to the south of Babylon.
207. GL 435.36-436.15.
208. Rudolph, Theogonie 192.
209. GR 311.11-24.
210. Drower, Mandaeans 95, n. 3; Rudolph, Theogonie 74.
211. GR 163.28.
212. GR 311.31-40.
213. Rudolph, Mandaeism 5-6.
214. Rudolph, Mandaeism 9-10.
215. Rudolph, Mandaeism 10.

CHAPTER IV

MANI'S WORLD-RELIGION

1. The standard-bearer of dualism

To many people, journalists of all kinds among them, 'Manichaean' has the same meaning as 'dualistic', although, more often than not, they never use the term 'dualistic' itself and perhaps do not even know it. The popularity of the word 'Manichaean' - by using it one proves that one is an erudite person - must not lead to the conclusion that Manichaeism is the dualistic doctrine par excellence; in popular opinion Zoroastrianism also makes this claim. We shall, however, see that Manichaean doctrine is ideologically more extremely dualistic than many other Gnostic systems, and, moreover, it has the strictest way of life of all Gnostic sects.

What then makes it the standard-bearer of dualism? It is difficult to say. A connection, perhaps, may be even an identification with Zoroastrianism, because after all Mani, the founder, although born in Mesopotamia, was an Iranian? Or the fact that one of the greatest minds in Antiquity, and even of European history, Saint Augustine, was a Manichaean in his younger years? Or is it because Manichaeism can rightly be called a world-religion of long standing, since from its birth-place in Babylonia it spread very widely and subsisted for many centuries? In the west it spread over almost the whole of the Roman Empire, surviving until well into the sixth century; in the east it made its way through Turkestan to China and Mongolia. In China it managed to subsist until after 1300. This means that the Manichaean religion reached its greatest extension and had its longest span of life in regions far beyond the ken of medieval people.

2. The rediscovery of Manichaeism

During the thousand years that elapsed between the end of the Western Roman Empire and the Renaissance, Manichaeism as such, as a specific doctrine in its own right, seems to have been forgotten in the west, although Manichaean ideas were still current, but under other labels, like Paulician, Bogomil, or Cathar.

It was only in the time of the Reformation and the Renaissance that Manichaeism was, so to speak, 'rediscovered'. It was a period of 'back to the sources' - to the sources of the Bible, of Christian dogma, of the Church, of art, and what not. In the wake of this 'archaeological' movement, forgotten ancient religions were brought to light again. The first scholars to mention Manichaeism were the so-called 'Magdeburgenses Centuriatores', the authors of the first Protestant ecclesiastical history, composed by Flavius Illyricus and his colleagues, and published in Basel in the years 1559-1574 under the title of 'Ecclesiastica historia Ecclesiae Christi'.

In 1569 the Roman-Catholic author Gabriel Dupréau, in his dictionary of heresies, accused Luther of being close to Manichaeism [1]. The Lutheran scholar Cyriacus Spangenberg defended the Reformer against this charge; he did this in a book of 1578, the first monograph to be devoted to Manichaeism [2]. For our purpose it is not necessary to pursue this historiographical enquiry further; suffice it to say that around 1600 research on Manichaeism was well under way [3].

Although the sources began to flow abundantly, for a long time there appeared no works of synthesis, partly because Catholic-Protestant controversy still flared up occasionally [4]. In the years 1734-1739 Isaac de Beausobre published a bulky work on Manichaeism in two volumes [5]. As Julien Ries states, this is the first summarizing study of the sources, western as well as eastern. But unfortunately his critique of the sources was biased, for Beausobre remains a controversialist. His whole work is governed by his preoccupation to justify the Reformation. He showed a tendency to see in Manichaeism a draft of Protestantism before Protestantism. But his great merit, says Ries, is to have brought together the hitherto scattered oriental data, and to have shown that the dualistic doctrine of Mani had an oriental origin [6].

3. Modern scholarship on Manichaeism

Although interdenominational warfare still continued, in the beginning of the nineteenth century "Mani, the Christian heretic, made place for Mani, the founder of a universal religion" [7]. It was the great German historian of religion, Ferdinand Christian Baur, who was the first to bring about this fundamental change in the perception of Manichaeism; it is not a heresy, he argued, but a new religion [8]. Baur had read several scholars who defended the thesis that Manichaeism was a reformed Zoroastrianism. While he agreed with this point of view, he insisted that Buddhism also had influenced Iranian religion. This had the effect of directing the attention of the scholarly world to Indian influences on Mani's doctrine [9].

Around the middle of the nineteenth century important and intriguing Arab sources were discovered and published which threw new light on Manichaeism. This led some scholars to believe that Manichaeism was not an Indo-Iranian doctrine. Fr. Spiegel, for instance, freely admitted that there was an Iranian connection, but, he says, Mani's aspirations were, so to speak, world-wide; Spiegel suggested that the real source of Mani's thought might be Babylonian cosmology [10].

It was in particular the German Assyriologist Konrad Kessler who, in publication after publication during the last quarter of the nineteenth century, defended the supposed Mesopotamian (Chaldaeo-Babylonian) origin of Manichaeism with all his might [11]. With the acerbity that so often characterizes scholarly discussion, Kessler was attacked from all sides. But he had his supporters too, among them nobody less than

Harnack who saw in the doctrine of Mani a Babylonian Gnosis, Semitic rather than Iranian [12].

In the last decade of the nineteenth century and again in the beginning of the twentieth important new sources were discovered. It was already known then that extremely ancient documents had circulated in the region of Turfan (T'u-Lu-Fan), in the Chinese province of Sinkiang, just to the east of the most eastern ridges of the Himalayas. From 1893 onward excavations were conducted there, first by the Russians, followed by the Germans. A mass of Manichaean documents was unearthed, most of it in Middle Persian, the language of Iran under the Sasanians, and partly in Sogdian, old Turkish, and Uigur. These finds eloquently testified to the great interest many nations had in Manichaeism.

In 1900 a Taoist monk found a recess in one of the grottoes of the 'Thousand Buddhas'; these are situated fourteen miles to the south-east of the town of Tun-Huang, in the province of Kansu, on the frontier of Chinese Turkestan. This recess contained a great number of ancient manuscripts, of Manichaean origin as they proved to be; a seal attached to one of the documents revealed that the library was immured in 1035. Alerted by this news, an English scholar arrived and bought five thousand of them; he was followed by a Frenchman who acquired another lot. These texts are in Chinese, Tibetan, and Sogdian, and in an Iranian dialect. Publication of the Turfan and Tun-Huang finds began almost immediately but has not been completed even now [13].

Finally, North-Africa yielded some of its treasures. In 1918 an important document dating from about 400 came to light in the vicinity of Tebessa in Algeria, near the frontier with Tunisia. In 1930 a German scholar was able to buy from a merchant in Cairo a whole collection of Manichaean texts dating from the fourth century, written in the Coptic language; they came from a cave near Medinet Madi in the Fayum [14]. It is obvious enough that all these finds have enormously enriched our knowledge of Manichaeism. Furthermore, the place-names mentioned show how far and wide Mani's influence ranged.

4. The present stance of scholarship

Ries describes the present state of scholarship with regard to Manichaeism as follows. On the question of its origin and the kind of Gnosis it represents, there are two streams of opinion. First, there are those who base themselves mainly on the oriental sources; they see in Mani a Gnostic who borrowed his world-religion from Iran. The chief protagonist of this school is the Swedish scholar Geo Widengren. The other school starts from the western documents, Coptic, Arabian, Greek, Latin, and Syriac, and concludes that Mani founded a Gnosis that closely resembled the Gnostic systems of the Graeco-Roman world. In this context one must mention the small but classical work of Henri-Charles Puech [15]. On one point, however, the two schools agree entirely : Mani was a hardly to be surpassed dualist.

5. Mani's life

a. Place and date of Mani's birth and his parents

Tradition always speaks of Mani as 'the Babylonian'. He was born in that country, indeed, very probably in the township of Mardinu on the left bank of the Tigris, not far to the south of the Sasanian capital Ctesiphon, the ancient Seleukeia of the Seleucids, now al-Mada'in [16]. The name 'Mani' was common enough in this part of Babylonia; Greeks and Latins sometimes rendered it as 'Manikhaios, Manichaeus' which may have been derived from the Syriac 'Mani Hayyah' = Mani the Living [17].

The date of his birth is known with the greatest exactitude : April 14, 216 [18] - a very rare phenomenon in the ancient world. How do we know this so precisely? Because in some autobiographical texts the prophet himself supplies sufficient astronomical and historical information to pin down his birth-date to the day, the month, and the year mentioned [19].

Of Mani's parents only one thing is absolutely certain : his father was called Patek/Patteg/Pattig (Iranian) or Patiq (Syriac) [20]. Patek was no Babylonian but a Median, probably born in Hamadan, the country's ancient capital Ecbatana [21]. In all probability this Patek was a man of high birth; he may have been related to the then reigning royal house of the Parthian Empire, the Arsacids [22]. The name of Mani's mother varies from document to document, but Puech is fairly certain that her name was Maryam [23]. We may be rather sure, he thinks, that she too had a royal lineage; she belonged to the family of the Kamsarakan, a branch of the House of the Arsacids [24]. Before Mani's birth Patek migrated from Media to Babylonia; it is not known why [25].

b. Arsacid and Sasanian religious policy

When Patek settled in or near Ctesiphon, it was still the seat of the Arsacid dynasty in the person of the Emperor Ardewan (Ardavan or Artabanus) V. But on April 24 (or 28), 224 A.D., this ruler was dethroned and killed by one of his military commanders, who, after his coronation in 226, became the first emperor of the Sasanian House as Ardashir (Artaxerxes) I. This also meant that the Parthian rulers were relieved by Persian ones [26].
Puech mentions the supposition that is sometimes made that Mani's religious activity might have been directed against the new dynasty, probably usurpers in his eyes, related as he was to the disposed royal house. The new rulers clung to the ancient Iranian religion, and Mani could have tried to undermine their position by preaching a totally new creed. But Puech thinks that there is no sufficient ground for this theory [27]. Did the change of dynasty indeed signify a volte-face in a religious respect? It has often been contended that the tolerant, liberal, and philhellenic religious policy of the Arsacids made place for the harsh and intolerant Zoroastrianism of the Sasanians. It is true, of course, that Zoroastrianism, or Mazdaism, in time became the official state religion, favoured in every respect by the monarchs, this to the detriment of other creeds [28]. The leading thought was that Persia (with her diversified population)

should be a unified nation, with a national government and based on a truly national religion.

But a few objections might be raised. First, Zoroastrian orthodoxy had not remained as pure and undiluted as is sometimes supposed. In the period under consideration there existed a less orthodox, heretical branch of the original creed of Zoroaster, namely Zervanism [29]. Zoroaster acknowledged one supreme deity, Ahura Mazda (hence the name 'Mazdaism' for his creed); his starting-point, therefore, was monotheistic. Dualism began one stage lower, with two opposed spirits, Spenta Mainyu, the Beneficent one, and Angra (or Ahra) Mainyu, the Evil one. In the Zervanite myth a vague entity, Zervan (or Zurvan), Time, was the father of twins, Ormuzd (Ahura Mazda) and Ahriman (Ahra Mainyu). The Sasanian state church, says Widengren, was "a merger of Zervanite Magi ... and Zoroastrian fire-priests ... In this way a Zervanite stream originated in Sasanian Iran, so strong that we can speak indeed of a Zervanite coloured Zoroastrianism. It proved possible to describe the situation in these terms that the Zoroastrianism of the Sasanian period was really only a Zervanism" [30].

The second objection is that the first Sasanians were more liberal than is generally thought. It seems that Ardashir I (226-242) and his successor Shapur I (242-273), while certainly favouring Zervanism, were still somewhat hesitant about the course to be followed. Neither of the two, says Widengren, may rank as the real founder of a Zoroastrian-Zervanite state-church. Shapur in particular did not put obstacles in the way of Manichaeism [31].

c. Patek's religion

To return now to Mani's father. Patek seems to have regularly visited in Ctesiphon 'a temple of idols', according to an Arab source. The temple of which creed? This is not stated [32]. We do not know which religion Patek professed nor whether the temple in question was a cult-place of his own creed. But the phrase 'temple of idols' does not sound as if a Zoroastrian fire-temple is meant [33]. Anyhow, for three days on end Patek heard a voice coming from the interior of the sanctuary commanding him : "Patek, do not eat meat! Do not drink wine! And keep away from women!" This took place at a time that his mother was already pregnant of the future Mani. It is possible that Patek obeyed the injunction to abstain from women, for the same source tells us that he "sent for his son and brought him to the place where he stayed himself. After this he (Mani) grew up in his (Patek's) home and in his (Patek's) religion" [34]. This can have taken place in 219 or 220 after the child had been weaned at the breast [35]. The inference must be that Patek, for some years already, had been living apart from his wife.

d. The sect of the Mughtasila

What was the new religion of Mani's father? To all intents and purposes it must have been that of the 'Mughtasila'. Our Arab source says : "Patek joined a community of people in the region of Dast-i-Maïshân (in the southern part of Babylonia) that was known under the name of al-Mughtasila, that is 'those who wash themselves', the remains of which sect are still to be found in this region and in the marshes until our own days (= ca. 1000)" [36]. Did Patek join a sect of Baptists? Our thoughts of course fly immediately to the Mandaeans who were Baptists and who lived and still live in this region, the Shatt al 'Arab. The decisive question, however, is : were the Mandaeans established in southern Iraq way back ca. 220? It does not seem very probable [37].

Did the Mughtasila constitute a Baptist sect? This is, at first sight, not impossible; Baptist sects proliferated in the region between the Jordan and the lower Euphrates. Theodore bar Konaï speaks of the Mughtasila as 'the pure' and 'those who wash themselves' [38]. They were obviously given to frequent ablutions, but this ancient author does not speak of baptism proper [39]. On the other hand, Mani himself spoke of them as 'Baptists' [40]. Their purity was accentuated by their wearing white garments; without any doubt they were leading a strictly ascetic life. Since Patek was ordered to abstain from sexual intercourse, after which he joined the Mughtasila, the inference must be that this sect rejected marriage and sexuality (which the Mandaeans did not).

Our Arab source, the 'Fihrist' of Ibn an-Nadim, knows somewhat more about those Mughtasila. He speaks of 'the Sabaeans of Bata'ih'; the Bata'ih is the marshland of the Shatt al 'Arab where the Euphrates and the Tigris unite. "They practise ablutions and wash everything they eat. Their head is called al-Khasyah. It is him who gives the law to his community. He pretends that there are two fields of being, male and female ... They are of one accord with the Manichaeans on the two principles" [41].

e. Was there a relation between the Mughtasila and the Elkasaites?

This text makes up happy with a proper name : al-Khasya, which name makes our thoughts jump to the 'Elkesai', the sect of the Elkasaites (Elkesaites, Elcesaites). A prophet or founder called 'al-Khasyah' probably never existed [42]. The sect is said to have appeared around A.D. 100 along the Euphrates. We come on firmer ground only a century later, around 220, when we hear of a book of 'Elxai'; this book was believed to have brought down from heaven by an angel of gigantic proportions [43]. A book of Elxai really existed; a Syrian, Alcibiades of Apamea, brought it around 220 to Rome [44]. Only fragments of it have been preserved [45].

Alcibiades preached the Elkasaite doctrine in Rome and later perhaps also in Caesarea in Palestine but was forcefully combated by Hippolytus and Origen; Epiphanius mentions its existence at the end of the fourth century [46]. This author says that Elkasaites were Jews; the favourite aim of their propaganda were the Judaizing Christian groups that flourished in the broad region stretching from the Jordan and the Dead Sea through Syria and northern Arabia onto the Shatt al 'Arab. They went on vegetating for some centuries; we saw that Ibn an-Nadim said that they still existed around 987 [47].

Elkasaitism can best be characterized as a syncretistic religious ideology in which Jewish, Christian, and Gnostic influences amalgamated. "They are neither Christians nor Jews or pagans; they are a middle sort or rather nothing at all", sneered Epiphanius [48]. Having a sacred book of their own, Elkasaites did not put much stock in the Bible. They rejected Paul and all his letters; since they abhorred every kind of sacrifice, they repudiated all books and passages in the Old Testament referring to sacrifices. "In fact,", says Bareille, "they utilized Scripture for hardly anything else than for giving a semblance of orthodoxy to their doctrine" [49]. In the book of Elxai they possessed "the precious and unique pearl that enclosed all the mysteries of salvation which must not be disclosed to the first comer, because not all men are faithful and not all women are straightforward" [50].

Elkesaites may have been Jews but their disdain of the Bible is as un-Jewish as it is un-Christian. Their boasting of a special revelation of their own is typically Gnostic, just as their wish to keep it secret and reserved only for an élite. This attitude is equally un-Hellenic, for Elkesaites held that, since everything had been revealed in their book, the wisdom of Egypt and the philosophies of Pythagoras, Plato, e tutti quanti were superfluous [51].

The Elkesaite system is monotheistic [52]; the usual ditheism of the Gnosis is not to be found in it. The highest and sovereign God himself is the creator; there is no mention of a lower and evil-intentioned Demiurge. But it is not orthodox Christianity because Jesus of Nazareth is not the Son of God; there is no real Trinity. In fact, Elkesaites are not interested in Jesus. God has a son indeed who, however, is a creature, albeit a very great and privileged one. This son went through many manifestations and incarnations, the first one of these being Adam. The Holy Spirit is presented as a female angel [53], which again is a Gnostic feature.

The Elkesaites remained Jewish in so far that they practised circumcision, kept the Sabbath, and obeyed the injunctions of Mosaic Law [54]. But they were vegetarians and did not bring carnal and bloody sacrifices. The place of the sacrificial fire is taken by water. The new adherent became a full member by complete immersion into water, but contrary to Christian usage, baptism could be repeated later as a a means of forgiveness for grave sins.

The great problem is whether or not the Elkesaites and the Mughtasila were identical. Ibn an-Nadim clearly was of the opinion that they formed one and the same sect. There are indeed many striking points of resemblance; they existed in the same period and in the same region. Both were ascetic, both rejected bloody sacrifices, and both gave water rather than blood the place of honour in their ritual. But their doctrines and customs did not resemble each other exactly. An important point of difference was that the Elkesaites made marriage obligatory. "They hated virginity, condemned continence, and forced (their members) to contract marriage" [55]. But the Mughtasila were a non-marrying sect. Why else would Patek have joined them after having been ordered by the voice to abstain from women and sex [56]?

We saw, however, that Ibn an-Nadim, obviously referring to the Mughtasila, spoke of their 'two fields of being', male and female; in these 'two fields of being' he saw two principles. In this respect, he thought, they were identical with the (later) Manichaeans. The Elkesaites, I wrote, did not acknowledge two gods; so far as we know the Mughtasila did not either. An ancient text suggests that, according to Elkesaite doctrine, there was a conflict between 'the king of the future things' (God) and 'the king of the present things' (the son of God). The last mentioned said that the whole world belonged to him, but that he would present it to the higher king, if he would prostrate himself and adore the son (cf. Mt. 5). He said this because he knew that when the higher king did this, the son would have him in his power. This smacks, if not of ditheism, then in any case of dualism [57].

It is not possible to obtain absolute clarity on the relationship of Elkesaitism and Mughtasilism. But it seems that they were very close [58]. Mani must have heard of the two principles very early in his life; they were in the very air he breathed [59]. The mental climate in which he grew up was one of gnosticizing, of élitism, of asceticism, of esoterism, and above all, of dualism.

f. Young Mani as a Mughtasila

Surroundings like these did not remain without influence on the precocious boy; "even when young he spoke words of wisdom" [60]. Members of the sect testified how Mani had lived among them. "Since your earliest age you lived in our midst for the good, faithful to our prescriptions and to the rules of conduct in our Law." Mani himself was quite content with having been a Mughtasila. He called this period his 'years of nursing'. "It was then that I joined the religion of the Baptists in which I grew up. Because of the youth of my body I was protected by the power of the light-angels and the very great powers who were charged by Jesus-Splendour to stand guard over me. It was thus that, since my fourth year until the moment that I acquired physical maturity, I was protected by the hands of very holy angels and the powers of sanctity" [61].

Two things must strike us. First that 'protected'. Protected against what? In all probability against sin, against evil. And next we detect a sentiment of being the object of special attention from above. These things amount to an early feeling of 'apartheid', probably stimulated by the seclusion in which the sect lived. True enough, the Prophet told this to his disciple Salmaios in retrospect, but that he had an early notion of being chosen is by no means unlikely.

g. On the road to 'apartheid'

At the age of twelve the deeply religious boy had a revelation. An angel who was called 'tawn' came to him and spoke : "Leave this cult (of the Mughtasila), for you are not one of its adherents. Upon you are laid purity and refraining from bodily lusts, but it is not yet time for you to appear openly, because of your tender years" [62]. This same source states that the angel came from 'the King of the Gardens of Light', "and from what he said, it was God exalted". In other words, the revelation was backed by the highest possible authority. The meaning of the word 'tawn' is given as 'companion'; what is meant is a double, a sort of twin [63], a spirit that must live 'with him, accompany him everywhere, and come to his aid always"[64]. It is not impossible that with this spirit the Holy Ghost is meant [65].

h. The dissident

The adolescent had his problems with the Mughtasila, and they with him. He no longer believed that all those lustrations had any sense [66]. "Every baptized (washed) food that is evacuated and expelled by the body does not distinguish itself from food that is not baptized" [67]. Why wash vegetables? This does not cleanse a person from evil. What Mani sought was moral purity. "The purity of which Scripture (= Jesus in the Gospels) speaks is that purity that comes from being able to distinguish between light and darkness, life and death, living waters and dead waters. This is the true purity which you were ordered to put into practice" [68]. One sees already emerging the doctrine of the two principles.

Mani did not believe in the redeeming power of water but in something quite different which put him at a very great distance, not only from Elkesaites and Mughtasila, but also from baptist Jewish sects, Christians and Mandaeans alike. "The purity of which we spoke ... is acquired by means of Knowledge ..., according to the commandments of the Saviour. Knowledge delivers the soul from death and destruction" [69]; this became his basic credo.

There must have been much discussion, not always of a serene kind, between the Mughtasila and their ever more deviant member. His indignant co-religionists reproached him that he was choosing the pagan way. "He will go the heathen and eat Greek bread. For we heard him saying : 'One must eat Greek bread'. Likewise he said that it is good to take beverage, grain, vegetables, and fruit-things that our fathers took care not to consume" [70]. Elkesaites and Mughtasila ate only unleavened bread; to eat something else ('Greek bread') meant apostasy [71].

The exasperated elders then cited Patek and asked him to explain the behaviour of their son to them. But he said : "Call him yourself and try to make him understand reason". So the young man had to appear in person before the convocation. His accusers chose the mild way. "Since your infancy you are with us and you have always persevered in our prescriptions and the observances of our Law. What happened to you? For you now oppose our Law, you reverse and reverse our doctrine. The road you are taking diverges from our way" [72]. Friendly as this admonition was, it also makes clear that the bridges had already been blown up. Mani answered that he did nothing but follow the example of Jesus who ate with sinners and publicans; he did not distinguish between bread and bread, between vegetable and vegetable [73]. What he next said virtually meant that not he was the heretic, but they themselves. For Elchasai, the founder, was not interested in ablutions [74]. At this point in the discussion the synod came very near to becoming aggressive against Mani; it was only at the entreaty of his father that the elders let go the culprit [75].

Of course, this report is of a later date, long after Mani had broken with the sect, and may, in consequence, contain a certain amount of rationalization. But there can be no doubt that it more or less faithfully renders the tension that at that time prevailed in the community.

j. Mani's mission

There could be no other outcome than a final breach. The period of gestation lasted twelve years, for Mani had reached his twenty-fourth year, when the angel tawn manifested himself to him for the second time. "The time is fulfilled for you to come forth and to give the summons for your cause." This makes it clear that Mani, once having become an adult, was conscious of having a cause of his own. The angel went on : "Peace for you, oh Mani, from myself and from the Lord who sent me to you. He has chosen you for his mission, and commanded you to summon in your own right, to preach the gospel of his truth as from his presence, and to carry on in this (mission) with all of your perseverance" [76]. The decisive words are 'in your own right'. Mani was no longer an Elkesaite or a Mughtasila.

k. The date of Mani's first public appearance

Mani must have waited some months before coming forward in public. Since this event was of the greatest importance to the Manichees, as the foundation date of their Church, they tried to ascertain it with the utmost exactitude. "Marcion appeared nearly a hundred years earlier", says Ibn an-Nadim, "Ibn Daysan appeared about thirty years after Marcion." Ibn Daysan is the Gnostic Bardesanes who lived 154-222. He 'flourished' around 185. It is evident that Ibn an-Nadim gives Mani some sort of Gnostic ancestorship. We come nearer to the event in question, when he writes : "Mani appeared during the second year of the reign of Gallus the Roman". This Gallus is the Roman Emperor Vibius Gallus Trebonianus (251-253); the Arabian author must be in error here, since the second year of this ruler is ten years after Mani's first public appearance. Gordianus III (238-244) was emperor then. We come closer to an accurate dating with this communication : "He (Mani) came forth (publicly) on the day of the sovereignty of Shapur (I) Ibn (son of) Ardashir, when the crown was placed on his head. It was Sunday, the first day of Nisan (April), when the sun was in Aries" [77]. Shapur I was emperor of Persia from 241 to 272. In spite of this precision, there still remains some doubt with regard to what Burkitt called 'the Pentecost of Manichaeism' [78]. On the authority of S.H. Taqizadeh, Puech and others prefer April 9, 243 [79].

l. What did Mani look like?

This seems the right moment, before we continue with Mani's travels and his doctrine, to ask what he looked like. There are portraits on some ancient coins that probably give his likeness. Some of these coins were found in Charakene in southern Mesopotamia; others were minted during the reign of King Peroz of Kushan in the third century (this king was a Manichee). They show the face of a man who is looking to the right; he has thick, wavy hair falling into the neck, a straight nose, and a pointed beard. Several scholars believe that this is an authentic portrait of Mani [80].

We have also a kind of 'movie' in which we see Mani entering a house; this 'movie' is the lively description of a meeting, as we find it in the Acta Archelai. We are in the home of a well-to-do man, Marcellus; bishop Archelaus is also present. They have been listening to an exposition of Manichaean doctrine by a certain Turbo, a disciple of the prophet. And then suddenly Mani himself arrives. He has made a long voyage to be able to argue with the bishop. "With him he brought selected young men and girls, twenty-two in all ... He went in to pay his respects to Marcellus. When he saw him, Marcellus stood surprised at the design of his dress. For he wore a kind of shoes which colloquially use to be called 'three-soles'; furthermore, he had a mantle in different colours looking like azure. In his hand he had a rather thick staff of ebony. Under his left arm he carried a Babylonian book. His legs were covered with differently coloured breeches, one leg red, the other a kind of leek-green. His facial expression resembled that of an elderly Persian doctor and general" [81].

m. Mani's missionary activities

At the time of his first public appearance Mani, now twenty-seven years old, must have felt lonely. However, he had two companions who were "in accord with his doctrine"; Ibn an-Nadim calls them Shamun (Simeon?) and Dhakwa (Zako?) [82]. One of our sources reports that Mani began his public activity by preaching to his own family. "The things that the twin (= the Tawn, the Spirit, the Paraclete) had taught me I divulged and communicated to my father and the elders of my family. When they had heard this, they were converted" [83]. "His father", says Ibn an-Nadim, "was also with him, watching what was happening to his cause" [84].

Mani began his missionary work in public in the capital, Ctesiphon, where he visited baptist communities [85]. He soon travelled on. There can be no doubt that the great example for Mani as a missionary was the indefatigable apostle Paul [86]. "Paul too went out and preached [87] ... But not one of the (other) apostles has worked as I did" [88]. But Tardieu rightly points out the difference between the apostolate of Paul and that of

Mani. Paul preached the Christ, "and him crucified"; Mani preached Mani who is 'the seal of the prophets', and who is the twin of the Spirit, that is, who identifies himself with it. Another difference is that Paul remained in Asia Minor, Greece, and Italy, within the confines of the Roman Empire; Mani travelled eastward, even as far as India [89]. This means the difference between an Hellenistic oriented and an orientally directed mission.

From Ctesiphon he probably went to the north of Babylonia. An ancient source has it that "they (Mani and his companions) entered the Roman Empire" [90]. If this is correct, they must have crossed the Euphrates into what are now the eastern provinces of Turkey and the eastern parts of Syria. This expedition cannot have lasted long [91], for soon enough they went south again, to the Shatt al 'Arab where Mani boarded a ship bound for India [92]. "I (Mani) travelled (on a ship) to the country of the Indians" [93]. Puech leaves us a choice of several reasons why he left the Sasanian Empire. Did he feel threatened? Did he want to learn from the Buddhists? Or was the apostle Thomas his example who, according to tradition, had made the same voyage to India and had founded Christian communities there [94]?

Mani landed in the region where the Indus flows into the Indian Ocean [95], in Balutchistan, in the southern part of present-day Pakistan. There he visited the kingdoms of Makran and Turan, to the west of the river [96]. He seems to have had some success there : "I preached to them the hope of life and chose for them a good selection" [97]. His stay in Balutchistan did not last long, perhaps not more than a year [98].

n. Mani's encounter with King Shapur I

Mani returned by ship to 'the land of the Persians', by which the Iranian heartland Persis is meant, and from there, equally on the sea-road, to the Shatt al 'Arab [99]. It is possible that he made a very important convert there, Firuz (or Peroz), a brother of King Shapur I; perhaps this man was viceroy in southern Babylonia. An old legend relates an event of this kind, embellished with many picturesque details [100]. True or not, it was Firuz who brought Mani into the presence of the king himself [101] who received him with great honour [102]. This encounter must have taken place in the capital. Doubtless Firuz was deeply impressed by Mani's personality, or else he would not have taken this initiative [103].

By a stroke of good fortune we are in the possession of an autobiographical fragment in which Mani described how he was received by the shananshah, the King of Kings [104]. The prophet was greeted by the emperor with these words : "Whence are you?", to which the answer was : "I am a doctor from Babylon". This means, says Ort, that Mani wanted to state that he had miraculous powers; he proved this by relating some miracles he had actually wrought [105]. The Fihrist reports that it was Shapur's original intention to have Mani executed, but when he saw "on his (Mani's) two shoulders what resembled two lamps of light, ... he felt in awe of him and felt well disposed towards him". The outcome of this first interview was that Mani obtained the royal permission to preach his creed throughout the Empire [106]. Shapur obviously felt a great sympathy for the prophet, for he was admitted two times more into the august presence [107]. He even was a member of the imperial retinue for several years [108]. If we may believe the Neoplatonic philosopher Alexander of Lycopolis, he served on the staff of the Iranian army during a campaign against the Roman Empire [109].

o. Further missionary travels

The missionary activity of Mani brought him far and wide, and lasted a great many years. He was active in the whole of the Sasanian Empire and perhaps even beyond its frontiers, in Turkestan and Kashmir. He also sent out his disciples as missionaries, to Egypt for instance [110]. Although looked upon favourably by the Emperor, the Manichaean creed did not become the official state religion. Widengren supposes that Shapur did not wish to commit himself and preferred to keep two options open, that of Manichaeism and that of the old Zoroastrian religion. His personal sympathies may have been with Mani's doctrine, but on political grounds he was not ready to decide for Manichaeism and, in consequence, against Zoroastrianism [111].

p. Mani's end

Thirty years later Shapur I died, probably in April 273; he was succeeded by his son Hormizd I. Mani's relations with this king were as friendly as those with his predecessor [112]. During his short reign the prophet was active in Mesopotamia. But already a year later Hormizd died, to be succeeded by his brother Bahram I (274-277). Now the long smouldering conflict between Mani and the Zoroastrian Magi came to a head. And far more than his father and his brother the new emperor was on the side of the Magi.

Mani must have guessed what was in store for him. He was forbidden by the emperor to travel to the kingdom of Kushan; obviously the government kept an eye on his movements. To his followers he said : "Look at me and satisfy yourselves, my children, for I shall bodily withdraw from you" [113]. The prophet travelled by boat on the Tigris to Ctesiphon as though he would visit the city of his birth for the last time; he then went on to Belapat (Gundishapur), a Sasanian residential town. As soon as the local Magi heard that their adversary had arrived, they accused him at the court.

Soon enough Bahram ordered him to appear before him [114]. When he arrived at the gate of the palace, the king was still at table and had not yet finished his meal. He had with him Karter, the chief of the Magi, Mani's principal accuser. Seeing Mani, the emperor broke out at once : "You are not welcome!". "But why?", Mani retorted, "What did I do wrong?". Bahram said : "I have sworn an oath that I would not allow you to enter this country", and angrily he continued : "What should we need you for, since you do not go to war nor do you hunt? But perhaps you are needed to play the doctor and to prepare medicines. And you not even do this". Bahram probably remembered that Mani had told his father Shapur that he was a doctor; obviously he saw this as a fraud.

Mani quietly answered that he had always done good to the royal family. He had driven out many devils and demons and had cured many of illnesses. He had even called back not a few from the brink of death [115]. The king, laughing angrily at this, now reproached the prophet that he had converted one of the kinglets, turning him away from the Zoroastrian faith. "From whom did you learn the things you teach?" Mani answered that he had not had a human teacher but had his doctrine revealed to him from above [116]. "But why", said the king, "did God give this revelation exactly to you, and not to us (the emperors), although we are the masters of the whole country?" "Such was the will of God", was the answer of the prophet [117], " ... You may do with me what you want. The Emperors Shapur and Hormizd honoured me in every respect."

The king then gave an order to put his opponent in irons [118]. Three young rowdies brought him to a prison where he was bound with chains weighing four stone together [119], one around his neck, three on his hands, and three on his feet [120]; the poor man could hardly move under this weight. We do not know how long exactly he was able to endure this torment; the indications in the sources vary from four to twenty-six days [121]. It cannot have lasted long : he was sixty years old and emaciated by fasting. He found the opportunity to arrange his affairs, particularly who was to succeed him as head of the community [122]. Puech thinks that Mani was imprisoned on Wednesday, January 31, 277, and succumbed on Monday, February 27 [123]. So afraid was the king of his adversary that he ordered his servants to wave torches over the corpse to see whether he was really dead [124]. Later the body was buried in Ctesiphon.

6. Mani's literary output

Mani was a prolific author who wrote, says an-Nadim, "seven books, one of them in Persian and six in Syriac, the language of Syria" [125]; in all probability this 'Syriac' was East-Aramaean [126]. These were the Book of Mysteries (or Secrets), the Book of Giants, the Shâbuhrâgan (this is the book in Persian, dedicated to Shapur I), the Treasure of Life, the Pragmateia, the

Living Gospels [127], and the Epistles of Mani. To this list, given by Ibn an-Nadim [128], the Book of Psalms and Prayers (this was partly composed by the prophet himself), and the Kephalaia (discussions between the Master and his disciples) may be added [129]. This looks impressive enough, but in fact very little of it is extant, not one work completely; of some books only the title remains. Of the Book of Mysteries we possess no more than three quotations [130].

7. The main characteristics of the Church of Justice

The movement that we use to call 'Manichaeism' really bears the name of 'the Church of Justice' or 'the Religion of the Light' [131]. It is, if we follow Puech, characterized by three main features. First of all, it was a universal religion [132]. It was thought of as the religion that would eventually be the only one, after it had won over the whole world. It was never claimed that Mani was the sole possessor of the Truth. Since the beginning of mankind there had been prophets of Truth; the first of these was Adam, followed by Seth, Noah, Abraham, and more particularly Buddha, Zoroaster, and Jesus. These last three, with Mani as the fourth, are the 'apostles'[133].

Mani is 'the seal of the prophets' [134]; with him prophecy becomes complete [135]. "In the last of times prophecy came through me, Mani, the messenger of God the truthful" [136]. "God called you for his apostleship", the Tawn said to Mani, "and now your mission is to invite people to the Truth; you must proclaim in his name the Gospel of Truth" [137]. Mani was greater than the other apostles. ""Not one of the apostles who were sent performed things like these" [138]. The guarantee of the Truth is that Holy Ghost was in Mani, or rather that he was identical with the Holy Ghost. "All that happened and all that will happen was revealed to me by the Paraclete ... I became one body and one spirit (with him)" [139].

The second characteristic, which is a consequence of the first one, is that Manichaeism is a missionary religion [140]. We have already seen how far and wide Manichaean missionaries preached the faith. Its third hallmark is that it is a 'religion of the Book' [141]. In the last resort it was based on Mani's own seven books. In contrast to other founders of religions, like Buddha or Jesus, who wrote nothing at all themselves, and whose doctrines were codified by their disciples, Mani left to posterity a considerable body of scripture by his own hand. Puech thinks that this "assured to Manichaeism a remarkable dogmatic stability"; there were no heresies and only a few schisms [142].

Puech warns us not to see in Manichaeism 'a kind of theosophic syncretism', although it is certainly true that many elements of other religions went into its making [143]. Mani himself was perfectly conscious of this. "Scripture, Books of Wisdom, Apocalypses, parables, and psalms of anterior Churches were assembled from everywhere in my Church for the wisdom I revealed to you. Just as a stream joins another stream to form together one mighty current, so the ancient books were inserted into my writings; and they form a great wisdom, such as former generations never saw" [144].

Rather than speak of 'syncretism', Puech would prefer the term 'Gnosis'. Mani grew up in a Gnostic environment and, in all probability, considered Marcion and Bardesanes (Ibn or Bar Daysan) as his forerunners [145]. And still more important, Mani's own mental stance and religious attitude were thoroughly Gnostic [146]. We are now on the threshold of Mani's doctrine.

8. Mani's dualistic starting-point

a. The two principles

The psychological and anthropological starting-point of Mani is that man feels himself abandoned in a bad world. But his theological premise is that God is all-good. He is the Light. "His substance is beautiful, excellent, noble, clear, pure, fragrant, lovely to see. His soul is good, noble, wise, beneficial, knowing. His work is the good, the salvation, the benefit, the joy, the order, the coherence, the agreement" [147]. As in all other Gnostic systems it is considered inconceivable that such a good God could be responsible for an evil world.

To explain the existence of evil, a second principle is needed, the principle of Darkness. To quote the same source again, "the substance (of Darkness) is ugly, imperfect, lowly, dejected, evil, stinking, horrifying to see. Its soul is bad, lowly, foolish, damaging, ignorant. Its work is evil, destruction, despondency, confusion, disconnection, dissension" [148]. It should be noted that among the oppositions between Light and Darkness also Knowledge-Ignorance figures. In this way Mani's dualism is presented. It is an ontological dualism of the most radical sort : there is a split in Being itself. There is no common monistic principle from which both principles would derive [149].

The opposition of the Light and the Dark is one way to express this dualism; that of Good and evil is another, and that of God and Hulê (Matter) a third. But no matter how it is called, the opposition is always absolute; its elements are uncreated, eternal [150], and equivalent, with no relationship whatsoever between them [151]. With regard to the opposition God-Hulê, there has been some discussion among scholars on the question whether this is Mani's own expression; this has been doubted because 'hulê' is Greek, and Mani probably did not know Greek. But the word 'hulê' was also used by the Syrians and was known to Marcion; a plethora of contemporaneous sources mention it in a Manichaean context [152]. This is important because this connects Manichaeism with other Gnostic systems in which matter is invariably bad.

In Manichaean texts the two principles are alternatively called 'natures', 'substances', 'fundaments', or 'roots' [153]. The favourite term is 'roots' because this leads to the concept of the 'Trees' : the Tree of Life, or the Good Tree, which is the Light, and the Tree of Death or the Bad Tree, which represents Darkness and matter [154].

b. Two 'gods' or one?

Augustine makes his Manichaean opponent Faustus say that in Mani's system there is only one god. "Nowhere in our dissertations the name of two gods is heard. It is indeed true that we confess two principles, but one of these we call 'god' and the other 'hulê', or, as we commonly and according to our usage say, 'demon'" [155]. Augustine was not impressed. He, a former Manichee himself, had always understood that his co-religionists spoke of two 'gods'. To say that there is only one seemed a word-play to him, since both principles are acting as gods. "The issue at stake is not a word but the operation" [156].

Baur in his turn remained unimpressed by this remark of the Father of the Church. "In the refusal to give the name of god to the evil principle just as (it is given) to the good one, lay the admission that, from the very first, one principle is decisively subordinated to the other. Dualism resulting from polytheism remains true to its real character only when it puts both principles next to one another. But when it considers, if only according to the name, the one as god and the other as a demon, then it is already on the road to become an absolute monotheism" [157]. In other words, Baur was of the opinion that Mani did not profess an absolute dualism but a relative one.

This seems to me a far-fetched conclusion. Faustus explained to Augustine that one must not assign the same term to two different things. "When a doctor is speaking of health and illness, he does not mean to say that there are two healths. And if we speak of warm and cold, we do not intend to say that there are two warmths. Different things merit different names, and since good and bad are by no means the same, we must not, in consequence, give them the same name" [158]. But Faustus did not want to say that the evil principle is in some way dependent on the good one; on the contrary, what he wanted to stress is their immense difference. Naturally the same name would have brought them closer to each other, but Faustus rejected this possibility

9. The origin of Mani's dualism

a. Did it stem from Iran?

Baur believed that Mani's system "nowhere approached the Zoroastrian system of religion closer than in its dualism ... In this dualism Mani ... remained entirely faithful to the religious doctrine in which he, as a Persian, had been raised" [159]. In more than one respect this is a glib statement. In foregoing volumes I occasionally gave vent to my opinion that the idea that all dualism had its origin in Iranian dualism is a scholarly idiosyncrasy. As soon as the term 'dualism' is heard all heads turn in the direction of Iran. Iranian dualism evidently is some sort of nuclear explosion the fall-out of which is discernible everywhere and in all ages. Although Mani was an Iranian by birth, there is no reason to suppose that he trod in the footsteps of Zoroaster. We have not the slightest indication that Patek, Mani's father, was a Zoroastrian. And if he was one, he abjured Zoroastrianism in order to become a Mughtasila. This was the religion in which Mani was raised, not Zoroastrianism.

Widengren too finds it 'self-evident' that "Mani took his starting-point in the ancient Iranian dualism". Nevertheless, he detects in Baur's point of view 'a lack of logical clearness'. "Dualism is expressed in the Iranian religion with far greater precision than in Manichaeism. This (Iranian) dualism originates in an incessant fight between the two principles, the good one (Ahura Mazda =) Ohrmazd, and the evil one, (Ahra Mainyu =) Ahriman. These principles are twins and had to choose for good and evil in the beginning of time. Ahriman chose for evil, whereas Ohrmazd decided for the good" [160].

This is, of course, not an exact rendering of the original doctrine of Zoroaster, but of a later heresy, called Zervanism, as Widengren correctly explains. However, even in this more radical, or less relative, version of Iranian dualism, there is a monistic common principle, Zervan (Time), from which the two opposed principles or beings emanate; in Zervanism dualism sets in one stage lower [161]. Such a common starting-point, however vague or vacant, is entirely absent in Manichaeism. If Mani really took his cue in Zervanism - which I strongly doubt -, then he effected a radical change in it. It is not really important that his bad principle was not named 'god'. What is decisive is that every source we possess portrays the principles as totally independent from each other; in Mani's system Being is existentially split into two.

b. Could something in Mani's early years have been the cause of his dualism?

Let us speculate for a moment on the origin of Mani's dualism. Some of our sources say that Mani was lame. "Some people say that he had two deformed feet, and others that it was only his right foot" [162]. It is, of course, tempting to discover in this physical defect the origin of his dualistic ideology. Williams Jackson suggests this when he says that "through his whole disposition, in particular when he really was born with a bodily infirmity, we can detect his exceptional idealism and cultivation, coupled with a visionary gift" [163]. And Puech states this in as many words : "This infirmity might serve to explain, partly, his abhorrence of the body, his acute awareness of the brutality and the congenital imperfection of this evil world, perhaps even the meditative and artistic tastes of his soul, all that was delicate and somewhat morbid in his ideal" [164].

How nice it would be if we could explain the origin of dualism in this charmingly simple way! But there are, alas, a few objections. The first is that although Ibn an-Nadim's Fihrist is generally considered a reliable source it must not be overlooked that it was written seven centuries later. There are no contemporary Manichaean texts saying that Mani was an invalid; the passage in the Acta Archelai that described him so carefully did not mention that he limped. Perhaps Ibn an-Nadim himself expressed some doubt when he wrote : "Some people say ..." [165].

Secondly, to explain Mani's dualism in this way seems to me to be an example of the reductionism that is so common in psychoanalytic circles. Psychanalysts are fond of monocausal explanations; the circumstance which determined a whole psychic make-up must be found as far back in a person's life as possible, preferably already in his earliest infancy. I am thinking here of another well-known man who also had a club-foot, Lord Byron the poet, of Hitler who had only one testicle, and of the German Emperor William II with his deformed left hand. In all those cases the deformity is by some scholars seen as a sufficient and convincing explanation of the course which a life took. If Hitler had been anatomically equipped in a normal way, we would not have had World War II, seems to be the inescapable conclusion.

Such a monocausal approach neglects other, equally or even more important factors that may have influenced the formation of a character. Let us, for instance, take the case of Byron. The fact that he had a loosely-minded spendthrift for a father and a flitter-brained and unstable woman for a mother, combined with their having separated early in his life, will have had its impact too. Let us consider this for the case of Mani. If it were possible that the fact of his being lame affected his mentality, there was yet another factor in his life that may have played a role in the formation of his incurable dualism.

Children derive their positive or negative ideas from the quality of the world around them, and more particularly from the quality of the relationship of their parents. If this relationship is harmonious, the child comfortably ensconces itself in the primeval trinity of father-mother-child; it learns in this way that there is nothing wrong, neither with the world nor with itself. Its world-view becomes 'holistic'. But if the parental couple lives in discord, and, especially, when it comes to a divorce, the effect on the child may be very serious and totally disrupt its view of life. For then it sees demonstrated that there is no fundamental and initial harmony, and that the two basic sides of life do not combine, but, on the contrary, oppose or perhaps even fight each other.

This may apply to the case of Mani. For the first result of his father's conversion to Mughtasilism was that the household was broken up. Because Patek's new community did not approve of relations with women, Mani's mother was left behind when the father went southward with his son. This means that young Mani grew up as a 'motherless' child, in a one-parent family, since his father had rejected his mother as superfluous. Would this not have affected his attitude to life, to the world? It may have taught him that to be religious, to lead a religious life, meant to reject one side of the world and to turn unconditionally to the other. If this was indeed the beginning of Mani's dualism, then it must have been strongly fortified by his education in the Mughtasila religion, since this doctrine was profoundly dualistic.

10. Two worlds and their sovereigns

a. Two contingent worlds

"The light shining existence was contiguous with the dark existence, with no barrier between them. The Light contacted the Darkness on its surface. The Light is limitless in height, as well as to the right and the left, while the Darkness is limitless in depth, and also to the right and the left" [166]. This description depicts the original state of equilibrium in which the two principles find themselves. The terms 'contiguous' and 'no barrier between them' should be not understood to mean that there was an overflow from one principle to the other, and vice versa. It means that there is no void in being; the two principles together are Being, and there is nothing else.

The word 'frontier' is used by the Shabuhragan, where it says that "the two (principles) do not touch each other at any point except on the side where they have a frontier" [167]. The word 'frontier' must be thought of as 'impassable frontier'. A Pahlevi text expresses the situation very clearly in these words : "The coexistence of the two principles implies a common frontier as (there is between) the sun and the shadow without there being between them any interval or distance" [168]. This signifies that Evil is autonomous and exists in its own right, without owing anything to the Light; from all eternity Light and Darkness are living apart. A more dualistic ontology cannot be imagined.

b. Two sovereigns

Both regimes have their own sovereign. The king of the luminous world is called 'Father of Greatness"; the title of the other ruler is 'King of Darkness'. Both realms consist of five 'mansions' which must be conceived of as emanating from their respective sovereigns. The 'mansions' of the light world are Intelligence, Reason, Thought, Reflection, and Will; those of the dark world are Smoke (or Fog), the World of Fire, the World of Wind, the World of the Waters, and the World of Darkness [169]. This makes it clear that the first world is a world of the mind, of rationality and thoughtfulness, whereas the characteristics of the second world denote chaos and disorderliness.

One should think of the realm of Darkness as a building with five floors of which the World of Darkness is the lowest. Each of these mansions has its own special archon, a demon, a lion, an eagle, a fish, and a serpent. These animals are in fact aspects of their sovereign [170]. The whole dark kingdom is teeming with hideous beasts, demoniacal bipeds, quadrupeds, birds, fishes, and reptiles [171].

The difference between the two worlds is accentuated most strongly. In the realm of the Light there is nothing but peace and harmony [172]. The highest god is praised in the most glowing terms; in all his properties and qualities he is most perfect. He possesses all wisdom and is incomprehensible in his greatness. His is a luminous and blessed land. But the dark world is peopled with unruly beings; horrible winds blow over it, it is full of smoke. Its five abodes are really pestiferous [173].

In the World of Darkness there is incessant movement. Its inmates try to ruin each other; they hurt, kill, and corrupt one another [174]. Matter, in the view of the Manichees, is a living thing, but disorderly and uncoordinated [175]. It is the wicked ruler himself who keeps the turmoil going; he "had swallowed, gulped down, and corrupted, passing from right to left and descending below, while all the time corrupting and slaying anyone who opposed" [176]. This world is one of discord, strife, and uproar [177].

11. An offensive against the upper world

a. Particles of the Light captured by Darkness

The infernal movement at last becomes so violent that the Archon is, so to speak, pushed higher and higher by it, until he reaches the upper frontier of his realm. Having risen thus high, he suddenly perceives 'the flashings of the Light' in the upper world [178]. "He then rejoiced mightily and was filled with admiration; with might and main he wanted to break into the higher world, rob it, and mingle the Light with his Darkness". And so "Matter marched on ... with his demons and idols, with fire and water, against the Light as it appeared (to him)" [179]. And not without success! For "they (the particles of the Light) intermingled with him, coming into contact with his ingredients" [180].

This event is the Manichaean equivalent of the Fall : the unspeakable happens, Light is being absorbed by Darkness. An ancient source stresses that the beings of the lower world have no inkling of a god enthroned in the Light nor whether they could go unpunished when they invaded the luminous world [181]. But if it is true that the King of Darkness was wholly ignorant of the Light-World, it is equally true that the upper world knew nothing of its counterpart. "So after it (the Light World) had come to know about him (the ruler of the realm of Darkness), it made him known to the world of discernment which is the world of Knowledge, then to the world of the unperceivable, then to the world of intelligence, and then to the world of forbearance" [182].

b. An inconsequence pointed out

The Manichaean position shows an inconsequence here which ancient authors were not slow to point out. "How can Darkness see the Light?", asked Titus of Bostra, "If it is capable of seeing the Light, it is not Darkness" [183]. And Alexander of Lycopolis judges it ridiculous that there would be an upward movement from Darkness to Light. Why does an object go upward? Only because it is pushed upward, like a stone thrown into the air. Since there is no other solution, argues Alexander, then it was God himself who raised Hulê up. With inexorable logic this scholar goes on to explain that, if Hulê had a longing for the light, it cannot have been wholly bad [184].

It would certainly have been difficult for Mani to explain these objections away. But he was forced to accept this subtraction from his fundamental dualism because he had to make clear why good and evil are intermingled in this world. This mixing of good and evil would never have occurred if the good had not acquiesced in it [185]. On the other hand, evil had to accept the existence of the good. "The people of Darkness loved the Light from the very first; however violently they wanted to possess it, they were yet not ready to extinguish it" [186]. Alexander of Lycopolis even goes so far as to postulate an intermediate element. "Now if there are only God and Hulê as first principles, could there be any other conclusion than that there is something in the middle? If there is nothing (in between), the two (principles) remain unmixed. Therefore, it is rightly stated : if the extremes intermingle, there is necessarily something in the middle, so that they are connected" [187]. Alexander is carrying the argument ad absurdum here; Mani would never have admitted that there was an intermediate element. Rather than swerving from his basic dualism, he was ready to accept an anomaly in his system.

12. Celestial counter-measures

a. The suffering god

The mansions of heaven got upset by the sudden attack of the army of Darkness. The supreme Father could have ordered the five aeons (mansions) to go to war against the forces of Darkness, but he was unwilling to do this since, as he said, "it is for peace and the good that they were created by me" [188]. To a certain extent even God proves powerless against the onslaught of evil. Using violence would have been incompatible with his absolute goodness. He is no Zeus or Jahve. "He has neither fire to operate with nor lightning and thunderbolts nor water to cause a flood or iron or any other weapon of this kind" [189]. It is a strange idea that God remains constricted by his own superior qualities.

Another ancient author proves astonished that the Manichees should say that "the realm of their god cannot be shocked by anything ...; but all the same we see that the god of the Manichees according to them comes under the pressure of evil" [190]. But Baur remarks that this is the consequence of the war between the opposing forces; since the army of Darkness took the initiative, the supreme god must in the first instance appear as suffering [191].

b. The Mother of Life

The Father of Greatness has no other means of retaliation at his disposal than his goodness. This is what Theodore bar Konaï means when he makes the Father say : "I shall go myself and combat them" [192']. That is, he will act through his essence. In this way, as Widengren says, he passes from contemplation to activity [193]. "The Father had nothing to punish evil with because there is nothing of badness in the house of God. Therefore, he sent out a force that we call 'psuchê' into Matter; it would be the death of Matter if later this force would be separated from it" [194]. This means, a life-giving force emanated from the Father.

It was Alexander of Lycopolis who called it 'psuchê.' Titus of Bostra speaks of "a power of the good, not a discernible light, but rather, so to speak, a projection of the godhead"; he has it that Mani himself spoke of the all, a world-soul, that is [195]. It obviously is the principle of life in the material world. It is also a creative force. "God emitted a good soul, as a particle of his own substance; through the mixture and blending of this ... the enemy (Matter) became tempered and a world was made" [196]. The abstract idea of a power or a soul was made more concrete by dubbing it 'the Mother of Life' [197].

c. Primordial Man enjoins the battle with Darkness

This Mother of Life emits an emanation from herself which becomes Primordial Man, or the First Man [198]; he is not to be confused with the biblical Adam. Faustus says he was made 'of the substance of God' [199]. This First Man was appointed by the supreme godhead to do battle with the Darkness [200]. His armament was formed by five elements, also called his 'sons', his 'soul' and 'deities' : air, wind, water, light, and fire [201]. Thus well-equipped Primal man descends to the frontier of the other world, 'close to the belligerents' [202].

But the enemy is not easily to be outdone. He too, called 'the Ancient Devil' by Ibn an-Nadim, arms himself with five elements : smoke, flame, obscurity, pestilential wind, and clouds [203]. A long and hard battle between Primal Man and the Ancient Devil ensued [204]. Augustine says that during the fight the opposite elements got mixed, smoke with air, darkness with light, bad fire with good fire, bad water with good water, bad wind with good wind [205]. At last, Primal man is overcome by the forces of Darkness; the Devil gulps down his five 'sons' [206].

This signifies nothing less than that elements of the celestial world have become engulfed by Darkness; it looks as though obscurity has triumphed. The material destined for the creation of the world will be an impure mixture of higher and lower elements. The outlook is pessimistic enough since, as one source says, the enemy has devoured Primal Man's armament 'which is his soul' [207]. But perhaps not all is lost; perhaps the loss is not real but only a strategem. Sometimes a general sacrifices part of his army in order to save the rest of his troops [208]. Or a good shepherd may leave one lamb to the lion in order to bring his herd into safety [209]. One could also postulate that not Primal Man but his enemy was the loser. "The good one (= the godhead) sent out a force which he gave a name according to his own idea (= Primal Man), as a bait for Hulê ... And this (Hulê), apprehended by a voracious appetite, in some way or other was bound like a wild beast" [210]. He became like a fish on the hook. In this way Hulê might be brought to its senses.

d. The meaning of this move

What this all means will be evident. The situation of the world and of mankind may be miserable, our prospects may be gloomy, for particles of the Light have become imprisoned in the lower sphere. But through the grace of the Father the enemy will not have the last word. Because the Light remains the Light and cannot be extinguished, there still is a glimmer of hope. It also explains why there are so many opposites in this world, "that one thing is good and another bad, so that this mixture and union of the two principles is revealed through the opposition of things down here" [211].

13. Contrarieties in the lower sphere

The elements of the mixture oppose each other indeed : Life (or Light) and Matter do not suffer one another gladly. "In the combination of Matter and psuchê dissimilars are joined. Through this mixture, matter contracted something vicious, and psuchê got in distress." The splendour of the soul becomes somewhat obscured by its contact with Matter [212]. On the other hand, when the five sons of Darkness had devoured the sons of Primordial man, "this (food) became for them a sweet mixed with a deadly poison" [213].

This fundamental contrariety in the second sphere must not be seen as necessarily negative or destructive. No cosmogony is possible without it. Let us ask Baur to take the floor to demonstrate this. "In the Manichaean system the creation of the world cannot be anything else than the reciprocal limitation of the basic forces that oppose each other. The extremes meet from both sides in a middle ground which for both parts is the ultimate measure. The absolute Good and the absolute Evil bind and bound each other reciprocally; a harmonious relationship originates in which the oppositions balance each other, as we see in the existing order of the world. This restriction and this bounding of the good are lying in the necessary, not be lifted barrier set to it by Evil through its sovereign activity which is independent of the Good ... The Good reveals the superiority that is its due because of its nature and that, in consequence, cannot be denied even in the Manichaean system; in this way it subjects itself to and complies with the limitation that is conditioned by the primordial opposition. Thus it becomes for Evil too the ordering and purposive principle ... This limitation, this measure, and this purposing is the essence of the Manichaean cosmogony" [214].

14. A twofold rescue operation

a. Primal Man recovered

The rescue operation can begin now. Deep down in the abyss Primal Man at last regains consciousness; seven times he directs a prayer to his Father [215]. "The Father heard him and sent out another power that emanated from him" [216]. There occurred, in fact, a sequel of emanations. First, the Father evoked the 'well-beloved of the Lights', and he in his turn summoned the 'great Ban' (Architect), and the Ban evoked the Living Spirit, and the Living Spirit summoned his five sons (another quintuplet) : the Ornament of Splendour (intellect), the great King of Honour (understanding), Light-Adamas (spirit), the King of Glory (thought), and the Bearer (cogitation). The Living Spirit, accompanied by his five sons, descended to the realm of Darkness and there found the Primal Man with his five sons. Now something curious happens. Living Spirit utters a cry resembling a sharpened sword; this cry is answered by Primal Man. Both the call and the answer become hypostatized and, together with Living Spirit, return to the world above [217].

Once again the meaning of this will be clear. A human being feeling imprisoned in this world realizes that he is called to a higher existence and joyfully answers the call. Both call and response transcend the dualistic divide between the two worlds; that they become hypostatized signifies that their effect will not be lost, since they are stronger than Evil.

When Call and Reponse arrive in the luminous world, Living Spirit 'assumes' Call, and the Mother of Life Response [218], in other words, they identified with these two entities. The Spirit and the Mother descend together, discover Primal Man deep down in Darkness, and rescue him by reaching him the right hand which he takes [219]. This is the aetiology of the firm handclap which plays such a great role in Manichaean ritual. "The first right hand is that which the Mother of Life gave Primal Man ... In consequence of this mystery it is the origin (viz. of the custom of the handshake) that exists among men when they give it to one another" [220].

Cleansed and pure Primal Man appears in heaven before the Father. "Primal Man was assumed in the aeons of the Light ... He bent his knee and adored the god of Truth and all the aeons of the Light [221] ... A voice came to him from on high that spoke : 'Sit at my right hand, my firstborn, until I make your enemies your footstool under your feet" [222]. The salvation of Primal Man out of the pit of Darkness and his safe return to the luminous world are the prototype of the course of the Manichee's life. It also deserves attention that the future Redeemer, Primal Man, must first be redeemed himself. This is typically Gnostic. The idea is that a Redeemer who did not go through all it himself will not be able to save mankind.

b. The search for Primal Man's armour

But by no means all is well yet. Primal Man may be back now where he belongs, but he has left his armour behind. This means that celestial elements are still enclosed in Matter and will have to be collected and brought back to the Light-World. This is not going to be an easy task! Once again Living Spirit marched out, together with his five sons. They killed the archons of the lower world and flayed them; from their skins the Mother of Life spanned the firmament, from their bones the mountains were made, and from their flesh and excrements the earth [223]. The lower one descends, the viler the material.

15. The cosmic structure

The defeat of the enemy implies that the structure of the cosmos has come into existence. This structure is fairly complicated, for there are ten firmaments, or heavens, in all, and eight earths. The material they are made of consists of particles of Light mixed with elements of Darkness. The King of the World of Light "made one angel responsible for bearing the heavens, and another for raising up the earth" [224]. Heavens and earth are, therefore, the apanage of the Light-King; that they exist is his work. In Manichaean doctrine there is no separate evil-intentioned Demiurge. If the reader might have come to suppose that realms of Light and Darkness are now entering into sort of Entente cordiale, he or she is sorely mistaken. The fundamental dualism remains unshaken. Around the lowest of the earths the Light-King has a trench dug, and behind this trench a wall is raised, just as around a town, "so that none of the Darkness separated from the Light could get out". For into this lowest world he has thrown Darkness [225].

The particles of the Light that have become embroiled with those of Darkness are, so to speak, in three different states of aggregation : there are those which, in spite of their contact with Darkness, remained wholly pure, then those which were defiled only slightly, and finally those that became thoroughly soiled [226]. From the first category the King of the Light-World fashions the sun and the moon. The light he has sifted out of the Darkness becomes 'a Column of Praise' which is 'almost certainly the Milky Way' [227]. If this is correct, then the Milky Way is the luminous conveyor-belt along which the 'magnificats, sanctifyings, good words, and deeds of righteousness' are transported on high. From the human world "this is thrust into the sun, then the sun thrusts it into the Light above it (= the Milky Way), in the world of praise, in which world it proceeds to the higher unsullied Light" [228]. The task of the sun and the moon is to shield the divine world from Matter and to transmit what remains of the Light in Matter to God [229].

All other entities in the universe are made of either slightly or heavily sullied Light-particles which means that they are no good. Particularly the five planets belong to the domain of obscurity. It is a peculiarity of Manichaeism that they are not put on one line with the sun and the moon which was the common view not only in Antiquity but in Gnostic circles too. Whereas sun and moon reign over Sunday and Monday which, in consequence, are the propitious days, the other days are governed by the planets which makes them inauspicious. "The Manichees say that there are two substances, the one good, the other bad. From this (the bad one) five contrarious powers result. They say these are five days of malignity. They assert that two (days) are good, those of the sun and the moon, which they say to consist of a superior substance" [230]. Or as Simplicius puts it, the sun and the moon are 'of the portions of the good', and the others 'of the portions of evil' [231]. The Kephalaia calls the five planets "the malefactors who perform all evil and wickedness everywhere in that land (the world), above and beneath, in every creation, in the dry and the humid, in trees and in the flesh (= the body)" [232]. So everything and everyone in the sublunar world is governed by the forces of evil. The dualistic split is carried over into the Manichaean concept of the week.

16. A new offensive from above

Once again a massive offensive is staged from above. The Mother of Life, Primal Man, and Living Spirit incessantly implore the Father of Greatness to come to their aid, for there are still particles of Light hidden in the material world. A third emanation takes place which leads to the conception of the 'Third Envoy'; this envoy becomes the father of the twelve 'Virgins of Light' in whom the reader will recognize the twelve signs of the Zodiac. These Virgins are the personifications of superior virtues, like wisdom, truth, and justice [233]. The Envoy constructs an ingenious machinery, a 'sphaira', something resembling a water-wheel; its wheels are wind, water, and fire [234]. This paddle-wheel is turned by the King of Glory (one of the sons of Living Spirit) and the sun and the moon; it serves to pump up the particles of Light from the sphere of Darkness and refine them [235].

The salvaged particles of Light are, in fact, the souls of the elect. Once liberated they ascend along a column of light until they reach the moon. By absorbing the particles of Light it grows into a full moon; this process takes two weeks. In the next two weeks the moon is waning; this means that the souls are transferred to the sun whence they return to the Kingdom of Light [236].

The victory is not yet complete though. The Third Envoy makes another attempt, 'less mechanical', says Puech ironically [237]. The Envoy assumes the shape of a Virgin of the Light which implies that he is androgynous. Radiantly nude he appears in the sun, and 'the seduction of the archons', of the ruling powers of the world of obscurity, begins. Suddenly we are confronted with the sexual imagery which is so common in Gnostic ideology and which makes such a strange contrast to their abhorrence of all that is sexual. The female demons see the Envoy in his male shape, the male ones as female.

Excited by lust, the males eject their semen, which contains particles of the Light, and let it fall on the earth. From this semen five trees come and from them the plants. The female demons give birth to 'abortions'; these too fall on the ground and eat the buds of the trees. In this curious way male and female elements cooperate to bring forth the animal world [238]. Flora and fauna, in consequence, have a demoniacal origin but contain particles of the Light. Animals are worse than plants; they eat plants, and in doing so assimilate the luminous particles which are in the plants. This makes it extremely difficult to free the sparks of Light, particularly because the demons keep a watchful eye, ever ready to chase away those wanting to undertake the work of liberation [239].

The great offensive from above was not a complete success. Although some of the luminous particles are salvaged, the forces below have succeeded in stowing away others of it. Worse is to come.

17. A sweeping design

For a long time Matter, to be thought of as personified - it is sometimes given the name of 'Az' = concupiscence [240] - has been exposed to the offensive from above. But now it plans to retaliate with a grandiose project, nothing less than a counter-creation. This counter-creation is to serve as a hermetic prison from which the luminous particles that are still contained in Matter cannot escape. The chief of the demons takes action. Afraid of the force of the celestial light, he asks his cronies to deliver up to him that part of the Light that is still in their possession. "With it I shall fashion an image of the great being that appeared to us full of glory." The 'great being' refers to Primal Man. There is after all nothing original in his design since the chief demon works after a celestial model [241]. "Then the kingship of the Light will belong to us, and we shall be free of the life of the Darkness." This is really a sweeping design! The outcome must be that the lower world will take over the celestial realm.

"The demons, having not the slightest hope of keeping the Light with them, conceded to offer it to their ruler; they did not despair of continuing to reign through this device ... Since they were a promiscuous lot, consisting of males and females, their chief ordered them to copulate with another. Having intercourse together, the males communicated their seed, and the females became pregnant. What was born resembles their parents; they inherited the greater part of the qualities of their parents (i.e. they too were demons - F.). The prince seized them, rejoicing in this excellent gift ... He ate them and derived great strength from this food, because there was in it not only strength but still more astuteness and a sense of wickedness coming from the ferocious race of their parents. He then called his wife to him who had come forth from his own tribe. Having intercourse with her he sowed in her an abundance of the evils he had devoured himself. To this he added not a little of his mind and power. This he did in order to give form and shape to everything that he brought forth" [242]. This comes from Augustine.

Theodore bar Konaï relates it somewhat differently. In his account the chief ruler is called Asaqloun, a son of the King of Darkness. "He said to the abortions : 'Give me your sons and daughters ...'; they brought these to him; the male ones he ate, and the females he gave to his wife Nabrod" [243]. In both versions the totality of the luminous particles is now concentrated in these two, apparently far beyond the grip of the higher powers. The real end of the cosmogony in Manichaean terms is to secure what remained of the Light in the lower world for the powers of Darkness. It should be noted that sexual intercourse is considered the means to propagate evil.

18. The creation of Adam

a. Adam as a microcosmos

The time has now come for the creation of the first human beings; this is the result of a demoniacal conspiracy and takes places behind the screen erected by the demons. The King of Light must have nothing to do with it. "Nabrod and Asaqloun copulated; she conceived and had a son by him and gave him the name of Adam; she conceived again and bore a daughter and gave her the name of Eve" [244]. If Adam and Eve are the parents of mankind, then our grandparents are demons!

The Kephalaia shows itself highly interested in the shape of Adam, but it has a low idea of Eve. Adam is, in fact, a microcosmos. "The whole cosmos, on high and below, is related to the human body." Then follows a description of this body, going from top to toe. For instance, "from his neck downward to the region of his heart he is related to the ten firmaments ... From his heart downward to his diaphragm (?) he is related to the air; his genitals are related to the great earth ... In this way the little body is related to the great cosmos, in the firmaments, in its orderings, in its mountains, walls, and vehicles". This means that man is closely connected with the physical world which spells no good : "His flesh is related to the vehicle of Darkness" [245]. In short, Adam, and all mankind with him, has a material, that is, evil origin [246].

b. The function of human sexuality

Just as one would expect, all the vices of the archons are to be found in mankind too, in particular sexual lust and the desire to copulate, by means of which the enclosed particles of the Light are transmitted to other bodies, although they themselves always remain imprisoned [247]. The introduction of sexual procreation is a serious setback for the work of redemption; strong counter-measures are now needed. Such is 'the heritage of the demoniacal origin of man'. There is no reason for him to extol himself; after all, "the human race came into being through a repellent mixture of cannibalistic and sexual actions" [248]. On the other hand, this vile body contains particles of the Light and will, for this reason, interest the King of Light. "The great prince of Darkness generated Adam and bound in him a great part of God (i.e. of the King of Light = particles of the Light - F.) that had been bound in all the foetuses of the archons of Darkness which they had given him to eat" [249]. Augustine even states optimistically, on the authority of the Manichees themselves, that "Adam had in his soul a very great part of the Light and a very small part of the adverse race" [250].

c. The dark side of Eve

There exists from the very first a great difference between Adam and Eve, that is between man and woman. In Adam, as I have already pointed out, most of the light particles are to be found. He has two souls, one good, one bad, or a good pneuma and a bad soul ('psuchê'). Other ancient authors spoke of two 'natures' in man, but whichever term is chosen, it invariably denotes a vicious split in the inner core of the human being [251]. Fundamentally, man is attracted by the Light, for his pneuma is incapable of committing evil, but his soul has a strong taste for the bad, made as it is from dark particles. This brings man under the spell of concupiscence and forces him to do evil. In Eve the mixture mainly consists of dark particles and contains very few luminous ones. In so far as she too has a pneuma, it is extremely weak. She is invincibly allured by evil and constitutes a great danger for Adam. "They (the archons) similarly created Eve and gave her a portion of their own concupiscence in order to deceive Adam, and in this way the mould of the world was shaped by the demiurgical power of the archon" [252]. In this antithesis of Adam and Eve we see the man-woman dualism that is so frequent in Gnostic systems [253].

19. The appearence of Jesus

a. Jesus a mythical figure

It is at this juncture that Jesus makes his appearance in Manichaean doctrine - rather late in the day, as Bardy remarks [254]. He adds that, with Jesus, "Christianity appears for the first time in Manichaean dogmatics" [255]. However, Jesus appears solely as a mythical figure, not as the historical person of the Gospels; Mani's Jesus has nothing to do with orthodox Christian doctrine. "When the fire angels beheld the light of God and his goodness which passion had despoiled and made captive in those two who had been born (= Adam and Eve), they asked al-Bashir (= the 'Teller of Good Tidings', in all probability the Third Envoy)" [256], the Mother of Life, Primal Man, and the Spirit of Life to send to this ancient offspring (Adam) someone to free and save him, to teach him Knowledge and righteousness, and to rescue him from the devils [257] ... So they sent Isa (= Jesus, and with him a deity who sought out the two archons (Nabrod and Asaqloun) and imprisoned them" [258].

Not a word is said of Jesus' human life. "He has no need of a dove or of baptism, nor of a mother and brothers, and perhaps not of a father" [259]. Instead, it is reported how he begins by beating down the evil powers in the cosmos. "The Jesus of the splendour ... resembles a man who is sent to eradicate (tares) and to burn an enormous field (sc. with bad fruits) with fire ..., so that they would not grow again ... He fulfilled his will among the numerous (evil) powers" [260]. Jesus the splendiferous then approaches Adam whom he finds lying in a deathlike sleep, blind and deaf, deprived of all Knowledge, thirsting for revenge, a victim of the wicked demons [261].

b. Jesus the spender of Knowledge

But Jesus knows that there is yet a higher spirit in man, his 'nous' [262], in which the light particles are concentrated. In this nous of man Jesus in fact recognizes himself, for he is **the** nous; in consequence, man, at least his pneumatic part, is an image of a higher power, of Jesus himself who is "the power and wisdom of God; his power lives in the sun, his wisdom in the moon" [263]. He is, as Baur writes, "the spirit of the Light and the sun, drawing to himself all the luminous elements in matter. But he is also the God who works in man as a higher principle and giving him the right Knowledge of everything that can elevate him above Matter" [264].

"Jesus awoke Adam from his deathlike sleep to free him from an overwhelming spirit [265] ... And he proceeded to speak to ... Adam, enlightening him about the Gardens (of Paradise), the deities, Hell, the devils, earth and heaven, sun and moon [266] ... And then Adam examined himself and knew who (he was) [267]." This is the central and decisive moment : Adam receives Knowledge, the 'gnoosis'; he becomes a' knowing' being. And this Knowledge immediately performs its redeeming function : "The soul of the blessed (Adam is meant but it equally applies to every Manichee - F.) became intelligent again and rose up" [268].

Jesus "made him stand upright and taste the tree of life". In other versions it is the tree of the knowledge of good and evil; this is then identified with Jesus himself, as "the Knowledge that is in the world"; whoever accepts him has the discernment of good and evil" [269]. It is only logical that in this version Paradise is identified with the world. "And Adam looked around him and wept, and raised his voice with the violence of a roaring; he tore his hair, beat himself, and said : 'Woe, woe to the maker of my body and the jailer of my soul and the rebels who enslaved me" [270].

c. A warning against women

Jesus has a stern warning to give to man now. "He caused him to fear Eve, explaining to him that she was forbidden, and that he should restrain himself from (going to) her and making him afraid to approach her, so that he obeyed" [271]. Eve obviously is a hopeless case; she has not been 'awakened', that is, she did not receive the redeeming Knowledge. Instead, her femininity is associated with sexuality. Once again the Gnostic-dualistic abhorrence of sexuality and the Gnostic depreciation of women comes to the fore.

20. Mankind spoils the liberation process

a. Eve as the tool of the demons

The scene seems now set for the final act, the definitive liberation of mankind and the return of the imprisoned particles of the Light to heaven. But once again the redeeming process is slowed down, and this time it is the fault of mankind itself, for, not heeding the warning of Jesus, it begins to propagate itself, that is, to transmit the enclosed luminous particles to ever new generations, always further down the ages. By a cunning move Adam is persuaded to start this process.

"The (male) archon (Asaqloun) reverted to his daughter who was Eve, and because of the lust that was in him, had intercourse with her." Motives of incest are by no means rare in Gnostic ideology; they form part of its predilection for inclusive thinking. "From her he begot a son who was disfigured and of a ruddy complexion. His name was Cain, the Ruddy Man. Then that son had intercourse with his mother, by whom he begot a son who was white and whose name was Abel" [272]. This double incest means that Cain at once was the father of Abel and his brother!

b. Cain and Abel

There is yet no end of incestuous relations. Cain once again sleeps with his mother and begets by her two daughters, the Daughter of Corruption whom he takes to wife himself, and the Wise of the Ages whom he gives to Abel. Both men were married to their sisters, while Cain's betrothed also became the aunt of Abel and his sister-in-law.

It now looks as though two races of men might originate, the corrupted and the wise. But Mani remains consequent : there is no innocence in the lower world, although it is true that "in the Wise of the Ages there was virtue from the Light of God and His wisdom". The world of Darkness shows an incredible toughness of resistance and proves almost invincibly resilient. One of the 'angels', that is to say, of the demons, brutally assaults the Wise of the Ages and fathers two girls with her. Their names bode no good : they are called Lamentation and Laden with Lamentation. Understandably enough Abel was not pleased; in spite of the Wise's protest, he remained stubbornly convinced that Cain had been this 'angel'. When Cain heard that his brother-son went about complaining, he 'brained him with a rock, killing him. Then he took the Wise of the Ages for a wife".

c. Eve seduces Adam

This long story is needed to explain why Adam fell into the trap of sensuality. The rapist 'angel' was indignant that Cain had taken the Wise, the mother of his daughters for a wife. Therefore he taught Eve 'the language of magic' which refers to magical incantations, "so that she could enchant Adam. This she proceeded to do, enticing him with a wreath of blossoms from the tree. When Adam saw her, he fell upon her in sensual passion, so that she gave birth to a male child who was beautiful and of comely countenance." But now the angel became still angrier, because it had obviously not been his intention that Adam should seduce Eve; very probably he wanted Eve for himself. Adam was so innocent that it was only too possible that he could beqeath this innocence to his offspring.

Repenting, Eve tried to kill her child, but Adam carried it off. Then the archons hacked down the trees and chased away the cows so that Adam would be unable to feed his boy on fruit and milk. But now Adam too took his refuge in magic; "he took the offspring and made circles around him". Over these circles he invoked the name of the King of the Gardens (the supreme godhead), Primal Man, and the Spirit of Life. "Then he communed with God ... and said : 'Even if I have committed a crime against you, this (child) who has been born has not sinned. Then one of the three hastened down with a wreath of splendor, which he brought in his hand to Adam. When the angels and the archons beheld this, they went their way."

d. Adam saved by Shatil

Nothing daunted, the demon resumes the attack. He "declared hostilities against Adam and those who had been born, saying to Eve, 'Show yourself to Adam, so that perchance you may bring him back to us". So she dashed off and aroused the passion of Adam, who had lustful intercourse with her. When Shatil saw him, he admonished him (Adam)." Shatil is a son of Adam; his name in all probability is identical with that of Seth [273]. In Gnostic texts Seth invariably is a paragon of virtue. Shatil "reproached him, saying : 'Come, you shall go forth to the East, to the Light and the wisdom of God!'. So he (Adam) departed with him and dwelt there until he died and went to the Gardens (of Paradise). Then Shatil with Lamentation and Laden with Lamentation and their mother, the Wise of the Ages, accomplished their course, with one idea of right and one way of life, until their deaths." In other words, they became Manichees. "But Eve, Cain, and the Daughter of Corruption went to Hell."

e. What this all means

What this long relation, as told in the Fihrist [274], means is that, first of all, there are two races of men, dualistically opposed of course, the redeemed who are destined for heaven = the Manichees, with their 'one way of life',

life', and the doomed, destined for hell = the rest of mankind. Bayard Dodge describes with admirable clarity what keeps the two races apart [275]. "This description is an allegory based on Gnostic ideas. Mani felt that man must free himself from sexual passion in order to be saved. Abel, the Wise of the Ages, and her daughters evidently represent righteousness, which must be freed from worldy lust, even if it entails sorrow. Cain, the Daughter of Corruption, the demon-angel, and Eve represent carnal passion. Adam impersonates man with his weaknesses, while Shatil reveals man's ability to overcome weakness and be saved."

21. The suffering Jesus

Throughout the ages, a running battle is going on in the world. There are two 'parallel actions', as Puech says [276], the line of Evil and the line of Salvation. This is the consequence of the fact that in this present world Light and Darkness are still intermingled. There are two powers in the world, which should not be thought of as good and evil but rather as active and passive, or as Alexander of Lycopolis expressed it, as a demiurgical one and a suffering one - suffering because it is mixed with Matter [277]. Some part of God is imprisoned in all created things. "Part of the nature of God is mixed with the heavens and the earth and under the earth, in all material bodies, dry and humid, in all flesh, in all the seeds of trees, herbs, men and animals" [278].

This hidden and enclosed part of God is sometimes understood as being the suffering Jesus who "is daily born, daily suffers, daily dies" [279], and "who hangs not only on the cross but on every tree" [280]. Augustine identifies the whole world with 'the cross of the Light' [281]. Jesus' passion and cross are no longer historical events, happening at a certain place and at a certain time; their historicity is not important at all. Instead, these events acquire mythical proportions and become omnipresent in time and space. "And finally, by the fact of crucifixion, Knowledge is given" [282]. We are suffering with and in Jesus, and Jesus is suffering with and in us; by the cross, "the wounds of the passion are manifested which our soul is suffering" [283]. This is a basic idea of the Manichees, that of 'Jesus patibilis', the suffering Jesus, a Jesus who is not only our Redeemer but must be redeemed himself, and by us [284].

22. The prophets and the Church

The Kephalaia gives us the list of the great prophets of mankind. It opens with Adam and Seth, then come Enoch, Noah, and Abraham. Buddha is mentioned also as well as Zoroaster, and then, of course, Jesus, who came 'spiritually ..., without a body'; he sent out his apostles and with them went Paul [285]. There have always been people who were ready to listen to these prophets but the greater part of humanity preferred the lead of Eve and Cain. Once again we discover the second of the two great dualisms of the Gnosis, that between the chosen and the damned.

After the death of Paul the Church fell into decay. "They left justice behind them and the narrow, difficult path and preferred ... the broad way." Then there came a just one who belonged to the realm (= the Light World) but after him it again went downhill with the Church [286]. The 'just' one refers to Marcion. But finally Mani appeared who called himself 'the apostle of Jesus Christ through the will of God the Father'; with these words he began his 'Epistola fundamenti' [287]. After Mani people no longer have an excuse to be on the wrong side since they have been sufficiently enlightened. They now know that the great paddle-wheel is working by means of which the luminous particles will be scooped up from the Darkness in order to be, via Sun and Moon, transported back to Heaven [288]. The big point, however, is how to come onto this wheel. But Mani has taught how to perform this.

23. The three seals

We are well informed on Manichaean morals by saint Augustine. Three seals are attached to a Manichee, one on his mouth, one on his hand, and one on his womb [289].

a. The seal on the mouth

The seal on the mouth prevents a Manichee, as the reader may guess, from lying, from uttering blasphemies, and from speaking evil, especially of God; it is even forbidden to swear [290]. But the faithful should not only be careful about what goes out of the mouth, but also about what goes into it.

Manichees are vegetarians, they do not eat meat, and are teetotallers, they do not drink wine. Although animals are very bad creatures, nevertheless they too contain particles of the Light. If people eat their flesh, then these particles will pass into human bodies which makes their liberation more difficult. For normally, when an animal dies a natural death, the last luminous sparks left in it are freed [291]. It is a grave sin, directly against God, to eat meat. Repentant Manichees confess : "By taking living bodies as food and drink with the ten tops of our fingers that resemble serpents's heads, and with our thirty-two teeth, we do evil and give trouble to God" [292].

Wine is strictly prohibited; it will be a shocking revelation to the lovers of a good glass that it is made from the bile of the devil [293]. Only sweet, non-alcoholic drinks, like apple-juice, are permitted, and these only in small quantities. Since milk and eggs are equally forbidden, the pious Manichee is to a large extent dependent on green stuff, in particular onions, mushrooms, pears, and other fruit, like melons [294].

The Manichaean rule prescribed regular fasting; how frequent the fast-days were is difficult to say; that there were many of them is certain. It seems that on Sundays every adherent had to fast, and to this the really elect added Monday. There was a fast of two days at every new moon, and every year one of thirty days [295]. So much for the seal on the mouth. All this strict abstinence shows how negatively the Manichee thought of things created; as much as he could he tried to avoid contact with them.

b. The seal on the hand

The prohibitions following the seal on the hand are equally severe. Of course, killing was forbidden, but this implied far more than homicide and murder. It also involved carrying arms and going to war. One should not kill an animal, however vile and impure it might be; nobody has a right to the spark of Light it contains. If we believe the Acta Archelai, the restrictions were so severe that they made life almost impossible. "Who eats bread, but it is necessary to eat bread, becomes bread; who kills a chicken becomes a chicken." Manichees do not, like Mandaeans, believe in the sacramental properties of water. "Who washes himself in water injures his soul." And "he who walks on the earth hurts it; and he who moves his hand damages the air" [296].

If a Manichee obeyed these injunctions to the letter, he would be condemned to total inactivity and immobility. But did he really take them literally? There seems to have been ways to circumvent them. "If they (the Manichees) want to eat bread, they must pray first, and then say to the bread : 'I did not mow you nor mill you nor kneed you nor put you into the oven; somebody else made you and brought you to me; therefore, I eat you in innocence" [297]. Perhaps they used similar incantations to enable them to do what is inevitable.

What is most important is that all this shows how deeply the Manichees abhorred this world; their attitude to it was fiercely dualistic. In principle, they would prefer to have nothing to do with it and to live ethereal lives, touching nothing, not even eating. Even their vegetarianism was a concession; they would rather take no food at all. In this way they could associate already with the luminous world above, if not in reality - since they still had to eat, they still had to tread the earth -, then in any case mentally. Or must we say 'knowingly'? For it was exactly the fact that they 'knew' about these things that put them apart from the dumb masses.

c. The seal on the womb

If the reader now sits bemoaning the awful lot of the Manichee who made his own life so difficult, I must caution him or her that there is worse to follow. For there was also a seal on the womb! This meant 'selfcontrol and chastity' [298], and this in the most absolute sense. The act of sex implies that evil is propagated from one person to another, and that, perpetually, the sparks of Light remain enclosed in Matter. In consequence, a true Manichee is forbidden every form of sexual activity; it is intrinsically evil [299]. The true Manichee should for ever remain virginal and shun all contact with women (Manichaeism is a male affair; it has nothing to say to women). If someone is not able to live without female company, he should not make her a mother. It is far worse to procreate children than to indulge in sensual pleasure; one should, therefore, if needs be, take a concubine rather than marry [300].

24. The faithful Manichee a strict dualist

By faithfully observing the strictest obligations of the creed, the true Manichee will become an out and out dualist. To him the problem with the world (and with human life) is that it is such a muddle. As the result of a cosmic catastrophe, part of the Light has become submerged in Matter. Man is no exception to this : he too is a mixture of good and bad, of the Light and the Dark. The whole series of operations, undertaken by the powers above, had only one aim : to restore the original dualism through which the upper and the nether world were neatly separated from each other. The higher powers, and in the last resort particularly Jesus, busy themselves in collecting once again the particles of the Light and reintegrating them into the luminous world from which they came.

Man is their main object. By acquiring the redeeming Knowledge - that is, by becoming a Manichee -, he will be able to realize that he is a strange compound of light and dark, but this essential Knowledge is sufficient to separate the two. He will become conscious and free, in contrast to the others who will remain dull and ignorant. At death, the redeemed Manichee will return to heaven. Or rather, not 'he', not his vile material body of course, but only his pneuma, his spark of Light. But for the unknowing there will be no escape [301].

Baur very aptly summarizes Manichaean moral teaching in the following words. "Manichaean doctrine, in accordance with its whole tendency, especially with regard to the second and third seals, aims at severing all ties which bind man to the material world. If Matter constitutes the evil principle, then all contact with Matter, with everything that serves to foster physical life, that keeps it going and propagates it, is sin and continuation of that original sin that connected the divine soul that sprang from the Light with a material body" [302].

25. At the hour of death

a. The death of a Manichee

"When death comes to one of the Elect, Primal Man sends him a light shining deity in the form of the Wise Guide. With it are three deities, who bring a drinking vessel, clothing, a headcloth, a crown, and a diadem of light. A virgin accompanies them who resembles the soul of that member of the Elect ... They take the member of the Elect and garb him with the crown, the diadem, and the garments. They place the drinking vessel in his hand, and mount up with him in the Column of Praise (= the Milky Way) to the sphere of the moon, to Primal Man and the Mother of the Living, to where he at first was in the Gardens of the Light. As for the body ... which is abandoned and cast down, the sun, the moon and the light shining deities abstract from it the forces which are the water, fire, and ether (= the elements, the earth deserves no mention), and which ascend to the sun, becoming divine (n.b. the reader should note that these elements do not enter the upper world - F.). But the rest of the body is flung to the lower regions" [303].

The words 'where he at first was', highly illuminating as they are, should not escape our attention. The Redemption is, in fact, a work of recuparation; what has fallen down from above into the world is recovered. Here lies a great difference with Christianity. Whereas the Christian is oriented to a future where he or she will be fully himself, with body and soul, such as he or she never was before, the Manichee, and the Gnostic in general, is directed to the past; what he wants is the restoration of a situation that has already existed.

b. The death of a non-Manichee

But "when death comes to an evil man (= a non-Manichee) who is enslaved by craving and lust, the devils attend him, taking hold of him, chastising him and showing him horrible things. As those (good) deities are also present with the same garments (= as presented to the good man), the evil man supposes that they have come to save him. But, instead, they have come to reproach him, to remind him of his evil deeds, and to substantiate proof of his having neglected to aid the Elect. Then he continues to vacillate in the world and in torment, until the time for punishment, when he is cast down to the underworld" [304].

What the strange expression 'vacillating in the world and in torment' signifies is explained by (Pseudo-)Augustine. "Those who, through love of the world, have let themselves stray from the luminous way ..., who, what's more, have by their persecution afflicted the holy Church (of the Manichees) and the Elect who observe the celestial precepts, will be excluded from the beatitude and the glory of the holy Kingdom ... They will remain glued to this horrible globe over which they must stand guard. Thus their souls will remain attached to the things they loved so much. They will stay abandoned on this obscure globe" [305].

26. Manichaean apocalypse

The process of the recuperation of the Light particles will take an immensely long time. Even the Elect are not wholly safe : some sparks will inevitably escape them and start roaming about again. But finally the end comes. It will be ushered in by the outbreak of the 'Great War'. We read about this in the Manichaean 'Coptic Homilies'; during this war the faithful Manichee will be subjected to endless tribulations. Its outcome is the final victory of the Church of Justice. "The new generation (of Manichees) will come and firmly take possession of its goods" [306]. Part of those who constitute the 'unknowing' will as yet be converted to Manichaeism.

Then comes the Last Judgment. Christ will separate the good and the bad. Henceforward Jesus and the Elect can live in safety. But this peaceful period is only an interlude. Soon enough Jesus and the Elect will return to heaven together with the protecting deities of the cosmos [307]. Left to itself the cosmos will fall to pieces and burst into flames [308]. The confragation will last for 1.468 years and will purify Matter so that the recoverable particles of the Light can escape and surge upwards [309]. But all the rest, including Matter, concupiscence, sexuality, gender [310], demons, the damned [311], and, according to some schools, even the hopelessly soiled particles of Light, will be rolled into one great ball [312]. This will be lowered into the deepest pit that will be then covered with a gigantic stone [313]. It is a grandiose vision which makes one think of the closing scene of Wagner's 'The Twilight of the Gods' in which, under the thundering tutti of the orchestra, the burning Valhalla sinks into the flooded Rhine, while Brünnhilde, the last of the gods, disappears on horseback into the blazing glow.

The universe now returns to its original state. "After the restoration of the whole cosmos the restoration of the two natures follows; the archons live on deep down in their realm, and the Father up there, after recovering what was his" [314]. Baur, however, rightly concludes that the triumph of the Light is not complete, insofar as the realm of Darkness, although rendered harmless, continues to exist. We should not overlook the possibility that, moreover, part of the Light may be trapped under the great stone so that not all souls have been saved [315]. This would mean, says Titus of Bostra, that "God finds out that his own nature is being punished" [316]. With this riddle a Manichee must be content to live.

27. The Church of Justice

I shall now turn to one of the basic characteristics of the Church of Justice, as the Manichees themselves called their Church, which will dispose of a problem that, probably, has kept the bewildered reader occupied for some time already. How is it possible that Manichaeism continued to exist for more than a millennium, if the the movement was so strictly against marriage, procreation, and sex? In view of this a Manichaean community would have been doomed to extinction within a lifetime. Or was it the case that every Manichee succeeded in winning at least one convert, in order to replace himself when he died? Human laxity in general, inevitable apostasies, and particularly premature deaths would have prevented this. The real solution of this problem is that there were two classes of faithful, the Electi and the Auditores; the diminishing ranks of the Electi were replenished by recruits from the Auditores.

a. The Electi

It is self-evident that the observance of the strictest Manichaean morals was far beyond the capacities of most people. Only a small number was ready and able to live up to them. These were the Electi, the Chosen; they were the really 'just', the only authentic members of the Church [317]. Their purity was expressed by the fact that they went clad in white; even their hats were white. They lived together in religious communities which sometimes included some women and children. I don't know whether these were the repudiated wives and offspring of the men, but in any case there were no relations between them. The men despised all women. "With regard to women, they (the men) must consider them as empty and deceitful appearances; they must not be taken in and embarrassed by their sensual charms, just as a bird that, flying high, will not perish in the net" [318].

An Elect would live completely detached from this world, without any contact with it except, as Puech archly remarks, for the necessity of feeding himself [319]. Having received the 'seal of the hand', they were no longer allowed to work, to gather food, dig out vegetables, or even pluck an apple or cut off a corn-stalk. For their living they were thrown on charity; "with perfect dignity they await alms ; if nobody gives them these, they go out begging to provide for their needs" [320].

The task of collecting and preparing foodstuffs for the Electi fell to the Catechumens. When one of these reached a dish to an Elect, he (the Elect) expressed his deep indignation for the fact that he had to eat by cursing the server; he then swore that he had had no part in the crimes that were committed in order to prepare this food (for instance, mowing grain). After that, he absolved the server. This daily ritual was necessary because food is material and, for this reason, bad. But food also contains particles of the Light which, via the body of the Elect, will return to the celestial realm [321].

b. The Auditores

The Auditores lived a less strict life. But they too observed a code of high morality, the 'Ten Ordinances' : no idolatry, no killing, lying, stealing, adultery, no magic, etcetera [322]. However, they were allowed to perform ordinary work, to marry and have children, and even to eat meat and drink wine [323]. It goes without saying that they had to lead a devout life of praying and fasting. The faults they made by violating the seal of the hand were to be made good by giving alms to the Electi. Their good works might ensure their being reborn in the body of an Elect [324].

c. The relationship of Electi and Auditores

Puech speaks of two concentric circles here, the inner and far smaller one of the Electi, and the other, much larger of the Auditores. The authentic Church of Justice is formed by the Electi; the Auditores are no more than auxiliaries to make life possible for the Electi [325]. The relation between the two groups cannot be dubbed dualistic. The Elect says to the Auditor : "You are my brother, you are our companion wandering with us to the Land of the Light" [326]. Augustine, who was in the know, assures us that, in the opinion of the Manichees, the two groups form one Church [327].

But just as the Electi were dependent on the Auditores for their physical survival, the Auditores were spiritually dependent on the Just. As a consequence of the strict moral code, the acts of the Auditores were criminal in themselves, but they became pious by transfer because they were performed on behalf of the Perfect. As Puech formulates it, "the place that he (an Auditor) occupies has no justification and no sense except in function of the person of the Elect who concentrates in himself all the powers and all the operations which are necessary to accomplish the work of Salvation" [328].

Baur wrote in the following terms about the distinction between Electi and Auditores. "In general the Electi and the Auditores relate to one another in the same way as the Gnostics used to distinguish between pneumatic and psychic people; as the hylics stood on the third step, so, according to Manichaean opinion, the third class was formed by all those wo lived outside the community of the Manichees and who entirely belonged to the material world. However strictly and consequently Manichaeism exerted itself to carry through its dualistic world-view, it was, at least here, forced, in order not to turn the ethico-religious aim of life into an unsolvable riddle, to introduce an intermediate term between spirit and matter and to postulate in this way a gradual transition from the one to the other of the opposed principles" [329].

I feel unable to detect this gradual transition, and in consequence I see no lessening of the dualistic tension. The terms 'pneumatics, psychics, and hylics' are used nowhere in Manichaeism. The comparison with other Gnostic systems is not helpful. In those Gnostic systems that, like Valentinianism, acknowledge the existence of 'psychics', the term refers to people who are not Gnostic but might become so. But they could just as well turn into hylics. Manichaean Auditores, however, are members of the Church of Justice; together with the Perfect they stand over against the massa damnata. So they do not constitute an intermediate group. How Baur could state that they formed a transition between the two principles remains a riddle for me.

d. The hierarchy of the Church of Justice

The Church of Justice was hierarchically structured. At least in the first decades of its existence it had a supreme head, the 'archêgos', who resided in Babylonia but later transferred his seat to Samarkand. Mani himself appointed twelve apostles who later were succeeded by the twelve Masters or Teachers. Furthermore, there were seventy-two bishops and three hundred and sixty presbyters [330].

e. Manichaean sacraments

The Manichees knew only two sacraments, baptism and the eucharist [331]. Baptism was reserved for the Elect; the Auditores were only cathechumens. It is not impossible that those Electi who from their earliest youth had lived the strict life, were never baptized; they did not need an act of purification. But probably Auditores who decided to join the Electi received baptism; in view of the great distance separating the Elect from the Auditores, says Baur, the transition had to be marked by a ritual [332]. But here a problem arises. We know that Mani attached no value to water rituals; "they (the Manichees) do not believe that baptism with water works salvation for whosoever" [333]. Could it be that they baptized with oil [334]? According to Augustine, they ascribed a healing and purifying effect to oil [335].

Whereas the existence of a Manichaean baptismal rite remains somewhat dubious, there can be no doubt that the Electi celebrated the eucharist. It was only for them; the Auditores did not take part. Augustine more than once mentions a eucharistic celebration [336]. Since the Auditores were not even allowed to be present, Augustine, who never was more than an Auditor, derived what he knew about the eucharist from hearsay [337]. Very probably the daily meal of the Electi had a sacramental meaning, because consumption of food meant the liberation of the light particles in it. But once a year there was a solemn eucharistic feast. Since the use of wine was forbidden to the Perfect, they seem to have substituted water for it.

f. Early missionary activities

Already during his lifetime Mani sent out missionaries to preach the new creed in Syria and Egypt. Some disciples at an early date visited Jerusalem [338] and the faith was preached in Judaea. In the fourth year of the Emperor Aurelianus, that is in 274, a certain Akuos came from Mesopotamia to Eleutheropolis in the region of the Jordan [339]. Their success was great, for we see a whole array of Fathers of the Church take up arms against the Manichees in Syria, where a certain Thomas arrived [340], and in Palestine; their presence along the Jordan is attested until well in the seventh century.

It must have been around the year 261 that the first Manichee reached Egypt; he was bishop Papos who came with a stock of Manichaean scripture, and who later was followed by the already mentioned Thomas [341]. Already around 300 the Egyptian Manichees were numerous enough to induce the bishop of Lycopolis to write a book against them.

g. Roman reactions

Oddly enough, not only the Christian authorities became uneasy about the new sect but also the Roman officials [342]. Around 290 a Roman proconsul in the east reported to the emperor, Diocletian, about it. The supreme ruler obviously saw it as a great danger for the imperial cult. He reacted with a prescript which is said to be the first official document in which Manichees are mentioned. He ordered a formal persecution of them, because the Manichees, "with their execrable morals and the savage laws of Persia, threatened to infect in some way the modest and tranquil Roman nation with their pernicious poison". The mention of Persia suggests that very probably the Emperor saw Iranian fifth-columnists in the Manichees in a period during which the Empire was constantly at war with the Persians. The Manichaean chiefs must be burned together with their books and the goods of the Manichees must be confiscated [343].

h. Further expansion in the west

In spite of this and other imperial counter-measures, the creed spread westward along the African coast of the Mediterranean. Manichees became numerous not only in Egypt but also in the Maghreb [344]. Three famous Manichees of Tunisia, the triumvirate of Faustus, Fortunatus, and Felix, became the opponents of Saint Augustine with whom they had long discussions. From North-Africa Manichaeism spread into Spain and from there into Gaul, without, however, winning a great following in these countries, or so it seems. In contrast, the presence of a great number of Manichees in Italy during the fourth century is well attested; there were communities in Rome and in Milan. Even during the fifth century several bishops of Rome took measures against them. But, as I have stated earlier, in the west Manichaeism gradually lost its original vigour and finally disappeared from the religious scene.

j. Successes in the eastern world

Far greater and far more durable was the success of Manichaeism in the east [345]. Before 300 it penetrated into Arabia and even reached Mecca. The Fathers of the Church in Asia Minor polemized assiduously against the sect because it was numerous there. It had adherents even in the highest

Byzantine circles; we see several rulers act against it. Manichees within the orbit of the Byzantine Empire are still mentioned in the ninth century, but after that date very little is heard of them.

From Mesopotamia, Manichaeism travelled eastward to Persia and met with great success there. Here too it was persecuted, but this did not stop its triumphal march. It is said that around 1000 the great majority of the population of the residential town of Samarkand (now in the Republic of Uzbekistan) adhered to Manichaeism. Still further east the sect reached Central Asia. For a long time flourishing communities existed in Turkestan, in Mongolia, even in China proper.

But everywhere the Manichees met with fierce resistance. In the west pagans as well as Christians opposed them; in Persia they were not popular with the Mazdaist emperors and clergy, and later they were persecuted by the Moslims. In China the officials saw a great danger in Manichaeism for the authentically Chinese ideology. In Central Asia it was not persecuted but there it had to endure the rivalry of Buddhism. In these regions the Church of Justice managed to subsist until about 1300; for the rest, the eleventh century saw the end of Manichaeism.

28. Conclusion : Manichaean dualism

Throughout this chapter I have used my key-words 'dualism' and 'dualistic' only sparsely. I felt no need to explain at every turn how deeply dualistic Mani's doctrine is; this continuously strikes the eye. But let us now summarize what we have found. The two main dualistic elements of every Gnostic system are present here too, only in a more radical form than usually is the case. These are the split between the upper and lower worlds, and the division of mankind into those who will be saved, and those who will be doomed.

The bitter enmity between the celestial powers and those of the material world leads to a protracted battle between them in which the heavenly forces in the end gain the victory. The fact that the archons of the lower world succeed in capturing a small part of the luminous particles for good does not turn the absolute dualism into a more mitigated variant. The light particles have become so soiled and obscured that they, no longer recognizable as light, have become an integral part of the Darkness.

Equally, the fact that in the Church of Justice there is a class of second-rate Manichees, the Auditores, should not lead to the conclusion that, by the introduction of a medium term, the anthropological dualism becomes less. Since the Auditores form part of the Church of Justice, they do not stand in the middle between the Just and the damned, performing a kind of osmotic function.

Abhorrence of all that is material and physical are characteristic features of every Gnostic system, but besides Manichaeism there is scarcely another to be found in which it leads to such radical consequences. Almost everything comes in for a death sentence : work, touching things, treading the earth, food, particularly meat, wine, social intercourse with non-Manichees, even with Auditores, even with one another, since marriage, procreation, and sexuality in general are strictly forbidden. The whole habitus of Manichaean Electi shows that nothing on this earth has any meaning or value for them. They simply hate life!

NOTES TO CHAPTER IV

1. Gabriel Dupréau, De vitis, sectis et dogmatibus haereticarum. Cologne, 1569.
2. Cyriacus Spangenberg, Historia Manichaeorum, de furiosae et pestiferae hujus sectae origine. Ursel, 1578.
3. See for this passage, Ries, Études manich. 18-28.
4. Ries, Études man. 33-36.
5. Isaac de Beausobre, Histoire ciritique du Manichée et du Manichéisme. Amsterdam, 1734-1739.
6. Ries, Études man. 39.
7. Ries, Études man. 48.
8. Baur, Man. Rel.syst. (see Bibliography).
9. Ries, Études man. 67.
10. Ries, Études man. 81.
11. Ries, Études man. 81-85.

12. Ries, Études man. 85-89.
13. Ries, Études man. 210-211; G. Bardy s.v. 'Manichéisme. Sources manichéennes', Enc.théol.cath. 9.2., 1849-1850, Paris, 1927.
14. Ries, Études man. 215-216. This collection is a bad shape.
15. Puech, Manichéisme (see Bibliography). See also Nyberg, Forschungen 3-28. Useful is also Ort, Mani, Ch. I Survey of some important studies about Mani and his religion. The most recent bibliography is that by Alexander Böhlig s.v. 'Manichäismus', Theol.Realenz. Bd. XXII, Lieferung 1, 40-45. Berlin-New York (1991).
16. This is based on information supplied by Mani himself. The village of Mardinu is not known from other sources and no longer exists. In the eighth century the Syrian bishop Theodore bar Konaï wrote that Mani saw the light in Afrunya near Ghaukaï (lib.Schol., Mimra XI, 58). This town too no longer exists and is difficult to locate. See for a discussion of the identification of Mani'sbirth-place Puech, Manich. 34.
17. Puech, Manich. 32-33.
18. Albîrûnî, Chronology 121/122 and 190 has a disquisition on the dates of Mani's life.
19. Puech, Manich. 33.
20. His name is given in a diversity of spellings by a great number of authors, for instance in a Greek formula of abjuration as 'Patekios' (PG 1, 1468B, Paris, 1857), and by Theodore bar Konai, Lib. Schol., Mimra XI, 58 as 'Ptiq'; see Puech, Maich. 117, note 124.
21. But other birth-places in Media are also given, Puech, Manich. 118, note 126.
22. Puech, Manich. 36 is not sure of this kinship. Böhlig s.v. 'Manichäismus', TRE 22.1, 28, says that his being descended from the Iranian nobility is doubtful. Ort, Mani 195 and 199 : "His relation to the Persian royal family is not quite clear", but certain ancient data (Chinese and Arabic) "make it highly probable that Petek was a descendant from the Persian dynasty of the Arsacids".
23. Puech, Manich. 36. However, Tardieu, Manich. 5, thinks that a Christianizing Manichaean apologist gave her the name of Jesus' mother.
24. But, says Tardieu, Manich. 5, we also find in Christianity and Buddhism that the founder had princely ancestors; like Jesus, Mani was an only child.
25. Once again Tardieu, Manich. 5 : the same apologist **made** (my emphasis) his father into an emigrant leaving Hamadan for Ctesiphon, and Ctesiphon for Nahar-Kuthi, just as Joseph went from Nazareth to Bethlehem and from Bethlehem fled to Egypt. It looks rather far-flung. It may also be that Patek had some sort of palace in Ctesiphon and a country-house in Nahar-Kuthi, Widengren, Mani 30.
26. See Vol. V, Ch. I.3a.
27. Puech, Manich. 37.

28. See Vol. V, Ch. I.5f.
29. See Vol. V, Ch. I.5.
30. Widengren, Religionen 283.
31. Widengren, Religionen 43-245; Puech, Manich. 37-39.
32. According to Widengren, Mani 31, it might even have been a Buddhist temple.
33. Tardieu, Manich. 6.
34. Fihrist 773/774.
35. Decret, Mani 48.
36. Fihrist 774.
37. Widengren, Mani 32, is convinced that young Mani grew up in a southern Babylonian, Gnostic, Mandaean Baptist community. He admits that, although Mani was ordered to live ascetically, the Mandaeans were not ascetic; in order to solve this problem he postulates an ascetic branch of Mandaeism.
38. Theodore, Lib. Schol., Mimra XI.58.
39. Ort, Mani 201 : "It is quite understandable that historians of religions concluded from these terms (i.e. of Theodore) that the sect in question was a group of baptists. We wish to add, however, to this conclusion that our sources do not mention any form of baptism in the sense of a rite of initiation. The terms we mentioned above (i.e. of Theodore) may also lead us to the conclusion that the community in question was characterized by frequent lavations". Keph. VI.33.25-32 Mani himself says that "they (the Baptists) baptize by means of water-baptism", but it is by no means certain that he is speaking here of the Mughtasila.
40. Theodore, Lib.Schol., Mimra XI.58.
41. Quoted by Tardieu, Manich. 7/8.
42. However, Brandt, Elchasai 37-40, clearly holds him for a historical person. There exists yet another book on Elchasai, much more recent, a work in Italian. It was not present in the University Library of Amsterdam nor in any other Dutch, French, British, German, etc. library. After months of search the International Loan Service of the Amsterdam Library tracked it down in Italy. To send this book to Amsterdam and to me would cost an exorbitant sum. Furthermore, this would also cost much time, so that - as the librarian in Amsterdam assured me - it could easily arrive only in 1995, at a moment when, as I hope, this volume will already have been published. The book in question is by Luigi Cirillo, Elchasai e gli Elchesaiti. Un contributo alla storia delle communità giudeo-cristiane, Cosenza, 1984.
43. Epiph., Pan. 30.17; Hipp., Ref. 9.13.
44. Hipp., Ref. 9.13.
45. Hilgenfeld, Novum Testamentum fasc. 3, 151-176.
46. Epiph., Pan. 19.1-2.

47. Bareille s.v. 'Elcésaites', Dict.théol.cath. 4.2, 2235. Paris, 1924.
48. Epiph., Pan. 53.1.
49. Bareille s.v. 'Elcésaites', Dict.théol.cath. 4.2., 2237. Paris, 1924.
50. Hipp., Ref. 9.17; Bareille s.v. 'Elcésaites'. Dict.théol.cath. 4.2, 2237. Paris, 1924.
51. Hipp., Ref. 9.17.
52. Epiph., Pan. 53.1.
53. Hipp., Ref. 19.4.
54. Epiph., Pan. 19.5.
55. Epiph., Pan. 19.1.
56. For Brandt, Elchasai 136, this was sufficient reason to conclude that the Mughtasila did not have an Elkasaite origin.
57. Pseudoclementina, Homilia 8.21, PG 2. 237, Paris, 1847. Brandt, Elchasai 136, was of the opinion that the doctrine of the two principles was not originally Elkesaite but crept in from Iran.
58. According to Cirillo, Elchesaiti 138, we should, when comparing Elkesaitism and Mughtasilism (= 'i Battisti di Mani'), avoid two extremes. The first would consist in levelling the differences between the different groups of Elkesaites so that Elkesaites and Mughtasila would be virtually the same. The second is to argue as though the Mughtasila were totally independent of the story of Elkesaitism.
59. CMC 10-11 : "(Nachdem) mein Leib (von meiner Mutter) (?) im Kleinkindalter (?) bis zu meinem vierten Jahr (genährt worden war), trat ich (zu diesem Zeitpunkt) in die Glaubensgemeinschaft der Täufer ein. Als mein Leib im Jugendalter war, wuchs ich in dieser Gemeinschaft auf."
60. Fihrist 774.
61. CMC 11.12; this text goes on in this way : "Sie erzogen mich, indem sie mir Visionen und Wunder zeigten, die nur klein und sehr kurz waren, so wie ich sie ertragen konnte."
62. Fihrist 774. Of course, the comparison with the youthful Jesus has often been made. Widengren, Mani 32 : "Wir werden an den zwölfjährigen Jesus im Tempel erinnert". Tardieu, Manich. 13 : "Tout se passe comme si Mani enfant copiait Jésus enfant". Whereas it is true that Luke mentions the wisdom of the boy Jesus, the Gospels nowhere mention an angelic revelation to him.
63. The Arab word 'taw'am' signifies 'twin'.
64. Puech, Manich. 43/44.
65. Evodius, De fide 24.
66. CMC 44 : "Da trennte ich mich sogleich von den Normen jener Lehre, in der ich aufgewachsen war, und ich wurde wie ein Fremdling und Einzelänger in ihrer Mitte, bis der Zeitpunkt kam, zu dem ich aus jener Lehre austrat."

67. CMC 82.
68. CMC 84-85.
69. CMC 84-85; also citation nr. 5 : "... indem (ich) mit Weisheit und Gewandtheit in ihrer Mitte wandelte, das Ausruhen einhielt, kein Unrecht beging, keinerlei Schmerz zufügte, dem Gesetz der Täufer nicht folgte und nicht nach ihrer Art Reden führte."
70. CMC 87-88.
71. Once again some scholars are reminded of the disputes of Jesus with the Pharisees, Tardieu, Manich. 17.
72. CMC 90-91.
73. CMC 93.
74. CMC 94-95.
75. CMC 100.
76. Fihhrist 774/775.
77. Fihrist, 774/775. Idem in Keph. 14.31-32 : "In diesem selben Jahre, als Ardashir der König (?) (=Shapur I) (im Begriff war) die Krone (zu empfangen), da kam der lebendige Paraklet herab (zu mir) und redete ...".
78. F.C. Burkitt, The Religion of the Manichees. Cambridge, 1925, p. 3, quoted by Puech, Manich. 46.
79. Puech, Manich. 46; Böhlig s.v. 'Manichäismus', TRE 22, Lief. 1, 28, Berlin/New York (1991), mentions no date at all. CMC 18 : "Als ich vier und zwanzig Jahre alt war, in dem Jahre, in welchem Ardaschir, der König von Persien, die Stadt Hatra unterwarf und der König Schapur, sein Sohn, sich das Grossdiadem aufsetzte, am 8. (?) Tag des Monats Pharmuthi nach dem Mondkalender ...", this date is interpreted by Koenen/Römer as April 17/18, 240.
80. Williams Jackson, Person Manis 479/480.
81. Acta Arch. 14.
82. Fihirst 775, with note 144 by Bayard Dodge.
83. From a Middle Persian document, M49II, quoted Die Gnosis III, 80.
84. Fihirsty 774.
85. CMC, quoted by Böhlig s.v. 'Manichäismus', TRE XXII, Lief. 1, 29. Berlin/New York (1991).
86. Riès, Ét.manich. 236.
87. Keph. 13.20.
88. Keph. 101.26-27.
89. Tardieu, Manich. 27.
90. M2, in Die Gnosis III, 93; see Bohlig s.v. 'Manichäismus', TRE XXII, Lief. 1, 29, Berlin/New York (1991).

91. The same M2 text implies that, whereas Patek remained for a year there, Mani himself soon returned.
92. CMC 144; Keph. 186.6/7.
93. Keph. 15.25.
94. Puech, Manich. 44.
95. Keph. 184.24/25.
96. This is confirmed by a fragment found at Tourfan. Whether Mani travelled further northward and even visited the northern region of Gandhara is a matter of conjecture, Puech, Manich. 45.
97. Keph. 15.26/27.
98. Widengren, Mani 35.
99. Keph. 15.29-31, 185.15-17 and 186.6/7.
100. M47, translation in Widengren, Mani 36.
101. Fihrist 776.
102. Keph. 15.31/32.
103. Some scholars, and not the least important, believe that this encounter was 'the coming forth' of Mani, his first public appearance, as described by al-Nadim, Fihrist 775, and already related by me;'it might even have taken place on the coronation-day, Puech, Manich. 45/46, Widengren, Mani 36/37, Decret, Mani 60/61, Böhlig s.v. 'Manichäismus', TRE XXII, Lief. 1, 29, Berlin/New York (1991), whereas Ort, Mani 210, says that "there are no solutions for these (= chronological) problems". What makes me doubtful is that al-Nadim clearly treats the 'coming forth' and the encounter with the emperor as two distinct events separated from each other by the travels of Mani. One may also ask oneself whether the emperor, on such a crowded day as his coronation-day, would have found time and leisure to receive a travelling prophet who was totally unknown to him
104. This much damaged document is M566I, in Parthian, printed in Ort, Mani 51. It does not give the name of the king, but we may be sure, with Ort, Mani 215, that the ruler in question was indeed Shapur I.
105. Ort, Mani 215.
106. Fihrist 776, confirmed by Keph. 15.32/33.
107. Keph. 183.18-25.
108. Keph. 15.33-16.2.
109. Alex.Lyc., Tractatus 21. It is undecided, says Puech, Manich. 47/48, whether the campaign in question was that of 242-244 against Gordianus III, or that of 256-260 against Valerianus. Both are possible. If it were the first of the two, then Mani stood opposite Plotinus, the founder of the Neoplatonic school, who served in the Roman army as a volunteer.
110. Puech, Manich. 48/49.

111. Widengren, Mani 38/39.
112. Coptic Homilies, quoted in ort, Mani 219.
113. Coptic Homilies, quoted in Ort, Mani 221.
114. Coptic Homilies, Die Gnosis III, 95.
115. M3 in Die Gnosis III, 95/96.
116. CMC 64 : "Die Wahrheit und die Geheimnisse, über die ich rede, auch die Handauflegung, die bei mir ist, habe ich nicht von menschlichen oder fleischlichen Geschöpfen und auch nicht durch den Umgang mit Schriften empfangen."
117. Coptic Homilies 46, Die Gnosis III, 96/97.
118. Coptic Homilies 48, Die Gnosis III, 97/98.
119. 25 kilo.
120. Coptic Homilies 48, Die Gnosis III, 98.
121. See Puech, Manich. 138/139, note 210.
122. Coptic Homilies 50, Die Gnosis III, 98.
123. Puech, Manich. 52/53 and 139/140, note 216; see also Coptic Homilies 60, Die Gnosis III, 99.
124. Puech, Manich. 54.
125. Fihrist 797.
126. Widengren, Mani 77. See Lidzbarski, Warum schrieb Mani aramäisch? 250-254, and Rosenthal, Die Sprache Manis, 255-259.
127. Albîrûnî, Chronology 27.11 : "The Manichaeans have a Gospel of their own, in which they agree with the sects of Marcion and Bardesanes which also have 'a special Gospel'.
128. Fihrist 797-800.
129. Decret, Mani 76.
130. See for an overview Tardieu, Manich. 45-64, II Les oeuvres de Mani. Manichaean scripture is the subject of a two-volume work by Alfaric (see Bibliography).
131. Puech, Manich. 61.
132. Puech, Manich. 61-63.
133. Shabuhragan text quoted by Albîrûnî, Chronology 190.
134. Shabuhragan text quoted in Arabian by Ibn al Murtada in his 'Al-bahr, Az-zahhor', Kessler, Mani I, 355.
135. Puech, Manich. 62.
136. Shabuhragan text, quoted by Tardieu, Manich. 20.
137. Fihrist 775.
138. Keph. 16.9.

139. Keph. 15.19-24.
140. Puech, Manich. 63-66.
141. Puech, Manich. 66-68.
142. Puech, Manich. 67.
143. Puech, Manich. 68.
144. Keph. 154.
145. Keph. 13.27-34 says that after the apostle Paul the Church was 'scandalized' = became a scandal; "they left justice behind them". But then 'a just one, a true one, appeared who belonged to the kingdom. "He met ... (text unreadable); they worked in the Church of our Lord according to their power ... After them the Church fell into decay again." There can hardly be any doubt that these two just ones are Marcion and Bardesanes. See Puech, Manich. 150/151, note 268.
146. Puech, Manich. 70. "While, through its historical origins, Manichaeism is directly connected with anterior gnosticisms, it is, in its essence, a 'religion of salvation', of a Gnostic type." And "we will find back in Manichaeism all (the) characteristics of the Gnostic conception", Puech, Sur le Manich. 8 and 17.
147. asch-Scharashtâni, Religionspartheien I, 286.
148. asch-Scharashtâni, Religionspartheien I, 286.
149. Hans Jakob Pototsky s.v. 'Manichäism' in PW, Suppl.Bd. VI, 245 (Stuttgart, 1935) : "(Mani's Religion) verneint mit der äussersten Konsequenz die Möglichkeit, das Gute und das Böse auf **ein** (his emphasis) Urprinzip zurückzuführen ... Das Böse ist ein dem Guten selbständig gegenüberstehendes und nicht nur essentiell sondern ursprünglich auch existentiell von ihm getrenntes Prinzip (archê)".
150. Albîrûnî, Chronology 190 : "He taught that light and darkness are without beginning and end."
151. Epiph., Panarion 64.14.1 : "There is no intelligent agreement between them possible".
152. Puech, Manich. 161, note 286.
153. Puech, Manich. 74.
154. Puech, Manich. 160, note 285. The idea perhaps has a background in etymology since 'hulê' means 'wood', in Latin 'silva'. But the direct inspiration must have been the comparison of the good and the bad trees in Mt.7:17-19 and 12:33, and in the later text of Lc.6:43 from which it came to Marcion and through him to Mani.
155. Aug., Contra Faustum 20.1.
156. Aug., Contra Faustum 20.3.
157. Baur, Man. Rel.syst. 26. But Baur was refuted by an original source he cannot have known, a part of a Chinese Manichaean cathechism, the so-called 'Pelliot fragment", which says : "A person who asks to join our religion must know that the two principles of the Light and the Dark-

ness possess absolutely distinct natures", quoted by Puech, Sur le Manich. 29.
158. Aug., Contra Faustum 20.1.
159. Baur, Man. Rel.syst. 10.
160. Widengren, Mani 48/49.
161. See my Vol. V, Ch. I.5b.
162. Fihrist 794; o.c. 773 : "Moreover, he had a deformed foot."
163. Williams Jackosn, Person Manis 485/486.
164. Puech, Manich. 35.
165. See thesis IV in Ort, Mani.
166. Fihirst 777/778.
167. Quoted by Kessler, Mani I, 350.
168. Shkand-gumânîk vichâr 16.51-52.
169. Theodore bar Konaï, Lib.Schol., Mimra XI.313,16-17.
170. Keph. 30.33-31.2 and 77.23-78.3.
171. Puech, Manich. 75.
172. Aug., Contra Faustum 21.14.
173. From Mani's 'Epistula fundamenti', ed. A. Adam 28.
174. Aug., Contra Faustum 21.14.
175. Al.Lyc., Tract. 2.3 and 6.1.
176. Fihrist 778.
177. Titus of Bostra, Adv.Man. 1.16.
178. Fihrist 778.
179. Theodoret., Haer.fab.comp. 1.26. The reader will find a very clear account of the now ensuing war between both worlds in Puech, Sur le Manich. 32-59 'Les fondements théoriques du Salut : mythe cosmologique et anthropologique'.
180. Fihrist 778.
181. Titus of Bostra, Adv.Man. 17.
182. Fihrist 778; these are the five 'mansions' of the luminous world, but with different names.
183. Titus of Bostra, Adv.Manich. 19.
184. Alex.Lyc., Tract. 9.
185. Baur, Manich. Rel.syst. 48.
186. August., De nat. boni 42.
187. Alex., Lyc., Tract. 8.
188. Theodore bar Konaï, Lib.Schol., Mimra XI, (313) 59.

189. Theodoret., Haer.fab.comp. 1.26c.
190. Evodius, De fide 11.
191. Baur, Man.Rel.syst. 51.
192. Theodore bar Konaï, Lib.schol. Mimra XI, (313) 59.
193. Widengren, Mani 52.
194. Alex.Lyc., Tract. 3.
195. Titus of Bostra, Adv.man. 1.20.
196. August., De vera rel. 9.
197. Acta Arch. 7.3.
198. Acta Arch., 7.3.; Theodore bar Konaï, Lib.schol. Mimra XI (314) 59.
199. August., Contra faust. 2.3.
200. Fihrist 779.
201. Fihrist 779; Acta Arch. 7.3; Theodore bar Konaï, Lib.schol. Mimra XI (314) 59.
202. Fihrist 779.
203. Fihrist 779.
204. It is described in Keph. 67.23-70.7, but this text is heavily damaged.
205. August., De haer. 46.
206. Acta Arch. 7.4.
207. Acta Arch. 7.4.
208. Simplicius, Comm. in Epict. Ench. 34 (27). Poor editor of this work! Almost two centuries after its publication I was the first to cut this volume open!
209. Acta Arch. 28.2.
210. Titus of Bostra, Adv.Man. 1.12.
211. Baur, Manich. Rel.syst. 57.
212. Alex.Lyc., Tract. 3.
213. Theodore bar Konaï, Lib.schol. Mimra XI (314) 59.
214. Baur, Manich. Rel.syst. 61/62.
215. Theodore bar Konaï, Lib.schol. Mimra XII (314) 59.
216. Acta Arch. 7.4.
217. Theodore bar Konaï, Lib.schol. Mimra XI (314/315) 59.
218. Theodore bar Konaï, Lib.schol. Mimra XI (315) 59.
219. Acta Arch. 7.
220. Keph. 38.20 and 39.19-24.
221. Keph. 38.12 and 32/33.

222. Keph. 40.13/14. This text comes from Ps. 110:1 and is quoted five times in the New Testament (Mc. 12:36; Lc. 20:43; Acts 2:25; Hebr. 1:13 and 10:13). The word 'first-born', however, is a Manichaean addition.
223. Skhand-gumânîk vichâr 16.10-14.
224. Fihrist 781.
225. Fihrist 782.
226. (Pseudo)Gregory of Nyssa, De anima 208; Nemesius, De nat.hom. 2.48.
227. Fihrist 782, note 185 of Bayard Dodge.
228. Fihrist 782; Alex.Lyc. Tract. 3.
229. Alex.Lyc., Tract. 3.
230. Pseudo-Jerome, Indiculus de haeresibus 5, quoted by Puech, Manich. 171, note 321.
231. Simplicius, Comm, in Epict. Ench. 167 (272).
232. Keph. 168.7-16.
233. Theodore bar Konaï, Lib.schol. Mimra XI (316) 59.
234. Keph. 107.16-26 calles them 'vehicles' and 'garments'.
235. Keph. 112.25-113.25.
236. Asch-Scharahstâni, Religionspartheien I,289; Alex.Lyc., Tract. 4 and 22; August., De natura boni 44.
237. Puech, Manich. 80.
238. Theodore bar Konaï, Lib.schol. Mimra XII (316/317) 59; August., De natura boni 44; Keph. 136.1-13.
239. G. Bardy s.v. 'Manichéisme, dogmatique', Dict.théol.cath. 9.2., 1872, Paris, 1929.
240. Puech, Manich. 80.
241. This is also expressed several times by the Keph. 133.12-15, 134.2-4, 135.15-17 and 21-24, and still more
242. August., De nat.boni 46.
243. Theodore bar Konaï, Lib.schol. Mimra XI (317) 59.
244. Theodore bar Konaï, Lib.schol. Mimra XI (317) 59.
245. Keph. 169.29-170.19.
246. Acta Arch. 16.10.
247. Acta Arch. 16.7.
248. Widengren, Mani 63.
249. Commonitorium (vulgo Augustini) 4.
250. August., De mor.Man. 2.19.73.

251. The idea of man having two souls very probably stems from Beausobre, quoted to this effect by Baur, Man.Rel.syst. 163 : "Ainsi l'homme est animé de deux âmes opposées comme les substances d'où elles tirent leur origine". Others followed Beausobre on this point, but Baur himself did not agree. He found that it is very difficult "die Zweiheit der Seelen mit der Einheit des menschlichen Wesens und der Einheit des Bewusstseyns zu denken ..., da die Einheit des individuellen Lebens am wenigsten einen solchen Gegensatz der Principien zulassen zu können scheint" (p. 164). This is a holistic view, dear to moderns, but not natural to Gnostics. Baur cites Titus of Bostra, Adv.Man. 2.6 in support of his opinion, because this author spoke of 'natures' instead of 'souls' : "There are two opposed natures in us, so that we sometimes think evil things, and at other times good things". Does this distinction of 'natures' and 'souls' make much of a difference, especially if we take into account that they both 'think' ('enthumeisthai')? Another quotation, equally from Titus (1.23) : "The body of man is of evil, and the soul of the good, this soul either being uniform or consisting of opposites". Baur (165) infers from this that it is 'in jedem Fall eine und dieselbe Seele', but omits to mention that Titus added that "in consequence, the soul cannot have one structure (or composition, 'sustastis')", and also that "the body from itself does not brood on evil" (l.c.). Referring to Mani himself Titus said that, according to the prophet, "the soul is composed of good and bad, and that the rational part of it must be attributed to the good one (the godhead) and the irrational part to evil" (1.27). Anyhow, the soul is twofold. The authentic ancient source for there being two souls in man is saint Augustine who, after all, had been a Manichee himself. He wrote a short treatise entitled 'De duobus animabus contra Manichaeos'. In this (1) he spoke of 'two sorts of souls to which they (the Manichees) ascribe different and proper natures, so that the one is from the very substance of God, whereas with respect to the other they do not accept that it has God as its creator." But, when all is said and done, Baur (197) admitted that "die reine Lichtseele ... ihre Schattenseite (hat). Sie kann der Uebermacht der Finsterniss nicht widerstehen, mit welcher gleichsam ein Böses ihr den lichten Tag des Bewusstseyns raubt und in dunkle Nacht verkehrt, und sie aus dem Zustande der Freiheit in einen Zustand der Gebundenheit hinabdrückt".

252. Acta Arch. 12.2.

253. G. Bardy s.v. 'Manichéisme. Dogmatique', Dict.théol.cath. 9.2., 1877.

254. G. Bardy s.v. 'Manichéisme. Dogmatique', Di

255. G. Bardy s.v. 'Manichéisme. Dogmatique". Dict.théol.cath. 9.2., 1878.

256. Fihrist 778, with note 193 by Bayard Dodge.

257. Fihrist 783.

258. Fihrist 784.

259. Acta Arch. 50.

260. Keph. 53.13-54.14.

261. Document TIII,260, quoted by Puech, Manich. 260.

262. Keph. 157.18-19.

263. August., Contra Faustum 20.2.
264. Baur, Man.Rel.syst. 327/328.
265. Theodore bar Konaï, Lib.schol. Mimra XI (317) 59.
266. Fihrist 784.
267. Theodore bar Konaï, Lib.schol. Mimra XI (317) 59.
268. Puech, Manich. 82, quoting from a document S 9.
269. Acta Archelai 11.4.
270. Theodore bar Konaï, Lib.schol. Mimra XI (318) 59.
271. Fihrist 784.
272. Fihrist 784, note 196 by Bayard Dodge : "The word in Arabic is 'white' rather than 'blond', so that the color evidently has allegorical significance as 'good'".
273. Fihrist 786, note 203 by Bayard Dodge.
274. Fihrist 784-786.
275. Fihrist 786, note 205.
276. Puech, Manich. 82.
277. Alex.Lyc., Tract. 19.
278. August., De natura boni 44.
279. Evodius, De fide 34.
280. August., Contra Faustum 20.2.
281. August., Enarrationes in psalmos 140.12.
282. Alex.Lyc., Tract. 4.
283. August., Contra Faustum 32.7.
284. August., Contra Faustum 2.5.
285. Keph. 12.9-13.25; asch-Scharahstâni I.290.
286. Keph. 13.30-35.
287. August., Contra Epistolam 5.
288. Puech, Manich. 83.
289. August., De moribus Man. 19.
290. August., De moribus Man. 20-26.
291. August., De moribus Man. 36.
292. Kouastouanift-text, quoted by G. Bardy s.v. 'Manichéisme. Dogmatique', Dict.théol.cath. 9.2., 1879. Paris, 1929.
293. August., De moribus Man. 44.
294. August., De moribus Man. 29-30.
295. Fihrist 791; August., Sermo 236.2.

296.	Acta Arch. 10.
297.	Acta Arch. 10.
298.	Keph. 192.8/9.
299.	Alex.Lyc., Tract. 4.
300.	August., De moribus Man. 65; see G. Bardy s.v. 'Manichéisme. Morale', Dict.théol.cath. 9.2., 1889. paris, 1929.
301.	Puech, Manich. 85/86.
302.	Baur, Man.Rel.syst. 26.
303.	Fihrist 795.
304.	Fihrist 796; Bayard Dodge, the translator, comments that "the translation is free, to make the passage readable" (note 257).
305.	August., De fide 5.
306.	Homily-text, quoted by Widengren, Mani 70.
307.	Epiph., Panarion 66.31.6-7.
308.	Keph. 29.9-13; Alex.Lyc., Tract. 13.
309.	Keph. 54.13-19 and 75.21-26.
310.	Keph. 105.32/33.
311.	Keph. 104.6-20; Evodius, De fide 5.
312.	Keph. 105.5-14.
313.	August., De haer. 46.
314.	Epiph., Panarion 66.58.2; Alex.Lyc., Tract. 11. See also Puech, Manich. 84/85 and Widengren, Mani 70/71.
315.	Baur, Man.Rel.syst. 329.
316.	Titus of Bostra, Adv.Man. 1.31.
317.	Puech, Manich. 91.
318.	Chinese Manichaean tractate, quoted by G. Bardy s.v. 'Manichéisme. Eschatologie', Dict.théol.cath. 9.2., 1881. Paris, 1929.
319.	Puech, Manich. 90.
320.	Chinese fragment. quoted by G. Bardy s.v. 'Manichéisme. Eschatologie'. Dict.théol.cath. 9.2, 1881. Paris, 1929.
321.	Puech, Manich. 90/91.
322.	Fihrist 789.
323.	August., Ep. 236.
324.	August., Contra Faustum 5.10 and De haer. 1.46.
325.	Puech, Manich. 91.
326.	Keph. 221.2-4.
327.	August., De haer. 46.

227

328. Puech, Manich. 193, note 391.
329. Baur, Man.Rel.syst. 281.
330. August., De haer. 46.
331. There is no need for me to go deeply into the matter of Manichaean ritual. The interested should consult Puech, Sur le Manich. 235-394, 'Liturgie et pratiques rituelles dans le Manichéisme'.
332. Baur, Man.Rel.syst. 273.
333. August., De haer. 46. Also August., Contra duas Ep. 2.2.3 and 4.4.5 where he declares it to be (in Manichaean view) a work of the King of Darkness.
334. Turribius of Astorga, Epistola 5.
335. August., De mor.man. 39.
336. August., De actis 1.19, and Acta 3.
337. In De haer. 46 and in De nat. boni 47 Augustine says that there was a sexual element in this rite, but he adds that the Manichees themselves denied this.
338. Epiph., Panarion 66.5.1-3.
339. Epiph., Panarion 66.1.
340. Acta Arch. 44.
341. Alex.Lyc., Tract.; Widengren, Mani 118.
342. The relations between the Roman Empire and the Church of Justice are extensively treated by Lieu, Manichaeism, Ch. IV.
343. G. Bardy s.v. 'Manichéisme. Expansion', Dict.théol.cath. 9.2., 1864. Paris, 1929.
344. The spread of Manichaeism in the Roman Empire after the death of Mani is described by Lieu, Manichaeism, Ch. III.6.
345. The interested reader will find the detailed story of the eastward spread of Manichaeism in Lieu, manichaeism, Chs. VII, VIII, and IX.

CHAPTER V

LOOKING BACK AT THE GNOSIS

Part I Scholars and their opinions

1. How to introduce the Gnosis

People wanting to know what I am working on not rarely ask what 'that Gnosis' may be. Knowledge of this fascinating phenomenon is, to put it mildly, not widespread, not even among scholars, classical scholars not excepted. If such people prove genuinely interested I hand them a short essay on the subject, containing the bare outlines and written by me way back in June 1976 - my first 'publication' in this field. If they want to know more, I advise them to read first and foremost Jonas' 'The Greek Religion'; a further suggestion is the books of Leisegang and Rudolph, both called 'Die Gnosis'. But I have to explain then that the works of Jonas and Leisegang do not take the Nag Hammadi library into account, that incomparable set of authentic Gnostic documents. This defect may be remedied by the lecture of Filoramo's 'A History of Gnosticism'.

Many, of course, will wish to study original Gnostic writings at first hand, but, unfortunately, there exist no Gnostic texts that are purely explicatory; no cathechism, summary, or abstract of his religion was ever composed by a Gnostic believer. Furthermore, a phenomenon later referred to as 'the Gnostic religion' or 'the Gnosis', never existed. Instead, there were innumerable sects, often with widely differing opinions. There was not even, as in Christianity, a main Church or 'great Church'. An additional difficulty is that Nag Hammadi documents are opaque, sometimes to the point of incomprehensibility, and even beyond. They are repetitive, elusive, and replete with symbols and myths. Such texts were not written for inquisitive outsiders but for the initiated who were already in the know. Most of the secondary literature, moreover, is highly technical, written as it is by specialists in this field.

2. The drawbacks of specialization

True enough, beyond a certain point all scholarship becomes specialized, but there is an incredible amount of disagreement among Gnoseologues. I always thought that classical scholars in general are the most discordant group of scholars in the humanities; what one of them states is immediately pounced upon by another. But their discordance is easily surpassed by that prevailing among experts of the Gnosis. They often remind me of the Gnostics themselves who never proved able to attain that high degree of dogmatic agreement that is the hallmark of the Roman-Catholic Church. In fact, experts are not even unanimous on what is Gnostic and what not, in other words we possess no yardstick to determine with sufficient certainty whether or not a document is Gnostic. Just as the Gnostics of yore, Gnoseologues agree only to differ. I could not help thinking that this saying of Irenaeus : "Everyone of them thinks up something new every day", is also applicable to experts on the Gnosis.

Let me quote only one example out of many. Perusing the secondary literature on Simon the Magician, I collected the following statements about this remarkable man. 1. A man called Simon never existed - Simon is an historical person; 2. Simon lived in the first century - Simon lived in the second century; 3. Simon was the first Gnostic - Simon was not the first Gnostic - Simon was no Gnostic at all; 4. Simon is the author of the Apophasis megalê - Simon is not the author of the Apophasis megalê; 5. the most original and authentic part of Simon's ideology is the myth of Helen - the most original and authentic part of Simon's ideology is his divinization; 6. Irenaeus' report on Simon is the only reliable one we have - Irenaeus' report on Simon is utterly untrustworthy. I swear that all those opinions were expressed in publications to be found in the Bibliography of my Volume VII. All this compels one to regard these scholarly assertions as so many tentative hypotheses.

3. Christianity the origin of the Gnosis?

a. The hallmark of the Gnosis according to Simone Pétrement

The hallmark of the Gnosis, according to Simone Pétrement, is the concept of 'the separated God', the idea of a primal godhead who is alien to creation, the cosmos, and mankind. The real creator is another divinity, the Demiurge, who occupies a much lower stage in the divine hierarchy, so low that he often does not even know that there is yet another, a supreme godhead. But though the title of her book reads 'Le Dieu séparé' [1], it is not about the relationship of the two divinities. The subtitle says what it is really about, 'the origins of Gnosticism'.

b. The New Testament as the basis of the Gnosis

Mme. Pétrement takes issue with all those scholars who postulate a non-Christian origin of the Gnosis. There is not much talk nowadays of a possible pre-Christian origin, but there are savants who classify the Nag Hammadi texts into 'Christian' and 'non-Christian ones'. Pétrement admits that some of these texts do not show even the slightest trace of Christianity. But she backs out of this problem by stating that a great deal of study will be necessary before we are more or less sure about this alleged non-Christian character. Yet even if these texts were to be found to be non-Christian, this would still be no proof, she asserts, that they were **born** (her emphasis) outside Christianity [2].

This brings us to the kernel of her argument. Her main thesis, defended with admirable tenacity and vigour, and at great length, is that all Gnostic sects and all Gnostic systems without exception in the last resort have the New Testament, in particular the Gospel of John and the Pauline letters, as their spiritual background. The common source from which the whole Gnosis derives is biblical Christianity.

A biblical scholar will immediately protest that, in addition to Christian, there are many pagan elements to be found in Gnostic texts, Platonic for instance. Mme. Pétrement has no problem to readily admit this, but she disposes of this objection by stating that in its later stages the Gnosis began to drift more and more from its Christian moorings and, in consequence, became permeable to non-Christian influences. She also admits that much in her work is hypothetical but, she concludes, all taken together, the hypothesis of an basically Christian origin of the Gnosis seems to be by far the most solid one [3].

c. All Gnostic systems interrelated

This means that all that is Gnostic is interrelated and affiliated, because all Gnostic systems in one way or another are, to a certain extent, related to or dependent on certain tenets of the biblical creed. The result is that an imposing building rises before our eyes, a common system in which every Gnostic sect or text finds its allocated place. Should we follow the reverse order of Mme. Pétrement's argument, we would find at the farthest end, that is to say the nearest to us in time, the Ophites and the Sethians, characterized by her as 'twins'. Working backward in time, we see that the father of these twins is Valentinianism. She sees the last mentioned system as an attenuated form of the Gnosis in which the separation of God and world is much tuned down and the distance of the Gnosis from Judaism and Christianity considerably narrowed. She writes that she cannot rule out the possibility that the system of Valentinus, together with that of Carpocrates, emanates from Basilides, and through him from the Syrian school. Perhaps, she thinks, Basilides and Saturnilos were the first real Gnostics.

We are now in Syria. From Menander we reach back to Cerinthus, if such a person really did exist, and from him to Simon the Magician, with the same (Pétrement's) proviso. However, she admits that the ecclesiastical tradition according to which Simon is the father of the Gnostic heresy might contain 'a spark of truth'. We have arrived now in the near vicinity of the New Testament, not so much so because Simon is mentioned in the Acts of the Apostles, but rather on account of the alleged Gnostic tendencies of John and Paul. Simone Pétrement does not contend that Paul and John were Gnostics, but, she writes, there was much in their writings, and not only in theirs, that appealed to the Gnostics. But the real link between the New Testament and the Gnosis was Apollos, the Christian Gospel preacher, who is mentioned in Acts and by Paul. He is said (by Pétrement and others) to have preached, mainly in Corinth, a Gospel that was different from that of Paul and which was Gnostic (avant la lettre), or at least 'gnosticizing' [4].

We now stand gazing at a mighty tree in full splendour, with its branches, covered in rich foliage, from lowly beginnings rising ever higher and higher. It does not impair the tree's beauty that near the crown some alien looking shoots appear. The bed from which it arises is neatly delineated from the shrubbery around. But it is perhaps a minor flaw that the lowest part of the trunk is tenuous, almost too fragile to sustain this whole growth.

It seems to me that in Mme. Pétrement's beautifully organized and apparently so logical a structure something typically French becomes evident, a desire for rationality, for systematic constructiveness, for something 'Cartesian', one might say. At the same time, there is a historicist and evolutionist aspect to it. Historicist it seems because every element in it is linked, in chronological order, to another, earlier element and is seen to proceed from this earlier element, with, finally, one single historical source for the whole complex. Its evolutionist leanings become apparent in the development of the structure, starting and unfolding from modest and somewhat hardly definable beginnings and ending in an intricate complex in which all elements are organically connected with each other. In this way the author is paying homage to several influential intellectual tendencies at a time.

d. Pétrement's workmanship

Let us now take a look at her workmanship. Her erudition is certainly impressive; she is well acquainted with Gnostic scripture and other ancient sources, and is extremely well read in secondary literature. Her style is clear. She has many interesting remarks to make and offers some fascinating insights.

On the other hand, it is a very bulky book, running to more than six hundred and sixty pages of text. Exposed as he or she is to a constant barrage of arguments, the reader may be perhaps be excused if he or she slowly becomes somewhat tired. This present reader, for one, sometimes thought "the lady doth protest too much, methinks". The sheer bulk of the book proves that the author had an enormous lot of arguing to do in order to make her theses and hypotheses acceptable. Page follows page of dense argumentation, often very detailed, so that the reader often does not see the wood for the trees. The book would have gained if it had been carefully pruned; now it looks as though the author's whole collection of cards went into it.

In the course of her study Simone Pétrement takes issue with almost every other scholar in this field; in fact, I found no one with whom she wholeheartedly agrees. With whole schools, in particular with scholars who postulate the existence of a non-Christian Gnosis, she is in complete disagreement. I don't doubt that, if she had to review my Volumes VII, VIII, and the present one, in which three books the Gnosis is the main subject, she would hack them to pieces. She has to fight a lonely battle in the scholarly world, and an uphill one at that.

Inspecting her mode of argument more closely, we discover soon enough that she defends her theses very often in an hypothetical manner. Conditional statements abound. She constantly uses words and terms such as 'perhaps, possibly, presumably, if-then, might be, could be, assuming that ...'.

e. How the report on Simon the Magician is handled

A telling example of this is how she handles the report on Simon the Magician, as rendered in Acts 8:4-24. It is related there that a certain Simon performed great magic tricks in Samaria. But the apostle Philip converted him to Christianity. Then Peter and John came to Samaria, prayed over the new converts, and laid their hands on them so that they received the Holy Spirit. Simon then wished to have the same power the apostles had and offered money to them in order to get it. But Peter cursed him for this.

According to Pétrement, who remains somewhat doubtful about the historical existence of Simon, the report in Acts might indicate that he was the head of a Samaritan Christian community to which a certain degree of autonomy, with respect to the Church of Jerusalem (the Mother Church), had been accorded. He wanted to administer the sacrament that involved the descent of the Holy Spirit. Perhaps he hoped to play a role of importance. But he may also have wished to make the Samaritan Christians less dependent on Jerusalem. Samaritan Judaism had always jealously defended its independence; it would be only natural that Samaritan Christianity would do the same. But he did not aspire to put his Church wholly on its own, for his offer of money to Peter might have meant that he was ready to sustain the poor of Jerusalem. The authorities at Jerusalem indignantly turned down this offer. The idea that Simon wanted to buy the Holy Spirit might have been an interpretation post factum when the breach between Simon and the Mother Church was already a fact [5]. Yes indeed, if my aunt had them, she would be my uncle [6]!

Quite simply, this short passage in Acts does not support this elaborate reading. First of all, the founder of the Samaritan community was Philip. Once Simon was converted, he did not take over but stayed in the shadow of the apostle, "utterly surprised by what he saw happening" [7].

There is not the slightest indication that there was tension between the Church of Jerusalem and the infant Samaritan Church. Peter and John obviosuly were welcome in Samaria and acted there as the real authorities. How Simon's offer of money for acquiring the power of the apostles can be reinterpreted as an offer to send money for the poor of Jerusalem is anybody's guess. Pétrement's assumption that Simon as a result of the rejection of his offer broke away from the Mother Church is not warranted by the text which says that he submitted himself to Peter [8].

f. Simone Pétrement's theory of Apollos

Mme. Pétrement is by no means the only scholar to postulate a Christian Gnosis; on the contrary, this is a common topos of modern Gnoseology. But whereas almost all other scholars take the connection for granted, she is assidously looking for the link and tries to defend and reconstruct it. Now nobody contends that the Gnosis and orthodox Christianity are more or less the same thing; positing that both are autonomous interpretations of an original creed, everyone admits that these interpretations differ widely and in highly important respects. If we assume that there existed indeed a Christian Gnosis (do, non concedo), then it follows that Gnosis and orthodoxy at a given moment parted ways. When was that? And who effected the separation, whether or not it was consciously done?

One need only consult the contents of 'Le Dieu séparé' to find the answer : more than sixty pages are devoted to Apollos, far more than to any other biblical or Gnostic figure appearing in this book. This Apollos was an Alexandrian Jew who at a certain moment, when Paul was travelling through Galatia and Phrygia, came to Ephesus. He was an eloquent man, steeped in knowledge of the Bible. He had already been instructed in 'the way of the Lord', that is, in the Christian faith, but had only been baptized with the baptism of John, not with that of Jesus. This means that, technically spoken, he was not yet a Christian. This notwithstanding, enthusiastic as he was, he preached about Jesus in a detailed way; he even did this in the synagogues of the town. Having listened to him, a married Christian couple, Priscilla and Aquila, friends of Paul, instructed him in 'the way' more accurately.

Later he wanted to travel to Greece; he went there provided with letters of recommendation by the brethren of Ephesus. In Greece, and we may presume that Corinth is meant, he again began to preach, proving to the Jews that Jesus was the Messiah [9]. That Apollos took up his abode in Corinth follows from Paul's first Letter to the Corinthians. Right at the start he scolds his Corinthian Christians because there is disagreement among them. Everyone in the community seems to have his own slogan : "I am of Paul, I of Apollos, I of Kephas (Peter), I of Christ" [10]. This must mean that there was partisanship in the Corinthian Church. What exactly was the point at issue between the several parties is not explained.

Mme. Pétrement states that here the first indications of a **tendency** (her emphasis) towards Gnostic ideas become discernible. "It seems", she writes, "that principally the partisans of Apollos are concerned in this respect" [11]. We should keep in mind that Paul visited Corinth during the years 50-52, and that the most probable date of this letter is A.D. 55. On the strength of 1 Cor. 3:6 ("I planted, Apollos watered") we are justified in assuming that Apollos arrived in Corinth between 52 and 55. If this is correct, then the historical split-off of the Gnosis from Christianity, if we stick to Pétrement, began in this period.

The point is not that, in her opinion, Apollos was a Gnostic, whereas Paul was not. Neither of them was a Gnostic. In her opinion Saturnilos and Basilides were the first fully recognizable Gnostics, not Apollos therefore. Of course, in Paul the 'separated God', who in her theory is the hallmark of the Gnosis, is not be found. But she maintains that both of them, Paul as well as Apollos, were 'gnosticizing', and Apollos more so than Paul [12]. He went a step further on this road, but Paul would not have this. That was the conflict.

Another author too, to whom Pétrement refers, Brandon, holds the view, but without speaking of gnosticizing, that "an Alexandrian Christian of considerable personal prestige had taught among Paul's converts an interpretation of the Christian faith which was notably different from that expounded by Paul" [13]. This scholar regards "Apollos as a representative of a Church which was out of communion with that of Paul or at least not favourably regarded by it" [14]. This makes Apollos come dangerously near to being a schismatic.

So Apollos is introduced as the rival of Paul, as a near-schismatic, as the preacher of a doctrine deviant from that of Paul. The problem is that, in the report in Acts, there is not one word of disparagement about Apollos to be found. On the contrary, he is abundantly praised. What is said of his teaching is only that he, with the Old Testament as a witness, proved that Jesus was the Messiah. Paul in his letters is writing somewhat more neutrally, but in 1 Cor. 16:12 he calls Apollos his 'brother' whom he wanted to have with him on his travels. Since he intended to go to Corinth, this would have meant that he was ready to take with him a dangerous rival, to a town where this rival had already sown discord.

There was, indeed, partisanship in Corinth. But there were not only parties of Paul and Apollos, but also of Peter and even of Christ. The last two names are usually conveniently overlooked. Now we know absolutely nothing about the nature of this partisanship; we cannot even guess why people opted for Paul, Apollos, or others. But if differences of doctrinal opinion really came into play, what must we make then of an adherence to Peter or Christ? Must even Christ be seen as a deviant teacher? The chief of a schismatic community?

Paul for one does not make a choice between himself and Apollos; there should be no partisanship at all, he writes. "Whether it is of Paul or Apollos or Kephas ..., all is yours, but you are of Christ, and Christ is of God" [15]. Apollos and Paul are both no more than subordinates, collaborators of God, each working in his own way; neither of them is important, since it is God who gives the growth [16]. Would he have written this if Apollos was dangerously deviant with regard to doctrine? Wouldn't he, in that case, have stressed his own authority far more?

The evidence which Simone Pétrement adduces is necessarily circumstantial since, with one exception [17], Apollos is mentioned nowhere else. Not one Gnostic text refers to him. In both his first and second Letter to the Corinthians Paul is fighting adversaries. It is fairly common ground among biblical exegetes that these adversaries belong to two different groups; in the first letter they are gnosticizers and in the second Judaizers. But Pétrement throws them all in one heap. Disagreeing with many other scholars, she bluntly states that "the adversaries of Paul in the second Letter to the Corinthians are the same as in the first". In the time between the first and second letter the situation had not grown fundamentally different but had greatly deteriorated [18]. Since Paul himself nowhere mentions Apollos in connection with his later rivals, a lot of arguing is needed to show that he was the man behind this all [19]. So much for Apollos in his relation to Paul.

g. The 'gnosticizing' of Paul and John

Mme. Pétrement avers that "the interpretation of the New Testament remains essential for the study of Gnosticism" (printed by her in italics) [20]. The New Testament is the fountain-head from which literally all typically Gnostic elements spring. But she does not mean, of course, that there is a one-to-one relationship between it and the Gnosis, as if the New Testament were a kind of lexicon of Gnostic terms and opinions. She rather sees the New Testament's gnosticizing concentrated in John and Paul, and in Paul not really in all his epistles, but mainly in Colossans and Ephesians. If this last letter is not by Paul himself, it is in her opinion the work of a Paulinian. What Pétrement finds in Paul, but still stronger in John, is anticosmism (the rejection of the world) and anti-Judaism. Both are, indeed, constitutive elements of the Gnosis.

She believes that the gnosticizing of Paul becomes still more evident in John. "Not only the anticosmism but also the anti-Judaism increases from Paul to John." She adds that "in the beginning of the second century certain people criticized the belief in a God who was at the same time the creator of the world and the instigator of the Law (i.e. of Moses)" [21]. This would mean that such people were already close to the Gnosis.

Of John she says that "Gnosticism to a large extent proceeds from him. It also proceeds from Paul but more directly from John. Almost all Gnostics develop Johannine themes". It seems, therefore, that in John we have found the real starting-point of the Gnosis. Even Marcion, Pétrement adds, "adheres to a current of thought the starting-point of which seems to be the anticosmism and anti-Judaism of John" [22]. One wonders why Marcion rejected the Gospel of John, together with those of Matthew and Marc, and instead acknowledged that of Luke as the only (more or less) trustworthy one.

Who was John? 'John' was not John, the disciple whom Jesus loved. She admits that a very old ecclesiastical tradition ascribes the fourth Gospel to the beloved disciple, but she obviously is viscerally incapable of admitting that one who dubs himself 'the beloved of Jesus' could have written it [23]. As a possible reason why this disciple must remain anonymous she adduces that the real author may not have known his name [24]. No, the real author of the fourth Gospel, as the reader will have guessed already, was Apollos. Pétrement gives a number of reasons for her supposition [25], but admits that her theory is hypothetical and leaves a number of difficulties undiscussed [26]. What makes this so alluring for her is that, if it is correct, Apollos may be seen as at once the father of the gnosticizing tendencies in the New Testament, and also of post-biblical tendencies of this kind, and in the last resort of the Gnosis itself.

I do not disagree with Mme. Pétrement that there really is a gnosticizing strain in the New Testament. There certainly was, just as there are dualistic tendencies. Chapter IV of my volume VII bears the significant title 'Antagonistic, dualistic, and gnosticizing elements in the New Testament'. However, it is argued there that the New Testament is basically a homogeneous and undualistic book - rather an exception in a period in which dualism almost everywhere set the tone. Indeed, I enumerated there a number of dualistic tendencies that are not be found in the New Testament and which it never posits, for instance, that there are two sets of human beings, the elect and the doomed.

It is, however, true that a number of specific concepts that resemble that of the Gnosis occur in the New Testament, and in particular in Paul and John, for example, the terms 'aioon' and 'archoon', or the idea of the Law given by angels. Much is made of the contrast between 'flesh' and 'spirit' (pneuma) too. In the same chapter I argued that the occurrence of such terms does not turn the New Testament into a Gnostic tract; on the whole the book, Paul and John not excluded, takes a definite anti-Gnostic stance.

Were Paul and John in their alleged anti-Judaism forerunners of a Marcion who fiercely rejected everything Jewish, even the whole of the Old Testament? Paul had a running conflict with Mosaic Law. For him this Law, with the advent of Christianity, had had its day. But he also testified that, by means of that same Law, he had learned to live for God. He prided himself on being a Jew of the tribe of Benjamin, 'born and bred a Hebrew', even a Pharisee [27]. "Are they Hebrews? Me too! Are they children of Abraham? Me too!" [28]. He exhorts his converts from paganism to humbly acknowledge that they are spiritually dependent on Judaism [29]. Can such a man be suspected of anti-Jewish feelings?

It is true that the generic term used by John for the foes of Jesus is 'the Jews'. John shows Jesus as taking his distance from 'the Jews' and all that they stood for. But does this mean that John had definitely turned against Judaism? After all, it was John's Jesus who spoke the highly significant words that "salvation comes from the Jews" [30] - an utterance that surely would not have been underwritten by the Gnostics! And speaking to 'the Jews', Jesus declared that "Scripture (by which he meant the Old Testament) cannot be aside" [31] - a sentiment that would not find favour with Marcion! Basically, John too was not anti-Judaistic.

With regard to anticosmism, it must be understood that the Gnostics rejected the world lock, stock, and barrel : creation is bad, evil, deficient, destined to destruction. Mankind is included in this judgment; only the 'spirits' of the elect will be saved but not their bodies. Anticosmism of this kind is not be found in the New Testament. John, indeed, has many objections against 'the world'. But in his terminology 'the world' is not so much creation as such but mankind in so far as it is averse to God. This is not anticosmism. John is the one who wrote that everything was created by the Logos (and the Logos is God). "Without him nothing that is came into being" [32], and also that God "loved the world so much that he gave his only Son so that the world would be saved by him" [33]. Absolutely un-Gnostic words! If gnosticizing persons took their cue from John, they would have had to overlook these and other words by him.

h. 'Knowledge'

It is impossible to follow Mme. Pétrement's extremely long argumentation with the idea of refuting her. For this another book would be needed. I must restrict myself to only a few points. With regard to the word 'knowledge', in the sense in which the Gnostics used it, this scholar says that it is also found in Judaism and primitive Christianity. She then adds that "such an employment (of this term) certainly seems new with respect to the language of classical Antiquity; one does perhaps not find one single instance in pagan texts that are anterior to Christianity" [34].

This is a telling example of the obsessive industry with which Pétrement gives everything Gnostic an origin in Christianity. Her assertion is manifestly untrue; a few random checks in Plato would have shown her that she is wrong. Here I am obliged to refer the reader to my Volume VII, Chapter II, entitled 'Gnosis : its semantics and etymology'. In this long chapter I traced the history of the words 'gi(g)nooskein' and 'gnoosis' throughout the course of Hellenic and Hellenistic literature from Homer to Posidonius. The conclusion was that, from the first beginning, these knowledge-words were used by all the philosophers and poets in a peculiar sense that would later become that of the Gnosis, the sense of esoteric, and intuitive knowledge of higher and hidden things. Of course I cannot give the proofs here, but the reader will find all the relevant evidence in that chapter. The New Testament authors by no means 'invented' that meaning; on the contrary, they had ample literary evidence to draw upon.

j. Conclusion

It is true that there is a certain resemblance between biblical ideas and concepts and their Gnostic counterparts, superficial, I think, rather than fundamental. It does not follow from this that the Gnosis had its beginnings in early Christianity, as though it was, so to speak, an embroidery on originally biblical themes. A Proustian dictum is perfectly applicable here : "All things that are of the same period resemble each other" [35]. The first and second centuries A.D., and even some time before, formed a period in which all kinds of dualistic and gnosticizing ideas, concepts, and terms were freely bandied about. Whoever was interested could find them everywhere, for they are to be found in late Hellenistic philosophy, in Philo, in Essenian ideology.

In the period under consideration and in the area stretching from Egypt through Palestine and Syria into Asia Minor combustible material was lying about on all sides. It really needed no incendiary, not even a casually dropped spark, to set it on fire. As Peter Sloterdijk (or Thomas Macho) wrote, the Gnosis originated through self-ignition, just as a haystack sets itself ablaze, when its internal temperature oversteps a critical degree [36]. How and why the temperature was steadily rising I described in Chapter IV of Volume VI and in Chapter I of Volume VII. There is no need to turn to the New Testament exclusively for gnosticizing trends. The thing is not so much that ideas of this sort are found in it too; the real miracle is that amidst this great sea of dualism and gnosticizing it remained remarkably free from these.

The book of Mme. Pétrement is the fruit of an enormous intellectual effort. But it seems to me to be overheated. Hers is a system in which everything has to be allotted a place; there must be an organic whole that accounts for every element. I regret to say it, since I sincerely admire the great erudition and industry that went into the making of this book, but its author did not succeed in convincing me.

Part II Was there a Christian Gnosis?

1. A 'Christian' Gnosis

That there was a Christian Gnosis, or that the Gnosis was basically Christian is a well-known theme of modern scholarship. I met this term 'Christian Gnosis' so frequently in scholarly works of this and the previous century that it seems almost superfluous to quote one or other particular author. A few instances may suffice. In a recent interview on the radio, only a short time ago, I heard my compatriot Gilles Quispel, a world-famous expert on the Gnosis, assert that his own Christian (Protestant) confession was perfectly compatible with Gnostic doctrine; he even argued that the Gnosis is a deepening and enriching of his Christian faith.

In her book on 'The Gnostic Gospels' (see Bibliography) Elaine Pagels speaks (p. XXXIV) of 'gnostic christian sources' and of 'gnostic forms of Christianity'. Throughout her book she treats the Gnosis as a variant of Christianity, the other variant being orthodox ('Roman-Catholic') Christianity. "If we go back to the earliest known sources of Christian tradition ..., we can see how both gnostic and orthodox forms of Christianity could emerge as variant interpretations of the teaching and significance of Christ" (p. 148). We know that, after a few centuries, orthodox Christianity triumphed. In Pagels' view this was not a happy development. "To the impoverishment of Christian tradition, gnosticism, which offered alternatives to what became the main thrust of Christian orthodoxy, was forced outside" (p. 149).

2. How to approach this question

It is utterly impossible to broach this question of whether or not there was a Christian Gnosis in a neutral way. One approaches it either as an orthodox Christian (whether Protestant or Roman-Catholic) or as an agnostic or as a Gnostic (or sympathizer with the Gnosis). On the last pages of her book (pp. 150/151) Pagels explains why she has "devoted so much of this discussion to gnosticism". This is not because she advocates "going back to gnosticism - much less that I 'side with it' against Christianity" [37]. "I find the discoveries at Nag Hammadi enormously exciting", she writes, "since the evidence they offer opens a new perspective for understanding what fascinates me most - the history of Christianity". I find her standpoint wholly sympathetic - with this proviso that in this book I am concerned first and foremost with the history of dualism rather than that of Christianity.

Mrs. Pagels states that she is "a person concerned with religious questions". I can say the same of myself, but I feel that, in thorny questions like these, it may be helpful to be somewhat more specific. Let me, therefore, present my credentials. I am an orthodox Roman-Catholic, a regular church-goer, accepting as true what the Church of Rome authoritatively teaches as true - not more, as my father used to say, but certainly not less. If one now objects that, in consequence, my approach can never be objective, my retort is that it will certainly be different from that of the Gnostic or agnostic (but not really from that of the orthodox Protestant), but it would be wrong to state this difference in terms of objectivity and subjectivity.

I need scarcely explain why I am devoting so much space to the Gnosis in my series. It is the first of the great peaks in the history of dualism. Never before we have met such a complex of dualistic doctrine and sects. In this volume (and the next) I am writing about at time when religion seemed to go Gnostic and to become, by the same token, dualistic. This alone is a sufficient reason for me to occupy myself with the Gnosis. This scholarly stance would in itself not require the presenting of credentials. I am, nevertheless, just doing this in order to back up the attitude I am taking towards the endless reiteration of the idea that there was such a thing as Christian Gnosis.

I am not out to denigrate the Gnosis. In no way! I hope that the present volume shows that my treatment of it is as open and honest as I can manage - although I must admit that there are elements in the Nag Hammadi documents that I found strange and puzzling. I am helped, moreover, in my approach by the fact that I find the Gnosis, as a religious phenomenon, really fascinating. If it is an opponent of Christianity, it is one of great calibre, prompting me to mobilize all my mental and scholarly and even human resources to understand it. For this is what I really want, to understand it, not to combat it. I am neither an early Father of the Church nor a late one.

3. Confusion of terms

There is much confusion of terms and ideas in the postulating of a Christian Gnosis. As I will try to demonstrate, 'Christian' and 'Gnosis' are incompatible terms. It would advance the discussion on the Gnosis, on the origins of Christianity, on early Christianity, and on the relationship between it and the Gnosis immensely, if we were able to stop speaking of 'Christian Gnosis'. The claim that there was one does not do full justice to the intriguing phenomenon that the Gnosis represents. Positing a 'Christian Gnosis' means that it is thought of as an epiphenomenon of Christianity. I maintain that we should think of it as a wholly original, independent, and autonomous movement, as a movement sui generis.

4. Did the Gnostics see themselves as Christians?

Did Gnostics consider themselves Christians? The fact is that they rarely dubbed themselves so; hardly ever in the Nag Hammadi Library is this term used whether for Gnostics or for the orthodox [38]. To all intents and purposes, for the Gnostics orthodox Christians were a lesser breed, inferior people who were ignorant and who served the wrong God. We must assume that they found 'Christian' an odious term not fit to be applied to themselves. In most systems orthodox believers seem to have been grouped with the hylics, the hopelessly lost matter-people, as contrasted with the pneumatics, the spirit-people (the Gnostics).

5. Were Gnostics members of the Church?

But that Gnostics loathed the term 'Christian' does not mean in itself that they were not members of the Church. At least a number of them must have belonged to it, as the expulsion of some eighty Barbelo-Gnostics from the Church of Alexandria about 335 proves [39]. Of course, not all Gnostic groups consisted of members of the Church. Those who were members must have considered themselves the elite, the ones who really 'knew'; they despised the rest, not only the pagans but no less their fellow-Christians. In some systems, in that of the Valentinians for instance, some hope is held out to non-Gnostics in the Church, the great majority we must assume. It is more than probable that it were those people who are referred to as 'psychics' - 'soul-people' - who occupied an intermediate position between the pneumatics and the hylics. Psychics could eventually still become pneumatics, but if not, they would go the way of destruction with the hylics.

Insofar as Gnostics were indeed members of the Church, they must have led a fringe existence in it and have operated in a 'grey zone'. Let me mention a few curious facts. It is absolutely impossible to reconstruct a biography of Jesus from the Nag Hammadi texts. Mention is made of only three main events, his birth, his baptism in the Jordan, and his death - with this proviso that it was not the Saviour who suffered on the cross but somebody else. The ascension is an event that took place, not after his death but before it, because the Saviour returned to the Pleroma when the passion began. Whereas the role of Mary is reduced to virtually nothing, her husband Joseph is mentioned only once [40]; the names of Bethlehem and Nazareth never occur, and the apostles hardly ever. There is no talk of miracles nor of any other event in Jesus' life. And so on. Even less there is any mention of the Catholic Church [41].

One does not get the impression that ecclesiastical life was at the centre of the Gnostic interest. Gnostics who were members of the Church cannot have felt strongly attached to it. They had their own secret and esoteric doctrine, their own scripture, their own prophets, their own rituals, their own conventicles. They even had their own God, for the Father of all was not the God of Jews and Christians. But the minimal conceivable attachment we might suppose fades into complete nothingness, when we remember how fiercely, as related in Chapter IX of the present volume, the Gnostics combated the official Church with its hierarchy, its teachings, its understanding of the Bible, even its Saviour who, in Gnostic view, was only 'a dead man'.

One might ask why Gnostics wanted to remain members of an institution they loathed so deeply. Was it fear of persecution by ecclesiastical authorities? But, as I remarked earlier, these authorities, often in danger of their own lives, had no leg to stand on in this respect. Gnostics could be expelled, as sometimes happened. However, expulsion can not have meant much to them, living their own lives as they did. Did they hope to conquer the Church for their own ideology? They virtually abstained from partaking in ecclesiastical life; they did not try to push themselves upward on the hierarchical ladder. But had they have wanted to rebuild the Church in their own sense, they would have been forced to occupy positions of influence.

I can only think of one reason for their staying in the Church. I admit it is entirely conjectural; we have no evidence for it. But it seems to me to accord perfectly with their peculiar psychology. To be the only ones, in a large community, who really 'knew' what it was all about, who realized that they had been 'god' and would become 'god' again, even to a certain extent already were, must have given the Gnostics a sense of elation, a feeling of superiority. They could savour this feeling far better within the institution, with all those ignoramuses around them, than without it where they would exist more or less in a void. This feeling of superiority was enhanced rather than diminished by the opposition they met. That the unknowing did not understand them was a safe sign that they were right. Thus they formed a kind of (unauthorized and unrecognized) aristocracy in the Church, living by its own standards and despising the profane vulgus of the orthodox.

6. The name of Christian

Orthodox followers of Jesus Christ and adherents of his teachings call themselves 'Christians'; it was only a few years after his death that the faithful in Antiochia were indicated by this name for the first time [42]. Until this day members of the Roman-Catholic, Anglican, Orthodox, and Reformation Churches are called and call themselves by this name; they all belong to the large, although diversified, body of Christianity. But with the one exception of the Gospel of Philip I have found no Gnostic sects so calling themselves. And nowhere in the early Fathers of the Church are the Gnostics mentioned as Christians. In their view they obviously are not. It is only modern scholars who call Gnostics 'Christians'.

In the chapters of this volume we saw them being given many names : Sethians, Ophites, Cainites, Nicolaites, Valentinians, Basilidians, or Gnostics. It is true that we find these names in the books of the early Fathers of the Church, so that it remains possible that they were invented by these authors for the sake of convenience. But on the other hand, we know for certain that some of these sects called themselves 'Gnostics', and when the author of the Revelation of John warns the Christians of Ephesus and Pergamum against the Nicolaites, we may safely assume that his addressees knew who were meant.

When reading the Paraphrase of Shem, with its fierce polemic against Jews and Christians, I amuse myself with the idea of some modern scholar who falls over backwards to demonstrate that Gnostics were really Christians, just as much, although in a different way, as the orthodox. Judaism and Christianity, with their Law, their Bible, and their Jesus, meant nothing to Gnostics; they were works of the wicked Demiurge, full of deceit and ignorance.

If the contention one encounters so frequently in modern scholarship, that the Gnosis originated in Jewish circles, for instance in Alexandria, is true, then one must also accept the fact that such Jews have strayed incredibly far from their roots indeed. Stroumsa is one of the scholars who maintain that "the cradle of some of the earliest Gnostic groups was among Palestinian or Syrian baptist sects of Jewish background." But then he asks this pertinent question. "How did the passage from the Jewish God to the Gnostic Demiurge, from monotheism to dualism, come about?" And he gives the following answer. "It would seem ... that a hierarchical duality between God and His demiurgic angel did develop inside Judaism before the first Christian century, in order to answer the problem of biblical anthropomorphisms. The Gnostics who were obsessed with another problem, that of the existence of evil and its source, picked up this duality between God and the Demiurge and radicalized it by demonizing the Demiurge and identifying him with Satan ... The demonization process ... transformed a hierarchical duality into a **conflicting** (his emphasis) dualism" [43]. I do not find this answer wholly satisfying because the mental distance covered between the Jewish Jahve and the Gnostic Demiurge is so enormous; I can, therefore, hardly believe in a Jewish origin of the Gnosis.

7. Points of resemblance

It must be admitted that there are points of resemblance between both religions. The fact that both originated in the same period of history, the first century A.D., and in the same area of the world, the south-eastern corner of the Mediterranean, accounts for many similarities. Furthermore, the Gnosis was eclectic as well as syncretistic, so that we must not be suprised to discover many Jewish, Christian, and biblical items in Gnostic systems. But then it must be understood that those systems, albeit in a lesser degree, also drew on other, non-biblical sources, on Zoroastrianism and Zervanism, on Pythagoreanism and Platonism, on Hellenistic philosophies and Greek popular religious creeds like Orphism. What probably bedevils modern observers most is that both are religions of redemption; in this they profoundly differ from Greek official religion. But as we shall see, this is exactly the point where Gnosis and Christianity part ways.

I feel I can do no better now than let Ernst Haenchen take the floor. This is what he writes [44]. "Each of these two religions (Gnosis and

New Testament Christianity) develops an idea of God, man, and world. Both pictures sometimes resemble each other so closely that one might think that, when placed on each other, they would cover each other with their lines. But this impression is deceptive. Although the lines may coincide for a short distance or run almost parallel, they soon go apart in the most decisive way. Finally one discovers that every detail basically always betrays a peculiar spirit belonging to this religion or that."

8. Gnostics and the Bible

The first thing that strikes us is the great difference between Gnostic and apocryphal writings on the one hand, and the canonical New Testament on the other. Since the discovery of the Nag Hammadi Library, a great many fascinating and intriguing texts have come to light, but nothing that may be compared to the Gospels in the New Testament. True enough, there are texts that bear the name of 'Gospel' : the Gospel of Truth, the Gospel of Philip, the Gospel to the Egyptians, and others, the best known being the Coptic Gospel of Thomas. However, the four canonical Gospels all present a more or less coherent picture of the public life of Jesus of Nazareth, each of them written from a different point of view. Two of them, those of Matthew and Luke, have something to add on his birth and early youth. All of them culminate in the story of the Passion and the Resurrection.

Not one of the Gnostic or apocryphal Gospels does the same. Some of them restrict themselves to Jesus' childhood only; texts like the Book of James, also called the Protoevangelium [45], or the Latin and Greek Gospels of Thomas, are really infancy Gospels. They relate miracle stories of the boy Jesus; for instance, how, when on his way to the spring he broke his pitcher, he carried the water home in his garment. The Gnostic Gospel of Philip is a long theosophic speculation with hardly a trace of the biography of Jesus in it. The Coptic Gospel of Thomas has not the remotest resemblance to a biography but is, instead, a collection of sayings attributed to Jesus, only a small part of which appear in the canonical Gospels.

The scriptural sense is totally inverted by antinomian sects that exalt precisely those people such as Cain, the Sodomites, Korah, Judas, and still others, who incur a biblical condemnation. We should also not overlook the fact that by far the greater part of the Bible is passed over in silence in Gnostic texts. There are hardly any references, or none at all, to the Wisdom Books, while many of the great names and events in Jewish history are not mentioned at all.

The inevitable conclusion must be that Gnostic and apocryphal Gospels are very different from their canonical counterparts in plan and design. It must also not be lost from view that, so far, I have only spoken of Gnostic Gospels. In many another Nag Hammadi tractate there is hardly a reference to the Bible or none at all. It is true that a number of Nag Hammadi texts draw heavily on both the Old and New Testament citing many passages; but more often than not they embellish them and add words and phrases to give them a Gnostic colouring. Gnostic authors do not approach the Bible as an autonomous text in its own right composed with a specific end, but utilize it sporadically, whimsically, and arbitrarily, selecting some texts in order to support their own ideas, and others to combat and even vilify them. The attitude of Gnostics respecting Holy Writ is totally different from that of orthodox Christians : these respect the Bible as the source of truth par excellence, whereas Gnostics do not go farther than to admit that it might contain some grains of truth.

9. Gnostic language

The Bible is destined for everyone without distinction; for this reason it is couched in generally clear and understandable terms. Although Scripture doubtless contains some difficult or obscure passages, the book as a whole has always been read and enjoyed by very simple people without a smattering of literary education (I am thinking here of Rembrandt's old mother whom he painted while she was reading a heavy Bible tome).

Most Gnostic texts, on the contrary, present enormous difficulties to the reader; they are full of opaque phrases and obscure references. This is not surprising since they were destined for select groups of initiates who were knowledgeable about esoteric vocabulary and names. While the preaching of the Gospel by the apostles and their successors was a public affair, the contents of Gnostic texts were secret; their divulgation was often expressly forbidden.

10. History and its absence

This leads us to a very important point, that of the absence of history in Gnostic texts. The Gospels are meant to be historical reports. I know quite well that many a modern intellectual would object that they contain a good many mythological elements, but this is not the point at issue. This point is that the authors of the New Testaments books intended to present their stories as histories, as reports about persons who lived and events that took place in given times and in specific places, and that could be verified by contemporaries. These authors wrote either as eye-witnesses or they consulted eye-witnesses.

In Gnostic texts there are no references to times and places. Very few human persons occur in them, and only rarely a historical event is mentioned. What is related mainly takes place in a non-historical, pre-human, even pre-cosmic sphere. Gnostic authors are not interested in human history. Their documents are peopled with a great number of beings and entities that occur nowhere in the Bible or in profane history. In many Nag Hammadi and other tracts we meet figures like Abraxas, Astaphaios, Noria or Norea, Achamoth, Harmozel, Ororiael, Thautabaoth, and many, many more. Only people who are 'nourris dans le sérail' know who they are. This a-historical character of Gnostic texts is accentuated by the fact that in many cases their authors remain anonymous. The far more concrete nature of New Testament books is also demonstrated by the fact that they can be ascribed to specific authors.

A quotation from Jakob Taubes brings out very clearly what I mean here. "The theatre of myth (with which pagan myth is meant - F.) on which gods, men and things appear, is nature. Revealed religion has made this theatre empty. It strives away from nature and makes the 'true' God encounter mankind on the theatre of history. The theatre of the Gnosis is neither nature nor history but man's interior : soul, spirit, pneuma" [46].

11. Jesus Christ

The dominating figure of the New Testament is Jesus of Nazareth, a Jewish prophet and faith-healer, who went around in public for some years, preaching a new message. The Jewish authorities considered him dangerous, a risk to the safety of the people; they finally had him arrested and executed. New Testament authors identify this 'son of the carpenter' with 'Christ', the Messiah, the elected and anointed, the new and glorious King of Israel, foretold by the prophets for centuries. For this reason orthodox Christians have always spoken of 'Jesus Christ'.

Gnostic authors have a completely different approach. To them Christ is by no means the same person as Jesus. This Jesus is most of the time a rather insignificant person who lends his body as a temporary abode for Christ. Christ never has a body of his own; he is not organically connected with a body and has only one in appearance. It is for this reason that by far the greater part of the biographical details of the life of Jesus, as they appear in the canonical Gospels, are absent in Gnostic texts. If we did not possess these Gospels, we would not cull much information from Gnostic documents. There the spiritual Christ is uncomfortably paired with the vague figure of Jesus.

In many Gnostic systems it is not Christ who suffered on the cross since, as a pleromic and pneumatic being, he is incapable of suffering. The one who is executed on the cross is this Jesus or even Simon of Cyrene. Before the time of the Passion Christ has already returned to heaven. In my opinion Gnostics and orthodox Christians radically disagree, in particular, on the significance and role of Jesus of Nazareth. Now, when we speak of a 'Christian Gnosis', are we fully aware that the attitude of Gnostics and orthodox Christians with regard to the one who gave his name to Christianity is utterly different, so much so that they seem to speak of two different persons? Is it really no more than a 'variant' of Christianity, if the Gnostic Christ did not die on the cross? Shouldn't we rather fully acknowledge the immense distance between both views?

12. The notion of God

The notion that orthodoxy and the Gnosis have of God is utterly different. In the Bible God is a highly exalted being enthroned high above humanity, the cosmos, and the celestial host. He is no creature, he is not created; in this he is essentially different from everything and everybody else. Human beings, however devout or intelligent they may be, are incapable of grasping fully who or what God is; no description or approach will do justice to his greatness. Only God is able to have a complete understanding of himself. I guess a Gnostic would agree with this without difficulty. But the conformity stops here.

The God of Jewish and Christain faith is a creator-god; he has directly and so to speak with his own hands brought into being all that is, and in particular mankind. The many so-called anthropomorphisms in the Old Testament prove, not that he is human (which he isn't) but that he is really concerned with his creation, with mankind, and in a special way with the people of Israel. When it is stated that God after the Fall made clothing for Adam and Eve [47], or that he closed the door behind Noah and his family when they had entered the Ark [48], we are not confronted with a primitive theology, but with a God who is lovingly concerned with mankind. Jesus expresses the same idea when he says that the hairs on our heads are all counted, or that no sparrow falls from the roof without him knowing it [49].

With Jews and Christians God is by no means wholly unknowable, still less unapproachable. He has a name by which he may be known, Jahve. People pray to him in adoration but no less to implore his help and intervention, even in trivial things. Jews and Christians believe that God is present in their lives.

The Gnostic highest god is ensconced behind innumerable and interminable spheres, full of inimical powers that surround the cosmos. He remains effectively sealed off from all that is material, physical, concrete, human, in short, from creation. As Jonas puts it : "The deity is absolutely transmundane; its nature is alien to that of the universe which it neither creates nor governs and to which it is the complete antithesis" [50]. Jonas rightly speaks of this deity as of 'it', for it is an abstraction, although it is sometimes called 'Father' or 'Mother-Father'. Nothing could be more useless than to speak of its nature or to pray to it, for Gnostic treatise after treatise reiterates that it is unknown and unknowable. "The transcendent God Himself is hidden from all other creatures and is unknowable by natural concepts" [51]. In other words, there can be no Gnostic natural theology. The great difference between both religions in this respect can be framed in these terms. Whereas in Jewish and Christian orthodoxy God is at once immanent and transcendent, in the Gnosis the deity is only transcendent.

13. Heaven and Pleroma

Gnosis and Christian orthodoxy concur in this that both acknowledge an abode under God but above the earth and the cosmos. Christians call this abode 'heaven' or 'the heavens'. It is where God dwells, surrounded by angelic beings among whom some sort of hierarchy obtains. These angels are purely spiritual beings, all of them created by God. Furthermore, it is the place where the redeemed go to enjoy eternally the presence of God. Heaven is not hermetically sealed from the earth, as is proved by the fact that it is the destination of human people, in principle even of all mankind. But there is no one-way traffic : the Bible speaks of angels and celestial messengers visiting people on earth. And God himself, according to Jewish and Christian doctrine, inspired the biblical authors. Devout Christians are convinced that God leads their lives and helps them in every circumstance. They believe in God's Providence.

The Gnostic Pleroma is divided from the cosmos by an almost impenetrable barrier. We may well ask ourselves whether, in regard to

Gnostic doctrine, we are justified in speaking of 'creation'. A far better term would be 'emanation', a flowing forth from. Van Wersch [52] very aptly states that the Gnostic godhead is 'Being-in-movement'. We are light-years distant from Aristotle's 'Unmoved mover'. The first principle, or prime deity, expands itself into ever greater self-knowledge and self-realization. The Pleroma, or Fullness, proceeding from the first principle, is gradually filled with the godhead's emanations, mostly called 'aeons'. We heard of many of them in early chapters of this volume, of Barbelo, Sophia, Christ, Anthropos. The fact is that man, in principle, is not a doomed and rejected being but has his prototype in the upper realm. Even the cosmos in itself might be called a divine concept, but soon in the cosmogonical process the higher regions lose control of the nether world.

The idea of Pleroma, or Fullness, accounts for the fact that it is not always easy to distinguish the several emanations from each other; sometimes they seem to be one and the same entity but then again they are clearly distinct. Within the Gnostic view this is logical because the aeons form part of the All-One and partake in his divine identity (whereas biblical angels are not divine). It is also logical that the Pleroma only knows androgyny, sometimes even for the prime deity; it is often impossible to tell whether some entity is male or female or both at the same time. Androgynity, or bisexuality, is a hallmark of the Pleroma; it is the expression of its inclusiveness, its all-in-one. This explains why Gnostic theosophy does not abhor the idea of incest. It must also be pointed out that in the Bible celestial beings are not androgynous but a-sexual.

14. Ideas of gender

In Gnostic doctrine the existence of sexes on earth is a breach in the Pleroma, a dimunition of its fullness, even a mutilation. Originally, it was intended that mankind would be just as androgynous as the pleromic entities; that there exist masculinity and femininity on earth is a forceful proof that things went wrong down here. The sexes through their existence demonstrate the confused and degenerate state of the world. Just as androgynity is the expression of the Pleroma's inclusiveness, sexual 'apartheid' is the expression of the exclusivity that prevails in the cosmos. The consequence is that sexuality is deprecated, marriage and femininity underrated, and maleness extolled, since, as so often, women are seen as the paragons of sexual lust.

In the biblical creation stories the origin of the sexes is presented as intended and expressly willed by God; there is neither an androgynous model nor a primordial Anthropos. Human beings are originally created as male and female. They belong to one another in an monogamous union of which progeny is the welcome consequence. This means that sexuality as such is valued as God-given. Woman is basically the equal of man; where and when this is not the case it is not in accordance with the plans of God. I know that some readers will object that in the Old Testament women are discriminated against, and that Paul does the same in the New Testament. I have really no space here to go into this question more deeply, but this does not mean that I am dodging the problem which I treated at length, for the Old Testament in my Vol. IV, Ch. II1.12g-n, and for the New Testament in Vol. VII, Ch. IV.4g. I invite objectors to consult these sections.

15. Creation

In biblical theology, accepted by Jews and Christians alike, God is both the direct cause and creator of the cosmos, mankind included. It is by his express will and his own action that all that is came into being. Because God is the source of all goodness, what he made, mankind once again included, is essentially good. "And God saw that is was good" [53]. Jewish and Christian orthodoxy are both based on the idea of the conformity, not identity, of God and his creation. The cosmos, as God's handiwork, is imprinted with his seal and bears his mark. This applies in particular to man.

This conformity between God and man is expressed in the thrice repeated formula of Gen. 1:26-27 : 'in his image and likeness'. It is, therefore, possible for man to communicate with God, and for God to be present in history, in particular in Jewish history which is a history of salvation. In the Middle Ages the Schoolmen, in particular Thomas of Aquinas, would give to this conformity the name of 'analogia entis', the 'analogy of being'.

Nothing can be said of the Gnostic prime deity's role in creation for the simple reason that he did not create the cosmos. He is entirely innocent of creation and has nothing whatsoever to do with matter. Is it really conceivable that two religions, one of which vehemently denies any analogy between the first deity and the cosmos, and the other of which thrives on the concept of this analogy, can be called variants of the same thing?

Gnostic judgment on the cosmos, the present world, and mankind is entirely negative. They are real misfits, full of evil and ignorance, good for nothing. Gnostics abhor matter and all that proceeds from matter, and the body more than anything else. There will be no 'resurrectio carnis'; only the pneuma (of the elect) will return to heaven. For ordinary human beings, the unenlightened, it will be impossible to take the road back; because they are ignorant, they do not even know that they possess a pneuma and have a spark of the pleromic Light in them, or that there is a Pleroma and a highest deity.

The world is doomed to perdition; it will, with mankind, be done away with. There is no re-creation; there will not be 'a new heaven and a new earth'.

16. The Fall

In both religions a Fall occurs, an event that explains why, to put it mildly, the world might be a better and happier place than it really is. But they profoundly disagree on the question where it took place.

If we take the biblical creation story at its face-value, the Fall took place in Paradise and was caused by the first human beings, later called Adam and Eve. Seduced by the serpent, the embodiment of evil, they transgressed God's command not to eat from the tree of knowledge of good and evil. In view of later developments in the history of religions, this looks like an ironical comment on the Gnostic notion of Knowledge. Knowledge they were promised but what they came to know was only that they were naked. The Fall was the fault of humanity alone and absolutely contrary to God's intentions. And it is mankind that has to account for the consequences. Closely connected with the Fall are the concepts of guilt and sin. The Fall is sin, original sin, the basic sin of rebellion against God, from which all later sinfulness proceeds. Sin leads to guilt, a personal guilt that asks to be forgiven. Sinful man is looking for redemption.

In Gnostic systems mankind is entirely innocent of the Fall, although it is the miserable victim of it. Something went wrong beyond the scope of humanity, high up in the celestial sphere, long before mankind came into being. Perhaps we can speak of a Gnostic Fall only in a metaphorical sense, since it becomes by no means clear who caused what or what caused what. Even the term 'cause' is somewhat inappropriate since the Fall is something that just happened rather than that it was caused.

It is even quite possible that the derailment, as a metaphysical event, took place in the bosom of the first godhead himself. A principle of evil split off from the primordial deity and began its nefarious course downwards through the aeons towards the cosmos. It is never explained why this happened. It will be clear that this concept offers no room for sin or guilt. Both are concepts that hardly, or not at all, occur in Gnostic religion. The place of sin is taken by Ignorance. The ethical difference in Gnostic systems is not that between sin and forgiveness or between guilt and redemption but that between Knowledge and Ignorance. This Ignorance consists in the fact that unenlightened man does not realize that he is basically God; the split in his consciousness prevents him from 'knowing' who he really is. Knowledge, however, leads to perfect self-realization, that is to the divinization of the Self.

We may define the basic Gnostic attitude as being conscious of the tragic split in the deity which is repeated in the microcosmos that is man. My compatriot Stefan van Wersch, who wrote an intriguing book on the history of the Gnosis, is of the opinion that we must not first of all look into the bosom of the godhead but start from the self-perception of the Gnostic. He speaks of "the supposition that the Gnostic saw a certain disorder or a rending in their person as the essence of their 'Self', and that they, starting from the presupposition that they, in their innermost beings, were God, then construed the myth of the 'Fall' in order to explain this rending. In this way the disorder that some people may feel in themselves is sublimated into a divine principle"[54].

Needless to say, Jews and orthodox Christians never think of themselves as being 'God'; they do not identify with God. At the same time they do not suggest that the source of evil and sin is not themselves but must be located somewhere else, and certainly not in God who is, in their opinion, all-good and cannot be associated with any sort of evil or sin.

17. The Demiurge

Judaism and Christian orthodoxy confess only one God, the Creator of heaven and earth; there are lower celestial beings but these, having been created themselves, are not creators. Creation is the sole province of God Almighty. This is undiluted monotheism. In the Gnosis, on the contrary, we could, with some reserve, speak of a form of ditheism, of there being two gods. Since the highest deity is innocent of creation and has nothing whatsoever to do with matter, the existence of this world must be imputed to another being of a lower order. Mostly his character is bad; he is always ignorant of the Pleroma, and what he has made is evil or bungled.

This being is the Demiurge, the world-maker, the great ruler or archon of the cosmos; although he is called otherwise, by several names, he assumes the traits of the Jewish God Jahve. It is this bad and ignorant being who gave the (Mosaic) Law to mankind; this Law spells oppression, stupidity, darkness, lies. There are, therefore, two gods (although the Demiurge is rarely called so) in Gnostic systems, the prime deity who keeps a careful distance from the cosmos and mankind which he did not create and does not govern, and the Demiurge who, stupid and evil-intentional as he is, manages the affairs of this world in his own malevolent way. Compare this to the biblical God who is interested in and is taking care of mankind. At the close of the biblical revelation John will summarize this in three words : God is Love [55].

18. Revelation

This brings us to the role of revelation in both religions; there is a certain similarity between them on this point because both rely on revelation. But, according to orthodox theology, God himself need not to be revealed as the omnipotent creator of all that is. With the help of the human intellect he can be known, as Paul said, 'from created things' [56], by way of deduction that is. Whoever opens 'Denzinger', the famous collection of magisterial dogmatic pronouncements of the Roman-Catholic Church, will not find as no. 1 : 'God exists'.

The whole Bible, Old and New Testaments, is a book of revelation. According to Jewish and Christian faith God himself speaks in and through it explaining his plan and intentions with the world and mankind. Since his message concerns all mankind, it is directed to all men; it is all public, there is no secret doctrine. According to Jesus' last words on earth, it has to be proclaimed to all people [57].

The Gnosis too relies on revelation; in fact, the revelation, the 'call', is the Knowledge itself. The unknowable prime godhead can be known by no one and in no way, but Knowledge opens the way to him. It is not so that the enlightened Gnostic knows more about God than unilluminated ignorants, but he knows how to reach him, how to become united with him, after having passed through all the spheres. This 'call' is only given to a few elect; the rest are left in the dark.

19. Redemption

Both religions are essentially religions of redemption. According to orthodox Christian creed, Jesus is the Redeemer, the Saviour; salvation is effected by his passion and death on the cross. The cross is the instrument and the sign of salvation. In the Gnosis this plays no role at all. Redemption is effected by Knowledge; the Knowledge, the Gnosis, itself is the redemption. Who possesses this is eo ipso redeemed. This means that Gnostic Knowledge is in fact self-knowledge, with the consequence that redemption is self-redemption. In orthodox teaching it is impossible for man to redeem himself. In the Gnosis there is indeed a Redeemer, a Saviour, but his task is to impart Knowledge to the elect. This Redeemer is often Christ, but may also be Seth or some other figure.

Add to this that the cross offers redemption to all mankind (but one must live up to it; knowledge is not sufficient), whereas Gnostic salvation is destined only for the elect. The ignorant may go their own doomed way. This can also be expressed in another way. Orthodoxy is social, concerned as it is with the fate of all mankind, whereas the Gnosis is individualistic and interested only in the salvation of a few elect.

20. The conclusion

Should we ask an arbitrary number of people what is the exact opposite of Christianity, I guess almost all people would answer : paganism. But this answer would be wrong. For paganism is a natural religion (I am not speaking of David Hume's 'natural religion') using such elements as water and fire, bread and wine, priest and sacrifice, temple and altar, and many more; we could also think of apparitions, oracles, and revelations. All these elements return in Judaism and Christianity, especially in the Roman-Catholic and eastern Orthodox Churches. For this reason we must think of paganism, Judaism, and Christianity as cognate religions, because they share and are built on the same natural and basic elements. No, the real opponents are Christianity and the Gnosis. The dividing line is that of the analogy of being. This also accounts for the harshness of the battles between them; neither the Gnosis nor Christianity combated paganism with the same furor. In Christianity there is conformity between Creator and created; in the Gnosis there is not. Even the merest thought of such conformity between the highest god and creation is felt to be repellent and blasphemous.

I don't think that confounding the issues brings the history and the study of both Gnosis and Christianity really forward. Gnosis is a phenomenon in its own right, and must be explored as such; the same applies to Christianity.

Part III The place of the Gnosis in Anitiquity

1. 'Unbehagen in der Kultur'

Seen from the viewpoint of the mental history of late Antiquity, the Gnosis expresses an extremely deep 'Unbehagen in der Kultur', in the civilization of that period. All that was untoward in the culture, the history, and the religion of all previous ages, all the oppositions, all the failures flowed together in that great and fascinating movement that is called the Gnosis. It was confronted with 'what is wrong with the world' and attempted to find an answer to it. It did not look for a remedy, it was no revolutionary or reforming movement. What it wanted to discover was an escape - an escape from a world that did not 'work' and should be given up as hopeless.

2. Syncretism and autonomy

The Gnosis is often described as syncretistic, and this it certainly was, since it assembled and incorporated elements not only of the Hellenic and Hellenistic civilizations, but also from Egypt and Mesopotamia, from Judaism and Christianity and reworked them into a highly original, independent, and autonomous religious ideology. But this ideology was not homogeneous, for it broke, as in a prisma, its central tenets into a great number of aspects; there were, indeed, dozens and dozens of Gnostic sects. However, we may safely say that they agree on a small number of constitutive ideas.

3. The Gnosis, the contemporary world, and history

Although influenced from many sides, but at the same time existing in its own right, the Gnosis stood apart from all that was common and fundamental in the ancient world. Its doctrines were secret, its members were initiates who were forbidden to divulge what they knew. This kind of secrecy was foreign to the Graeco-Roman official religion, just as to Judaism and Christianity both of which loved to proselytize. There were not many really secret religious sects in Antiquity, perhaps even none at all. Maybe the only one which comes to mind here is Orphism, but, as I argued in Volume I, Chapter IV.10, and particularly in Volume VII, Chapter I.7a, this was a precursor of the Gnosis.

Gnostics were not interested in contemporary politics, because politics formed part of a world they held at a discount. There is in the Gnostic documents not a trace of the great historical event of these centuries, the foundation of the Roman Empire and how it expanded far and wide. I know of no Gnostic who occupied a political position of any importance. Add to this that Gnostics remained anonymous, with the exception of some founding-fathers and prophets of whose lives generally extremely little is known - this in a civilization in which people cared to be commemorated, preferably in an honourable way.

By the same token Gnostics did not take in interest in history, not even in the history of their own sects. Nothing that happened here below could be of any value or significance. However much Gnostics borrowed from Judaism, Jewish history as such did not figure in their writings; some of its greatest names are never mentioned. There is still less of Greek or Roman history; not one Roman emperor would be able to discover his name in Gnostic scripture. As a non-political and non-historical phenomenon the Gnosis was exceptional in Antiquity. Even the Jews whose books are basically of a religious and prophetic nature were much concerned with the politics of their time and with their own history.

4. Gnostic dualism

The refractory attitude of the Gnosis is perfectly mirrored in the fact that all its systems are dualistic to the core. In the preface to this volume I wrote that this dualism is twofold : there is the horizontal separation of the upper and the nether worlds, and the vertical division of mankind into the chosen and the damned. Gnostics throve on unsolvable oppositions; their whole mental world was moulded by these. The dualisms mentioned are by no means the only ones; every Gnostic system has its own special dualisms. Gnostics must have been curious people, of a special and rather rare stamp. They obviously were viscerally incapable of living without conflicts; I am not thinking of personal conflicts but of mental ones. They were always opposed to ideas that were current and commonly accepted in Antiquity, and, of course, in particular in their own environment. They even were incapable of living peacefully among one another, since, as Chapter IX of Volume VIII showed, they polemized often in acid terms against other Gnostic groups.

I think that most people prefer a holistic view of their situation to a dualistic one that is a picture of division and disharmony. We all tend to eliminate untoward elements, if not from our lives then at least from our memories (which are very malleable instruments!). And if we cannot succeed in suppressing our reminiscences, we try to embellish them. Only a short time ago I read of a British general who in 1928, only ten years after the end of World War I, told the men of his former regiment that the war had been the finest time of their lives. Had he told them this, when they stood in the trenches ready to attack, they would have booed him. That Gnostic dualists thought and argued in ways different from that of the rest of humanity proves how alienated they were from their contemporaries.

The world of Antiquity was not dualistic in the sense that dualism was its main constitutive element. This does not mean, however, that dualism was an unknown phenomenon in the ancient world. Quite the contrary! All the foregoing volumes have shown that dualistic oppositions often occurred and that they were very numerous - in all periods of history, in every region, and in all fields of life. Gnostic dualism had its forerunners and its models. But when all is said and done, whereas dualistic phenomena are not rare, dualistic systems are, and radically dualistic systems still more. It must be admitted that even in the Gnosis radically dualistic systems are the great exception. However, Gnostic dualism, whether or not radical, shows a very rare degree of intensity and coherence - it might even be said, of fanatical conviction.

There is more. If we consider the whole of the ancient world, as far as we have studied it by now, we may construe a descending scale of dualism as occurring in ancient civilizations. In the western world Hellas comes out on top as a society riddled with unsolvable oppositions; in the east, India. On the lowest level we find the least dualistic and most homogeneous and harmonious societies, in the east, China, in the west Israel, closely followed by Egypt.

Now the Gnosis originated in the south-eastern corner of the Mediterranean basin, in the region stretching from Egypt to Syria, that is in the least dualistic portion of the ancient world. If the Gnosis is so basically dualistic, why then did it not originate in Greece, as an offshoot from Orphism for instance? Or in Iran, in the wake of, especially, Zervanism? Or in India as an offspring of Buddhism which, by the way, was ideologically very close to the Gnosis? But, in fact, it came into being in those regions where dualism was not conspicuously present. If it is true that it began in Palestine, then it must be stated - and restated - that the Jewish religion and the Jewish society were the most homogeneous, the most 'all of a piece', of all Antiquity, though not without rifts and fissures. Almost the same applies to Egypt, its religion and culture, although with the same qualification.

In so far as Gnostic sects had Jewish founders, they had drifted very far from their moorings. Palestinian and Egyptian Gnostics found themselves at a very great distance from all and everything that surrounded them. Perhaps this was one of the reasons for keeping so much to themselves and for not sharing their redeeming Knowledge with all others, who, very probably, they considered incapable of understanding them.

5. Why the opposite view?

A very pressing question arises here. Why did the Gnostics take the opposite view? Why did they disagree with the basic tenets of the civizilation in which they lived? The general but as yet vague and inconclusive answer must be that they sought something that their culture or religion was incapable of giving them. They wanted the solution to a problem their own people could not privide them with, either because it was never acknowledged that there was a problem or because it was considered solved. We shall have to return to this.

In the first part of this chapter I quoted Simone Pétrement to the effect that ditheism was the hallmark of the Gnosis. I am not going to discuss whether or not this really was the main characteristic of the Gnosis, but Mme. Pétrement was certainly right in stating that most Gnostic systems recognized two gods, one the highest divinity of the upper world, the other the Demiurge of the lower world, the cosmos. With this ditheism, this two-gods-system, the Gnosis flew straight into the face of all religions of Antiquity. It is obvious to anyone that this was a categorical rejection of the strict monotheism of Judaism and Christianity. But it also denied what paganism stood for, the Olympian gods and the Roman pantheon in which they were later incorporated. The Graeco-Roman world knew neither of one god nor of two but of many.

Not even the Zoroastrian religion must be dubbed ditheistic, because it is basically monotheistic, with Ahura Mazda as the supreme god of the light, the ground of all being; Zoroastrian dualism sets in one stage lower, where two spirits, Spenta Mainyu, the good one, and Angra Mainyu, the evil one, are fighting one another. The only comparable case is Zervanism, an offshoot from Zoroastrianism, in which a good and an bad god, Ormuzd and Ahriman, oppose one another, although there is still a being above them, the vague entity called Zervan (Zurvan) or Time. But here an important difference with the Gnosis must be mentioned : whereas in Zervanism both gods are equal and coeternal, the Demiurge of the Gnosis is deeply inferior to the Pleromic god and in many cases does not even know that such a god exists. The nearest approach to Zervanism in Gnostic ideology is Manichaeism, but this too is no ditheism proper, since the second principle, Darkness, must not be called 'god'.

Why did the Gnostics turn away from the polytheistic as well as from the monotheistic 'model'? In this case the answer is clear enough : because they abhorred the cosmos. In Graeco-Roman polytheism the gods were not creators, they were part of the universe themselves; therefore they had to be rejected along with the doomed cosmos. In Judaism and Christianity the one and only God is the creator of heaven and earth, but the Gnostics did not want a real god as the creator of the cosmos. They did not want to lay the guilt of having made a failure of the world at the door of a supreme godhead. As a consequence, they needed a second divinity as the creator. To be perfectly clear, they did not consider the Demiurge bad, because he had made a bad world; it is the other way round : because the world is bad, its creator must be bad too.

6. The anticosmic attitude

This brings us to the profound anticosmic attitude of almost all cosmic groups. In this respect too the Gnostics were at variance with all Antiquity. The word 'cosmos' is Greek and means 'ornament'. In principle, the Hellenes saw the world as well-made and well-ordered. The polis in which they lived was supposed to be modelled after the great cosmos, just as individual man was a microcosmos made after the model of the macrocosmos. There was, according to Greek thought, a chain of being connecting the cosmos, the polis, and individual man. The gods themselves formed part of this whole and did not stand apart from it. How the cosmos, gods included, had come into being was not clear to the Greeks;, anyhow, the gods had not made it, and there was no Demiurge.

There is, however, room for a misunderstanding here. As Dodds correctly maintains, the Greeks in general saw "the whole vast structure ... as the expression of a divine order; as such, it was felt to be beautiful and worshipful; and because it was self-moving it was thought to be alive or informed by a living spirit ... For most men educated in the Greek tradition (this) remained common ground". This does, however, not mean that the parts of the cosmos were thought to be all of equal quality. To quote Dodds once more, "across the cosmic map Aristotle, following hints in Plato, had drawn a line which came to be generally accepted : above the line, beyond the moon, lay the unvarying heavens where the stars moved ...; below it lay the sublunar world, the domain of chance, mutability, and death. And in this glittering house of many mansions the earth appeared as the meanest mansion of all : it was held to be the compact of the mere dregs and sediments of the universe" [58].

This statement could seduce us into believing that the Hellenes saw the world just as the Gnostics did. They, the Gnostics, took a very low view of the world, indeed. The most we can say is that they thoroughly radicalized a thought that was current in the Hellenic world. However, the differences between their world-view and that of the rest of Antiquity are far greater than the (apparent) similarity. As we have seen so often in the preceding chapters, they too drew a line, but this was not a line within the cosmos, between its higher and lower sections, but one between the whole of the cosmos and the upper world. The totality of the cosmos was objectionable to them, not only the lower part, and they were far fiercer and more radical in their condemnation than any philosophical system of the ancient world.

Jews and Christians stood much further from the Gnostic point of view. They knew a Creator, Jahve, the God of heaven and earth. It was he who made the cosmos and saw that it was good; and he also made mankind and saw that it was very good. They considered the cosmos God's handiwork, so much so that they held that human beings can infer the existence of God from creation. Since the Gnosis bars the upper world of the godhead hermetically from the lower one, there was for them no possibility to conclude from creation to the existence of a God who would be its creator.

Since the cosmic world is not in any way connected with the Pleroma, and since in most Gnostic systems it is the work of an evil-intentioned Demiurge, it is considered an objectionable, vile thing, fit only to be thrown away. Gnostics take an equally low view of humanity; human beings are hardly better than matter. Their only redeeming feature is that they have a spark of pleromic light in them, although scarcely anyone is aware of it.

7. The 'all-or-nothing' syndrome

In this respect too the Gnostics took a position that was in total contrast to all that was dear to the ancients. If we start from their ingrained and cultivated dualistic mentality, this becomes comprehensible. To dualists it is always a question of all or nothing. Now nobody denies that the world has its imperfections and that man is not an ideal being. But for Gnostics those tares and defaults formed a sufficient reason to condemn and reject the world and all those who live in it. Idealists as they were, and not seeing their ideal realized here below, they postulate an upper world of the highest perfection, a real 'pleroma', that is, 'fulness'. This Pleroma is all and the All, whereas the world is nothing. Perhaps someone might object that the Platonic world of the Forms represents such an ideal world, but then it should be noted that this world was organically connected with the human world and gave sense and meaning to it.

Such a Pleroma was wholly unknown to the pagans; this ideal of total, of ontological completeness was entirely foreign to the Graeco-Roman world. The Christians did indeed use the term 'pleroma' for the hereafter, but this indicated another reality than that to which the Gnostic term referred. It was not the exact opposite of this world. Whereas 'Pleroma' is correctly translated with 'fulness', the Christian 'pleroma' should be rendered with 'fulfilment'. At death, for a Christian 'vita mutatur, non tollitur', life is not taken away but changed, as an old hymn says. Life is brought onto a higher plane but will not become fundamentally different. The good there was on earth will be there in heaven too, but in greater perfection. To this good the body too belongs, 'the temple of the Holy Ghost'. At the final fulfilment it will be rejoined to the soul - its own soul - to live forever in heaven.

8. The alien god

Let us return now to the Gnostic Pleroma. At the top of it, or sometimes even above it, the supreme Gnostic godhead resides. In opposition to Jahve, Zeus, Wotan, Amun-Re, or Ahura Mazda it has no proper name. Rather than of a 'he' we should speak of an 'it', because this divinity is not so much a concrete personality as an abstraction. It is not the creator of the cosmos; it is not in the slightest degree concerned with the fate of mankind. The Gnostic conception of the 'alien god', god the unknown, the inaccessible, the incomprehensible, even the unnameable, was completely foreign to the ancient world; it constitutes yet another form of apartheid.

Now while other gods of Antiquity, like Zeus, are no creators either, they, Zeus, Jahve, or others, take a great interest in this world and its inhabitants and personally intervene in their affairs. True enough, the interests of Zeus and Jahve are of a very different character, but this is not the point at issue here. The fact is that they are, so to speak, continually present.

That God almighty takes care of this world and of humanity is, in Christian theology, strongly underlined by the dogma of Jesus Christ being God and man at the same time - two natures, one divine, one human, in one person, as it is most succinctly expressed. By the same token, this dogma once more stresses that there is an analogy between God's world and that of man.

The Hellenic case is different but not essentially so. Iliad and Odyssey teach us that the Olympian gods were only too ready to descend to the earth, to assume human shapes, to produce offspring with earthly men and women, to take part in their wars, and what not. There were demigods, half-god, half man (but no God-man, all God and all man). With the Greeks too, the earthly and the divine orders were closely intertwined.

9. The Gnostic and the Christian Redeemer

Perhaps it will adduced that, just as Christianity, the Gnosis knew a Redeemer. Quite right! The concept of the Redeemer is of paramount importance in Gnostic systems. And just as Christ the Saviour was sent by God to this earth, so, at least in a number of Gnostic systems, the supreme godhead dispatches a Redeemer here below - a Redeemer who, in some systems, is his son. But if it is true that Christianity and Gnosis resemble each other in this respect, it would be superficial to leave it at this. We pass over in silence, since everybody is aware of it, the fact that the idea of redemption was entirely alien to the pagan Graeco-Roman world. In the Jewish religion, however, this notion was not entirely absent. Perhaps we should not speak here of a Redeemer but rather of a deliverer, a Messiah, who would, some time in the future, free Israel from al her oppressors and lead the people into a new age in which the chosen people would be the vanguard of humanity.

This idea of the promised Messiah was taken over by Christianity, with the proviso that, according to the Christians, this Messiah had already come in the person of Jesus of Nazareth, the Saviour. He, just as much God as the Father who sent him, came to redeem mankind, to take their guilt, their sins, upon himself, and to atone for these by his sacrificial death on the cross. His task it was to reconcile mankind with the Father and to reopen the gates of heaven. It must be expressly stated that the mission of the Messiah concerned the whole of humanity, nobody excluded.

Looking below the surface, we see that the Gnostic idea of Redemption differs considerably from the Christian concept. If there is a Redeemer - which is not always the case -, he did not appear in order to save all mankind. One cannot even say that he was out to save the Gnostics, for they, in so far as they were body and soul (matter and psuchê), would perish along with the non-Gnostics. The Redeemer's task is to collect the sparks of light that are scattered throughout the world. The Saviour's concern was to bring back to the Pleroma the 'pneumata, the luminous particles that were enclosed in the Gnostics. Only Gnostics were aware of possessing such a spark of light. I get the impression - but this matter remains somewhat unclear - that, at least in some systems, Gnostics are those who are endowed with a pneuma, whereas others are without it. Anyhow, it will be evident that the Gnostic Redeemer - or Redeemers, for they assume different shapes and names - did not descend to save mankind, but only a small part of it, and then not the whole human person.

10. The concept of election

This brings us to the concept of election. I believe that all civilizations foster the idea that some of their members are spiritually more favoured than others. I am not speaking here of social, financial, or political precedence. Hellenic culture as such did not know of election. There is perhaps one exception, that of the initiates of Eleusis who went home with the moral certainty that they were destined for immortality. But then, the mystery-cult of Eleusis was a divagation from the main cult; for the common run of Hellenes what happened in the great mystery-hall remained a secret, just as it remains a secret for us. The Greeks acknowledged that there were people beloved or favoured or privileged by the gods, but one cannot say that this amounted to an election.

Directing our attention to Judaism now, we discover something entirely different. Israel considered herself as the chosen people - a small nation, indeed, but selected among all the peoples of the world to be Jahve's own. The task of Israel was a twofold one : first to preserve the monotheistic idea, the concept of the one and only God, secondly to prepare the coming of the Messiah who would rise from her midst. The chosen people must not keep the benefits and blessings of the election to itself but, while ever remaining the vanguard, share them with all humanity; in the end all men would gather around the Mount of Sion in adoration of the true God.

This conception of divine election was taken over by the budding Christian Church. Since the Christians considered themselves the new Israel, even the true Israel, the 'verus Israel', they naturally saw in themselves the new chosen people on which the mantle of the Jews had fallen. They saw themselves charged with the same command : to proclaim and profess the one and only God. With regard to the Messiah, however, there was the telling difference of which I have already spoken : according to the Christians the Messiah had already arrived. But although the Christians felt that the Jews had gambled away their privileges, in the end, as Paul had prophesied, a chastened Israel would take the lead again, so that all humanity would be gathered around the altar of the Lamb.

I don't know from where the Gnostics took their idea of election. After all, it seems natural enough for small and secret groups to develop ideas of selection and election. Anyhow, the sentiment of being elected was one of the solid pillars on which Gnostic movements rested. They were separate, they were chosen, they were selected. But whereas the Messianic message of Judaism and Christianity was destined for all mankind, Gnostics did not prove interested in the fate of humanity. They kept to themselves and did not see themselves as the vanguard of the human race. They could not care less for their fellow-beings. The seal of election was the acceptance of the Knowledge. That the great majority of human beings were incapable of seeing the unique significance of this Knowledge or proved indifferent to it, only showed how much they deserved their fate : to founder in the final ruin of the world.

Summarizing this part of our discussion, we can state that it was characteristic of the mental stance of the Gnosis that it was antinomian. It went, and it did so apparently with relish, 'against the grain'. None of the concepts (or myths) of community, of belonging together, of forming one society, appealed to the Gnostics. There is hardly a Gnostic text, or perhaps none at all, from which we can conclude to the political or ethnic allegiance of the author (not to mention the curious fact that we hardly ever know the name of an author. The polis-idea of the Hellenes, the feeling of being the common subjects of a god-pharao, the restful sentiment of being protected and blessed by the Pax Romana, of organically forming part of Jahve's chosen people, or the idea of being members of the Mystical Body of Christ in the Church, all these notions were entirely foreign to Gnostics. What bound them together was the negative idea of not being like all the others. This made them take their distance from the concepts, myths, and practical realizations of community that were such a general feature of Antiquity, and, we might add, of all ages and civilizations.

11. The Gnosis as theosophy

If we study the Gnosis as a whole, without paying attention to the many diversions and differences that characterize it, we may safely attach the term 'theosophy, to it, by which I mean first of all that it was neither a theology nor a philosophy. I know perfectly well that 'theosophy' is a modern term but I cannot find an ancient equivalent for it. I feel that the modern theosophy of Annie Besant and Madame Blavatsky, whether consciously or not, owes much to the ancient Gnosis.

Gnostics were anti-philosophical. Of course, scholars will point out, as they did in effect, that Platonic, Neoplatonic, and other philosophical systems to a certain extent influenced Gnostic beliefs, but this did not turn these beliefs into a philosophy. By 'philosophy' I understand a systematic study of and an intellectual investigation into phenomena of a predominantly non-practical nature - although, naturally enough, philosophy has an influence on practical life.

Greek thought began with philosophy - that of the Presocratics - and was often not to be distiguished from science. In Hellenic and Hellenistic times philosophy and science developed side by side. Wilhelm Nestle has characterized this process as the transition from mythos to logos. Although the mythical view of the world did never wholly vanish from the Greek mind, perhaps not even from philosophy itself, the main trend of thinking, in any case of that of Hellenic intellectuals, was philosophical and scientific rather than mythical.

Judaistic, that is biblical, thought was decidedly unphilosophical. The earlier biblical authors were unacquainted with Greek thinking and, in consequence, did not react to it. Later biblical authors, those of the Hellenistic period, knew something of pagan philosophy but were averse from it, because it was heathen and worldly. All the same, references to it are obscure and rare.

The focus of Jewish thought was God from whom everything came and to whom everything referred. Were, in consequence, the biblical authors theologians? If by 'theology' we understand 'systematic theology', they certainly were not. Of course, we legimately speak of 'biblical theology'; this is perfectly in order as long as we are indicating by this term a coherent, intelligent, and understandable body of biblical tenets and opinions. We are surely justified in speaking of such a body, such a complex of thought, because there is one (already mentioned) focus of interest around which all other interests are grouped and to which they all refer. Biblical theology originates, perhaps not so much from the problem of the existence of God (which is simply taken for granted) but rather from the dependence of man on God, and from man's ideal response to God as well as his failure to respond. From these starting-points all the rest follows.

The Christian attitude is not essentially different. The New Testament does not contain a philosophy but it presents, if not a systematic, then a regular exposition of the teachings of Jesus of Nazareth, followed by the elaboration of these in the apostolic and pastoral letters, in particular those of Paul. It is doubtless admissible to speak of the theology of the New Testament. The points of interest of Jewish theology are still there, but there is now a new focus, the concentration on the role of Jesus Messiah.

Already before the last direct disciple of Jesus had died, these points of theological interest were taken up by Christian authors, beginning with Saint Clement of Rome, followed by a host of others, the early Fathers of the Church who have been quoted over and over again in these pages. The result was that in the period under consideration a regular Christian theology came into being.

The attitude of the early Christian theologians towards pagan philosophy was somewhat ambiguous. Some authors rejected it lock, stock, and barrel, precisely because it was heathen. But others, especially those who came from a pagan (Hellenic) background themselves and were grounded in Greek culture, were ready to accept at least part of its philosophy which they saw as 'pre-Christian'. I shall have occasion to come back to this in a later volume.

Returning now to the Gnosis, we see an entirely different picture. Let me repeat the fruitful idea of Karl Jaspers who spoke of the 'Achsenzeit', a period in which world-history made a complete turnabout. In the centuries between 600 and 200 B.C. a change happened from mythical presentations to logical and scientific thought. This process took place in a broad band of countries stretching fom Greece through Israel and India to China. The Gnosis, however, originating several centuries after the Achsenzeit, bred on myth; it thrived on speculations of a non-scientific, non-intellectual, non-historical, a-logical, and sometimes even anti-logical character. It did not shy away from contradictions.

12. Comprehensibility and incomprehensibility

A scholar who attacks Gnostic scripture will initially find him- or herself completely at a loss. But he or she should realize that Gnostic literature was not written to be understood by outsiders. I feel that even initiates did not comprehend all of it; probably the mysteriousness and the (not rarely occurring) incomprehensibility of the texts enhanced their worth and significance in their eyes. This too constituted a major difference with all other scripture of Antiquity, since normally ancient authors, pagan, Jewish, Christian, desired to be read and understood by as many people as possible. They were writing for the public eye, for even when their texts were in principle destined for a restricted and special group, nobody forbade outsiders to take them in hand. A case in point is the Septuagint, the translation of the Hebrew Old Testament into Greek, which made the book accessible to the whole ancient world.

13. Behind the times?

Were Gnostics behind the times? Were they a curious leftover from a previous age? Were they belated representatives of a more primitive mentality? Were they, so to speak, cultural fossils? Now, if we assume for a moment that they were indeed remnants of a world that had ceased to exist for long, we must admit that these remnants were fairly numerous. There were a great number of Gnostic sects, and the total number of adherents cannot have been small. We have no idea how many members each sect counted; some of them must have been very small and remained restricted to a special area. But others, like the Marcionite Church, the Valentinians, and the Manichees spread their wings over a wide area and must have counted a great many adherents. While some of them were of short duration, others prolonged their existence for several centuries. Manichaeism still existed until almost the end of the Middle Ages; Mandaeism subsists to the present day.

It is fairly possible, when all is said and done, that the 'mythical' mentality did not die out so completely as scholarly disquisitions seem to suppose. A cultural change is never definitive; something of the past, perhaps even much, remains and keeps manifesting itself. A good comparison would be with the Enlightenment. Its enthusiasts honestly believed that, if religion had to stay, it had to become a 'rational', undogmatic, and non-denominational religion. However, such a religion never materialized. Instead, millions of people still adhere to the old denominations, Protestant or Catholic, to say nothing of Islam.

Whenever and wherever some sort of Enlightenment movement originates - there was a Greek Enlightenment, starting with the Presocratics -, an anti-Enlightenment will accompany it. The Gnosis is the main representative of this anti-Enlightenment movement in Antiquity. In this respect it really was referring to the past. The Gnosis became the rallying cry for all those who were disaffected with many important and constitutive elements of ancient culture. But at the same time, it looked towards the future. The Gnostic heritage was never lost. Later movements could draw on it, and there were (and are) many of them. There is a main stream in western culture, but there is also an submerged stream that surfaces here and there and now and then. To this submerged stream the Gnosis belongs.

The Gnosis was the meeting-place of all those who disagreed with the culture of the society in which they lived. Left to themselves, they were probably unable to express what exactly agued them. The Gnosis provided the answer, and with the answer the solution. More than once in the course of these volumes I have stated that the Gnosis was dualistic to the core. It certainly was. But it also generated dualism, in the sense that it put people who perhaps were thinking or rather feeling in a vaguely dualistic sense firmly on their feet. One might say that it made dualism respectable, fashionable, at least for a great many people, establishing itself, as it did, in great and complex systems.

NOTES TO CHAPTER V

1. The title of her book is 'Le Dieu séparé' (see Bibliography).
2. Pétrement, Dieu séparé 15.
3. Pétrement, Dieu séparé 662.
4. Pétrement, Dieu séparé 657-662.
5. Pétrement, Dieu séparé 305.
6. "The modern clergyman has acquired in the study of the science which I believe is called exegesis an astonishing faculty for explaining things away", wrote the British novelist W. Somerset Maugham in 'The moon and sixpence'.
7. Acts 8:13.
8. Acts 8:25.
9. Acts 18:23-28.
10. 1Cor.1:11-12.
11. Pétrement, Dieu séparé 306.
12. Apart from short entries in encyclopaedias, the only monopgraph (49 pages) about Apollos is that of Schumacher (see Bibliography).
13. Brandon, Fall 25.
14. Brandon, Fall 139.

15. 1Cor.3:22-23.
16. 1Cor.3:5-9.
17. 1Tit.3:13.
18. Pétrement, Dieu séparé 350.
19. Schumacher, Apollos 22/23, is certain that Apollos' preaching did not really, that is to say, dogmatically, differ from that of Paul. Why else should Paul have called him 'brother'? But probably Apollos, who came from Alexandria, the preeminent seat of learning, possessed the greater erudition of the two and could express himself more eloquently and elegantly. It would not be surprising if some new Christians in Corinth, not without a tinge of snobism, would have preferred Apollos' teaching to that of Paul. The apostle himself, writing to the Corinthians, admitted that his introduction of the Gospel was couched in the simplest terms : "Milk I gave you, not yet solid food" (1Cor.3:2). Is it too far fetched to suppose that Apollos, who came later to the harbour town, was able to give them that 'solid food'? Although there was an Apollos-party in Corinth indeed, Paul nowhere reproaches Apollos for have organized it. In fact, when Paul exhorted the Corinthians to desist from their partisanship, Apollos had already left the city and was in Ephesus, where he met Paul. The best proof that the apostle did not think of Apollos as of a party-chief is that he urged him to return to Corinth, but this Apollos steadfastly refused to do for the moment (1Cor.16:12).
20. Pétrement, Dieu séparé 17.
21. Pétrement, Dieu séparé 24.
22. Pétrement, Dieu séparé 307.
23. Pétrement, Dieu séparé 401.
24. Pétrement, Dieu séparé 407.
25. Pétrement, Dieu séparé 385-397.
26. Pétrement, Dieu séparé 397-405.
27. Phil.3:5.
28. 2Cor.11:22.
29. Rom.11:17-18.
30. Jo.4:22.
31. Jo.10:35.
32. Jo.1:1-3.
33. Jo.3:16-17.
34. Pétrement, Dieu séparé 186.
35. Marcel Proust, Du côté de chez Swann. Pléiade edition of 'A la recherche du temps perdu', I 411.

36. Sloterdijk/Macho, Die wahre Irrlehre. Weltrev. I 25.

37. In this book Pagels seems to hold on to her own Christian (Presbyterian) confession. However, in a tv-presentation of 1991 that I saw in Dutch television, she got much nearer to the Gnosis, even to the point of having become a Gnostic herself.

38. With only one exception all the references to 'Christian(s)' are to be found in the Gospel of Philip (NHC 2.3).
1. (62) "If you say 'I am a Jew', no one will be moved. If you say 'I am a Roman", no one will be disturbed. If you say 'I am a Greek, a barbarian, a slave, (a) free man', no one will be troubled. (If) you say 'I am a Christian', the world will tremble. This is the person whom the (powers) will not be able to endure (when they hear) his name."
2. (64) "If you go down into the water and come up without having received anything and say 'I am a Christian', he has borrowed the name at interest. But if he received the Holy Spirit, he has the name as a gift."
3. (67) "It is appropriate that those who have (the truth) not only acquire the name of the Father and the Son and the Holy Spirit, but have acquired it on their own. If one does not acquire the name for himself, the name (Christian) will also be taken from him. But one receives them (Father, Son, Ghost) in the aromatic unction of the cross ... For this person is no longer a Christian but a Christ."
4. (72) "The Lord said it well : 'Some have entered the kingdom of heaven laughing and have come out. (They do not remain there - the) one because he is (not) a Christian, (the other because he regrets his action) afterwards."
5. (75) "And, (as a) Christian (people), we (ourselves do not descend) from the Jews."
6. (52) "When we became Christians, we had both father and mother."
7. (74) "The chrism is superior to baptism, for it is from the word 'chrism' that we have been called 'Christians', certainly not because of the word 'baptism."
Finally, one quotation from the Testimonium veritatis (NHC IX.3). (31) "The foolish think (in) their heart (that) if they confess 'We are Christians', they will be saved."
It is abundantly clear that these texts show a very special understanding of what 'Christian' signifies. First of all, the last quotation contains a remarkable deviation from orthodox doctrine which has it that baptism is the first and most necessary sacrament. It obviously is not baptism that makes one into a Christian (to say nothing of the false etymology). Text nr. 2 says implicitly that baptism in itself is not enough : some receive the Holy Spirit with it and others do not. Those who do are, of course, the Gnostics. The same in nr. 3 : some are privileged with a special relationship with the Trinity; they are the true Christians.

39. See Ch. VI.2 of the present volume.

40. The Gospel of Philip (NHC 2.3.73) : "The father of Jesus was Joseph the carpenter" - an unorthodox statement.

41. In 'The Tripartite Tract' (NHC 1.5) where 'the Church' is mentioned eight times, it always signifies the Gnostic community, not the Roman-Catholic Church. It is just the same in NHC 11.2, 'A Valentinian Exposition.'
42. Acts 12:26.
43. Stroumsa, Another seed 172.
44. Haenchen, Buch Baruch 317.
45. This name given to it by Guillaume Postel in the 16th century.
46. Jacob Taubes, Der dogmatische Mythos der Gnosis, cit. Sloterdijk/Macho, Weltrev. I, 244.
47. Gen. 3:21.
48. Gen. 7:17.
49. Mt. 10:29-30; Lc. 12:6.
50. Jonas, Gnost.Rel. 42.
51. Jonas, Gnost.Rel. 42.
52. Van Wersch, Gnost.occ. vloedgolf 23. This interesting and erudite book deserves a translation!
53. The refrain of the creation story in Gen. 1.
54. Van Wersch, Gnost.occ. vloedgolf 17/18.
55. Jo.1, 4:8.
56. Rom. 1:20.
57. Mt. 28:18.
58. Dodds, Pagan and Christian 6/7.

BIBLIOGRAPHY

I ORIGINAL SOURCES

A COLLECTIONS

CODEX MANICHAICUS COLONIENSIS. Der Kölner Mani-Kodex. Über das Werden seines Lebens. Herausg. Ludwig Koenen und Cornelia Römer. Abhandlungen der rheinisch-westfälischen Akademie der Wissenschaften. Sonderreihe Papyrologica 14. Opladen, 1988.

DIOGENES LAERTIUS, Lives of Eminent Philosophers II. Ed. and translated by R.D. Hicks. Loeb Classical Library 185. Cambridge (Mass.)/London, 1970 (1925 1).

GINZA. Der Schatz oder Das grosse Buch der Mandäer. Übersetzt und erklärt von Mark Lidzbarski. Göttingen/Leipzig, 1925.

DIE GNOSIS III. Herausg. Alexander Böhlig.

DAS JOHANNESBUCH DER MANDÄER. Einleitung, Übersetzung und Kommentar von Mark Lidzbarski. Giessen, 1905.

KEPHALAIA. Manichäische Handschriften des staatlichen Museums Berlin, Band I. Stuttgart, 1940.

THE NAG HAMMADI LIBRARY IN ENGLISH (NHL). Ed. James M. Robinson. Leiden, 1977.

B INDIVIDUAL AUTHORS

ADAMANTIUS
Dialogus de recta in Deum fide. Patrologia graeca 11. Paris, 1857.

ALBÎRUNI
Chronology of Ancient Nations. Translated and edited by C. Edward Sachau. London, 1879 (unveränderter Nachdruck Frankfurt, 1969).

ALEXANDER LYCOPOLITANUS
Tractatus de placitis Manichaeorum. Patrologia graeca 6.1. Paris, 1857.
An Alexandrian Platonist against dualism. Alexander of Lycopolis' Treatise 'Critique of the doctrines of Manichaeism'. Translation with introduction and notes by P.W. van der Horst and Jaap Mansfeld. Leiden 1974.

AMBROSIUS
De Paradiso. Patrologia latina 14. Paris, 1845.

AUGUSTINUS
1. Acta seu Disputatio contra Fortunatum Manichaeum. Patrologia 42. Paris, 1861.
2. De actis cum Felice Manichaeo. Patrologia latina 42. Paris, 1861.
3. Contra Faustum. Patrologia latina 42. Paris, 1861.
4. De duabus animabus contra Manichaeos. Patrologia latina 32. Paris, 1861.
5. Contra duas Epistolas Pelagianorum. Patrologia latinorum 44. Paris, 1841.
6. Enarrationes in psalmos. Patrologia latina 37. Paris, 1861.
7. Epistolae. Patrologia latina 42. Paris, 1861.
8. Contra Epistolam Manichaei. Patrologia latina 42. Paris, 1861.
9. De fide contra Manichaeos. Patrologia latina 42. Paris, 1861.
10. De haeresibus. Patrologia latina 42. Paris, 1861.
11. De moribus Manichaeorum. Patrologia latina 32. Paris, 1843.
12. De natura boni contra Manichaeos. Patrologia latina 42. Paris, 1861.
13. Sermones. Patrologia 33. Paris, 1861.
14. De vera religione. Patrologia latina 34. Paris, 1845.

AUTHORITATIVE TEACHING. NHC 6.3.
NHL 6.3. Introduced and translated by George MacRae. Edited by Douglas M. Parrott.

THE FIRST APOCALYPSE OF JAMES. NHC 5.3.
NHL 5.3. Introduced and translated by William R. Schroedel. Edited by Douglas M. Parrott.

THE SECOND APOCALYPSE OF JAMES. NHC 5.4.
NHL 5.4. Introduced and translated by Charles N. Hedrich. Edited by Douglas M. Parrott.

THE APOCALYPSE OF PETER, NHC 7.3.
NHL 7.3. Introduced by James Brashler. Translated by Roger A. Bullard. Edited by Frederik Wisse.

CLEMENS OF ALEXANDRIA
1. Homiliae. Patrologia graeca 2. Paris, 1857.
2. Stromateis. Les Stromates. Texte et traduction de Marcel Casier et autres. Series : Sources chrétiennes 38, 278, 279. Paris, 1954-1981.

COMMONITORIUM (vulgo Augustini)
Patrologia 42. Paris, 1843.

THE CONCEPT OF THE GREAT POWER. NHC 6.4.
NHL 6.4. Introduced by Francis E. Williams. Translated by Frederik Wisse. Edited by Douglas M. Parrott.

CYPRIANUS
Epistula LXXIIII.2. Corpus Scriptorum Ecclesiasticorum Latinorum. III.2. Vienna, 1871.

EPIPHANIUS
Panarion haeresium. Die griechischen christlichen Schriftsteller der ersten drei Jahrhunderte. Epiphanius I. Herausg. Karl Holl. Leizpig, 1915.

EPISTOLA FUNDAMENTI
Texte zum Manichäismus. Herausg. Alfred Adam. Berlin, 1954.

EUSEBIUS OF CAESAREA
1. Historia ecclesiastica. Die griechischen christlichen Schriftsteller der ersten drei Jahrhunderte. Eusebius II.1. Herausgegeben von Eduard Schwartz. Lepizig, 1903.
2. De vita Constantini. Patrologia graeca 20. Paris, 1857.

EVODIUS
De fide contra Manichaeos. Corpus scriptorum ecclesiasticorum Latinorum XXV. Prague/Vienna/Leipzig, 1891.

THE EXEGESIS OF THE SOUL. NHC 2.6.
NHL 2.6. Introduced and translated by William C. Robinson.

EZNIK of Kolb
Wider die Irrlehren. Der armenischen Kirchenväter ausgewählte Schriften der ersten drei Jahrhunderte. Herausgeb. Dr. Simon Weber. I. Band. Bibliothek der Kirchenväter, Bd. 57. München, 1927.

FILASTRIUS
Diversarum hereseon liber. Herausgeb. Fridericus Marx. Corpus Scriptorum Ecclesiasticorum Latinorum. XXXVIII. Prague/Vienna/Leipzig, 1888.

THE GOSPEL OF PHILIP. NHC 2.3.
NHL 2.3. Introduced and translated by Wesley W. Isenberg.

HEGEMONIUS
Acta Archelai. Die griechischen christlichen Schirftsteller der ersten drei Jahrhunderte. Ed. Charles Henry Beeson. Leipzig, 1906.

HIERONYMUS
Adversus Iovinianum. Patrologia latina 23. Paris, 1845.

HIPPOLYTUS
Refutatio omnium haeresium. Die griechischen christlichen Schrifsteller der ersten drei Jahrhunderte. Bd. 26. Hippolytus, 3. Bd. Ed. Paul Wendland. Leipzig, 1916.

THE HYPOSTASIS OF THE ARCHONS. NHC 2.4.
NHL 2.4. Introduced by Roger A. Bullard. Translated by Bentley Layton.

IRENEAUS LUGDUNENSIS
Adversus haereses. Contre les héresies. Eds. Adelin Rousseau and Louis Doutreleau. Vol. 2 Textes latin et grec et traduction. Paris, 1982.

JOSEPHUS, Flavius
Jewish Antiquities. Ed. Ralph Marcus. Loeb Classical Library. London Cambridge (Mass.), 1957 (1943 1).

JUSTINUS MARTYR
Apologia. Patrologia latina 6. Paris, 1857.

MARTAN FARRAXI OHRMAZDDATTAN
Skhand-qumânîk vichâr (La solution décisive des doutes). Une apologétique mazdéenne du IXe siècle. Texte pazand-pehlevi transcrit, traduit et commenté par Pierre-Jean de Menasce. Collecteana friburgensia N.S., fasc. 30. Fribourg (CH), 1945.

Ibn an-NADîM
Fihrist al-ulûm. Ed. Bayard Dodge, The Fihirst of an-Nadîm. A tenth-century survey of Muslim culture. New York/London, 1970.

NEMESIUS
De natura hominis. Patrologia graeca 40. Paris, 1863.

ON THE ORIGIN OF THE WORLD. NHC 2.5. and 13.2.
NHL 2.5. and 13.2. Introduced by Hans-Gebhard Bethge and Orval S. Wintermute.

ORIGINES
1. Contra Celsum. Patrologia graeca 11. Paris, 1857.
2. In Genesim homilia. Patrologia graeca 12. Paris, 1862.

PAPIAS
1. Argumentum Johannis ex codice Reginae Suetiae. Novum Testamentum domini nostri Jesu Christ Latine. Pars I. Eds. J. Wordsworth and H.J. White. Oxford, 1889-1898.
2. Prologus secundus ex codice Toletano. Ed. see above.

PSEUDOCLEMENTINA
Homiliae. Patrologia graeca 2. Paris, 1857.

PSEUDOGREGORY OF NYSSA
De anima. Patrologia graeca 45. Paris, 1863.

PSEUDOTERTULLIANUS
Adversus omnes haereses. Patrologia latina 2. Paris, 1844.

DE RESURRECTIONE. Epistula ad Rheginum. Eds. M. Malinine, H.-C. Puech, G. Quispel, W. Till, R. Mcl. Wilson, J. Zandee. Coptic text with English, French, and Zerman translations. Zürich, 1963.

ASCH-SCHARASTANI, Abu-'l-Fath' Muhammad
Religionspartheien und Philosophenschulen. Zum ersten Mal vollständig aus dem Arabischen übersetzt und mit erklärenden Anmerkungen versehen von Theodor Haarbrücker. I Die muhammadanischen, jüdischen, christlichen und dualistischen Religionspartheien. Halle, 1850. Reprografischer Nachdruck Hildesheim 1969.

SIMPLICIUS
Commentarius in Epicteti Enchiridion I. Ed. Iohannes Schweighaeuser. Epicteteae philosophiae monumenta. Tomus IV. Leipzig, 1798.

STEPHANUS
Decretoriae sententiae. Patrologia latina 3. Paris, 1844.

TERTULLIANUS
1. De anima. patrologia latina 2. Paris, 1844.
2. De carne Christi. Patrologia latina 2. Paris, 1844.
3. De ieiuniis. Patrologia latina 2. Paris, 1844.
4a. Adversus Marcionem. Patrologia latina 2. Paris, 1844.
4b. Adversus Marcionem. Ed. and translated by Ernest Evans. Oxford, 1972.
5. De praescriptionibus. Patrologia latina 2. Paris, 1844.

THEODORE BAR KONAÏ
Liber scholiorum. Livre des scolies. Traduit par Robert Hespel et René Draguet. Corpus Scriptorum Christianorum Orientalium. Scriptores Syri, Vol. 187. Louvain, 1981.

THEODORETUS
1. Epistulae. Patrologia graeca 83. Paris, 1864.
2. Haereticarum fabularum compendium. Patrologia graeca 83. Paris, 1864.

TITUS OF BOSTRA
Adversus Manichaeos. Patrologia graeca 18. Paris, 1857.

THE TREATISE ON RESURRECTION. NHC 1.3.
NHL 1.3. Introduced and translated by Malcolm Peel.

THE TRIMORPHIC PROTENNOIA. NHC 13.1.
NHL 13.1. Introduced and translated by John D. Turner.

TURRIBIUS OF ASTORGA
Epistolae. Patrologia latina 54. Paris, 1846.

II SECONDARY WORKS

A WORKS OF REFERENCE

Dictionnaire d'histoire et géographie ecclésiastiques. 12. Paris, 1953.

Dictionnaire de théologie catholique 1, 4.2, 9.1, 9.2, 15.1. Paris, 1923, 1924, 1927, 1946.

Encyclopedia of Philosophy 3 and 5. New York/London (1967).

Encyclopaedia of Religion and Ethics 8. Edinburgh, 1915.

The Encyclopedia of Religion. New York, 1987.

Europäische Enzyklopädie zu Philosophie und Wissenschaften 1. Hamburg (1990).

Paulys Real-Encyclopie der Classischen Altertumswissenschaft. Neue Bearbeitung herausgegeben von Georg Wissowa. Supplement-Band VI. Stuttgart, 1935 (PW).

Realencyclopädie protestantischer Theologie 12. Leipzig, 1903.

Theologische Realenzyklopädie (TRE). Band XXII, Lieferung 1. Berlin/New York (1991)

Theologisches Wörterbuch zum Neuen Testament 4.Bd. Stuttgart (1942).

Historisches Wörterbuch der Philosphie 7. Basel (1989).

B COLLECTIONS

BRIEFWECHSEL ZWISCHEN WILHELM DILTHEY UND DEM GRAFEN PAUL YORCK VON WARTENBURG. Buchreihe Philosophie und Wissenschaften 1.Bd. Halle, 1923.

DER MANDÄISMUS. Ed. Geo Widengren. Wege der Forschung. Band CLXXVII. Darmstadt, 1982.

DIE GNOSIS III. Der Manichäismus. Ed. Alexander Böhlig. Die Bibliothek der alten Welt. Reihe Antike und Christentum. Zürich, 1980.

CODEX MANICHAICUS COLONIENSIS. Atti del simposio internazionale, 3-7 settembre 1984. A cura di Luigi Cirillo. Studi e richerche 4. Cosenza, 1986.

C MONOGRAPHS

ALFARIC, Prosper, Les écritures manichéennes. Paris, 1918-1919.

BARC, Bernard, L'Hypostase des Archontes. Traité gnostique sur l'origine de l'homme (NH II.4). Bibliothèque copte de Nag Hammadi. Section 'Textes' 5. Québec/Louvain, 1980.

BAUR, Friedrich Christian, Das Manichäische Religionssystem, nach den Quellen untersucht und entwickelt. Göttingen, 1831. Photomechanischer Neudruck Tübingen, 1928.

BEHM, Johannes, Die Mandäische Religion und das Christentum. Leipzig, 1927.

BIANCHI, Ugo, Marcion : théologien biblique ou docteur gnostique? Vigiliae christianae 21 (1967).

BLACKMAN, E.C., Marcion and his Influence. London, 1948.

BOUSSET, Wilhelm, Hauptprobleme der Gnosis. Göttingen, 1907.

BRANDON, S.G.F., The Fall of Jerusalem and the Christian Church. A Study of the Effects of the Jewish Overthrow of A.D. 70 on Christianity. London, 1951.

BRANDT, Wilhelm August J.H., Elchasai, ein Religionsstifter und sein Werk. Beiträge zur jüdischen, christlichen und allgemeinen Religionsgeschichte. Leipzig, 1912.

BULLARD, Roger Aubrey, The Hypostasis of the Archons. The Coptic text with translation and commentary. Patristische Texte und Studien, Bd. 10. Berlin, 1970.

CIRILLO, Luigi, Elchesaiti et Battisti di Mani : Limiti di un confronto delle fonti. Atti del simposio 1984.

COREN, Stanley, The left-hander syndrom : the causes and consequences of left-handedness. New York/Toronto, 1992.

COULIANO, Ioan P., Les Gnoses dualistes de l'Occident. Histoire et mythes. Paris (1990).

CURRY, Haskell B., Foundations of mathematical logic. New York/San Francisco/Toronto/London (1963).

DECRET, François, Mani et la tradition manichéenne. Series : Maîtres spirituels. 1974.

DODDS, E.R., Pagan and Christian in an Age of Anxiety. Some aspects of religious experience from Marcus Aurelius to Constantine. The Wiles Lectures given at the Queen's University of Belfast, 1963. Cambridge, 1965.

DOUGLAS, Mary, Purity and Danger. An Analysis of the Concept of Pollution and Taboo. Ark Paperback. London, 1984 (1966 1).

DROWER, Lady Ethel S., The Mandaeans of Iraq and Iran. Oxford, 1932.

DÜRRENMATT, Friedrich, Die Physiker. Werkausgabe, Band 7. Zürich (1980).

FALLON, Francis T., The Enthronement of Sabaoth. Jewish elements in Gnostic creation myths. Nag Hammadi Studies X. Ed. Frederik Wisse. Leiden, 1978.

FAST, J.D., Materie en leven (Matter and Life). De samenhang der natuurwetenschappen. Publication of 'Natuur en techniek', 1932, 1977 1.

FILORAMO, Giovanni, A History of Gnosticism. Translated by Anthony Alcock (L'attesa della fine. Storia della Gnosi.) London, 1991 (1990).

FUNK, Wolf-Peter, Die zweite Apokalypse des Jakobus aus Nag Hammadi-Codex V. Neu herausgegeben, übersetzt und erklärt von --. Texte und Untersuchungen zur altchristlichen Literatur, Bd. 119. Berlin, 1976.

GÖDEL, Kurt, On formally undecidable Propositions of Principia Mathematica and Related Systems. With an introduction by R.B. Brainthwaite. Translation by B. Meltzer. Edinburgh/London, 1962.

GOETHE, Johann Wolfgang, Dichtung und Wahrheit. Goethes Werke IX. Hamburg, 1964 5.

GRANT, Robert M., The Mystery of Marriage in the Gospel of Philip. Vigiliae Christianae XV (1961).

HAENCHEN, Ernst, Das Buch Baruch. Ein Beitrag zum Problem der christlichen Gnosis. Gott und Mensch. Gesammelte Aufsätze. Tübingen, 1965.

HARNACK, Adolf von, Marcion : Das Evangelium vom fremden Gott. Eine Monographie zur Geschichte des Grundlegung der Katholischen Kirche. Texte und Untersuchungen zur Geschichte der altchristlichen Literatur. 3. Reihe, 45. Band. Leipzig, 1924 2 (1920 1).

HEIJENOORT, Jean (John) van, From Frege to Gödel. A Source Book in Mathematical Logic, 1879-1931. Cambridge (Mass.)/London (1977 3, 1967 1).

HERTZ, Robert, The Pre-Eminence of the Right Hand : A Study in Religious Polarity. In : (Ed. Rodney Needham) Right & Left. Essays on Dual Symbolic Classification. Chicago/London (1973). Translation of : La Prééminence de la main droite : étude sur la polarité religieuse. Revue philosophique 68 (1909).

HILGENFELD, Adolphus, Novum Testamentum extra canonem receptum. Fasc. 3 Elxai libri fragmenta collecta, digesta, diudicata. Leipzig, 1866.

HOFFMANN, R. Joseph, Marcion : On the Restitution of Christianity. An Essay on the Development of Radical Paulinist Theology in the Second Century. American Academy of Religion Academy Series. Chico (Ca.), (1984).

HOLL, Josef, Gott und Hölle. Der Mythos vom Descensus-Kampfe. Studien der Bibliothek Warburg XX. Berlin, 1932.

JACKSON, Abraham Valentine Williams, Die Person Manis, des Begründers des Manichäismus. Der Manichäismus (Ed. Widengren). Originally 'The Personality of Mani, the Founder of Manichaeism'. Journal of the American Oriental Society 58 (1938).

JAKI, Stanley S., The Relevance of Physics. Chicago, 1970 2 (1966 1).

JAMES, William, The Varieties of Religious Experience. A Study in Human Nature. The Fontana Library. Theology and Philosophy. 1971 (The Gifford Lectures 1901/1902).

JANSSENS, Yvonne, La Prôtennoia Trimorphe (NH XIII.1). Texte établi et présenté par --. Bibliothèque copte de Nag Hammadi. Section 'Textes' 4. Québec, 1978.

JONAS, Hans, The Gnostic Religion. The Message of the Alien God and the Beginnings of Christianity. London, 1992 (1958 1).

KESSLER, Konrad, Mani. Forschungen über die manichäische Religion. Ein Beitrag zur vergleichenden Religionsgeschichte des Orients. Bd. I Untersuchungen und Quellen. Berlin, 1889.

KIERKEGAARD, Sören, Die Tagebücher, 2. Bd. Gesammelte Werke 2. Ausgewählt, neu geordnet und übersetzt von H. Gerdes. Düsseldorf/Köln, 1963.

KOLAKOWSKI, Leszek, Metaphysical Horror. London (1988).

KROLL, Josef, Gott und Hölle. Der Mythos vom Descensus-Kampfe. Studien der Bibliothek Warburg XX. Berlin, 1932.

LADRIèRE, Jean, Les limitations internes des formalismes. Étude sur la signification du théorème de Gödel et des théorèmes apparentés dans la théorie des fondements des mathématiques. Doctoral thesis. Louvain, 1956.

LAYTON, Bentley, The Gnostic Treatise on Resurrection from Nag Hammadi. Edited with Translation and Commentary by --. Harvard Theological Review. Dissertation in Religion no. 12. Ann Arbor, 1979.

LEISEGANG, Hans, Die Gnosis. Stuttgart, 1955 4 (1924 1).

LESSING, Doris, Out of the Fountain. The Story of a Non-Marrying Man and Other Stories. Penguin Books, 1979.

LIDZBARSKI, Mark, Warum schrieb Mani aramäisch? Der Manichäismus (Ed. Widengren). Originally in Orientalische Literaturzeitung 30 (1927).

LIEU, Samuel N.C., Manichaeism in the Later Roman Empire and Medieval China. Wissenschaftliche Untersuchungen zum Neuen Testament 63. Tübingen 1992 (2. ed., rev. and expanded, 1985 1).

LOISY, Alfred, Le Mandéisme et les origines chrétiennes. Paris, 1934.

MACKIE, J.L., Truth, probability and paradox. Studies in Philosophical Logic. Clarendon Library 17. Oxford, 1973.

MAHÉ, Jean-Pierre, Le sens des symboles sexuels dans quelques textes hermétiques et gnostiques. Nag Hammadi Studies VII. Ed. Martin Krause. Les textes de Nag Hammadi. Colloque du Centre de l'histoire des religions (Strasbourg 23-25 octobre 1974). Ed. Jacques-É. Ménard. Leiden, 1975.

MARTEL, Jean, Dieu cet inconnu. Lyon, w.d.

MÉNARD, Jacques-É., L'Évangile selon Philippe. Introduction - texte - traduction - commentaire. Strasbourg, 1967.

MUSIL, Robert, Der Mann ohne Eigenschaften I. Rowohlt 1981.

NAGEL, Ernest & NEWMAN, James R., Gödel's proof. New York, 1958 (Dutch translation by J.M. Debrot, De stelling van Gödel. Utrecht/Antwerpen, 1975).

NOVALIS, Das philosophische Werk I. Schriften II. Herausg. Richard Samuel. Stuttgart, 1981.

NYBERG, Henrik Samuel, Forschungen über den Manichäismus (1935). Der Manichäismus (Ed. Widengren).

ORT, Lodewijk J.R., Mani. A religio-historical description of his personality. Doct. thesus Un. of Amsterdam. Leiden, 1967.

PAGELS, Eliane, The Gnostic Gospels. London, 1980

PAIS, Abraham, 'Subtle is the Lord ...'. The Science and the Life of Einstein. Oxford/New York, 1982.

PEEL, Malcolm Lee, Gnosis und Auferstehung. Der Brief an Rheginus von Nag Hammadi. Neukirchener-Verlag. 1974. Translation of the Epistle to Rheginus. A Valentinian Letter on the Resurrection. Philadelphia, 1969.

PÉTREMENT, Simone, Le Dieu séparé. Les origines du Gnosticisme. Series : Patrimoine-Gnosticisme. Paris, 1984.

PROUST, Marcel, Les plaisirs et les jours. Pierre Clarac (Éd.), Jean Santeuil, précédé de Les plaisirs et les jours. Bibliothèque de la Pléiade. Paris, 1971.

PUECH, Henri-Charles
1. Le Mandéisme. Son fondateur. Sa doctrine. Musée Guimet. Bibliothèque de diffusion. Tome LVI. Paris, 1949.
2. Sur le Manichéisme et autres essais. Paris, 1979.
3. Der Stand des Mandäerproblems (from the French). Der Mandäismus (Ed. Widengren).

RIES, Julien, Les études manichéennes. Des controverses de la Réforme aux découvertes du XXe siècle. Collection Cervaux-Lefort 1. Louvain-la-neuve, 1988.

ROBINSON, William C., The Exegesis of the Soul. Novum Testamentum XII (1970).

ROSENTHAL, Franz, Die Sprache Manis. Die aramäistische Forschung. Leiden, 1939. in : Der Manichäismus (Ed. Widengren).

ROUSSEAU, Jean-Jacques, Émile, ou De l'éducation. Oeuvres Complètes IV. Bibliothèque de la Pléiade. Paris, 1969.

RUDOLPH, Kurt
1. Entwicklungsgeschichte der mandäischen Religion. Der Mandäismus (Ed. Widengren).
2. Die Gnosis. Wesen und Geschichte einer spätantiken Religion. Göttingen (1980 2, 1977 1).
3. Mandaeism. Series : Iconography of Religions. Section XXI : Mandaeism. Leiden, 1978.
4. Die Mandäer. I Das Mandäerproblem. Göttingen, 1960.
5. Theogonie, Kosmogonie und Anthropogonie in den Mandäischen Schriften. Eine literaturkritische und traditionsgeschichtliche Untersuchung. Forschungen zur Religion und Literatur des Alten und Neuen Testaments. Heft 88. Göttingen, 1965.

RÜSTOW, Alexander, Der Lügner : Theorie, Geschichte und Auflösung. Leipzig, 1910.

SAINSBURY, R.M., Paradoxes. Cambridge (1988).

SCHOPENHAUER, Arthur, Preisschrift über die Grundlage der Moral. (Herausg. Wolfgang von Löhneysen) Sämtliche Werke III. Stuttgart/ Frankfurt a.M., 1962.

SCHUMACHER, Rudolf, Der Alexandriner Apollos. Eine exegetische Studie. Kempten/München, 1916.

SCOPELLO, Maddalena, L'exégèse de l'âme. Nag Hammadi Codex II,6. Introduction, traduction et commentaire. Nag Hammadi Studies XXV. Ed. Martin Krause. Leiden, 1985.

SÉGUR, Philippe Comte de, La campagne de Russie. Mémoires du Géneral --. Collection Nelson. Paris, w.d.

SÉVRIN, Jean-Marie
1. L'Exégèse de l'âme (NH 2.6). Texte établi et présenté par --. Bibliothèque copte de Nag Hammadi. Section 'Textes' 9. Québec, 1983.
2. Les noces spirituelles dans l'Évangile selon Philippe. Le Muséon LXXVII (1974).

SLOTERDIJK, Peter, Die wahre Irrlehre. Über die Weltreligion der Weltlosigkeit. Weltrevolution der Seele. Eine Lese- und Arbeitsbuch der Gnosis von der Spätantike bis zur Gegenwart I. Herausg. Peter Sloterdijk/Thomas H. Macho. Artemis & Winkler Verlag (1991).

SMITS, Rik, De linkshandige Picador : over links- en rechtshandigheid. Amsterdam, 1993.

SNOW, Charles Percy, The Two Cultures and a Second Look. An expanded version of The Two Cultures and the Scientific Revolution. Cambridge, 1974 (1959 1).

STROUMSA, Gedaliahu A.G., Another seed. Studies in Gnostic Mythology. Nag Hammadi Studies XXIV. Leiden, 1984.

TARDIEU, Michel, Le Manichéisme. Series : Que sais-je. Paris, 1981.

VEILLEUX, Armand, La première Apocalypse de Jacques (NH V,3). La seconde Apocalypse de Jacques (NH V,4). Bibliothèque copte de Nag Hammadi. Section 'Textes' 17. Québec, 1986.

VOLTAIRE, Traité de métaphysique (1734). Oeuvres complètes II. Oeuvres philosophiques. Paris, 1829.

WEINBERG, Steven, Dreams of a Final Theory. New York (1992).

WERSCH, Stefan van, De gnostisch-occulte vloedgolf. Van Simon de Tovenaar tot New Age. Kampen (1990).

WIDENGREN, Geo, Die Religionen Irans. Die Religionen der Menschheit, Band 14. Stuttgart (1965).

WILSON, Robert Smith, Marcion. A Study of a second-century Heretic. London, 1980 (photostatic reprint of London, 1933).

WHITEHEAD, Alfred North/RUSSELL, Bertrand, Principia mathematica I. Cambridge, 1927 2.

GENERAL INDEX

Abel, 20-21, 30, 78, 195-198
Abraham, 69, 84, 171, 199, 240
Achsenzeit, 277
Acts of the Apostles, 36, 232, 237
Adam, 7-8, 9, 13, 19, 21, 28, 29, 30-31, 113, 117, 132-137, 139-140, 141-142, 160, 171, 191-193, 193-194, 195-198, 199, 254, 258
Adamantius, 102, 103
Adamites, 137
Afrunya, 214
Ahra see Angra
Ahriman, 81, 157, 175, 267
Ahura Mazda, 157, 175, 267, 271
Akuos, 210
Albîrûnî, 214, 219, 220
Alcibiades (a Syrian), 159
Alexander of Lycopolis, 168, 180, 181, 182, 198, 210, 218, 221, 222, 223, 225, 226, 227
Alexandria(n), 22, 86, 235, 236, 245, 248, 280
Alfaric, Prosper, 219
Algeria, 154
Amann, É., 55, 98, 102, 106, 143
Ambrosius, 105
Amun-Re, 271
Analogia entis, 279
Ananus (High Priest), 36
Anatolian, 103
Androgynity, androgynous, 7-8, 12, 17, 24, 25, 27, 29, 32, 43, 256
Anglican, 248
Angra (Ahra) Mainyu, 157, 175
Anicetus, bishop of Rome, 53
Anselm of Canterbury, 65
Antiochia, 248

Antoninus Pius, 55
Antinomian(ism), 20, 69, 78, 84, 95, 113, 250
Antitheses, work of Marcion, 56, 63, 100
Apelles, 86-91, 105
Apellians, Apellicians, 86
Aphrodite, 19
Apocalypse of James (the First), 34-35
Apocalypse of James (the Second), 35-36
Apocalypse of Peter (Gnostic treatise), 40-42
Apollos, 232, 235-238, 239, 279, 280
Apostles, 11, 52
Aquila, 236
Arab(s), Arabia, 92, 114, 115, 153, 155, 158, 159, 165, 211, 214, 216, 219
Aramaic, 115, 144
Archelaus (bishop), 166
Ardashir I (Artaxerxes), 156, 157, 165, 217
Ardewan V (Ardavan, Artabanus), 156
Aristotle, 256, 269
Ark of the Covenant, 66
Armenia, 93
Arsacids, 156, 214
Asia Minor, 55, 56, 167, 211, 241
Asia(tic), 86, 103, 212
Assembly (French), 8
Assyriologist, 153
Astaphaios, 24
Astrological, 16

Augustine, Saint, 58, 151, 174, 190, 198, 199, 209, 210, 211, 220, 221, 222, 223, 225, 226, 227
Aurelianus (Roman emperor), 210
Authoritative Teaching (Gnostic treatise), 36-38

Babel, 140, 149
Babylon(ian)(s), 103, 110, 114, 149, 151, 153, 154, 155, 156, 158, 166, 167, 168, 209, 215
Baghdad, 108, 111
Bahram I, Sasanian emperor, 169-170
Balutchistan, 167
Bar Konaï see Theodore 143
Barbelo, 42, 256
Barbelo-Gnostics, 245
Barc, Bernard, 47
Bardesanes (Ibn Daysan), 165, 171, 220
Bardy, G., 99, 147, 193, 214, 224, 225, 226, 227
Bareille, G., 105, 105, 160, 216
Basel, 152
Basilides, 54, 83, 231, 236, 248
Bata'ih, 159
Baur, Ferdinand Christian, 153, 174, 175, 182, 184, 194, 205, 208, 209, 213, 220, 221, 222, 223, 224, 225, 226, 227
Beausobre, Isaac de, 152, 153, 213, 224
Beelzebub, 77
Behm, Johannes, 143, 149
Belapat (Gundishapur), 169
Benjamin, tribe of, 240
Besant, Benjamin, 275
Bethge, Hans-Gebhard, 22
Bethlehem, 214, 245
Bianchi, 103, 104
Bible, biblical, 21, 26, 36, 73, 75, 87, 113, 152, 160, 235, 246, 248, 249, 251, 252, 254, 255, 257, 258, 261, 276, 279
Bisexuality see Androgynity
Black Sea, 53
Blackman, E.C., 56, 61, 65, 71, 76, 97, 98, 100, 101, 102, 102, 107

Blavatsky, Madame, 275
Bogomil, 152
Böhlig, Alexander, 214, 217, 218
Book of Adam see Ginza
Book of James, 250
Book of John see Drasha
Bousset, Wilhelm, 48, 57, 81, 99, 103
Borsip(pa), 140, 149
Brandon, S.G.F., 236, 279
Brandt, Wilhelm, 215, 216
British, 111, 116, 154, 265, 279
Brünnhilde, 205
Buckley, Jorun J., 145, 146
Buddha, 171, 172, 199
Buddhism, Buddhists, 153, 167, 212, 214, 266
Bullard, Roger A., 14, 15, 18, 20, 47, 48, 51
Burkitt, F.C., 165, 217
Byron, Lord, 177
Byzantine (Empire), 212

Caesarea, 159
Cain, 12-13, 20-21, 78, 195-196, 199, 251
Cainites, 248
Cairo, 154
Canonical Prayer Book of the Mandaeans, 116
Capernaum, 61
Cathar, 152
Cerdo, 59-60
Cerinthus, 232
Ceylon, 113
Chabot, Jean Baptiste, 143
Chaldaean, 153
Cham, 114
Charakene, 165
China, Chinese, 151, 154, 212, 214, 220, 226, 266, 277
Christ (Jesus, Gnostic), 2, 3, 7, 10, 11, 12, 26, 41, 42, 59, 71, 72, 74-78, 79, 81, 83, 83, 89-90, 102, 161, 193-195, 195, 198-199, 199, 205, 253-254, 262, 281
Christian(s), 2, 5, 6, 9, 15, 34, 38, 39, 40, 53, 55, 59, 62, 65, 72, 77, 78, 81, 82, 84, 84, 92, 93, 94, 95,

96, 110, 111, 112, 113, 114, 131, 144, 152, 159, 160, 163, 167, 193, 210, 230, 232, 235, 243-263, 269, 270, 271, 272, 274, 276, 277, 281
Christianity, 5, 34, 64, 69/70, 71, 80, 92, 95, 106, 110, 112, 143, 160, 193, 204, 214, 229, 230-242, 242-263, 264, 267, 268, 272, 274
Christianizing, 214
Cirillo, Luigi, 215, 216
Clement of Alexandria, 54, 91, 97,, 101, 104
Clement I, bishop of Rome, 276
Codex Jung, 1
Concept of our Great Power (Gnostic treatise), 38-40
Constantine the Great, 93
Coptic, 154, 155, 250
Corinth(ian)(s), 232, 236, 237, 280
Ctesiphon, 155, 156, 166, 167, 169, 170, 214
Cyprianus, 99, 104
Cyprus, 92, 93

Dhakwa (companion of Mani), 166
Damascus, 93
Dast-i-Maïshân, 158
David, 70
Dead Sea, 159
Deir Ali, 93
Demiurge, 5-6, 21, 23, 25, 25-26, 26-27, 29, 38, 42, 59, 66-67, 66-67, 67-68, 68-69, 70, 71, 72, 76-77, 78, 79, 81, 82, 83, 88, 91, 93, 160, 230, 248, 249, 260-261, 267, 268, 270
Diocletian, Roman emperor, 93, 210
Docetism, docetist, 40, 74, 89, 97
Dodds, E.R., 269, 282
Dodge, Bayard, 217, 222, 224, 225, 226
Dörrie, Heinrich, 46
Drasha dYhaya, 115-116
Drower, Ethel S., 109, 110, 111, 113, 114, 115, 116, 142, 143, 144, 145, 146, 147, 149
Dualism, dualistic, 1, 3, 9, 12, 13, 14, 16, 20, 23, 22, 25, 32, 32, 37,

40, 43, 56, 57-58, 59, 64, 65, 66, 71, 73, 74, 77, 79-83, 87, 89, 90, 91, 94, 97, 100, 104, 108, 112, 113, 116, 117, 120, 121, 123, 125, 129, 132, 133, 135, 139, 145, 151-152, 153, 155, 157, 161, 172-178, 178, 181, 187, 193, 199, 201, 202-203, 208, 212-213, 239, 244, 249, 265-267, 279
Dupréau, Gabriel, 152, 213
Dutch, 281

Ecbatana, 156
Egypt(ians), 78, 92, 113, 114, 148, 160, 168, 210, 211, 214, 241, 263, 266
Elchasai, 164, 215
Eleleth, 15, 15, 21
Eleusis, 273
Eleutheropolis, 210
Elkasaites (Elkesaites, Elcesaites), 159-161, 216
Eloai, 24
Elxai, 159, 160
English see British
Enlightenment, 278
Enoch, 199
Ephesus, 55, 235, 236, 248, 280
Epiphanius, 54, 87, 88, 89, 90, 91, 92, 97, 98, 99, 103, 104, 105, 106, 159, 160, 215, 216, 220, 226, 227
Eros, 27, 28
Essenian(s), 144, 241
Eucharist, 11, 85, 112
Euphrates, 93, 110, 158, 159, 167
Europe(an), 109, 116, 151
Eusebius of Caesarea, 86, 88, 97, 105, 106, 106
Evans, Ernest, 99, 100
Eve, 8, 13, 19, 21, 29, 30, 49, 113, 117, 132-137, 140, 191-193, 193, 195-197, 199, 254, 258
Evodius, 216, 222, 225
Eznik of Kolb, 68, 76, 93, 98, 101, 102, 103

Fallon, Francis, 48, 49
Fathers of the Church, 46, 53, 55, 91, 210, 211, 248, 276

Faustus (Manichee), 174, 183, 211
Fayum, 154
Felix (Manichee), 211
Filastrius, 87, 99, 105, 106
Filoramo, Giovanni, 228
Fiore, Joachim da, 39
Firuz, brother of Shapur I, 167-168
Flavius Illyricus, 152
Flood, the, 38
Fortunatus (Manichee), 211
French,, 232 154
Funk, Wolf-Peter, 51

Galatia, 235
Gandhara, 218
Ghaukaï, 214
Gaul, 211
Genesis, Book of, 7, 8, 12, 18, 19, 21, 29, 49, 136
German, 57, 62, 95, 98, 116, 153, 154, 177
Ginza Rba, 115-116, 146
Gnosis, 1, 11, 14, 21, 57, 82-83, 84, 115, 121, 130, 132, 134, 136, 143, 154, 155, 160, 171, 199, Ch.V passim
Gnostic(s), Ch. I passim, 53, 55, 57, 61, 67, 69, 71, 73, 76, 78, 79-83, 87, 88, 90, 92, 95, 108, 113, 115, 116, 117, 119, 132, 135, 136, 141, 142, 151, 155, 159, 160, 165, 171, 186, 188, 193, 195, 197, 198, 208, 209, 212, 213, 215, 220, 224, Ch.V passim
Gnosticizing, 239, 242
Golgotha, 41
Gordianus III (Roman emperor), 165, 218
Gospel(s), 12, 36, 41, 60, 61, 63, 89, 95, 97, 193, 216
Gospel to the Egyptians, 250
Gospel of John, 61, 231, 239
Gospel of Luke, 49, 59, 61-62, 75, 216, 239, 250
Gospel of Mark, 49, 61, 239
Gospel of Mathhew, 48, 61, 239, 250
Gospel of Philip, 1, 4-14, 248, 250, 281

Gospel of Thomas, 250
Gospel of Truth, 250
Grant, Robert M., 12, 14, 46, 47
Greece, 167, 236, 266, 272, 277
Greek(s), 32, 43, 46, 55, 71, 82, 93, 155, 160, 163, 214, 241, 242, 249, 250, 263, 264, 267, 268, 269, 270, 271, 272, 273, 274, 275, 276, 277, 281
Gregory of Nyssa, 223
Gundishapur see Belapat, 169

Hadrian, Roman emperor, 54
Haenchen, Ernst, 249-250, 282
Ham (supposed son of Noah), 114
Hamadan, 156, 214
Harnack, Adolf von, 53, 55, 56, 60, 61, 64, 68, 69, 73, 74, 74, 79, 82, 85, 86, 90, 92, 93, 94, 95, 96, 97, 98, 99, 100, 101, 102, 103, 104, 105, 106, 154
Hatra, 217
Hauran range, 143
Hebdomad, 24
Hebrew, 240, 277
Hedrich, Charles W., 51
Helen, companion of Simon the Magician, 105, 229
Helen of Troy, 33
Hellenic see Greek
Hellenism, 142
Hellenistic, 82, 103, 103, 167, 241, 249, 263, 275, 276
Henoch, 78
Hierapolis, 55
Hilgenfeld, Adolphus, 215
Himalayas, 154
Hippolytus, 98, 105, 105, 159, 215, 216
Hitler, Adolf, 177
Hoffmann, 103-104
Holy Ghost, Holy Spirit, 234, 271, 281
Hormizd I, Sasanian emperor, 169, 170
Hume, David, 262
Hyginus, bishop of Rome, 55, 59, 98
Hymenaeus, 3

Hypostasis of the Archons, 14-22, 22

Ibn al Murtada, 219
Ibn Daysan see Bardesanes
Iliad, 271
India(n), 153, 167, 277
Indian Ocean, 167
Indus, 167
Iran(ian), 64, 81, 92, 103, 104, 108, 110, 114, 140, 147, 151, 153, 154, 155, 156, 157, 165, 166, 167, 168, 175, 211, 214, 217, 266
Iraq(is), 108, 109, 111, 158
Irenaeus, 53, 54, 59, 65, 97, 99, 100, 101, 102, 104, 229, 230
Isaiah, 25
Islam, 278

Israel (people), 12, 25, 66, 70, 91, 254, 266, 273, 277
Italy, 92, 167, 211

Jackson, A.V. Williams, 176, 217, 221
Jaldabaoth, 13, 16, 18, 24, 25, 27
Jahve, 17, 25, 66, 69, 182
James (apostle), 34, 36
Janssens, Yvonne, 52
Japhet, 114
Jaspers, Karl. 277
Jericho, 67
Jerusalem, 35, 85, 114, 234, 235
Jesus Christ, Jesus of Nazareth, 2, 10, 11, 12, 25, 34, 35, 39, 41, 42, 56, 57, 60, 61, 62, 67, 70, 98, 98, 111, 112, 114, 131, 143, 144, 145, 160, 163, 165, 171, 172, 214, 216, 217, 235, 236, 237, 240, 245, 248, 253-254, 254, 261, 271, 272, 275, 276, 281
Jew(s), Jewish, 6, 17, 24, 34, 36, 40, 59, 61, 63, 66, 69, 69, 69-70, 71, 70-71, 77, 78, 80, 82, 84, 89, 103, 109, 111, 112, 113, 114, 131, 144, 159, 160, 162, 235, 236, 240, 246, 248, 249, 250, 253, 254, 255, 257, 258, 260, 264, 266, 269, 274, 276, 277, 281

John, apostle, 58, 99, 232, 234, 238-241, 261
John the Baptist, 110, 111, 114, 115, 143, 235
Jonas, Hans, 228, 255, 282
Jordan, 56, 109, 118, 141, 142, 143, 158, 159, 210, 245
Joseph (father of Jesus), 214, 245, 281
Josephus, Flavius, 36, 144
Judaea, 210
Judaism, Judaistic, 40, 61, 64, 71, 80, 84, 95, 112, 113, 144, 145, 231, 240, 241, 248, 249, 260, 262, 263, 264, 267, 268, 273, 274, 276
Judaizers, judaizing, 60, 60, 62, 159, 238
Judas, 78, 251
Justin the Martyr, 57, 91, 92, 99, 105

Kamsarakan (Arsacid branch), 156
Kansu, 154
Karter (Magus), 169
Karun (river), 108
Kashmir, 168
al-Khasyah, 159
Kessler, Konrad, 153, 219, 221
Kind, Friedrich, 48
Korah, 251
Koran, 116
Kroll, Josef, 145
Kurdistan, 108
Khuzestan, 108
Kushan, 165, 169

Latin, 155, 220, 250
Law, Mosaic, 59, 60, 63-64, 69-70, 73, 77, 76, 80, 88, 100, 106, 160, 238, 240, 248, 260
Layton, Bentley, 43
Leisegang, Hans, 228
Letter to the Colossans, 238
Letters to the Corinthians, 236, 237-238, 280
Letter to the Ephesians, 238
Letter to the Galatians, 61, 84-85
Letter of Peter (second), 95
Letter to Timothy, 3

Lidzbarski, Mark, 116, 121, 130, 146, 147, 148, 219
Lieu, S.N.C., 227
Logos, 12, 241
Loisy, Alfred, 111, 113, 143, 144, 145, 146
Luke, 56
Luther, Martin, 37, 57, 106, 152
Lutheran, 152

MacRae, George, 51
al-Mada'in, 155
Macho, Thomas, 242, 281
Madonna, 19
Magdeburgenses Centuriatores, 152
Maghreb, 211
Magi (Zoroastrian), 169
Mahé, Jean-Pierre, 8, 45
Makran, 167
Mandaeans, Mandaeism, Ch. III passim, 158, 163, 201, 215
Mani, 80, 84, 108, 151, 153, 154, 155, 155-177, 181, 193, 196, 199, 209, 210, 212, 214, 215, 216, 218, 220, 223, 227
Manichaeans, 92, Ch. V passim, 278
Manichaeism, 80, Ch. V passim, 268, 278
Marcellus (context of Mani), 166
Marcion, Ch. II passim, 113, 165, 171, 199, 220, 239, 240
Marcionite (Church), 51, Ch. II, passim, 278
Marcus Aurelius, Roman emperor, 87
Mardinu, 155, 214
Mary (mother of Jesus), 2, 9, 10, 74, 89, 111, 245
Mary Magdalena, 10, 11
Mary Salome, 10
Maryam (mother of Mani), 156
Maugham, W. Somerset, 279
Mazdaism, Mazdaist, 156, 212
McLean, N., 84, 104
Mecca, 211
Media(n), 114, 156, 214
Medinet Madi, 154

Mediterranean, 96, 211, 249, 266
Menander, 232
Ménard, Jacques-É, 9, 11, 46
Mesopotamia(n), 110, 115, 151, 153, 165, 169, 210, 212, 263
Messiah, 70, 236, 237, 253, 272, 273, 274, 276
Middle Ages, 108, 109, 258, 278
Milan, 211
Mithraism, 103-104
Mithridates, 103
Modalist(s), 75
Mohammed, 111
Mongolia, 151, 212
Monism, monistic, 65, 81, 129, 132, 138-140
Monotheism, monotheistic, 113, 157, 160, 174
Moses, 69, 86, 88, 114
Moslims, 212
Mughtasila, 158-159, 159, 161, 162-164, 175, 177, 178, 215, 216

an-Nadim, Ibn, 159, 161, 165, 166, 170, 171, 176, 183, 218
Nag Hammadi Library, 1, 42, 228, 229, 230, 244, 245, 250, 251, 252
Nahar-Kuthi, 214
Nazareth, 143, 214, 245
Nebuchadnessar, 114
Nemesius, 223
Nestorian, 143
Neoplatonic, 168, 218, 275
Nestle, Wilhelm, 275
New Testament, 2, 3, 12, 35, 57, 56, 59, 60, 62, 64, 66, 71, 75, 89, 95, 96, 111, 144, 163, 223, 230-231, 232, 238, 239, 240, 241, 242, 250, 251, 252, 253, 257, 261, 276
Nicolaites, 248
Noah, 21, 78, 113, 114, 171, 199
Nominalism, 4
Norea, 21-22
North-Africa, 154, 211
Nyberg, H.S., 214

Odyssey, 271
Old Testament, 12, 57, 59, 62, 63, 64, 69, 71, 70, 74, 75, 78, 80, 81,

86, 88-89, 93, 95, 97, 106, 107, 112, 131, 145, 160, 237, 240, 251, 254, 257, 261, 277
Olympian gods, 267, 271
Ophite(s), 46, 231, 248
Origen, 47, 91, 105, 105, 159
Origin of the World (Gnostic treatise), 22-32
Ormuzd, 157, 175, 267
Orphism, 249, 264, 266
Ort, Lodewijk J.R., 168, 214, 218, 219, 221
Orthodox Churches, 248

Paganism, pagan, 262, 277
Pagels, Elaine, 243, 244, 280
Pahlevi, 178
Pakistan, 167
Pale, 241, 92, 93, 143, 144, 159, 210
Palestine, Palestinian, 249, 266
Papias, bishop of Hierapolis, 55, 98
Papos (Manichaean bishop), 210
Paradise, 7, 8, 18, 20, 27, 29, 31, 258, 279
Paraphrase of Sem, 248
Parthian, 156, 218
Parthian Empire, 156
Patek (Patteg, Pattig, Patiq), 156, 157-158, 161, 163, 177, 214, 218
Patriarchs of Israel, 77
Paul (apostle), 12, 57, 59, 61, 62, 77, 80, 81, 82, 84, 88, 95, 97, 160, 166, 167, 199, 220, 231, 232, 235, 236, 237, 238, 238-241, 257, 261, 274, 276, 280
Paulician, 152
Pax Romana, 275
Peel, Malcolm Lee, 1, 44
Pergamum, 248
Peroz, king of Kushan, 165
Peroz see Firuz
Persia(n), 156
Persis, 167
Persia see Iran
Persian, 56, 154, 170
Peter, apostle, 40, 42, 60, 234, 235, 236, 237
Pétrement, Simone, 82, 83, 104, 230-242, 267, 279, 280
Pharisees, 56, 217, 240
Philetus, 3
Philip (apostle), 4, 234
Philo Judaeus, 241
Philumenê, 86, 89, 90
Phrygia, 54, 235
Plato, 58, 99, 160, 241, 269
Platonic, Platonism, 134, 231, 249, 270, 275
Plotinus, 218
Polycarp, bishop of Smyrna, 53, 54
Polytheism, 66, 174
Pontus, 55, 61, 103, 103
Portuguese, 109, 110
Postel, Guillaume, 282
Pototsky, H.J., 220
Presbyterian, 281
Presocratics, 275
Priscilla, 236
Pronoia, 26, 27
Protestant(ism), 106, 152, 153, 243, 244, 278
Protoevangelium, 250
Proust, Marcel, 242, 280
Pseudotertullian, 55, 89, 97, 99, 105, 106
Ptah, 148
Puech, Henri-Charles, 108, 142, 155, 156, 165, 167, 170, 171, 176, 189, 198, 207, 208, 214, 215, 216, 217, 218, 219, 220, 221, 223, 224, 225, 226, 227
Pythagoras, 160
Pythagorism, 249

Quispel, Gilles, 243

Red Sea, 114
Reformation (Churches), 96, 152, 153, 248
Rembrandt, 251
Renaissance, 152
Revelation of John, 248
Rheginos, 1, 44
Rhine, 205
Rhodon, 86-88
Ries, Jules, 152, 153, 213, 214, 217

Robinson, William C., 50
Roman(s), 92, 93, 140, 155, 165, 210, 218, 264, 267, 268, 270, 272
Roman-Catholic Church, Roman-Catholicism, 12, 40, 53, 55, 56, 59, 60, 71, 81, 83, 84, 85, 87, 88, 91-97, 98, 98, 104, 106, 112, 143, 152, 199, 220, 229, 243, 244, 245, 246, 248, 261, 262, 274, 275, 278, 281, 282
Roman Empire, 92, 151, 152, 167, 168, 211, 227, 264
Rome, 53, 55, 56, 59, 60, 86, 86, 92, 98, 99, 159, 211
Rosenthal, Franz, 219
Rudolph, Kurt, 108, 110, 112, 113, 116, 119, 122, 128, 130, 132, 135, 138, 141, 142, 143, 144, 145, 146, 148, 149, 150, 228
Russian(s), 154

Sabaeans, 159, 49
Sabaoth, 17-18, 25-26, 48
Sabbath, 67, 84
Saddam Hussein, 109
Saklas, 16, 17
Salmaios (disciple of Mani), 162
Sam (supposed son of Noah), 113, 114
Samael, 16, 17, 25
Samaria, 232, 234, 235
Samarkand, 209, 212
Sasanian(s), Sasanian Empire, 154, 155, 156, 157, 167, 168, 169
Satan, 39, 54, 62, 64, 66, 81, 249
Saturn, 17
Saturnilos, 231, 236
Schaeder, Hans-Heinrich, 144
Schoolmen, 258
Schroedel, William R., 50
Schumacher, Rudolf, 279, 280
Scopello, Maddalena, 4, 50
Seleucids, 155
Seleukeia, 155
Sem, 114
Semitic, 115, 144, 154
Septuagint, 277
Sermon on the Mount, 73
Seth, 21-22, 171, 197, 199, 262

Sethians, 231, 248
Sévrin, Jeam-Marie, 50
Sex(ual)(ity), 7, 9, 11, 12, 13, 19, 27, 30, 34, 72, 82, 135, 137, 191, 192, 195, 202, 205, 206, 213, 227, 257
Shamun (companion of Mani), 166
Shapur I, 157, 165, 167-169, 169, 170, 217, 218
asch-Sharashtâni, 220, 223
Shatt al'Arab, 158, 159, 167
Shi'ites, 109
Simon of Cyrene, 253
Simon the Magician, 33, 105, 229, 230, 232. 234-235
Simplicius, 222, 223
Sinkiang, 154
Sinope (Sinop), 54, 55, 58
Sion, Mount of, 273
Sloterdijk, Peter, 242, 281
Smyrna, 53, 55
Sodomites, 78, 251
Sogdian, 154
Sophia, 9, 15-16, 17, 20, 22, 23, 24, 26, 27, 29, 30, 35, 42, 46, 256
Soul (On the) (Gnostic treatise), 32-34
Spain, 211
Spangenberg, Cyriacus, 152, 213
Spenta Mainyu, 157, 175, 267
Spiegel, Fr., 153
Stephen (deacon, first martyr), 36
Stephen I, bishop of Rome, 104
Stoics, 67
Stroumsa, Gedaliahu A.G., 248-249, 282
Sunnites, 109
Syncretism, syncretistic, 159, 171, 249
Syria(n), 34, 59, 92, 92, 110, 115, 143, 144, 159, 167, 170, 210, 214, 232, 241, 249, 266
Syriac, 155, 156, 170

Taoist, 154
Taqizadeh, S.H., 165
Tardieu, Michel, 166, 214, 215, 216, 217, 219
Taubes, Jakob, 252-253, 282

Tebessa, 154
Temple of Jerusalem, 40, 62
Tertullian, 61, 63, 64, 65, 67, 69, 75, 83, 85, 86, 88, 91, 92, 97, 98, 99, 100, 101, 102, 103, 104, 105, 106
Testimonium veritatis (Gnostic treatise), 281
Thebais, 92
Theodore bar Konaï, 143, 158, 182, 191, 214, 215, 221, 222, 223, 225
Theodoretus of Cyrus, 93, 101, 103, 104, 106, 221, 222
Theodorus of Mopsuesta, 104
Theosophy, theosophic, 171, 275-277
Thomas (apostle), 167
Thomas (Manichaean missionary), 210
Thomas of Aquinas, 258
Tiberius, Roman emperor, 62, 70, 75, 79, 98
Tibetan, 154
Tigris, 110, 155, 159, 169
Titus of Bostra, 180, 182, 206, 221, 224, 226
Torah, 111
Treatise on the Resurrection, 1-4
Trebonianus Gallus, Vibius (Roman emperor), 165
Trimorphic Protennoia (Gnostic treatise), 42-44
Tripartite Tract (Gnostic treatise), 282
Tun-Huang, 154
Tunisia, 154, 211
Tura dMaddai (legendary mountain), 114
Turan, 167
Turbo (disciple of Mani), 165
Turfan (T'u-Lu-Fan), 154, 218
Turkestan, 151, 154, 168, 212
Turkey, 167
Turkish, 54, 154
Turner, John D., 52
Turribius of Astorga, 227

Uigur, 154
Uzbekistan, 212

Valentinian(s), Valentianism, 2, 12, 13, 46, 53, 80, 231, 245, 248, 278
Valentinus, 52, 54, 83, 231
Valerian, Roman emperor, 93, 218
Valhalla, 205
Vegetarianism, 83, 200, 201
Veilleux, Armand, 50

Wagner, Richard, 205
Weber, Carl Maria von, 48
Wersch, Stefan van. 57-58, 256, 259-260, 282
Widengren, Geo, 155, 157, 168, 175, 182, 214, 215, 216, 218, 219, 221, 222, 223, 226, 227
Wilhelm II, German Emperor, 177
Wilson, R.S., 102, 106
Wintermute, Orval S., 22
Wisdom Books, 251
Wisse, Frederik E., 51
Wotan, 271

Yaldabaoth see Jaldabaoth
Yam (supposed son of Noah), 114
Yao, 24
Yaphet (supposed son of Noah), 114

Zandee, J., 18
Zervan (Zurvan), 157, 175, 267
Zervanism, Zervanite, 57, 65, 81, 103, 157, 175, 176, 249, 266, 267, 268
Zeus, 182, 271
Zoê, 17, 26, 28, 29, 30
Zoroaster, 81, 157, 171, 175, 199
Zoroastrian(ism), 57, 65, 81-82, 103, 151, 153, 156, 157, 168, 169, 170, 175, 249, 267